Human Rights and
African Airwaves

Human Rights and African Airwaves

Mediating Equality on the Chichewa Radio

Harri Englund

Indiana University Press
Bloomington and Indianapolis

This book is a publication of

Indiana University Press
601 North Morton Street
Bloomington, Indiana 47404–3797 USA

iupress.indiana.edu

Telephone orders   800-842-6796
Fax orders   812-855-7931
Orders by e-mail   iuporder@indiana.edu

Manufactured in the United States of America

Library of Congress Cataloging-in-Publication
Data

Englund, Harri.
   Human rights and African airwaves : medi-
ating equality on the Chichewa radio / Harri
Englund.
      p. cm.
   Includes bibliographical references and index.
   ISBN 978-0-253-35677-2 (cloth : alk.
paper) — ISBN 978-0-253-22347-0 (pbk. :
alk. paper) 1. Radio broadcasting—Social
aspects—Malawi. 2. Radio broadcasting,
Chewa—Malawi. 3. Nkhani Zam'maboma
(Radio program) 4. Public radio—Malawi. 5.
Human rights in mass media. 6. Malawi Broad-
casting Corporation. 7. Malawi—Social condi-
tions. 8. Ethnology—Malawi. I. Title.
   PN1991.3.M3E55 2011
   302.2344096897—dc22
                                        2011013555

1 2 3 4 5   16 15 14 13 12 11

For Mikael

4

Contents

Acknowledgments

Once again I have to register my debt to the many friends and acquaintances in Dedza District and Chinsapo Township in Malaŵi who not only suggested intriguing topics to research but also offered perspectives on them that helped me revise my initial interpretations. Because I have not used the services of research assistants for this book, I can do no more than thank my interlocutors collectively, all too aware that writing academic books may not be the best way to adjust this sort of debt.

I felt welcome at the Blantyre headquarters of the Malaŵi Broadcasting Corporation during the tenure of two successive pairs of director generals and deputy director generals. The employees I worked with may not want their names to appear here for reasons that will be evident to the readers of this book. However, having rather reluctantly been interviewed by some of them on the radio (twice in Chicheŵa and once in English), I believe I am not the only one in our relationship who enjoys the powers that come with representing others. This book bears witness to some of the ways in which they have exercised those powers under the constraining conditions of public broadcasting in Malaŵi.

A number of academics were generous enough to read or listen to parts of this book when it was a work in progress. Some offered their comments and criticisms in seminars or during casual conversations, others in writing, but it feels right to acknowledge them in equal measure: Georgina Born, Erica Bornstein, Matei Candea, Blessings Chinsinga, James Ferguson, Ørnulf Gulbrandsen, Sian Lazar, John Lonsdale, Giacomo Macola, Liisa Malkki, Tomas Matza, David Maxwell, Wapulumuka Mulwafu, Yael Navaro-Yashin, Isak Niehaus, Francis Nyamnjoh, Derek Peterson, Anthony Simpson, Sharath Srinivasan, Nikolai Ssorin-Chaikov, Marilyn Strathern, Megan Vaughan, Richard Werbner, and Wendy Willems. Dee Mortensen and the peer reviewers assigned by Indiana University Press had a profound impact on shaping the final version of this book.

The research for this book began during a project funded by the Academy of Finland. The final fieldwork and the period of writing were made possible by the support of the University of Cambridge and the Economic and Social Research Council (ESRC).

Human Rights and
African Airwaves

Introduction

Palibe cholakwika, "nothing is wrong," Yohane Banda assured the BBC in an interview in 2006. The father of Madonna's African child feared that the pop star would send the child back to poverty in Malaŵi if she became angry with human rights activists' complaints about the illegalities of the adoption case. The child would return to crushing hardship, a life of tedium and deprivation that could spell his early demise. Would the human rights activists feed the child once the clamor of the high-profile case had died down?

Banda's words in Chicheŵa, Malaŵi's most widely spoken language and a regional lingua franca, were barely audible amid the fury of English-speaking human rights activists in Malaŵi and elsewhere.[1] Their viewpoints were readily juxtaposed in the world media with Madonna's claims to compassion. Not only did the poorly formulated legislation and Malaŵi's failure to be a signatory to the convention on transnational adoptions expose the country to the whims of the rich and the famous. According to activists, Madonna's aims and methods were also morally wrong. Commenting on her alleged choice of the child from a parade of twelve pre-selected children, one activist likened the procedure to slavery, another to shopping.[2]

It is possible, without denying that the controversy over Malaŵi's adoption laws was necessary and worthwhile, to discern in Banda's concern an alternative perspective on the moral dilemmas posed by severe poverty and inequality. Transnational adoption does not need to entail the uprooting it represents to some of its critics.[3] It can become a part of the manner in which some poor people seek relationship with the affluent world, suggesting that "fostering" might be a more accurate term here than "adoption." In his interviews with the world media, Banda emphasized that he would not have allowed the adoption to take place if it had meant that the child was no longer his son.[4] When Madonna returned to Malaŵi in 2009 to court more controversy with her plan to adopt a second child, a meeting was arranged between Banda and his son. Now remarried with another young son, Banda commented that "David still resembles me, but he looks very much like his half-brother Dingiswayo." "I can't wait to see the two brothers reunite," he was also quoted as having said.[5]

These were not the words of a hapless and ignorant victim of a Western celebrity's vanity. With the world watching, Banda was asserting his relationship to his first son and thereby to all the security and prosperity that the son's association with a Western millionaire seemed to involve. Yet it was far from certain that the world would take note of Banda's perspective. Around the same time, a spokesperson for the Save the Children Fund in the United Kingdom pronounced, "The best place for a child is in his or her family in their home country."[6] The pronouncement matched the search for a proper order in the legal objections against Madonna's adoption sprees. Just as the law was expected to provide an unambiguous definition of various parties' rights in transnational adoption, so too was the pronouncement unambiguous about subjects belonging to particular communities. Banda's claim to a relationship in transnational adoption, his evocation of an obligation despite a breathtaking discrepancy in distance and wealth, could only complicate the order activists and experts sought to assert.

While neither Madonna nor transnational adoption will feature in the pages that follow, the broader questions raised by this example are at the heart of this book. What insight might be gained into rights and obligations if claims expressed in African languages were taken seriously by activists, academics, and policy-makers? The question of language—for instance, the sharply uneven opportunity to hear Chicheŵa and English in the world mass media—is important in both literal and metaphorical senses. Close attention to the African-language mass media can yield insights into the form and contents of claims that elude not only foreign observers and policy-makers but also some of Africa's own intelligentsia and human rights activists. As such, the attention to language raises in a more metaphorical sense the question of discursive resources and the extent to which African-language genres stand any chance of influencing debates on contemporary African conditions beyond the particular context in which they are broadcast.[7]

This book explores such questions through the ethnography of a popular radio program in Malaŵi. *Nkhani Zam'maboma* (News from the Districts) was launched in 1998 by the Malaŵi Broadcasting Corporation (MBC) to gather stories from the public. Its matter-of-fact style of presenting those stories defined it as a news bulletin. It is, however, rather different from the official bulletin that has retained an unmistakable bias toward the ruling party despite Malaŵi's transition to multipartyism in the early 1990s. The predictable accounts of presidential and ministerial engagements in the official news bulletin contrast with *Nkhani Zam'maboma*'s irreverent stories about folly among various other figures of authority. Both the contents and the richly idiomatic language of *Nkhani Zam'maboma* distinguish it from the MBC's didactic and partisan reporting, and the program's popularity has been matched by a steady supply of more stories from the public than its editors have been able to accommodate within the daily ten-minute broadcast. Rather than inciting violence or rebellion against those who have caused injury, the program gives more subtle insight into how obligations tying persons into mutual dependence have a certain prospective, aspirational quality. Told from the perspective of the downtrodden, the stories on *Nkhani Zam'maboma* have mediated moral debate outside the purview of political leaders, human rights activists, and aid agencies.

This book examines both the production and reception of *Nkhani Zam'maboma*. If studied with respect to the actual conditions of life and work, editors' views on professional service qualify much of the derision they have received since Malaŵi's airwaves were liberalized in the 1990s. Frequently denounced by foreign and local human rights activists, the MBC's news journalists have found in *Nkhani Zam'maboma* a particularly satisfying mode of public-service broadcasting. The bias and misinformation they allow in other programs appears to be indefensible, until perhaps the end of this book. At the same time, their creative editing of stories sent to *Nkhani Zam'maboma* has generated a nationwide audience that identifies and debates the abuse of power through idioms that are different from the vocabulary introduced by human rights activists and ostensibly democratic politicians. The opportunity here is to explore a public arena in which people, irrespective of their differences in age, gender, religion, and wealth, make claims on those who have caused them injury. The result is a discovery of equality whose consequences extend far beyond the case itself. We are asked to consider how equality as a condition of claim-making differs from equality as a utopian goal pursued under the auspices of human rights activists and democratic politicians.

The Silences of Human Rights Talk

Writing about African-language oral and aural genres, Ruth Finnegan has noted, "Just because some groups have not been listening (perhaps especially certain circles of intellectuals), it does not mean that no one has been speaking" (2007: 72). Of special interest to this book are those young secondary school and university graduates who came to occupy positions as volunteers and paid employees in non-governmental organizations (NGOs) after the political transition in Malaŵi. Many of them adopted human rights as the issue they wanted to promote in the new Malaŵi, but few showed any inclination to explore African-language genres, such as the one broadcast by *Nkhani Zam'maboma*, for insight into the experience and conceptualization of injustice. As I documented in my previous book, *Prisoners of Freedom: Human Rights and the African Poor* (2006), activists and volunteers working for human rights NGOs were often keen to appear as the vanguard of a universal moral and legal disposition. Their preference for English over African languages and their styles of dress, among other markers of identity, distinguished them from "the grassroots" they had identified as the beneficiaries of their knowledge. Condescension was never far from their minds, expressed as doubt over the intellectual capacities of the grassroots. A recent illustration comes from a consultant and NGO entrepreneur of Malaŵian extraction. Describing how he asks his ten-year-old daughter to comment on his writings before passing them on to the publisher, he concludes: "To communicate to the public in a generally low literacy environment, we must target the ten-year mind because the grasp and comprehension ability by most of our people is more or less at that level" (Malunga 2010: 27).

Paternalism about "our people" who have the mind of a ten-year-old owes much to a long history rarely appreciated by those who issue such judgments. Colonialism before independence in 1964 and presidentialism afterward etched such paternalism on the outlook of successive generations who had the opportunity to seek self-improvement through formal education. While true in this broad sense, the historical observation does call for qualification. The condition is somewhat specific to Malaŵi, where the relative absence of radical (whether populist or socialist) ideologies among the intelligentsia has undermined the commitment to social justice observed in some NGOs in other countries in Africa (Yarrow 2008). As research about NGOs develops in diverse world regions, it may also become more apparent how an NGO can display different features to different audiences, from its sponsors to its clients to its peers (Hilhorst 2003). Research carried out by NGOs themselves, moreover, indicates important differences in the methods and objectives of knowledge production among African intellectuals. NGOs' demand for short-term consultancies contrasts with the erudition associated, in Africa as elsewhere, with academic philosophy and social sciences (T. Mkandawire 2005: 32). The contrast that is of interest to this book, however, does allow for a measure of comparability between the NGO and academic segments of African intelligentsia. As discussed below, the contrast revolves around the value that different kinds of intellectuals have attributed to African ways of thought and practice. The question is whether condescension and admiration have actually shared common assumptions.

More than any other members of Malaŵi's intelligentsia, human rights activists provide an illuminating juxtaposition to the editors of *Nkhani Zam'maboma*. While both have been involved in generating knowledge about injustice, the form and contents of the claims they have mediated have been strikingly different. Activists' reluctance to listen to African-language genres has been consistent with their tendency to prioritize political and civil liberties over the full range of grievances Malaŵians have had about poverty and exploitation. One consequence of activists' emphasis on procedural democracy has been a secondary status attributed to socioeconomic rights. The Bill of Rights contained in the new constitution, for example, has failed to specify and even to recognize some of the key socioeconomic rights (D. Chirwa 2005). Moreover, when the Malaŵi Law Commission embarked on a review of the constitution in 2006, it identified issues other than socioeconomic rights as being in need of further elaboration (Mbazira 2007).[8] A brief look at Malaŵi's political economy lays bare the silences of this sort of human rights talk.

After three decades of autocratic rule under Kamuzu Banda, Malaŵi held the first competitive multiparty elections in 1994. The incoming president Bakili Muluzi, a businessman who had once been the secretary general of Banda's party, presided over unprecedented liberalization in politics and the economy. The new constitution put an emphasis on civil and political liberties, while the cultivation of cash crops such as tobacco was liberalized along with market-ing systems. Overall, the new government's interest in smallholder agriculture was halfhearted, with the liberalization of the fertilizer market spelling the end of subsidized inputs and deepening hardship for villagers cultivating overused land (Harrigan 2003).

Despite the new government's rhetoric on private entrepreneurship, Mala-ŵi's manufacturing sector contracted from 16 percent in 1994 to 12 percent in 1999 (Chinsinga 2002: 27). The rhetoric did encourage youths, in particular, to make their living as vendors and hawkers in Malaŵi's main urban centers, Li-longwe, Blantyre-Limbe, Mzuzu, and Zomba, trading in smuggled or imported commodities (Jimu 2008). The country is, however, unlikely to lose its rural outlook anytime soon, the proportion of smallholder farmers of the economi-cally active population having been nearly 79 percent in 1998 (National Statisti-cal Office 2002: 75). Eighty-five percent of the population lived in rural areas in 2008, with a difference of only one percentage between the censuses then and in 1998 (National Statistical Office 2010: 9). The human development index of the United Nations placed Malaŵi at the 164th position out of 177 countries in 2004. It also reported that 42 percent of the population lived below one U.S. dollar per day and 76 percent below two U.S. dollars per day.[9] Such levels of poverty were all the more striking in a country that had avoided large-scale civil strife throughout its independence.

The extent of inequality within Malaŵi is clear in the distribution of land and income. In the 1990s, 1.6 million smallholder families cultivated 1.8 mil-lion hectares of land, whereas three thousand estates owned 1.1 million hect-ares of agricultural land (UNDP 2001: 21). Only 9 percent of the smallhold-ers cultivated more than two hectares of land (UNDP 2001: 19). For the few in formal employment, salaries have always been low even by regional standards and marred by extreme inequality. In 2001, Malaŵi ranked as the third-worst country in the world in income inequality (UNDP 2001: 20). These inequali-ties translate into a permanent crisis in health care, with life expectancy drop-ping, largely because of the HIV/AIDS pandemic, from forty-eight years in 1990 to forty years in 1999 (UNDP 2001: 15).

After two terms in office and an unsuccessful bid to enter an unconstitu-tional third term, Muluzi stepped down in 2004 to pave the way for his hand-picked successor Bingu Wa Mutharika. A retired international civil servant with little foothold in Malaŵi's politics, Mutharika soon abandoned Muluzi and established his own political party. Leading a minority government dur-ing his first term, Mutharika faced a hostile opposition in parliament but enjoyed considerable support among the populace and the country's aid donors. A comprehensive victory in the 2009 presidential and parliamentary elections gave him a strong mandate for the second term. A change in rhetoric and policy accounted for Mutharika's popularity, geared not only against corruption in government but also in favor of smallholder farmers. Food security became one of the new administration's priorities, and backed by targeted input subsidies, some regulation of markets, and timely rains, Malaŵi produced a surplus of maize for consecutive years. Change was also palpable in urban areas, where vendors were removed from streets to designated, if overcrowded, markets.

The Millennium Development Goals, announced in the Millennium Declaration of the United Nations in 2000, gave the government a framework to monitor its progress in eradicating extreme poverty. According to its own report, the proportion of the ultra-poor dropped from 22 percent of the population in 2003 to 17 percent in 2006 and to 15 percent in 2007 (Government of Malaŵi 2008: 7). The positive results have been corroborated by more independent sources (see ODI 2010), but the achievements remain precarious. The poverty gap ratio—the average distance separating the poor from the poverty line—has changed little, thereby suggesting that some of the ordinary poor are never far from the condition of the ultra-poor (Government of Malaŵi 2008: 4). Moreover, support for smallholder farming can hardly produce sustainable benefits without political will to attend to the inequalities in land distribution.[10] Insufficient land has turned into landlessness in some parts of Malaŵi (Kanyongolo 2005 and 2008), and the predicament is not eased by increasing population density. Whereas on average 85 people lived on every square kilometer in 1987 and 105 people did so in 1998, the figure had risen to 139 people in 2008 (National Statistical Office 2010: 10).

Such matters of political economy rarely entered human rights talk after liberalization in Malaŵi. Particularly during Muluzi's regime, Malaŵi's public arenas, as mediated by ostensibly democratic politicians and human rights activists, entertained little else than the rhetoric of civil and political liberties, with the concept of human rights itself translated into Chicheŵa as *ufulu wachibadwidwe*, "birth-freedom" (Englund 2006: 47–69). Few Malaŵian activists sought to "open up" (An-Na'im 2002: 5) the concept of human rights to address the actual experiences and debates among the populace. They failed, as such, to contribute to the making of a human rights concept that might be genuinely universal, forged at the intersection, or friction (Tsing 2005), between apparently incompatible interests, practices, and metaphysics—"African" no less than "Western" (see Fernythough 1993; Zeleza 2004).[11] This book seeks to redress this deficiency by exploring public broadcasting in Malaŵi since the democratic transition for alternative insights into rights and obligations. Crucial to such a project is the realization that certain ways of making claims on other people can be just as widely publicized as the definition of human rights that NGOs adopted as their own. The reason why these claims have received little attention from activists and their foreign donors is twofold. On the one hand, voiced in Chicheŵa, they have escaped the attention of Malaŵi's expatriate community, many of whom never acquire fluency in the first language of about 70 percent of its population, a language that is understood by even more Malaŵians.[12] On the other hand, by not announcing themselves as alternatives to the human rights discourse, these claims have been easy to ignore among activists.

Liberalism on the African Airwaves

Studies of liberalism in Africa, particularly those that have seen its prospects dimmed by the shadows of colonial legacies, have emphasized the co-existence of two modes of rule, one designed for urban-based citizens with rights and the other for the rural majority living as the subjects of traditional institutions (see, e.g., Ekeh 1975; Mamdani 1996). A corollary has been a series of dichotomies that stifle analysis, including those between the Western and African ways of governance, modernity and tradition, individual and society, and liberalism and despotism. The interest in examining *Nkhani Zam'maboma* in conjunction with a particular form of human rights talk is to move from such dualism to a more nuanced understanding of multiple orientations within liberalism.

Such a project is not without precedents in the study of Africa. One precedent was set in the anthropology of Africa by those studies that, through detailed descriptions of egalitarian and inegalitarian practices as simultaneous possibilities, decoupled rights and obligations from a simplistic juxtaposition between individual and society (Fortes 1949; Gluckman 1965; see also Shipton 2007).[13] Another pertinent precedent is the recent revisionist history of nationalism in so-called British Central Africa, where the authoritarianism of post-independence regimes has threatened to erase from the historical record the liberal aspirations among some early African nationalists (Macola 2010; Power 2010). These precedents in scholarship alert us to the inadequacies of assuming that liberalism in its manifold forms is necessarily alien to Africa, or that Western discussions on the subject have little to gain from the study of Africa. In the twenty-first century, liberalism demands fresh ethnographic engagement in a double sense. The first is the liberalization of broadcasting and publishing, along with politics and the economy, in which new media products such as *Nkhani Zam'maboma* are embedded. The second is liberalism as an internally diverse moral outlook that feeds the ethnographer with implicit assumptions about the way the world is (or ought to be).

Ethnography on the production and reception of *Nkhani Zam'maboma* engages with the ways in which the mass media have been enlisted to support liberalization in Africa and elsewhere. As an aspect of foreign and nongovernmental aid since the end of the Cold War, media assistance has sought to promote an imported institutional framework of liberal democracy (LaMay 2007). The freedom of expression has been seen as an essential component of other freedoms in a democratic society, as outlined, among many other documents, in the Declaration on Principles of Expression in Africa by the African Commission on Human and Peoples' Rights in 2002. It calls for "full respect for freedom of expression" in order to assist "people to make informed decisions" and to facilitate and strengthen democracy. The declaration emphasizes "the particular importance of broadcast media in Africa, given its capacity to reach a wide audience due to the comparatively low cost of receiving transmissions and its ability to overcome barriers of illiteracy" (quoted in ARTICLE 19 2003: 5–6).

Nkhani Zam'maboma, associated as it is with Malaŵi's only public broadcaster, is as much entangled in mainstream liberal public arenas as it seems to offer alternatives to them. By the same token, the perspectives that emerge in the course of this book are by no means a straightforward rebuttal of liberal assumptions. It is not the freedom of expression as a value that is under dispute here. As far as journalism is concerned, at issue are the actual conditions of work and aspiration that some liberal prescriptions may overlook (Hasty 2005; Nyamnjoh 2005a). As the following chapters will show, *Nkhani Zam'maboma* has mediated engagement with injustice among both journalists and its listeners without recourse to the kind of assertive and individualistic claim-making that human rights activists have seemingly promoted.[14] Yet the purpose of ethnography is not simply to offer a special case that goes against generalization, as if African-language broadcasts could only have localized, parochial, or vernacular import (see also note 11). Such a purpose would allow those who do deploy "Africa" as a category of thought to proceed without significant challenge (see Ferguson 2006). The task is, rather, to make ethnography explore and test the liberal assumptions that often inform the definition of problems and solutions in contemporary Africa.

Stories broadcast on *Nkhani Zam'maboma* seem particularly pertinent to an exploration of equality rather than liberty within the vast repertoire of liberal thought.[15] They describe the disappointment that the figures of authority (husbands, wives, parents, chiefs, religious leaders, healers, teachers) cause when they forget or abuse their obligations toward their subjects. The perspective on equality gained through these stories is not simply peculiar to Malaŵian culture, as if equality could only be identified within discrete cultural worlds and was therefore a concept without any measure of generality (for an anthropological critique, see Fardon 1990: 580–581). The specter of cultural particularity is acute in the study of Africa, because scores of scholars and politicians have proposed a categorical distinction between Africa and the West. A pan-African sensibility has often inspired assertions, such as Kwasi Wiredu's, of a "deep difference between African communalism and Western individualism" (2009: 16). Such African alternatives have done little to dispense with the organizing assumptions of liberal thought itself, most notably the distinction between society and individual. This is evident in the ease with which the value attributed to communalism can be either positive or negative. The critics of African communalism use precisely the same form of argument as do its defenders, such as when Africans are portrayed to be so mired in communalism that they are unable to recognize "the values of secularism, personal privacy, and individualism" (Howard 1990: 170; see also Donnelly 1989).

A mere shift of perspective from rights and liberty to obligations and equality would not, in other words, resolve major conceptual issues bequeathed by liberal thought. "I am because we are; and since we are, therefore I am" (Mbiti 1970: 141) is an uplifting catchphrase to champion African values, such as in South Africa after apartheid, but it is not a description of human relationships in their messy actuality. The catchphrase has, however, the merit of regarding relationships as intrinsic to human existence rather than as something to which pre-social individuals must adjust themselves. African intellectual production does, therefore, present genuine opportunities to move beyond positions that derive from theories that are the problem in the first place. This book seeks to contribute to such a project through ethnography, recognizing that intellectual production is not confined to the intelligentsia.

The intellectual challenges underlying this book, alluding to some of the greatest conundrums in liberal thought, may seem not only intractable but also preposterous in a study ostensibly devoted to an African-language debate on the moral dilemmas posed by severe poverty and inequality. Indeed, some Africanists have expressed indignation at anything that smacks of theoretical and conceptual reflection (see White 2007). Such an attitude diminishes the study of Africa, assuming as it does that ethnographic and historical observations on Africa are neither mediated by assumptions and concepts derived from other contexts nor capable of confronting their universalist pretensions. At the same time, the choice of empirical domains for such exploration can itself be influenced more by what Euro-American academia considers cutting-edge than by actual practices in contemporary Africa. For example, the author of a pioneering anthropological book on Second Life, the online virtual world, has remarked, "It is hard to find a place today where the Internet isn't influencing people, and it is important for anthropologists to think about the cultural and political ramifications of new technologies" (quoted in Winnick 2008: 21; see Boellstorff 2008).

Social scientists may well want to avoid becoming bystanders in debates about the effects of new media technologies, but one contribution the study of Africa can make is to put such effects in perspective. In 2005, 0.07 percent of the Malaŵian population were internet subscribers (Government of Malaŵi 2008: 44). Although the indirect significance of the internet was undoubtedly greater than what this figure suggests, it shows that those interested in mass-mediated public arenas in Malaŵi should not overlook other domains to investigate. The reach of the radio makes it the foremost mass medium in Malaŵi, as in many other African countries, a medium which is far more widely accessed than newspapers and television, as well as the internet. Above all, in their rush to appreciate the new media, social scientists may confuse what is technologically cutting-edge with what is theoretically innovative. The mundane battery-powered radio can broadcast claims that go to the heart of the intellectual challenges confronting contemporary debates about liberalism and equality.

Old or new, media technologies do present ethnographic fieldwork with methodological dilemmas. In this regard, the study of radio broadcasting is not unlike the study of the internet and mobile telephones in Africa (see e.g., Buskens and Wobb 2009; de Bruijn et al. 2009). Both require, if they aim at giving insight into a range of users and media professionals, the capacity to traverse several sites during fieldwork. By the same token, this book arises from the serendipity offered by long-term village- and township-based fieldwork. This fieldwork both suggested *Nkhani Zam'maboma* as a topic and gave insights into its position in the everyday circumstances of its public. It was villagers in Dedza District and peri-urban dwellers in Chinsapo Township near the capital Lilongwe, my interlocutors for several years before I developed an interest in this topic, that drew my attention to the program. The fieldwork for this book took place between 2003 and 2008, in total for eighteen months, but much of it built on familiarity acquired through regular periods of residence in Dedza since 1992 and in Chinsapo since 1996. Villagers' and township dwellers' reflections on the stories broadcast on *Nkhani Zam'maboma* emerged both without my prompting in a variety of everyday situations and when we specifically sat down to listen to them, either live on the radio or by playing back my recordings. In 2003 and 2006 I recorded over five hundred stories, and I also obtained additional stories from the transcriptions held at the MBC. Apart from seeking comments on certain linguistic elements, I had, especially at the beginning, few questions to ask during the broadcasts. My interlocutors' elaboration on stories they had just heard was in itself a valuable opportunity to revise my own understanding of what those stories had said and how they could become entwined with their listeners' lives.

I first visited the headquarters of the MBC in Blantyre in 2001 as a part of my research on the translation of human rights discourse. This research introduced me to the MBC's top management and its senior Chicheŵa editors, contacts that proved important when I decided to conduct fieldwork in the newsroom where *Nkhani Zam'maboma* was edited. Although the management and employees at the MBC were consistently welcoming in their approach to me and my work, it was only after several months that I achieved enough trust among editors to be given complete freedom to read all the material that was sent to them and to compare their edited versions to the originals. This crucial aspect of my research had been delayed by the editors' initial denial that they changed much in the stories they decided to broadcast. The more our rapport deepened, the more I realized how much creativity they brought to bear on *Nkhani Zam'maboma,* a source of professional pride often compromised by other aspects of their work for the MBC. Further insights into the material and moral conditions of these journalists' lives emerged when I was invited to their homes in Blantyre's townships and to their villages of origin.

Inegalitarian Aspirations

The media professionals whom human rights activists and other observers often call "state broadcasters" are unlikely candidates for anything else than a demonstration of illiberal tendencies on the African airwaves.[16] A focus on *Nkhani Zam'maboma* certainly does not exculpate such tendencies in the MBC's other programs. But it offers a perspective on the liberalization of the airwaves that provokes questions a more obvious choice of topic would not enable us to face. The first chapter discusses the emergence of commercial and community radio stations in Malaŵi, and while some of them have succeeded in aligning their broadcasting with the liberal value of non-partisanship, the very popularity of *Nkhani Zam'maboma* demands attention. The world its stories depict is resolutely hierarchical, but the capacity of listeners to send in such stories regardless of their differences in age, gender, religion, and wealth is itself a consequence of liberalization. Accordingly, the fascination its broadcasts evoke, and the nationwide public it generates, are features of the liberalized public arenas the MBC's critics wish to defend. By connecting the MBC's journalists to their predominantly impoverished public in villages and townships, *Nkhani Zam'maboma* offers an opportunity to investigate what the liberal value of exposing injustice might mean to them all.

Such a topic also presents a corrective to a trend in the study of Africa that examines twenty-first century African life-worlds through the fantasies and aspirations of youths and new elites. Whether they are secondary school students (Simpson 2003; Stambach 2000) or urban-based business and NGO professionals (Ferguson 2006: 113–154), Pentecostals immersed in the prosperity gospel (Gifford 2004) or young men enthralled by hip-hop (Ntarangwi 2009; Weiss 2009), insights emerge into how Africans pursue their desires under the conditions of globalization. These insights are themselves a corrective to misguided ideas about Africa's isolation from the rest of world. Because these scholars are not all saying the same things about Africa's place in globalization, they also sustain a lively debate about the precise nature of contemporary African aspirations. Alongside the global circulation of images, sounds, and modes of identification exist media, however, by which Africans imagine the cross-cutting relationships that tie them to their families, neighborhoods, villages, and nations. In fact, by emphasizing Africans' involvement in globalization, scholars may swing the pendulum too far from what might actually be their everyday concerns and aspirations. The popularity of *Nkhani Zam'maboma* suggests that rather than globalization being an everyday concern, such significance is properly assumed by the conduct of personal relationships. It is an everyday concern in the quite literal sense of stories about relationships being broadcast on a daily basis.

Stories about personal relationships, as has already been alluded, have more than localized or parochial import. By the same token, they do much else than make Malaŵians aware of their intimate aspirations and constraints. They summon into being a national public at a time when nationalism appears to be on the wane in Africa, eroded by widespread migration and displacement, transnational religious and youth movements, and global NGO networks. While the generation of a national public in this case owes little to nationalism, the specific features of *Nkhani Zam'maboma* also make it a medium that transcends the confines of the national. The language of broadcast cuts across ethnic and national boundaries. Chicheŵa has long ceased to be the language of the Cheŵa, with Malaŵians of various ethnic origins acquiring it as their first language in the past few decades (Centre for Language Studies n.d. a). It is also spoken as the first language across Malaŵi's boundaries in Zambia and Mozambique, whose border regions have always been within the orbit of the MBC's broadcasts. Perhaps the most decisive feature that makes this national public transcend its own confines is the imagination of relationships of varying scale. As examples in this book will show, the public deliberations and personal reflections that stories inspire often move seamlessly from the scale of the personal to the national to the transnational.

Nkhani Zam'maboma enriches our understanding of liberalism on the African airwaves not only because it emanates from a broadcasting house that few observers would include in their list of liberal institutions in the new Malaŵi. It does so also because of the perspective it affords on the fundamental liberal value of equality. The challenge here is to understand what constitutes equality in the absence of an egalitarian ideology. As mentioned, stories uphold rather than subvert the hierarchical order in which figures of authority have obligations toward their subjects. Equality is intrinsic to the way in which authorities themselves are subjected to the desires of their dependents. More precisely, equality is a condition of the very claim dependents can place on their masters, benefactors, and leaders. It is by no means obvious that spaces for making such claims—and the equality they entail—have been abundant in Malaŵi. In this regard, *Nkhani Zam'maboma*'s mass-mediated space for taking authorities to task gives meaning to equality in relation to the widespread poverty and inequality that may make more conventional liberal prescriptions ineffective. That the hierarchies those claims uphold are actively desired by claimants also calls into question the specific content the freedom-focused human rights talk has given to equality.

An obvious contrast with this human rights talk is the way in which equality is not imagined as an attribute of mutually independent individuals. Neither individualism nor communalism captures the sense of equality as a condition of relationships within which claims are made. Intrinsic to relationships, equality requires no vanguard of progressive intellectuals and activists for its realization. Here is another contrast to human rights talk: whereas Malaŵian human rights activists have assumed the role of a vanguard in their efforts to introduce the new vocabulary of rights, the editors of *Nkhani Zam'maboma* do not assert their separation from the public they seek to serve. It is important to understand the different temporal horizons involved in this contrast. Human rights, in Malaŵi as elsewhere, have a certain utopian quality to them (Goodale 2009). While activists may in practice pursue incremental changes, the idea of human rights as the guarantee of equal freedoms and opportunities may well evoke a utopia, a distant future which may never arrive but which animates the vanguard in the present. By contrast, equality as a condition of relationship within which a claim is made is very much a matter of the present. The hierarchies those claims hope to make productive belong to the near rather than distant future, attainable before long though not predictable in their effects.[17]

The interest in juxtaposing *Nkhani Zam'maboma* with human rights talk is more descriptive than normative. This book comments on the *practice* of human rights rather than on the theory of human rights disconnected from the consideration of any actual form of life. Even if a fresh perspective on the nature and prospects of liberalism in Africa may thereby be achieved, the alternative to human rights talk is no panacea, nor is the objective to attack the idea of human rights. How *Nkhani Zam'maboma* might be criticized is also an aspect of this ethnography. It is a truism that there is more than meets the eye in the diverse idioms, narratives, and concepts through which people describe their relationships to themselves. When the rich attribute moral value to generosity, they can obscure the privileged standpoint from which they issue such an injunction (Moore 1986: 301). In Marshall Sahlins's memorable, if overly rhetorical, phrase, "Everywhere in the world the indigenous category for exploitation is 'reciprocity'" (1972: 134).

Critique, however, may come far too easily to social scientists. The capacity for seeing through the smoke screens of self-serving idioms, for seeing more than meets the eye, is not their prerogative. The debate that stories on *Nkhani Zam'maboma* provoke often interrogates not only authorities' complacency but also the purpose of the program itself. It is imperative to explore Malaŵian critiques of *Nkhani Zam'maboma* before issuing a social-scientific verdict on it. Both the critique and the celebration of the program by its editors and public attest to the powers of the imagination, released from the "deficient, illusory, deceptive, or suspect status" (Castoriadis 1997: 215) attributed to it by much of Western philosophy. No longer situated within the confines of "a psychological or ego-logical horizon" (Castoriadis 1997: 245), not to mention its re-

duction to the domain of the arts, the imagination assumes a profoundly social character, an inter-subjective sphere of experience and argument within
which alternatives to dominant perspectives can attain collective purchase.[18]
Whether such alternatives are best described as resistance to dominant perspectives is a moot point, one this book addresses with reference to the specific conditions of aspiration and constraint in twenty-first-century Malaŵi.

Outline of the Book

The chapters in part 1 begin to explore in detail the philosophical, historical,
and ethnographic issues this book seeks to engage. The particular history and
contemporary circumstances of public-service broadcasting in Malaŵi are the
focus of chapter 1. Against the easy dismissals of MBC journalists as passive
vessels of state propaganda, the chapter outlines the colonial and postcolonial
legacies within which they have pursued their profession. The new rhetorics
and regulatory frameworks of public-service broadcasting have attracted the
attention of politicians, human rights activists, and media analysts both inside
and outside Malaŵi. *Nkhani Zam'maboma,* which has the policy of not including politicians in the range of authorities its stories depict, has been deemed
unpolitical and therefore beyond the purview of these acrimonious debates on
Malaŵi's media.

Chapter 2 discusses how anthropologists have, more often than not, made
implicit assumptions about equality instead of subjecting it to a sustained anthropological consideration. Scandalized by inequality, anthropologists have
been reticent about the concept of equality that has informed their critiques.
Further evidence of unexamined liberal and illiberal assumptions creeping into
analysis is obtained through a consideration of how the conceptualization of
African alternatives has been harnessed to variously expose, subvert, and support liberal predilections. Deliberative democracy, counter-publics, and news
journalism provide examples of themes that have developed liberal thought in
relation to the study of mass media.

MBC journalists' pride in serving the government, as opposed to mere partisanship, is an observation that is developed further in chapter 3. A convergence
between the experiences of the impoverished public and the editors of *Nkhani
Zam'maboma* is a major theme here. Long-standing grievances within the MBC,
combined with worsening financial difficulties, generated frustration and resentment similar to that among the rural and urban poor, a convergence also
evident in both editors' and their public's interest in stories about witchcraft.

However, anthropology's own tendency to isolate witchcraft as a domain of discourse comes under consideration when it is observed that such stories by no means constituted the majority of stories broadcast on *Nkhani Zam'maboma*. This comparison between analytical and moral alternatives among journalists and anthropologists raises the question of equality in knowledge production.

Part 2 examines the contents and production of *Nkhani Zam'maboma*. Chapter 4 gives an overview of its recurrent topics and the regional and rural-urban distribution of stories that were broadcast. The conventions that made the program a new genre on Malaŵi's airwaves involved mixing the news format with features of long-established verbal arts. The analysis here is more textual than elsewhere in the book, but such an examination is crucial for understanding how stories assume their efficacy, and how they relate to other genres of storytelling, from news broadcasts to popular literature. It is also vital for recognizing the difference between the program's moral imagination and the didactic tone prevalent in Malaŵi's public culture. A discussion of several examples of stories substantiates these points and gives a flavor of what was broadcast.

The ethos of equality that this discussion of topics and their treatment begins to identify is carried forward by the ethnography of editorial aspirations and practices in chapter 5. Editors' creative input has included both the insertion of idiomatic expressions and the revision of perspectives in stories they have received from the public. The editing of stories for broadcast is also examined in the context of the editors' treatment of rejoinders and their rejection of some stories. Non-partisanship as public service becomes particularly evident in editors' refusal to broadcast stories involving politicians of any persuasion. After considering examples of editorial interventions in detail, the chapter concludes by presenting some key differences between this journalistic ethos and the movement of public journalism in the United States and elsewhere. A fundamental contrast revolves around what constitutes news. Whereas in public journalism news assumes the condition of novelty when it reveals inequalities, for the editors of *Nkhani Zam'maboma* it is the equal standpoint for making claims amid all-too-apparent inequalities that marks it out as a news program.

Chapter 6 ends this part by taking a closer look at editors' principles of verification and the insights they give into the relationships within which stories assumed their impact. As examples of testimonials, stories that were broadcast contrast in illuminating ways with testimonial practices in human rights reporting. This contrast receives more ethnographic analysis in a detailed consideration of so-called correspondents, listeners who became regular suppliers of stories. The MBC had no means to formally recognize them as contributors. Often somewhat marginal in the localities where they lived, correspondents could, however, achieve local renown through their association with *Nkhani Zam'maboma*. One correspondent's methods of verifying stories are given as an example of the consistent pattern by which the truth of a story was often a function of personal knowledge about relationships.

The shift of focus in part 3 from production to reception examines the effect the program's ethos of equality had in diverse everyday situations. Whereas chapter 6 describes the frequent supply of stories from some areas, the site of fieldwork on which chapter 7 reports was, for its inhabitants and for the ethnographer, remarkably invisible in *Nkhani Zam'maboma*. Silence on the radio could, however, speak volumes, as the chapter demonstrates through the case of a village headman. The conflict with his subjects evolved in the common awareness that a story about a similar scandal in a neighboring chiefdom had been broadcast on *Nkhani Zam'maboma*. The possibility of his misdemeanors becoming the subject of another broadcast played a significant role in disciplining the headman. Instead of being based on assertive and direct claims, this disciplining shows the powers of silent claims in the particular aesthetic of claim-making mediated by *Nkhani Zam'maboma*.

The program's disciplinary effects are explored further in chapter 8, which considers not only the program's popularity but also its critiques among Malaŵians. Suspending a social-scientific critique, the chapter explores arguments and viewpoints among born-again Christians, who were the program's most vociferous critics. They favored a comparable program of testimonies on an evangelical radio station. This comparable program both contradicted and extended the potential of *Nkhani Zam'maboma* to mediate an ethos of equality in claim-making, demonstrating that the alternative was not as disconnected from its opposite as critics suggested. Chapter 9 concludes the book by reviewing the alternative this ethnography presents to liberal thought on equality and obligation, and to the assumption among some scholars and policy-makers that Africa lacks institutions to monitor the abuse of power.

Texts, Transcriptions, and Translations

Any ethnography that is based on a substantial corpus of texts struggles to strike the right balance between analysis and a readable account of what those texts say. The ethnography of *Nkhani Zam'maboma* also faces the additional challenge of translating those texts and making at least some of the background knowledge they require available to readers who do not participate in the life-worlds they depict. I have opted for offering extracts from several stories across the chapters, with the original Chicheŵa words given either in brackets or in notes. To counter the unfortunate result of not rendering the stories in full, the section of appendixes provides the transcriptions and translations of those stories that have been considered in more detail in the chapters. All translations were done by me, as were the transcriptions, unless stated otherwise. Chicheŵa uses very few special characters, and I have relied on the Chicheŵa Board's (1990) revised edition of its orthography rules.

PART 1

Human Rights,
African Alternatives

1

Rights and Wrongs on the Radio

"Government says it is committed to ensuring that rural areas are developed." Broadcast in the main news bulletin of the Malaŵi Broadcasting Corporation (MBC) in 2006, this headline did not announce news in any obvious sense.[1] Novelty was less important than the timeless legitimacy of the state, whatever the composition of the government conducting its affairs.[2] The headline, in point of fact, was itself timeless. The year of its broadcast could have been any of Malaŵi's independence since 1964, when after three decades of Kamuzu Banda's autocratic regime, the country was ruled by two ostensibly democratic presidents, Bakili Muluzi (1994–2004) and Bingu wa Mutharika (2004 to the present). When I first arrived in Malaŵi in the twilight years of Banda's regime, it was the MBC's weather forecast that represented to me the station's disregard for imparting information. I discovered that the weather forecast had had the same refrain for decades, regardless of the season: "The winds will be light and variable but gusty in stormy areas." With its caveat and tautology, it seemed to sum up an ethos whose principal interest was to broadcast platitudes that would apply to *any time* and *anywhere* in Malaŵi.

Ethnographic fieldwork has enabled me to appreciate what lies beneath the predictable news headlines and the unchanging weather forecast. Villagers and township dwellers I worked with on other research projects drew my attention to *Nkhani Zam'maboma* at the dawn of the new millennium, the period when new private radio stations had, it seemed to me, consigned the MBC to its long overdue oblivion. Here was a program, I came to learn, which engaged Malaŵians' imagination of power and injustice far more effectively than the various civic-education initiatives of human rights organizations that were all the rage. Once admitted to work as an ethnographer in the newsroom, I also came to realize the value of this program for the MBC journalists' self-esteem. It was one of those rare programs in which professionalism as public service could flourish. Excruciating personal dilemmas and profound inequalities inside the MBC gave me insights into how state broadcasters experienced and negotiated the problems of bias and misinformation they were so often accused of (see chapter 3). *Nkhani Zam'maboma* also complicated another, less often remarked, facet of the MBC. It stood in contrast to the didactic tone of much else that was broadcast there and elsewhere in Malaŵi. The didactic tone was based on the unquestioned value of developmentalism as a justification for the delivery of paternalist messages to the impoverished masses. *Nkhani Zam'maboma* enabled the poor to make claims, however remote the form of those claims was from the ones promoted by human rights activists and aid agencies.[3]

It should be clear, therefore, that *Nkhani Zam'maboma* complicates rather than exculpates the work of the MBC. Yet precisely because the journalistic practices informing the program, and the claims and comments it inspired in villages and townships, provide an alternative perspective on Malaŵian engagements with human rights, obligations, poverty, and inequality, this perspective also necessarily questions the ease with which human rights organizations have condemned the MBC. ARTICLE 19—an international organization whose name evokes the Article 19 of the Universal Declaration of Human Rights that calls for the freedom of expression and open access to information— has called MBC journalists "slavish apparatchiks" (n.d.: 13). A look at the history of public broadcasting in Malaŵi certainly makes such seething strictures understandable, but the opportunity to explore critics' own convictions should not be lost. Human rights organizations' criticisms of media outlets draw on the expectation that the individual human being ought to be independent in forming opinions and accessing information no less than in pursuing his or her life on the basis of those opinions and information. By so doing, however, human rights activists may miss out on other ways of generating knowledge and claims about injustice, not least within the very institutions they criticize. One interest in regard to *Nkhani Zam'maboma* is its capacity to circumvent certain journalistic practices that have long been implicated in perpetuating injustice.

The Paternalism of Public Broadcasting

The BBC started broadcasting in Britain in 1922, and two years later a broadcasting station was established in South Africa, followed by one in Kenya in 1927 (Mytton 1983: 52). The first stations on the African continent, including the one in Harare (then Salisbury) from 1932 onward, were aimed exclusively at white listeners. The Second World War gave the colonial governments a reason to start broadcasting to African audiences, primarily as a means of informing them about their relatives conscripted to fight in the war. Radio Lusaka, launched in 1941 in Zambia (then Northern Rhodesia), expanded to become the Central African Broadcasting Station. After the end of the Central African Federation, it dissolved into three different national broadcasters, including the MBC.[4] Radio Lusaka was the first station in Africa aimed exclusively at Africans, and its broadcasting in African languages pioneered a policy favoring African languages in broadcasting in British colonies (Fraenkel 1959: 17). The policy was somewhat different in French territories, where French was given priority in broadcasting (Mytton 1983: 53).

The first receivers for Radio Lusaka were placed on public sites such as administrative centers, chiefs' courts, and mission stations (Fraenkel 1959: 17). This initiated a pattern by which radio listening has been as much a public as a private phenomenon in Africa (Larkin 2008: 71). The British language policy was, however, conducive to creating a mass audience based in domestic settings, and the ownership of receivers expanded rapidly in British colonies. Technological progress was crucial to this expansion. Wireless sets requiring electricity from main power supplies were soon supplanted by the "Saucepan Special" powered by large batteries, itself made obsolete in the 1950s by the arrival of transistor radios (Mytton 2000: 23). Although initially more expensive than the "Saucepan," transistor radios did not require expensive batteries, and a flood of imports established the portable radio as a feature of everyday life among many Africans. As discussed below, Malaŵi is one of those African countries where the radio has held its own as virtually the only mass medium. The history of technology is evident in the Chicheŵa word *wayilesi* (wireless) that is still the most common term for radio in Malaŵi.

The production of an African public was inseparable from the wider colonial project of creating subjects that could be ruled and enlightened at the same time (van der Veur 2002: 82–85). In this regard, it is instructive to compare the BBC's early intentions at home and the nature of its journalistic and organizational influence on emerging radio stations in Africa. The question of paternalism in the British model of public service broadcasting remains a moot point (see, e.g., Fortner 2005: 29; LeMahieu 1988: 145–148), but it is clear that class differences did cast a shadow over the BBC's inception. The ideal of service was "animated by a sense of moral purpose and of social duty on behalf of the community, aimed particularly at those most in need of reforming—the lower classes" (Scannell and Cardiff 1991: 9). Recent theoretical currents in the social sciences, inspired by Michel Foucault, have ingeniously discerned the exercise of power in various reformist projects to improve the lives of the disadvantaged (see, e.g., Cruikshank 1999; Rose 1999). Such a perspective may, however, gloss over significant differences in the ways in which paternalism could inform broadcasting in Britain and Africa.

Both sides had their pioneers, whose ideological commitments illuminate genuine differences in the nature and extent of paternalism in broadcasting. Harry Franklin was the director of information in the colonial administration when he started Radio Lusaka. One of his explanations for the initiative to start broadcasting to an African audience stated that "formal educational methods, taking perhaps two or three generations to produce a comparatively civilized African people capable of working reasonably well in the development of the territory, were too slow in the face of the obvious possibilities of rapid advance in Central Africa. We believed that if broadcasting could reach the masses, it could play a great part in the enlightenment" (quoted in Fraenkel 1959: 17). Compare this statement with the words of John Reith, the first director general of the BBC: "Our responsibility is to carry into the greatest possible number of homes everything that is best in every department of human knowledge, endeavour and achievement, and to avoid the things which are, or may be, hurtful" (1924: 34). Among his many examples, Reith mentioned the broadcasting of opera—"a comparatively small number of people were in a position to hear opera before" (1924: 175)—and children's programs that "may serve as an antidote to the harm which is being wrought on the children of the present day by the conditions under which they live" (1924: 185). Both Franklin and Reith were enthralled by the idea of enlightenment, but their approach to those they deemed to be in need of it (African natives and British lower classes) was not identical. "It is better to over-estimate the mentality of the public than to under-estimate it," Reith (1924: 34) wrote, alluding to the promise of public broadcasting as a class leveler.[5] For Franklin, "a comparatively civilized" public had to be *produced* before it could assume its role in the development of a society.

Much as revisionist perspectives on colonialism emphasize a process of negotiation and mutual influence between the colonizer and the colonized (see, e.g., Dirks 1992), it may not be accurate to view broadcasting in Africa in the same terms as other colonial intrusions. Broadcasting stations in Africa assumed a singular organizational form, one that was more centralized and more closely supervised by governments than, for example, the BBC ever was (Fardon and Furniss 2000: 9; Nyamnjoh 2005a: 47).[6] State monopoly over broadcasting intensified after independence in countries such as Malawi. It was only in 1998 that the legal status of the MBC shifted from a state broadcaster to a public-service broadcaster (ARTICLE 19 2003), and even then, as discussed below, the transformation was more apparent than real. The effects of state supervision and censorship on the MBC were particularly severe during the period of one-party rule under Banda.[7] Similar problems during the era of multiparty democracy, the more immediate context for *Nkhani Zam'maboma*, are discussed below and in chapter 3.

The problem with a perspective that focuses solely on state monopoly, then and now, is its inability to portray *Nkhani Zam'maboma* as anything other than an aberration from the norm. By making the program seem almost accidental in the perennial condition of bias and misinformation, the perspective prevents insight into the complexities of production and reception in the history of the MBC. It was precisely because the MBC's news and reports were so implausible that critical listenership started to evolve in Malawi. Jack Mapanje, an academic and poet who was detained without charge toward the end of Banda's regime, has recalled that "what appeared in the local papers, what was heard on the radio, was often irrelevant to the meaning of the event" (2002: 183). Under such circumstances, the "faculty of speculation and quick perception of events had to be highly developed" (2002: 183). The faculty of speculation did not become redundant with multiparty democracy, nor was it the prerogative of Malawi's intelligentsia. It was on the foundation of this critical listenership that the success of *Nkhani Zam'maboma* was erected.

At the same time, state monopoly and paternalism have long co-existed with a desire to elicit participation from listeners. White directors at the Central African Broadcasting Station cherished their trips to rural areas to record local music (Fraenkel 1959: 25), and nostalgia for a similar program, known as *Nyimbo Zam'maboma* (Songs from the Districts) and discontinued in the 1990s because of financial difficulties, was intense among the MBC's senior journalists during my fieldwork. The involvement of listeners through letters and interviews was a concern at the MBC even during the darkest years of postcolonial dictatorship. In the early 1980s, an MBC journalist, drawing the historical connection to British broadcasting a little too definitely, commented with considerable optimism: "It is good to see that the rigidity of the structure inherited from the BBC is being quickly broken down in order to allow the broadcaster and audience to interact positively" (quoted in Wedell 1986: 288).

These complexities call for careful consideration of contradictory practices within the apparently stifling approach to public broadcasting. The intent is not so much to justify those practices as to recognize the forms of critical reflection that both broadcasters and listeners have had at their disposal. The Central African Broadcasting Station provides another unlikely example of such a space for alternatives. Reminiscing about Pepe Zulu, the station's ambitious and argumentative Nyanja (Chicheŵa) announcer, a white broadcaster noted, "In most offices I knew in the Rhodesias he would have been dismissed after a week, perhaps because a semi-literate white girl employed as a filing-clerk would complain that he was a 'cheeky kaffir'" (Fraenkel 1959: 50). Mutual suspicion and the low levels of formal education among MBC journalists are significant, but it is also necessary to consider how the oppressive conditions of their work have themselves given rise to subtle forms of critique and claim-making. At the same time, complexity is magnified by the simultaneous possibility that the idea of public service, expressed as serving the government of the day, does attach genuine pride to their work.

Radio Nation

The launching and early days of *Nkhani Zam'maboma* will be traced in chapter 4, but it is important to note that it emerged in the context of unprecedented competition on Malaŵi's airwaves. In the aftermath of the Catholic bishops' pastoral letter in 1992—the first publicly voiced criticism of Banda's regime in years—the minister of state announced the government's endorsement of a free press (Chimombo and Chimombo 1996: 26). After the democratic transition, the National Broadcasting Policy, drawn up by the Ministry of Information, determined in 1998 that radio broadcasting was to be liberalized with immediate effect, backed by a new Communications Act in the same year (ARTICLE 19 2003). In anticipation of competition from private radio stations, the MBC launched its Radio Two in 1997 to offer more popular music and innovative program formats than the conservative Radio One was able to accommodate.[8] One of the innovations was to broadcast Radio Two around the clock, as opposed to the nineteen hours of Radio One per day, whereas Radio Two's use of English and Chicheŵa contrasted with Radio One's own innovation to start broadcasting news bulletins in seven languages.[9] Although its broadcasting style assumed a youthful outlook, Radio Two sought to cater to a broad range of listeners, including programs on children, cooking, sports, the disabled, and agriculture. Some of the topics were therefore the same as on Radio One, but Radio Two explored new interactive methods through, for example, talk shows and phone-in programs. An internal document at the MBC explained their popularity as a result of "instant listener participation and feedback thus underlining the radio's most striking feature which is immediacy."[10]

The present-day congestion on Africa's airwaves makes it easy to forget how recent the diversification of radio broadcasting is on the continent (Fardon and Furniss 2000: 3; van der Veur 2002: 93). When the first multiparty elections for over thirty years were held in Malaŵi in 1994, only two radio stations operated in the country: the MBC and an Evangelical Christian FM station run by the African Bible College and largely dependent on programs from the United States (Chipangula 2003: 24). The excitement created by the pastoral letter, read in the Catholic churches throughout Malaŵi (see Englund 1996a; Schoffeleers 1999), gathered momentum despite the MBC's campaign of misinformation and pro-government reporting.[11] For those who could access them, foreign stations such as the BBC's World Service and the South African Broadcasting Corporation proved far more informative sources than the MBC. It was only in 1998 that two more radio stations started to broadcast in Malaŵi, followed by a steady trickle of applications for a broadcasting license. By 2006, sixteen radio stations (including the two MBC stations) were operational in Malaŵi, nine of them boasting nationwide coverage, intermittent problems with transmission notwithstanding.[12]

While the MBC has remained the only public radio, the programs and objectives of private stations are diverse. In 2006, eight of these sixteen stations had a Christian broadcasting profile, whereas only one station—Radio Islam—catered to Malaŵi's Muslim population, which made up about thirteen percent of the country's population (National Statistical Office 2002: 39). The rest of the stations tended to have a commercial outlook aimed at urban audiences, often using more English than Chicheŵa in their broadcasts. Some stations have, however, been thorns in the democratic governments' flesh, such as Radio Maria, a Catholic station, during Muluzi's regime and Joy Radio, owned by Muluzi, during Mutharika's. The Zodiak Broadcasting Station will require special comment later in this chapter for its ethos of reporting, largely in Chicheŵa, that closely resembles public-service broadcasting. Chapter 8 will also consider one popular program of a Christian station as an example of

how some Malaŵians seek alternatives to *Nkhani Zam'maboma*, itself the quintessential alternative to much else that is broadcast on Malaŵi's airwaves.

This diversity of radio broadcasting attests to the medium's unrivaled position among Malaŵi's mass media. The situation has, just as the relatively recent
diversification, broader African resonances. Across the continent, "African
public cultures at the national level are—not only still but increasingly—radio-
driven cultures" (Fardon and Furniss 2000: 16–17; see also Zeleza 2009: 26).
Malaŵi had no television station until 1999, although satellite television, drawing mainly on South African entertainment channels, had become available in
1993 to those few who could afford it (Chipangula 2003: 24). Television Malaŵi
was launched by the government in 1999, separate from the MBC and yet in its
editorial policy prone to draw similar criticism for partisanship. Its lack of technical and editorial capacity has kept its supply of programs narrow, barely war-
ranting the status of national television, further compounded by Malaŵians'
general lack of means to purchase television sets.[13]

The history of print media predates that of broadcast media in Malaŵi,
but it has not been able to acquire similar national coverage and reach as radio.
Central African Times was established in 1895, changing its name to *Nyasa-
land Times* and then to the *Daily Times* (Chipangula 2003: 21; Patel 2000: 163).
Aimed at a white readership, it was the only newspaper until 1959, when Aleke
Banda started *Mtendere pa Ntchito,* a publication to inform Malaŵians about
issues around employment and politics, complemented in the same year by
Malaŵi News, a more openly nationalist newspaper and also initially owned by
Aleke Banda.[14] The Blantyre Print and Publishing Company owned the *Daily
Times,* but when Kamuzu Banda acquired the majority stake in it in 1969, it
heralded the end of press competition in Malaŵi for almost three decades. The
Daily Times and *Malaŵi News* adopted identical editorial policies, and as the
virtual personal property of the head of state, they based their coverage of national issues on sycophancy. Various short-lived magazines appeared in Banda's Malaŵi, but they were severely constrained by a small reading public and
the government's stringent conditions on publishing.

The print media blazed a trail in media diversification during the transition to multiparty democracy. Between the ministerial announcement in 1992
and the national referendum on the system of governance in 1993, over twenty
privately owned newspapers had appeared (Chimombo and Chimombo 1996:
26; see also M. Chimombo 1998). Several of them were owned by politicians
and, as a consequence, adopted the practice of partisan reporting. Nonetheless,
the vibrant press media, in some cases using more languages than English and

Table 1.1. Media Consumption in Malaŵi

Listens to radio at least once a week:	
Men	67 %
Women	52 %
Reads a newspaper at least once a week:	
Men	14 %
Women	7 %
Watches television at least once a week:	
Men	8 %
Women	5 %

Source: National Statistical Office 2003: 24

Chicheŵa, contributed to the thrill of political pluralism, particularly in urban areas. High printing costs and the small market, however, made this flourishing rather short-lived. Although newspapers continue to emerge and disappear, Malaŵi currently has only two newspapers with a well-established readership, advertising revenue, and distribution: the *Daily Times* and the *Nation*, including their weekend editions.[15] Yet in 2004 the former had a daily circulation of sixteen thousand and the latter of ten thousand copies (Neale 2004), pitifully small figures in a country of some eleven million people. Even if newspaper reading is often a public or shared event, just as radio listening is, these publications lack the capacity to reach most of rural Malaŵi for both infrastructural and linguistic reasons. Their copies do not move far beyond cities and district centers, and their Chicheŵa supplements on weekends are a poor consolation to a population that is, in the main, unable to read English.[16]

The superiority of radio over other mass media is demonstrated by the 2002 survey carried out by the National Statistical Office (2003) for American, British, and Canadian governmental foreign-aid agencies. Its results provide a poor substitute for the regular radio listenership surveys the office conducted in the 1960s and 1970s.[17] However, the 2002 survey does show that radio listenership far exceeds newspaper readership, not to mention television viewing (see table 1.1.).

The same survey found that 58 percent of Malaŵian households owned at least one radio, as opposed to only 3 percent that owned a television (National Statistical Office 2003: 16–17). The 2008 National Population and Housing Census reported that 64 percent of households owned a radio, a significant increase from the 50 percent recorded in the 1998 census (National Statisti-

cal Office 2010: 20). The 2002 survey mentioned above showed that the pos-
session of radios was more frequent in urban households (81 percent) than in
rural ones (55 percent). Yet when compared with the ownership of bicycles, a
type of goods more common in rural than urban households, the significance
of radios to rural Malaŵians appears more clearly. It was more common for a
rural household to own a radio (55 percent) than a bicycle (44 percent). Together with the practice by which people listen to the radio in many other settings than the privacy of their own houses, these figures lend support to the
contention that the radio is the foremost mass medium in Malaŵi.

Regulating the Freedom of Speech

In Africa, the diversification of radio broadcasting, recent as it is, has emerged
in countries where the link between government and broadcasting has generally been even closer than between government and the press (Mytton 1983:
63). In Malaŵi, a maze of draconian legislation had to be demolished to pave
the way for the diversification. Section 60 of the Penal Code, for example, made
publishing or broadcasting "false news" liable to life imprisonment (Chipangula 2003: 23). The 1968 Censorship and Control of Entertainment Act empow-
ered the Censorship Board to ban a wide range of publications, notoriously including world-class authors such as George Orwell and Wole Soyinka (Africa
Watch 1990: 70–75; Kanyongolo 1995).

Along with tacit habits of self-censorship, the legal and institutional legacies of media control have been difficult to undo. As a preliminary step, a code
of conduct was formulated in 1993 by pressure groups and the Public Affairs
Committee, a non-governmental forum initiated by lawyers and religious leaders (Patel 2000: 167–168). The MBC was the code's primary target, its news
journalism thought to be in need of a serious overhaul, fairness and accuracy
to be ensured by the new practice of editorial independence. The new repub-
lican constitution gave weight to these sentiments by including in its Bill of
Rights articles on the freedom of expression and the press, and on the right to
access information. Malaŵi had acceded to the *International Covenant on Civil
and Political Rights* in 1993 and had ratified the *African Charter on Human and
Peoples' Rights* in 1990 (ARTICLE 19 2003: 2). Together with the provisions on
the right to the freedom of expression in these international treaties, the new
constitutional framework has sought to replace censorship and state control
with a remarkably liberal disposition.

Malaẁian media analysts have been unanimous in their criticism of poor journalistic standards during the early attempts at media pluralism (see, e.g., Chimombo and Chimombo 1996: 32; Chipangula 2003: 25–26; Patel 2000: 164). The many newspapers that appeared as the democratic transition commenced were, in Mapanje's words, "ecstatic about the new freedom" and "ebullient to the point of being irresponsible" (2002: 178). For many of these critics, a lack of professional training among Malaẁian journalists has at least partly accounted for the low standards, both in the language used and in the partisan or unanalytical reporting. The training that was offered in Malaẁi during Banda's regime was given by senior colleagues to new employees, while a select few could learn creative writing from the English faculty of Malaẁi's only university until the 1990s (Chipangula 2003: 27–28). Those who could find funding and government clearance to study journalism outside Malaẁi were even fewer. In the late 1990s, the Malaẁi Polytechnic began to offer a diploma course on journalism, later upgraded into a degree course, but the most ambitious initiative in this regard was funded by the European Union. It helped to launch the Malaẁi Institute of Journalism in 1996, the country's premier school of journalism, complete with its own radio station.

Although, as the case of the MBC will indicate, some media houses have continued to employ new journalists with little regard for their background training, a certain professionalization has increasingly come to characterize journalism in Malaẁi. The transition heralded the establishment of various professional bodies, such as the Media Council of Malaẁi, the Journalists' Association of Malaẁi, the Press Clubs of Blantyre and Lilongwe, and the Malaẁi Chapter of the Media Institute of Southern Africa. Through seminars and press statements, many of these organizations have sought to raise the level of professionalism among Malaẁian journalists and, at the same time, to defend the freedom of expression. The Media Council, for example, proposed a code of ethics in 1995 (Chipangula 2003: 27; Patel 2000: 170). It included, among others, accuracy, correction, objectivity, and the distinction between news and opinions as the key objectives of the journalist's profession.

Professional bodies have few means of enforcing their objectives on practicing journalists. By contrast, an ominous continuity in the prerogatives of the state extends from the autocratic era to multiparty democracy, albeit under different legal and institutional guises (compare Ogbondah 2002). The Censorship Board has given way to the Malaẁi Communications Regulatory Authority (MACRA) as the principal public institution to police the media. Established in 1998 in conjunction with a new Communications Act, MACRA has courted controversy through its unilateral warnings and interventions. It was established as an autonomous and independent regulatory body to take over the functions performed until 1998 by the Malaŵi Telecommunications Corporation Limited, but the underlying act has attracted criticism in Malaŵi and abroad (see, e.g., ARTICLE 19 2003; Patel 2000: 170–173). Apart from transforming the MBC from a state broadcaster to a public service broadcaster, the act empowers MACRA to license and regulate broadcasters and to monitor their activities.

Among the problems that media analysts and human rights activists have identified in the act are the powers it grants to the minister of information and the state president to direct MACRA's decisions. The act mentions in several of its sections that MACRA may "seek the general direction of the Minister" on carrying out its duties from general regulatory issues to more specific decisions pertaining to the telecommunications and postal sectors. Section 19 states that MACRA may refuse license applications if so directed by the president in the interest of national security. Its board members, including the chairperson, are all presidential appointments, while two members—the secretary to the president and the cabinet and the secretary for information—are ex officio members. For media critics, it is little consolation, after this presidential prerogative, that the act excludes ministers, members of parliament, and persons holding party-political positions from membership on the board.

The interest MACRA's rulings have generated is another indication of broadcast media's significance. The regimes of both Muluzi and Mutharika have been implicated in its controversial directives and thereby in assaults on the freedom of expression. Yet these directives have been less successful in enforcing regulation than in provoking arguments and legal processes. During both regimes, many of MACRA's interventions were thinly veiled attempts to protect the privileged status of the MBC and Television Malaŵi. For example, one of the threats MACRA issued during Muluzi's regime was the withdrawal of the Malaŵi Institute of Journalism's license on the grounds that it broadcast news (ARTICLE 19 2003: 1–2). Similar contests over the right to broadcast news have marred MACRA's relations with other private stations, but the results have been, as in many other controversies, unsuccessful from MACRA's point of view. Indeed, by threatening to withdraw licenses, MACRA only attracted attention to the unlicensed status of the MBC and Television Malaŵi, despite their being subject to the same act of 1998 as everyone else. The public broadcasters were, somewhat sheepishly, licensed in 2004.

When the minister of information in Mutharika's administration threatened in 2007 to close four private stations because their licenses had expired, she not only drew criticism for speaking on MACRA's behalf but also inadvertently brought to the public realm the exorbitant fees that broadcasters were expected to pay for their licenses.[18] Charged in United States dollars in a country with precarious exchange rates, the license fee stood at U.S.\$5,000 and the frequency fee at U.S.\$7,180 in 2007. During Mutharika's regime, the harassment of private stations took many forms, but it was often clear that the target was one station in particular, Joy Radio. According to MACRA's records in 2006, its directors included the former president Muluzi, his wife, and his son, himself a member of parliament. One of the directives in 2007 ordered private stations to seek permission from MACRA before they engaged in live broadcasting.[19] The directive affected a number of stations, not least because the scope of "live broadcast" was left vague, but it was widely understood to have been prompted by Joy Radio's live broadcasts of Muluzi's speeches. In 2005, Mutharika had resigned from the United Democratic Front, then the ruling party that had sponsored his election campaign and was widely seen as Muluzi's personal property. After Mutharika's show of defiance, Muluzi's comments on the new government became increasingly vitriolic.

Courts soon resolved the issue of live broadcasts in private stations' favor, but MACRA continued to be implicated in Joy Radio's troubles. While the 1998 act has nothing to say about live broadcasting, its Section 48(7) does prohibit political parties and organizations from holding a license. Ministerial innuendos about politicians owning radio stations preceded MACRA's action on Joy Radio.[20] Its attempt to close down the station on the grounds of its ownership by politicians was successful for only three days until the court granted Joy Radio an injunction to resume broadcasting.[21] What the case brings out clearly is MACRA's close ties to the government. Shortly before the issue of ownership had been used as a reason to close down Joy Radio, the State House had suggested another avenue to pursue the station. In a press statement, it had warned the United Democratic Front and "its mouthpiece" Joy Radio "against tarnishing the image of His Excellency the President, Dr Bingu wa Mutharika."[22] A detail in the statement led to an intervention by authorities. It said that the station's manager was "a Zambian national who disguises as a Malawian citizen." It added that the "government will not accept foreigners who were involved in clandestine and fraudulent activities in the days of Mr Muluzi to confuse Malawians." A day after the press statement was released, officers from the Department of Immigration interrogated the manager's mother and other elders to establish his background.[23] The manager claimed to have been in Zambia as a refugee before Muluzi's ascension to power had brought democracy to Malaẁi.

The involvement of the media and courts in publicizing and countering MACRA's directives indicated a good deal of opposition to its subservience to the government. Much as this kind of opposition kept the freedom of expression a plausible prospect in Malaẁi, it is important to note another side to these controversies that locked the government and MACRA into disputes with private broadcasters, politicians, and human rights activists. Caught up in these disputes, MACRA failed to notice how *Nkhani Zam'maboma* mediated debate on rights and wrongs in Malaẁi. When I interviewed MACRA officials in 2006, they proudly took me to see the MACRA Media Monitoring Unit. With some aura of objectivity, it followed the news coverage on the major radio stations and produced weekly reports on what the officials defined as political news. While several receivers blasted out at the same time, the unit's officials filled out forms asking about the name of the political party mentioned and whether the news was positive or negative. Their findings were published in weekly reports to show the relative proportion of airtime given to different parties on different stations, with elaborate graphs and diagrams complemented by brief comments on how "balanced" the news coverage was.[24] When I asked about *Nkhani Zam'maboma,* MACRA's officials looked indifferent and said they had not received any complaints about it. Because they had defined "political news" to include only political parties, this program fell beyond their purview. MACRA ensured, for its part, that an entire domain of moral imagination on the public radio was free from governmental supervision.

Public Service on a Shoestring

The 1998 Communications Act, as mentioned, reconstituted the MBC as a public-service broadcaster. A number of high-minded objectives were given in section 87 to guide it in this newly defined mission. The MBC was to base its work on "respect for human rights, the rule of law and the Constitution," to "function without any political bias," to "support the democratic process," and to "provide balanced coverage of any elections." A board of directors, consisting of eight persons, came to govern the MBC and had the final responsibility for policy. The director general and the deputy director general were in charge of day-to-day operations. Media analysts and human rights activists were quick to note that, as with MACRA, a presidential prerogative to appoint officials retained the distinct possibility of political interference in the affairs of the MBC (see, e.g., ARTICLE 19 2003: 21–22). Seven of the eight board members were presidential appointees, and the eighth member was a senior civil servant, the secretary for information. Editorial independence, analysts noted, was not specifically mentioned as a value or an objective.

News coverage and reporting by the MBC have largely confirmed analysts' and activists' fears of bias, in spite of the transfer of presidential powers from Muluzi to Mutharika. The castigation of opposition parties, described as hate speech by some analysts (see Kayambazinthu and Moyo 2002), was carried out with abandon in news bulletins and other programs during Muluzi's regime, seldom tempered by an effort to solicit views from the people who were abused. The control and manipulation of information became a major preoccupation for Muluzi and his government, but because the luxuries of one-party rule were not available to them, they had to operate rather more cunningly than had been necessary during Banda's regime. While the apparent achievement of human rights as civil and political freedoms could always be evoked as a rhetorical device to distract attention from the new regime's dismal record in poverty alleviation, clandestine and corrupt methods were equally important. A report by ARTICLE 19 (2000: 60–71) uncovered two task forces in operation toward the end of Muluzi's regime. One was headed by the minister of information and involved senior figures from the MBC and the Malaŵi News Agency. The other was constituted within the MBC, answerable to Dumbo Lemani, Muluzi's henchman. According to this report, the aims of the two task forces were largely the same—to produce disinformation that would benefit the United Democratic Front (UDF) and damage the opposition.

Reporting on the elections has often revealed the MBC's partisan outlook particularly clearly. An exception was the 1994 general elections, the widespread expectation of a transition aiding critical and balanced reporting on the MBC (see Patel 2000: 168, 174). This observation on the capacity and willingness inside the MBC to embrace the conventions of public broadcasting is significant for my discussion of its newsroom practices later in this book. However, election coverage has not sustained this critical momentum after 1994. By the time of the 1999 general elections, the UDF had established itself as the custodian of the MBC, and it enjoyed more coverage than any other party during the campaign period (ARTICLE 19 2000). Codes of conduct, agreed between journalists, political parties, electoral officers, and media consultants, have become common at the onset of election campaigns, but the MBC has found little incentive to follow them. In 1999, the acting director general countered complaints about the MBC's broadcasts of Muluzi's campaign speeches by stating that he was covered "as State President and not as UDF president" (ARTICLE 19 2000: 17). A lack of vehicles was also given as a reason why the MBC did not cover the campaign rallies of opposition parties. The opposition's best chance of publicity on the MBC lay in paid advertisements rather than in coverage in news bulletins. Little had changed by the 2004 general elections. "For every one minute of news time given on MBC of benefit to all the opposition parties combined," one analyst reported, "13 minutes were given to the ruling alliance" (Neale 2004: 184).

It was only after Mutharika had resigned from the UDF in 2005 that the parliament—the institution that human rights activists thought should be in charge of monitoring the MBC (see ARTICLE 19 2003: 22)—started to take a critical look. Although Mutharika founded his own Democratic Progressive Party (DPP), he could not amass enough support among parliamentarians to establish a majority government. The MBC switched its loyalties, however, to suit the interests of the new DPP government, and a new director general and his deputy were appointed in 2007. Parliament had already cut the allocation for the MBC and Television Malaŵi by half in the previous year when it accepted the 2007–2008 national budget on the condition that the public broadcasters were given only one kwacha each. This nominal figure made it unnecessary to hold a vote that giving no allocation at all would have required. For the financial year 2008–2009, the government proposed to spend M.K.30 million on merging the MBC and Television Malaŵi into Malaŵi Broadcasting House. This plan came to nothing when the parliament decided to uphold the nominal figure for the second year. A lack of change at the MBC and Television Malaŵi was given as a reason. "They have become purely propaganda and hate stations," an opposition spokesman said, adding: "They are promoting disunity."[25]

It was, of course, politically expedient for the opposition to forget the broadcasts of hate speech on the MBC during Muluzi's regime. New programs, billed as "political cartoons," were cited by the opposition as particularly offensive, but it is important to realize how these programs, along with new business practices, were seen by the MBC's directors as the dawn of a new era. As discussed in chapter 3, the directors professed commitment to making the MBC a self-financing institution by expanding its advertising revenue and streamlining its operations. At the same time, a sense of humiliation and outright distress became palpable within the institution. Patricia Kaliati, Mutharika's choleric minister of information, was hardly consistent in her views on the MBC, sometimes lambasting its journalists for wastefulness and a lack of professionalism in covering politics,[26] and at other times—in fact, most of the time—expecting an automatic slot in the news bulletin whenever she wanted to contradict or disgrace other public figures in Malaŵi. Confused by the simultaneous imperatives of self-financing and serving the government, MBC journalists have also had to face the unprecedented predicament of delayed and incomplete salary payments.[27] The top management was humiliated when the director general's official car was impounded by the police over a M.K.26 million debt that the MBC owed to the Copyright Society of Malaŵi in unpaid royalties.[28] However, the sense of insecurity has been especially pronounced among many long-standing employees without major managerial roles, their frustration compounded by considerable inequalities within the institution and by enormous salary increases for its controllers.[29]

Material inequalities indicated the MBC's capacity to raise funds despite the punishment unleashed by parliament. It is apparent that not all of these funds came as a result of the new management's business strategy. Aid agencies continued to enlist the MBC as a vehicle for their developmentalist programs (see below), and even the government found ways and means to finance it. After the continuing payment of governmental subventions was revealed in the print media in 2007,[30] the MBC's management had to look for other ways of accessing government money. Bank overdrafts were written, using, as a top official at the MBC explained to me, the bank that belonged to the very government that was not supposed to fund the broadcaster. An element of humiliation did accompany these strategies to raise funds. The MBC had to use its transmitters as collateral to get bank overdrafts. A *de jure* public institution was thus reduced to a *de facto* private entity.[31]

The competition on Malaŵi's airwaves ensures that other stations have attempted to quench the public's thirst for news that informs and surprises. The use of Chicheŵa, breaking news about both local and national issues, and innovative program formats made the Zodiak Broadcasting Station, a private radio station launched in 2005, the most successful contender for the mantle of public-service broadcasting. Some of its innovations, such as broadcasting live from parliament, were promptly rejected by MACRA—only to have them handed over to the MBC to implement.[32] At the same time, Zodiak's success made the MBC's claim to public service more pressing. Many journalists with whom I spoke at the MBC spontaneously considered themselves to be in competition with Zodiak more than with any other broadcaster in Malaŵi. Although one appeared to be a governmental mouthpiece and the other a genuinely independent broadcaster, the founding director of Zodiak himself embodied the ambiguity between the two orientations. Gospel Kazako had worked for the MBC for many years before launching Zodiak, and in 1996 he was quoted as saying, "MBC has to support the government of the day" (AR-TICLE 19 2000: 17). The pride in serving the government, and its association with journalists' own sense of public service, can be genuine, strong enough to withstand assaults by budgetary problems and politicians' interference.

Enduring Developmentalism

What media analysts and human rights activists, in their commitment to condemning political bias, often leave unmentioned is another important continuity in public broadcasting across Malaŵi's different post-independence regimes. The continuity is developmentalism, the very vagueness of "development" permitting commonalities to persist in spite of the three governments' differences in style and substance. For the MBC, as for so much state- and donor-sponsored cultural production in the so-called developing world, the effect has been a didactic mode of engaging with the beneficiaries of development (compare Abu-Lughod 2005: 57–108). Entertainment, education, and information have often been seen to depend on each other in this mode of transmitting messages. The paradigms of developmentalism have changed, however, and the MBC has had to revise paternalist programming with more participatory ideas. Perhaps one reason why developmentalism has not attracted human rights activists' attention is a fundamental similarity between their approach to the so-called grassroots and the didactic methods deployed by governments and their collaborators. When they all have defined Malaŵi's majority as ignorant masses needing enlightenment from outside, developmentalism, particularly in its participatory guises, has seemed too natural to warrant comment (see Englund 2006: 117–122). What is interesting about *Nkhani Zam'maboma* is the way that it affords—for its editors if not for human rights activists—an alternative mode of engaging with the impoverished public.

The news headline with which this chapter began is an apposite and, as mentioned, timeless expression of the developmentalism that has tied successive governments and the MBC together. The onset of independence, in Malaŵi as elsewhere in Africa, was heavily dominated by the agenda of nation-building, and the eradication of "the unholy trinity of ignorance, poverty, and disease" (T. Mkandawire 2005: 13) was a project that legitimized the new African states. Nationalism may have fared somewhat worse than developmentalism over the decades, but a strong presidentialism has continued to identify the nation's fortunes with its sovereign leader.[33] Banda's annual "crop inspection tours," during which he visited carefully selected farms to ascertain yet another "bumper harvest," evolved into virtually incessant campaigning during Muluzi's era. Toward the end of his era, Muluzi often traveled with a convoy of trucks loaded with maize to be distributed for free as a part of the spectacle of his visiting the poor. Although, or perhaps because, Mutharika adopted a more technocratic approach to poverty alleviation, few of his speeches failed to mention development, the appellation "expert on development" (*katsiŵiri wa chitukuko*) becoming a regular feature of his praise songs. Closely associated with presidentialism, development was thus "a statist and elitist project" (T. Mkandawire 2005: 17), whatever new rhetorics the transition to multiparty democracy brought. The MBC may have lost some of its status as a key institution in nation-building, but the persistence of developmentalism has made it indispensable to every government.

The impact of developmentalism on the MBC is, however, merely an aspect of developmentalism pervading public life in Malaŵi, from the arts to academia. Critics have pointed out the didactic aesthetics of Malaŵian literature, an aesthetics in which the eagerness of authors to deliver moral and pragmatic lessons has often displaced any attempt at representing complexity and ambiguity (Moto 2001; H. Ross 1998; but see Englund 2004b). Other art forms were also enlisted by Banda's government and other agencies in the pursuit of development, with much Chicheŵa drama, for example, harnessed to advance health and agricultural issues or to eulogize Banda (Magalasi 2008: 163; but see Barber 1987: 44). In the twenty-first century, the stranglehold of developmentalism on academic life has appeared nowhere more clearly than at the University of Malaŵi. Not only are consultancy reports for governmental and non-governmental agencies a lifeline for many social scientists whose university salaries are barely sufficient to meet basic needs. Inaugural lectures by new professors in subjects such as linguistics and English literature have also sought to demonstrate relevance by highlighting the subjects' intimate relation to the project of development.[34] Under such circumstances, Malaŵi's intelligentsia has rarely commented on how the very pervasiveness of the notion of development has made it amenable to stirring up discontent and criticism. One comment to such an effect from another context of African academia is, for example, the recognition that the experiments in structural adjustment in Africa during the 1980s were largely "development against the people" (Ake 2000: 87). Post-developmentalist currents in Euro-American academia, reducing development to a discourse to be deconstructed, need not, therefore, be the only response to the apparent lack of imaginative African perspectives on development.

As a relational concept, "development" invites reflections on what the future may hold for oneself and one's country, and what life is like in other places and for other people—all issues that can challenge the status quo (see Bornstein 2005; J. H. Smith 2008). For broadcasting, the question is whether, and to what extent, development has been able to appear as a contentious issue. As has been seen, the need for listener participation was recognized by MBC journalists already in the early 1980s (Wedell 1986: 287–288). Even earlier, a farm forum project on the MBC had allowed agricultural extension workers to facilitate group discussions on agricultural issues. The concept of radio listener clubs, central to the deployment of mass media in development projects beyond Africa, gathered momentum during the 1990s through the combined effects of political liberalization and participatory methods. The Development Broadcasting Unit was established as an administratively independent department within the MBC in 1999, coinciding with the emergence of community radio stations sharing similar aspirations to promote participatory development.

"Community radio," however, encompasses a variety of initiatives, all claiming to serve local people but in many cases owned and operated by religious organizations, transnational NGOs, or the government (see Kasoma 2002; Myers 2000; Opoku-Mensah 2000). Moreover, radio listening clubs, whose deliberations provide community radios with program material, have been shown to be affected by gender and age hierarchies in Malaŵi, discouraging the kind of dialogue they are expected to facilitate (Manyozo 2005; Mchakulu 2007). For example, despite their inclination to support a rights-based approach by which rural Malaŵians are invited to engage with so-called service providers, programs of the Development Broadcasting Unit were found to perpetuate docility rather than engagement (W. Chirwa et al. 2000: 11–20). Although constituting the majority of members in radio listening clubs, women spoke less than half of the time taken by men, while the longest time was taken by service providers. Their expert-like advice brought a distinct flavor of top-down developmentalism to the apparently democratic deliberations.

These critical observations do not dismiss community radio listening clubs as failures. Although the emancipatory rhetoric of participatory development may attach unrealistic expectations to such clubs, the space they have opened up for public debate in rural Malaŵi is unprecedented. At the same time, however, their shortcomings have reflected problems common to many participatory approaches, such as the limited extent to which the poor themselves actually set the agenda for their participation.[35] Moreover, while agriculture, income generation, reproductive health, and food security have been recurring topics in radio listening clubs, their analysis has rarely ventured beyond the immediate request a so-called community can place on a particular service provider (see Mchakulu 2007: 258). The discussions have, therefore, been localized, the connection between local deprivation and national and transnational political economy never explicated. Developmentalism, in its participatory guises, has here assumed affinity with the civic-education projects of human rights organizations in Malaŵi. Rather than advocating poor people's claims and rights, teachings in these projects have in subtle ways allocated responsibility for poverty to the poor themselves.

Just as participants in civic-education sessions have been able to refuse the role assigned to them by their educators (Englund 2006: 114–117), so too has the controlled framework been subverted in radio debates. Writing about a local radio station in Benin, Tilo Grätz (2000:117–118) has described how debates organized as a part of civic education have taken unexpected directions when the examples cited by participants have contradicted presenters' and invited specialists' "correct opinions." However, alongside debate and phone-in programs there exist program formats more closely supervised by their sponsors, whether local or transnational NGOs, bilateral aid agencies, or the European Union. In Malaŵi, a common practice has been to employ actors or comedians to drive home the didactic messages. Story Workshop, a Malaŵian drama NGO, has often been enlisted to produce plays according to the specifications given by aid agencies and human rights NGOs.[36]

For instance, one short play, sponsored by the NGO Action Aid and broadcast in 2006, conveyed little ambiguity about impoverished parents' ability to send their children to school.[37] The broadcast began with the catchy tunes of a song that described sending girls to sell goods in the market rather than to school as "crushing their freedom" (*kuŵaphwanyira ufulu wawo*). It went on to state that "let them study so that they will be independent" (*asiyeni aphunzire adzakhale odzidalira*). The notion of *kudzidalira*, "to be independent and to look after oneself," was expounded in the ensuing dialogue that took place between a female teacher and a single mother. In an answer to the teacher's complaint that the mother had sent her daughter to sell scones in the market, the mother retorted that "you have a job and receive money at the end of the month to help your children, what about me?"[38] The teacher commented, "Why don't you sell on your own? Schooling increases opportunities for women to be economically independent."[39] The mother's observation that she did not have a husband to support her made the teacher say that neither did she, but because she went to school, "I look after myself on my own" (*ndimadzidalira pa ndekha*). The dialogue ended with the mother agreeing that she would have averted poverty through schooling, and she therefore promised to send her daughter to school.

Just as radio listening clubs may provide an important new opportunity for deliberation despite the shortcomings of participatory development, the play described here can also encourage fresh reflections on female education and advancement. However, a crucial aspect of *Nkhani Zam'maboma* inhered in the form it assumed in contrast to these governmental and non-governmental attempts at enlightenment. The disconnection between its sponsors and editors, along with its official status as a non-political program, was vital to the alternative it presented. The sponsoring companies—typically advertising goods such as cooking oil, soap, and paint—showed no interest in interfering with editorial decisions. As will be seen in chapter 4, *Nkhani Zam'maboma* emerged within the developmentalist disposition, but once it was reconstituted in response to the input from its listeners, it was subject to neither didactic developmentalism nor party-political expediency, the two vices of the MBC. The moral imagination fostered by *Nkhani Zam'maboma* inevitably surpassed the confines of "personal independence" (*kudzidalira*) and "freedom" (*ufulu*) inculcated in the broadcasts designed by aid agencies and human rights NGOs. *Nkhani Zam'maboma* enabled a radically different form of claims, one that made development a contentious issue and, more often than not, exposed personal independence as an unlivable fiction. It showed that, for the editors of the program, the transcendental value of development could not be reduced to developmentalism. It was this subtle sense of alternative claims that restored some professional pride and satisfaction among journalists working under the MBC's often stifling governance.

2

Obligations to Dogs

Between Liberal and Illiberal Analytics

Walking the dog was never a task Joseph Chisale cherished. Tending the garden of his European master, who was the only doctor at the nearby rural clinic, was a far more agreeable pursuit, and even cooking for the master involved skills and responsibilities that made the occupational category of "houseboy" a source of some respect in the village. Twice a day the master's Alsatian, the dog that had traveled with him from Europe, had to be taken for a walk, each time Chisale wondering whether the master's residence in his own village was such a blessing after all. Insolent children would run around him during the promenade, the cheekiest of them trying to provoke barking from the exotic creature. Adults would maintain a polite façade, their smiles and greetings, Chisale often felt, concealing their commiseration over the humiliation brought by a lack of opportunities in the village. Chisale suspected that the master would not have had the courage to face the commotion his outings with the dog would have caused in the village. The master's residence there had done nothing to change his status as a stranger, or to improve his communication skills in Chicheŵa.

One day the Alsatian got into a fight with a village dog. Chisale rushed to separate them, but was himself bitten by the village dog. The word reached the master quickly, and he left the clinic straight away. He went first to his dog, ignoring Chisale, who was nursing his wound. Alarmed at the injury his dog had sustained, the master wasted no time and lifted the dog into his car. Leaving Chisale behind to look for assistance at the local clinic, he drove off to Lilongwe, the capital some 250 miles away, to seek a veterinarian's opinion. The master had never gone to such lengths, Chisale observed ruefully, when his employees and their family members had fallen ill. Nor were the master's parting words considered tactful. He told his two night watchmen to stay awake at night because the dog that had performed their work would be gone for a while.

As the companion species of human beings (Haraway 2003), dogs have a rather different moral status in Malaŵi than in the country where the master came from. The needs of dogs would never take precedence over those of humans in Malaŵi, much as they can be valued as hunting partners or guards. Dogs are most often ignored in Malaŵian villages and townships, their oblivion punctuated with the violence of discipline. They are beaten with abandon even by those who would not inflict such methods of discipline on children. As such, the master's behavior added insult to Chisale's injury. The master's love for the dog was symbolic of a much wider predicament than the pain Chisale felt on that fateful day. Not only was it humiliating for an adult person, a respected member of the village, to make his living as a servant to a dog. That the master would put his dog's welfare before anyone else's was also a clear indication of his lack of commitment to his employees and neighbors. When telling the story, Chisale did not abstract the master's medical profession from the obligations he was expected to have toward those who prepared his meals, cleaned and guarded his house, and kept his garden in order. Rather, the master's failure to impart his medical knowledge after the incident merely confirmed that his love for the dog was greater than his love for the people on whom he depended.

The alternative newscast *Nkhani Zam'maboma* could have carried Chisale's story. I heard it when I visited his village with our mutual friend before I had properly started to follow the program. Stories like Chisale's—animated by moral argument without necessarily delivering moral lessons, rich in allusions that are not made explicit—are the stuff of everyday life in Malaŵi, and the success of *Nkhani Zam'maboma* rested on its championing and further refinement of popular narrative conventions. One could be reminded of a story heard on the program during an everyday encounter, just as other stories were often prompted by what was heard on the radio. I was reminded of Chisale's story when, several years later, *Nkhani Zam'maboma* did broadcast a story about the relationship between animals and white people.[1] Goats were reported to have disturbed the village funeral of a seventy-two-year-old man. The mourners heard them crying in their enclosure near the deceased's house where the wake was being held. The goats eventually managed to escape and came to jump around the coffin. One of them even ran ahead of the funeral procession to lead it to the graveyard, where the bereaved were said to have struggled to keep the goats away from the burial site. The report ended by explaining that "the goats were European breed, they were used to people" (*mbuzizo ndi zachizungu, zinazolowera ndi anthu*).[2]

The two-way influence between stories broadcast on the radio and stories told in everyday encounters raises a host of questions explored in the course of this book, such as the way in which mass-mediated stories generated a sense of a wider public even for incidents not reported by *Nkhani Zam'maboma*, and how editorial oversight guaranteed a consistent genre despite the program's apparent proximity to its public. For this chapter, one recurrent theme of stories broadcast on *Nkhani Zam'maboma* serves to introduce the program's particular moral outlook. The recurrent theme is the emphasis on obligations, on the relationships that tie masters and servants in mutual dependence.

Grief-stricken goats are alien to the obligations Malawians perform in funerals, just as the care that Chisale's master gave to his dog defined his separation from the villagers closest to him. Dogs and goats figure in Malawian reflections on white people because they afford a perspective on how strangers keep themselves as strangers. By committing themselves to the welfare of animals, white people are seen to make a statement about the separation between them and Malawians. Whether or not it commented on the habits of white people and their four-legged friends—as will be seen, stories broadcast on *Nkhani Zam'maboma* mostly did not—storytelling that addressed moral and existential quandaries in everyday experience presented a popular alternative to the human rights talk that had become ubiquitous after the democratic transition. Claims by rights-bearing individuals did not feature in such stories, however much their subjects and narrators may have been exposed to human rights talk.

While it is certainly true that the oppressed have in various historical contexts turned the language of rights to their own benefit (Ishay 2004), it is important to examine closely other ways in which they might express their claims and expectations. Such examination is, however, riddled with potential pitfalls. Research that identifies an alternative discourse may too easily assume that it is driven by a conscious challenge to the prevailing idea of rights, as though alternatives could only arise through acts of resistance. Moreover, a sense of obligation as duty has long been intrinsic to some concepts of human rights, most recently in the philosophical literature on involuntary poverty and human rights (see, e.g., Hertel and Minkler 2007; Pogge 2002; Sengupta 2007). Obligation as duty or responsibility exercises liberal theorists, because it can entail both the negative duty of how not to deprive persons of access to basic necessities and the positive duty of protecting their opportunity to earn a subsistence income (Ashford 2007). Even when they call for global solutions to global problems, the contributions to this debate often rest on an ethical and normative individualism that is at variance with the specific sense of obligation in the mass-mediated storytelling explored in this book.

The ease with which communitarian and illiberal standpoints suggest themselves as alternatives to individualism also requires caution. This chapter seeks a way out of the analytical impasse by placing the possibility of equality, rather than the rights-obligations balance, in the foreground. At the same time, the axiomatic individualism among liberal theorists is not countered simply by the common social scientific urge to unmask ideologies. Anthropological critiques of inequality, for example, can be unimaginative as long as they remain quiet about the concept of equality that spurs them. Two domains of inquiry are particularly pertinent to this book. The first concerns the prospects of alternatives to Africa's socioeconomic ills as theorized by Western and African scholars. The second concerns the debates on the liberal public sphere, counterpublics, and news journalism that illustrate how the question of equality has appeared in the study of mass media.

The Enigma of Equality

"One great challenge to any morally sensitive person today," Thomas Pogge (2002: 197) writes, "is the extent and severity of global poverty." It is immediately apparent to Pogge's readers that "any morally sensitive person" is a highly circumscribed category, a member of "us" contemplating, with great difficulty, the poverty that "they" suffer from. "We live in extreme isolation from severe poverty," Pogge observes. "We do not know people scarred by the experience of losing a child to hunger, diarrhea, or measles, do not know anyone earning less than $10 for a 72-hour week of hard, monotonous labor" (Pogge 2002: 4). Pogge touches here on a critical issue without really addressing it. Liberal egalitarianism seems shallow if it is never confronted by experiences and viewpoints among those who get classified as the global poor. The issue is not so much to insist on liberals undoing the spatial distance between themselves and the poor, whether at home or abroad.[3] Rather, the question is what difference it would make to engage liberal egalitarianism with the viewpoints of those it presumes to assist. Without such engagement, the debate rarely proceeds beyond this or that textbook definition of equality, its scope associated variously with opportunities and resources, the debate typically focusing on the prospects of distribution and the perils of domination (see Temkin 1993). These are serious issues, but their underlying view of the world, composed of discrete subjects such as nations and individuals, may too easily assume that the goal is a formal relation of equality between independent entities (compare Ferguson 2006: 22).The English concept of equality, after all, arose as a term of measurement (R. Williams 1983: 119). Claims that demand relationship can get dismissed as pathological clamor for dependence. Obligations to dogs appear natural when human beings are thought to exist in mutual independence.

Contemporary liberal theorists are often acutely aware of deficiencies in classical liberalism. Their unease arises in part from new topics of inquiry that have traditionally received unsatisfactory attention from liberal theorists: world poverty (Pogge 2002 and 2007), gender inequality (Ackerly 2008; Nussbaum 2000), and international migration and displacement (Benhabib 2004). These liberal critics continue to subscribe to individualism, albeit with an appreciation of the objections that this doctrine has encountered over a long period of time. Individualism here is ethical and normative, the foundation on which liberal egalitarianism is erected, and not a denial of the "constitutive attachments" (Kelly 2005: 9) that make up individual identities everywhere. Banal arguments and counter-arguments between liberals and communitarians, incited by statements such as "communitarians often champion culturally embedded social identities that are highly paternalistic" (Talbott 2005: 12), are thereby replaced by a good deal more sophisticated analysis.[4]

Martha Nussbaum, for example, insists that "the separate person should be the basic unit for political distribution" and that women, rather than be seen as "parts of an organic entity, such as the family is supposed to be," are to be regarded as "political subjects in their own right" (2000: 247). Crucial to this view is the principle of each person as end, their separateness thought to be evident not only on theoretical grounds but also in poor people's subjective experience of hunger and hard physical labor (Nussbaum 2000: 57) and in "the empirical fact of bodily separateness" (Nussbaum 2000: 60). While liberal theorists may disagree on the exact scope of structural reform, they are in no doubt about personal autonomy as both the means and end.

This sophistication does little to properly open up the question of person-hood. Nussbaum's "empirical fact of bodily separateness" flies in the face of ethnographic work on how bodies can be repositories of human and non-human relationships, as in the experiences of affliction and healing, or the very means by which persons come to know their involvement with other beings, human and non-human (see, e.g., Csordas 1994; V. Turner 1968). The refusal to dispense with the notion that persons are, or ought to be, autonomous individuals is no accident, of course. It betrays a commitment to that other linchpin of liberal thought: liberty. Nussbaum wishes every life to have "the preconditions of liberty and self-determination" (2000: 60), while Pogge's goal is to free the poor from "bondage and other relations of personal dependence" (2002: 197).[5]

Where little moral value is attached to persons being separate from one another, does the concept of equality have any meaning in analyzing such circumstances? It does, but only if the concept is dissociated from egalitarian ideology. A measure of universality is retained against cultural particularity when equality is understood to be a condition of relationship, not between mutually independent parties but precisely a condition of the relationship that makes them subjects in the first place. It is vital to realize what is entailed by the distinction between equality as a condition of relationship and equality as a goal pursued by governments and individuals. "To pose equality as a goal," Jacques Rancière (2004: 223) argues, "is to hand it over to the pedagogues of progress, who widen endlessly the distance they promise that they will abolish." For Rancière, the pedagogues of progress have included practically every major figure in the history of Western philosophy, always eager to theorize the condition of those "at the bottom," always loyal to the proposition, traceable to Plato: "Let all do their business and develop the virtue specific to their condition" (Rancière 2004: 220). In this history of knowledge production, philosophers have always thought *for*, and not only about, the poor, assuming that the shoemaker does nothing else than shoemaking, least of all philosophy. Rancière (2004: 165–202) does not spare sociologists either, finding a comparable division of intellectual labor evident in Pierre Bourdieu's work, which claims to take the side of the downtrodden against the arrogant and self-serving classes at the top. It does so, according to Rancière, by explaining backward the same thing as the philosopher-king, however much the downtrodden are shown to speak for themselves and to recognize their misery. In this sociology, "all recognition is a misrecognition, all unveiling a veiling" (Rancière 2004: 170).

Rancière's reading of Western philosophy and sociology suggests intellectual resources to engage the subject of equality in a novel way, irrespective of how much justice his provocations do to the authors he discusses (see also chapter 6). It would be ironic, however, if his thoughts on equality provided a new panacea. As intellectual resources, they must be confronted with intellectual resources gained through ethnographic fieldwork and analysis.[6] Central to this concept of equality is its disconnection from some perpetually elusive goal of public policy and its implication in the very possibility of human relationships. By the same token, equality as a notion is delivered from its association with personal autonomy and separateness. Stories broadcast on *Nkhani Zam'maboma* often depict injustice and exploitation. Told from the perspective of those who find themselves subjected to such abuse, they draw attention not so much to the infringement of individual rights as to powerful offenders' fundamental dependence on those they have caused injury. By illustrating how equality inheres in the moment of claim-making, these stories show the general import of *Nkhani Zam'maboma* and the parochialism of liberal egalitarianism. Far from erasing differences and hierarchy in the name of equality, *Nkhani Zam'maboma* enables the Malawian poor to assert relationships within differences. Severe poverty does not flatten out differences; it lays bare the differences that constitute subjects (compare Hirschmann 2003: 227–229).

Anthropologists, whose discipline is perhaps best suited to uncovering alternatives to prevailing academic and policy orthodoxies, have had relatively little to say about equality. Too often the common social-scientific penchant for unmasking ideologies has appeared to be all that anthropologists have to do, even when new insights into equality have begun to emerge. For example, Nigerian narratives about corruption that deploy rumors and metaphors can be appreciated for their ingenuity, but they are criticized for keeping "the structures that sustain inequalities" from "overt assessment and condemnation" (D. Smith 2007: 153). Yet even if anthropologists appear to know how to unmask the causes of inequality, they are rather more coy about the notion of equality that informs the unmasking in the first place. When an anthropologist reports that the subjects of her study are in the habit of "masking relations of inequality" through all manner of euphemisms and fictive kin terms (Abu-Lughod 1986: 99), the reader is left to ask in vain what might constitute equality in her case.[7]

Apart from their enthusiasm for unmasking, anthropologists have found it difficult to offer novel insights into equality for two additional reasons. The first is their tendency to discuss equality as an ideology or practice that is embraced by some civilizations but not others. One example, now largely discarded, has been the juxtaposition of hierarchical structures in India with the ideology of egalitarianism in the West (Dumont 1980 and 1986; see also Appadurai 1988; Béteille 1986; Rio and Smedal 2009). Another instance, still a source of fresh scholarship, has been the study of stateless societies, particularly hunter-gatherers (Riches 2000; Solway 2006; Widlok and Tadesse 2005). This scholarship has debated, among other things, the impact of new property relations on the equality of outcome that has been characteristic of these societies. It has also offered a rare link between anthropology and political philosophy, with theorists of anarchism regularly drawing on anthropology in a way that their liberal counterparts do not (see, e.g., Clark 2007; Taylor 1982).[8] At their best, anarchist theorists discover in anthropology intellectual resources "to expand political imagination by displaying the availability to us of alternative ways of life" (Clark 2007: 140–141). However, by focusing on particular, small-scale societies, increasingly through historical rather than contemporary ethnographic material, these theorists as much confine as expand the political imagination. Not only does the historical and ethnographic record show that competition over followers and resources has been intrinsic to stateless societies in Africa (Iliffe 2005: 100), the alternative moral and political discourse described in this book does not stem from Malaŵians' desire to dispense with the state or other institutions of governance. Moreover, to align the debate on equality too closely with the concerns of anarchism also exposes it to all those negative images of Africa that regard it as the continent plagued by the "coming anarchy" (Kaplan 1994; see also P. Richards 1996). It is as though the study of Africa was doomed to remain in the margins, unable to contribute, however critically, to a mainstream debate on equality and human rights.

Anthropologists' aversion to the mainstream explains the second reason for their tepid treatment of equality as a subject of enquiry.[9] As David Graeber, a self-styled anarchist anthropologist, has put it, "liberal" is a term that many anthropologists cannot pronounce "without a snort of contempt" (2004: 98). Here they enter an unholy alliance with past and present conservatives who have used the term as a form of abuse (see Kelly 2005: 5). While clearly distinct in style and substance, what unites critical anthropologists and conservatives is their rush to see in liberalism a phenomenon without variations, facilitated by their unwillingness to recognize that neither liberal regimes nor liberal thinkers can be reduced to a set of essential properties. John Gray has suggested that liberalism encompasses "family resemblances" (2000: 20–21) rather than having an essence. Insofar as equality is a central value to some liberals while liberty has that status for others, certain strands of liberalism, as is widely recognized in political philosophy, are akin to certain forms of anarchism and socialism (see, e.g., Carter 1971: 109–110). Categorical dismissals of liberalism as a moral and political theory beg the question of whether scholars are well served by *illiberal* assumptions seeping into analysis.

African Alternatives

The study of Africa presents examples of unexamined liberal and illiberal predilections guiding debate on human rights, poverty, and inequality. At the same time, it provides illustrations of how alternatives are all too often proposed, quite inadvertently, within the categories of thought derived from the political and intellectual adversaries themselves. The conundrum is well recognized among African intelligentsia, particularly in philosophy (see, e.g., Appiah 1992; Hountondji 1983; Mudimbe 1988 and 1994), but for empirical research, the issue of liberalism suggests specific questions that can benefit from ethnography. One controversy revolves around the question of whether those African countries that have pursued liberal democracy since the late 1980s are actually any closer to achieving liberal institutions and procedures.

Bruce Berman's (2004) argument illustrates the view that the continent is characterized by lack and absence insofar as liberal democracy is concerned. His argument merits attention, because it is based on long-term research and reflection, not on an ill-informed concern about the Dark Continent and the coming anarchy.[10] Berman (2004: 45) places the colonial legacy of bureaucratic authoritarianism at the heart of his analysis when he argues that patronage systems and divisive ethnic loyalties have undermined the emergence of civic trust. Africa is, Berman contends, marred by the absence of "a disinterested professional cadre" (2004: 52) who would run civil service without an ethnic or political bias. His model for such a development is the history of Europe, where "a protracted and difficult process" (Berman 2004: 43) resulted in universal trust in abstract and depersonalized institutions. The argument is, as such, unabashed in its Eurocentrism and its commitment to a liberalism that posits formal equality among autonomous individuals as the precondition of democracy.

It may seem paradoxical that negative images also bedevil what would appear to be a total reversal of Berman's argument, his liberal point of view supplanted by an illiberal one. The paradox is made possible by a current in Euro-American social theory that has resurrected, notably through Agamben (1998 and 2005), an interest in the work of Carl Schmitt (e.g., 1985), infamous for his association with the Nazi regime in Germany (see also Dyzenhaus 1998; Kalyvas 2008: 79–193). The interest derives from Schmitt's claim that exclusion is intrinsic to liberal democracy, the apparently democratic right to wield sovereign power over life inseparable from wielding it over death. John and Jean Comaroff (2006), who prefer "the postcolony" (wherever it may be) to "Africa" as a category of thought, seize on this notion to explain the conjunction of liberal experiments and increasing crime. They are thereby able to propose an integral link between sovereign violence and criminal violence, one redefining the other, such as when law is used to authorize predation and criminalize political opposition. It is not, in other words, that postcolonies in Africa lack liberal democracy. Once the power to decide on crime and disorder is understood to define liberal democracy, they have it in obscene proportions.

The negativity that unites Berman's and the Comaroffs' perspectives has the effect of dispensing with anything that might constitute virtue, civility, or obligation for people living the horrors they describe. Note, for example, how the Comaroffs' concept of lawfare preempts the association between law and justice by defining it as "the resort to legal instruments, to the violence inherent in the law, to commit acts of political coercion, even erasure" (2006: 30). The Comaroffs are, however, far too well versed in postcolonial studies to follow Berman in his Eurocentrism. They give copious examples of a similar "dialectic" between law and disorder in Europe and North America, but insist that it appears more inflated in postcolonies. The reasons are, as in Berman's obverse case, historical, including colonial legacies and postcolonial structural adjustments that exacerbated inequalities. Yet precisely because this aspect of liberal democracy appears inflated, "postcolonies are hyperextended versions of the history of the contemporary world order running slightly ahead of itself" (Comaroff and Comaroff 2006: 41). It is in these margins of the world where "tectonic shifts in the order of things" are experienced first, "most visibly, most horrifically" (Comaroff and Comaroff 2006: 41). Perhaps this vision is not so disconnected from Eurocentrism after all—postcolonial disorder and lawfare are compelling because they afford a glimpse of horrors to come in Euro-America. Whatever else it does, the vision, with its eye for tectonic shifts, evokes an apocalypse far more encompassing than the nightmares of Afro-pessimism.[11]

Where are the intellectual resources to appreciate Africans' efforts to live their lives as moral beings amid the all too obvious inequalities, impoverishment, and exploitation? Hardly in these dismal readings of liberal democracy in Africa, whether they focus on its lack or its abundance. They join a long line of theorists who have, in Africa and beyond, sought to account for the persistence of inequality in democracies by revealing just how powerless the poor and the marginalized are. The tendency is, as the above discussion of Rancière's (2004) work suggests, to speak on behalf of the poor, or against them, if their preferences seem pathological. Underlying this tendency is, in Barbara Cruik-shank's words, the impossibility "to speak in the voice of the voiceless without first constituting their inability to speak for themselves" (1999: 34). One alternative is to assert, with Achille Mbembe, that subjects "have internalized authoritarian epistemology to the point where they reproduce it themselves in all the minor circumstances of everyday life" (2001: 128). This assertion has the merit of freeing analysis from a simplistic juxtaposition between domination and resistance. It comes, however, with the cost of making complicity in power look ever more insidious and ubiquitous, as if conversations about authority could not also evoke the value of obligation and mutual dependence (Lonsdale 2004: 77). Above all, the hierarchy these conversations may end up sustaining is not necessarily a function of internalizing authoritarian epistemology but of equality that elicits recognition of a relationship between subjects and rulers.

It is tempting to respond to the perspectives described above by adopting the viewpoints of those African intellectuals and politicians who have sought positive engagement with African social life and thought. Much as this rich field of reflection does offer insights into the problems of liberalism in Africa, familiar difficulties with derivative discourses remain. In independent Africa, one of the most intriguing attempts to imagine political and intellectual alternatives to domination by former colonial masters revolved around the idea of African socialism. For some theorists, it presented an opportunity to celebrate and standardize "indigenous socialism" that included "communal ownership of land," "the egalitarian character of society," and "the extensive network of social obligations" (Friedland and Rosberg 1964: 5). The vision was to transform the scale of this indigenous socialism "from the parochial kinship unit to the nation" (Friedland and Rosberg 1964: 8). The imagination of the nation as family was by no means restricted to socialist experiments or Africa, and paternalism embodied by the head of state became the norm even in those African countries that never pursued socialism, such as Malaŵi (see Schatzberg 2002). Yet as subsequent critics have pointed out, the Marxist concept of "false consciousness" was no less attractive to African socialists than to their counterparts elsewhere, often resulting in summary dismissals of so-called African tradition (T. Mkandawire 2005: 12).[12] Variations in the actual implementation of socialism became noteworthy—from Marxist-Leninist vanguardism in Mozambique to so-called humanism in Zambia—and they may have been even more significant had not a hostile international environment stalled these experiments.[13] Yet while it has become easy to assert that no country in Africa was "fully socialist" (Sindima 1995: 118), deeper intellectual problems, particularly as they also pertain to more recent transformations, should not escape from view. As Igor Kopytoff observed already in 1964, the emerging elites were building "a new pan-African social mythology whose vocabulary remain[ed] essentially Western" (1964: 55). The communalism that had signified primitivism for Western missionaries and explorers was given a positive value without serious attention to how accurate the notion was in the first place.

It is the persistence of this vocabulary that unites otherwise diverse philosophical and political perspectives on Africa. The first generation of post-independence African intellectuals, some of whom were co-opted by new governments, was indeed pan-African in its cultural outlook, searching for an identity in a common African heritage rather than in ethnicity (T. Mkandawire 2005: 18). Some of the philosophical equivalents survive until the present time, with concepts such as *ubuntu* or, in Chicheŵa, *umunthu* presented as the cornerstones of a particularly African view of existence (see, e.g., Mbiti 1970; Sindima 1995). Although always of interest to some African intellectuals, particularly to those in the diaspora, this philosophical pan-Africanism was revived by South Africa's delivery from the yoke of apartheid. The coinage to focus the attention was the African Renaissance, albeit a curiously European notion in some of its elaborations (see, e.g., Magubane 1999). By comparing Africa's rise to Europe's defeat of medieval obstacles to progress, the program of African Renaissance risked writing history through alien analogies (compare Mamdani 1996).[14]

What the vocabulary of pan-African values has contributed to the debate on liberalism is, among other things, a rather crude distinction between individualism and communalism. "Individualism is the invention of Western society" (Lumumba-Kasongo 2005: 15), runs a rather typical charge against the narrow idea of liberal democracy that has been marketed in Africa. Much as this critique is informed by concerns over colonial legacies and an exploitative political economy, the difference between Africa and the West tends to assume metaphysical qualities. "The metaphysics of African societies," Tukumbi Lumuba-Kasongo writes, "are characterized more by the principle of collective existence than that of individualism" (2005: 16). The idea that Africans are particularly bound by group loyalties is merely an instance of the inversion mentioned above by which a sign of primitivity for Westerners was turned into a positive resource for African nationalists. Elements of this inversion inform the African Charter on Human and Peoples' Rights, approved by the Organization of African Unity in 1981 and presented as an African response to overtly individualistic human rights (see, e.g., Mutua 2002). Yet by making collective rights conditional on recognition by the state, the charter has rarely been used to challenge postcolonial authoritarianism (Hastrup 2001: 60; Lindholt 2001).[15] In a similar vein, some politicians found it expedient to hide their long-standing authoritarianism behind the façade of African culture (T. Mkandawire 2005: 18).

It is precisely because individualistic laws and procedures did come to define liberal democracy in Africa that critics' attempts to envision alternatives must be taken seriously. Claude Ake was undoubtedly correct to assert that "in Africa's search for democracy, there is very little in the experience of the established democracies to guide it and a great deal to mislead it" (2000: 31). The question is how to appreciate particular histories and the values they have generated without succumbing either to cultural essentialism or to the idea of "Africa's pathological exceptionalism" (see Zeleza 2003: 282). Ake himself went beyond abstract communalism by emphasizing the materiality of membership, such as "the involvement of everyone in promoting the common good" and "sharing the burdens and the rewards of community membership" (2000: 184). What individualistic prescriptions in policy and politics have tended to obscure, not least in Africa, is the impossibility of affording personal autonomy. Membership based on a certain conviviality has instead been a precondition of human existence (Nyamnjoh 2004).

Conviviality is not dictated by the brute fact of material survival alone. The need is to describe the moral and existential considerations subjects bring to bear on their material predicament, but the thrust of the above discussion is to advise caution with a descriptive vocabulary that derives from the same source as individualism. Communalism, the idea that persons are mere parts of a whole, is the obverse of individualism and, as such, the other side of the same coin (Englund 2004a). Caution is all the more advisable when both Ake

(2000: 184) and Lumumba-Kasongo (2005: 21) conclude their critiques of liberal democracy with calls for genuine equality. Insightful as they are, these critiques based on a notion of Africans' distinct social character fall short of specifying what equality might entail when it is decoupled from the confines of the individualism-communalism debate.

Anthropology must be attentive to its mandate to explore intellectual and political alternatives in the most unexpected domains, propelled not by exoticism but by a desire to engage a mainstream debate with observations it would not otherwise encounter. Storytelling and other forms of African-language use, for example, demand a degree of intellectual equality to be accepted as intellectual resources on a par with the theories of liberal critics and African intelligentsia. Even in Malaŵi under Banda, popular drama groups offered outlets for African-language deliberations on the predicament of severe poverty (Barber 1987: 44–46). Their idioms and style were different from the ones deployed by university students, whose plays tended to be situated in either folkloric or middle-class realms. More broadly, whether it is ritual language (Apter 2007), songs and oral poems (Vail and White 1991), or oracular expression (Barber 1991), anthropologists and historians working in Africa have long demonstrated the powers of African languages to mediate wide-ranging political and moral reflection and practice. Storytelling that summons a mass-mediated public to consider inequality and obligation arises from this well-established strength and addresses conundrums that are directly relevant to the prospects of liberalism in Africa.

Publics and Counter-publics

The distant needy are often as much aware of inequality as those liberal theorists who have made their condition a subject of moral and political deliberation. One major source of awareness for both sides is the mass media, even if they rarely consume the same media products. While the media makes images and ideas of possible lives elsewhere available to the poor (Appadurai 1996: 35), it also contributes to their awareness of how unevenly poverty has been distributed in the world (Fassin 2007: 277–278). A wide range of media, not least rumor and other narrative genres, makes the world contract for Malaŵians and indicates that the work of the imagination is by no means spurred by the electronic media alone (compare de Vries 2001; Englund 2007a; Mazzarella 2004; van de Port 2006). The specific interest of *Nkhani Zam'maboma* is how it summons, through its use of the lingua franca Chicheŵa and its coverage of the whole country, a national public to consider inequality and obligation. It is a genre that liberal theorists in the affluent North are highly unlikely to ever encounter, confined as they are, in spite of all the media flows in their own lives, to debating world poverty amongst themselves.

It is, nonetheless, precisely through topics such as the public sphere and deliberation that liberal theorists have come to revise some of liberalism's key tenets. The concept of publics refers to audiences of a distinctive kind, most often mass-mediated and, as such, physically absent from each others' lives. Whether they are imagined to be vast or limited, publics are convened by a specific medium or performance, their members anonymous and yet alike in one respect or another (Barber 2007: 139–140). "A public is a relation among strangers," as Michael Warner (2002: 74) has written. The role of print media in producing national publics is by now a classic insight in historical scholarship (see B. Anderson 1983), but debate continues as to whether those publics are democratic and the extent to which the mass media enables or corrodes democratic aspirations. Jürgen Habermas's (1989) work, which has cast a long shadow over this debate, presents a particular view on the emergence of the liberal value of equality.

The bourgeois public sphere came to replace, according to Habermas, a theatrical display of authority in late eighteenth-century Europe. Crucial was a broader legal and economic transformation by which a public composed of autonomous and equivalent individuals became a feasible notion, further advanced by new cultural institutions such as coffee houses, clubs, concerts, and newspapers. For Habermas, the bourgeois public was "from the outset a reading public" that became "the abstract counterpart of public authority" (1989: 23). Rational debate, carried out in coffee houses and newspapers, was key to Habermas's notion of the civil society that the emerging public sphere entailed. Subsequent scholarship has, however, taken issue with several of his assumptions, pointing out, among other things, that this democratic public sphere actually excluded women and certain other categories of people (Fraser 1992). Rationality is another assumption that has come under fire, along with the dualisms of private and public, and ethics and aesthetics, that Habermas's argument is seen to rest on (see, e.g., Gardiner 2004). The conflictual and contradictory aspects of the public sphere, some of them embodied as much as argued, therefore hold special interest to Habermas's critics.

The flurry of criticism aimed at Habermas's argument should not obscure its own status as critical theory. Habermas's intent was to account for the erosion of the democratic public sphere that had provided a counterpoint to state authority, a critique he pursued in his later work through a normative theory of communicative reason (see Habermas 1996). One culprit in the decline of the democratic public sphere is the mass media, its increasing commercialization allocating unprecedented power to those with capital to distribute their views. It is this dismal view of the mass media—once the cornerstone of the democratic public sphere, now one of its worst enemies—that affords considerable affinity between Habermas and other theorists of the public sphere. One area of discussion is associated with so-called deliberative democracy, an instance of attempts to nuance prevailing orthodoxies about liberal democracy. Already by emphasizing citizens' participation in the weighing of different policies, theories of deliberative democracy mark a step away from the narrow definition of democracy as voting and electoral competition (Chambers 2003). This is also an arena in which scholars have elaborated their critique of Habermas's focus on communicative reason. A heightened sense of sociocultural diversity, for example, has enabled them to challenge a difference-blind model of rationality (Benhabib 2002; Valadez 2001; M. Williams 2000). This development has led to work on the aesthetic and embodied dimensions of deliberation (Tarnopolsky 2007), and on interior, rather than merely public, deliberation (Fearon 1998; Goodin 2003). Doubt has also been raised as to whether Habermas's normative stance has helped to move the debate from democratic procedures to actual outcomes (Paley 2004).

These critical directions in scholarship will inform much of this book, but it is necessary to pause on critics' distrust of the contemporary mass media. The reason why many theorists of deliberation, themselves liberals of various kinds, have a rather low opinion on its prospects is precisely the commercialization and consequent triviality of mass-mediated views and debates. "Citizens," a typical charge against deliberation goes, "are more likely to look for debates on television, newspaper editorials, or magazine stories than undertake lengthy and costly studies of economics" (Pincione and Tesón 2006: 19). The reliance on the media does not warrant high hopes, because, according to another critic, "the press perpetuates misunderstandings of what people want, probably as often in pursuit of the facile 'good story' as for political objectives" (Stokes 1998: 136). Theorists of deliberative democracy thus join hands with media critics, who have also bemoaned the stranglehold of corporate ownership on the expression and diversity of opinions in the public sphere (see, e.g., Bourdieu 1998; Herman and Chomsky 2002). What should give us pause, however, is not this well-taken concern over corporate ownership but the paucity of ethnography on media production and consumption in critics' diatribes.

Their interventions too often rely, in Henry Jenkins's words, on "melodramatic discourse about victimization and vulnerability, seduction and manipulation" (2006: 247).[16]

Although anonymity defines publics, not all of their members can remain anonymous to the ethnographer. Even a public as vast as the nation has to be approached by living among those who consume media products designed for a national public. The results are often different from what a purely textual analysis can offer, such as when television serials are shown to enter social worlds whose conditions do not match the national ideal they depict (Abu-Lughod 2005; Mankekar 1999). Anthropological perspectives on the media thus often go beyond the concept of reception in media studies, whatever convergence the use of ethnographic methods has brought between the two fields of study.[17] Yet ethnography does not nuance or challenge media critics' tirades only by showing how media consumers can be more astute than these critics think. The study of media production is equally important, the diversity of settings where anthropologists have studied journalistic practices opening up fresh questions about professionalism and political involvement (see Bird 2010; Boyer 2005; Boyer and Hannerz 2006; Hannerz 2004; Hasty 2005; Ståhlberg 2002). In much of Africa, as discussed in the previous chapter, media production has long operated under the shadow of colonial and postcolonial repression (Nyamnjoh 2005a: 39–53). This historical observation already suggests important variations in the constraints that trouble media critics. In Malaŵi, state control has been compatible with a professional ethos of public service that corporate control has been observed to undermine elsewhere.

To the extent that a national public co-exists with publics produced by various genres and media, and is itself more complex than what official rhetoric suggests, repression and control cannot be the whole story of media production and consumption. However, in the study of pluralism, a notion of counter-publics may present itself rather too swiftly, in spite of being a welcome antidote to Habermas's theory (Negt and Kluge 1993) and a useful tool in some ethnographies (see, e.g., Hirschkind 2006). Insofar as counter-publics "contravene the rules obtaining in the world at large, being structured by alternative dispositions or protocols, making different assumptions about what can be said or what goes without saying" (Warner 2002: 56), *Nkhani Zam'maboma* hardly summoned a counter-public, whatever its divergence from the official news bulletin. This contention also questions the ease with which scholars have looked for signs of resistance in oppressive conditions, bypassing the possibility that impoverished subjects seek relationship with those who abuse them.

Finally, another historical observation from Africa reminds us that the print and electronic media, while undoubtedly distinct in their reach and impact, are only recent modalities in the long-standing multiplication of imagined communities (Barber 2007: 145; Barber 2009). Mass-mediated publics have to be understood in the context of other genres and performances by which Africans have commented on the obligations of those in authority.

New Perspectives on News

The allusion to a comparison between *Nkhani Zam'maboma* and the MBC's official news bulletin suggests important variations in media products that fall under the same category. *Nkhani Zam'maboma* and the official bulletin did share a number of features: both were prepared in the same newsroom, often by the same journalists, and both were presented in the same matter-of-fact tone without additional commentary. Both types of news were also known as *nkhani* (stories) and distinguished from rumors (*mphekesera*) and fictional narratives (*nthano*). However, while the official news was, for both the MBC's journalists and their public, notorious for bias and misinformation, stories broadcast on *Nkhani Zam'maboma* were true (*zoona*). Such a status, as will become clear in subsequent chapters, by no means shielded *Nkhani Zam'maboma* from controversy that often took issue with the veracity of some of its contents. What merits consideration here is the way in which ethnographic research on this program contributes to recent insights into the diversity of news as a media form, raising questions about the values of novelty and objectivity in liberal views on media production and, by the same token, about the very distinction between production and reception in media studies. The prospect of increasingly democratic media practices in emerging news journalism requires particular attention, for it lays bare one more instance of equality as a goal informing analysis.

For journalists in the MBC's newsroom, novelty, as the previous chapter already suggested, was less important than broadcasting the timeless legitimacy of the state in official bulletins. Endless reports on the inauguration of schools, bridges, roads, clinics, and development schemes did not appear to be a source of tedium in their work. On the contrary, journalists distinguished, in confidential conversations with me, such reports from items with unsavory bias toward a political party. The next chapter describes their personal tribulations when asked to broadcast biased news they considered offensive. Even the most uncritical account of the state president's speech could, however, be compatible with their professional ethos. The reference to the president as "the leader of this country" (*mtsogoleri wa dziko lino*), such as in a news broadcast in 2003, is one example of upholding an institution despite the incumbent's indisputable shortcomings.[18] The bulletin that had this news as its main item, taking most of the broadcast time, was edited by journalists who later described to me their unease with food shortages and the president's unconstitutional bid for a third term during the early years of the new millennium. They defended this and numerous other news of its kind by pointing out that leadership (*utsogoleri*) outlived its incumbents and was a crucial subject of national broadcasting.

That this subject was not interrogated in the spirit of critical inquiry advocated by human rights organizations and media observers betrayed the distance between liberalism and the MBC journalists' professional ethos. The irony, of course, is that the president had in the MBC a platform to not only assert his government's commitment to development and his intolerance of ministers who did not perform. Muluzi also used every opportunity he had to claim the liberal values of democracy and human rights as his own. The news broadcast in 2003, reporting on his speech in a predominantly poor township in the capital, highlighted the difference between his government and the one-party state that had preceded it by drawing attention to new economic freedoms and the improved status of women and youths. Whether broadcasting such news was a mere ironic (or tragic) appropriation of liberalism by illiberal means cannot be properly answered, however, without due regard for what else constituted the professional ethos of the news editors.

Much as they were different, the official bulletin and *Nkhani Zam'maboma* did not stand in a relation of power and its resistance to one another. An element of catharsis did attach editors to *Nkhani Zam'maboma* against the confines of both language and politics in the official bulletin. But *Nkhani Zam'maboma*'s perspective on the dark side of authority and leadership also complemented the official bulletin's celebration of legitimacy and development. It showed how the incumbent did become the subject of deliberation when the register shifted from uncritical reporting to moral argument. The liberal insistence on revealing the abuse of power was not an alien value to editors, but it would be simplistic to reduce editors' preference for a more subtle claim-making to the imperative of self-censorship. The abuse of power found its limits in the mass-mediated effort to influence rather than to overthrow the incumbent.

The study of these continuities and discontinuities between different forms of news contributes to the nascent study of news practices by anthropologists. Moving beyond the sociological unmasking of power relations behind journalists' claims to the transparency of news (see, e.g., Altheide 1976; Tuchman

1978), anthropologists have begun to take more seriously what is unusual about news among media forms: its claim to be "an accurate reflection of reality" (Bird 2010: 5). Unmasking power relations may be a less urgent task than investigating, ethnographically, what such a claim might entail in the highly diverse contexts of news production and reception. The sociological critique has largely derived from studying newsrooms and elite journalistic communities in the North (Wahl-Jorgensen 2010). By contrast, recent ethnographic work recognizes a fuller range of domains and participants in the worlds of news. A particularly intriguing parallel between apparently disparate worlds derives from the intersection of production and reception in both the resource-poor settings of the South and the opportunities offered by the new media in the North.

For reception studies, at the heart of these emerging insights is a move away from "the primacy of news content" that "privileges the individual acts of reading" (Peterson 2010: 171). Reception has conventionally been approached as a process by which individual readers, viewers, or listeners decode messages sent to them by mass media. However, radio, for example, is not only the programs it broadcasts but also a material object that enables or inhibits interactions among its audiences depending on the economic and material conditions in which it is located, as Debra Spitulnik (2002) has demonstrated through the case of Zambia. In Zambia, as in Malaŵi, mobile receivers extend radio listening to those who do not own them, their circulation throwing light, among other things, on how personal status is entangled with material objects and how the boundaries of home may not be the same as in the North. Above all, close studies of radio listening may reveal the ways in which news items assume their meaning and impact within the relationships of everyday life.

A similar discontent with individualistic perspectives informs new approaches to news production. Largely prompted by new possibilities for coproduction through digital information and the internet, anthropologists contrast the current situation to pioneering sociological studies in which "the journalist always stood as a productive presence" at the center of analysis (Boyer 2010: 242). New standards of objectivity may be in the making when new technologies recast old convictions about conflicts of interest, libel, and plagiarism (see Vesperi 2010). Venerable media outlets, particularly newspapers, face unprecedented pressure to adapt or to lose revenue. A source of fear and uncertainty for some journalists, the new opportunities for co-producing news and other media forms with their publics can also be greeted with enthusiasm by those who wish to subvert the corporate stranglehold on mass media (compare Henry 2007; Jenkins 2006).

The most promising outcome so far of this unlikely convergence of studies from the South and the North is the prospect of an increasingly sophisticated idea of what constitutes publics. It was noted above that publics addressed by particular media forms are characterized by anonymity and the mutual equivalence of their members. The critique of individualism in both the reception and production of news permits a finer sense of not so much mutual equivalence as mutual dependence. Studying news as an encounter between journalists, the sources they depend on, and their audiences that actively process what they are given as news can lead to a notion of publics as networks (see Rao 2010). Journalists' own involvement in their audiences' life-worlds—and the multiple types of journalism that exist beyond the newsroom—militate against the view that journalists are located entirely outside the public their media products help create. Although some media critics and human rights activists may prefer a flat network, an intrinsically democratic process of news gathering and dissemination, hierarchical networks are more likely.[19] Much depends on the historical and economic setting of publics, thereby cautioning against too perfect a parallel between the resource-poor media worlds of the South and the new media technologies of the North.

The case of *Nkhani Zam'maboma* shows how Malaŵian broadcasters were deeply committed to journalism as a distinct profession. MBC journalists' ethos of public service did facilitate a certain identification with the rural and urban poor they envisioned as their primary audience, an ethos further enhanced by the material difficulties and rural attachments they shared with this audience. Yet as the chapters in part 2 of this book demonstrate, despite purporting to broadcast stories in virtually the same form as they were received, the editors of *Nkhani Zam'maboma* did not forfeit a certain authorial prerogative. Equality, in other words, again appears in a rather more complex guise than what both the moral individualism of liberal theorists and the critical sensibilities of social scientists can allow for. As a news program within which the downtrodden could assert, as subjects capable of making claims, their constitutive equality with their masters and leaders, *Nkhani Zam'maboma* was itself based on hierarchies of knowledge production. Those who see in emerging and interactive news journalism a domain in which to pursue equality as a goal will also find an alternative view in subsequent chapters. They discuss how the hierarchies of knowledge production affected listeners' different capacities to interpret the details of stories they heard on the radio. A key observation, unsettling to conventional liberal sensibilities, is that those differences were compatible with equality as a condition of hierarchical relationships.

3

Against the Occult

Journalists and Scholars in Search of Alternatives

A story broadcast on *Nkhani Zam'maboma* in 2003 told of a woman who had been found alone in a rural graveyard at midday, lying on top of a tomb.[1] On closer inspection, villagers discovered a bag next to her. It contained a razor blade, a needle, and a bottle of blood. The woman had sought to dispel suspicions that anything sinister was at issue by claiming that she did not know what she was doing because she was drunk. The story went on to report that the woman had good employment in the commercial capital Blantyre and that the villagers who had found her suspected that she had wanted to protect her job against possible dismissal. They also thought that the visit to the graveyard had been occasioned by her desire to find a charm (*chizimba*) for making bricks used in building a modern house (*nyumba yamakono*). Her first husband was reported to have left her because of her witchcraft (*ufiti*), while she had bewitched her second husband to stay at home with the couple's children.

While discussing this and other contributions to *Nkhani Zam'maboma* with villagers in Dedza District and township dwellers in Chinsapo near Lilongwe, Malaŵi's capital, I was often struck by the ease with which people were able to elaborate on the details of a story. Allusions which they discerned opened up a wider set of issues than was immediately apparent to the ethnographer. Stories about visits to graveyards when there were no funerals were familiar enough to me after years of fieldwork in rural and urban Malaŵi. The scandalous nature of such stories arose from breaking the rule, known even by children, that no one should visit a graveyard outside funerals, at least not without a permission obtained from the chief. The visits were invariably sinister in these stories, and a remarkably consistent exegesis of the above story was offered to me in both Dedza villages and Chinsapo Township. Listeners elaborated on it by pointing out that clandestine visits to graveyards were ordered by healers who had been approached by supplicants looking for personal benefits such as success at work.[2] This widely shared understanding received more detail when some listeners claimed to know the words uttered in such exchanges. A healer would begin the process by asking the supplicant, "Are you courageous?" (*kodi mwalimba mtima?*). If the answer was affirmative, the supplicant was sent to a graveyard to collect a charm or activating agent for the healer's concoction (*mankhwala*). The visit to the graveyard, known as "attaining a charm" (*kukwanitsa chizimba*), required courage, because the person came into contact with corpses, either by digging them up or by conjuring them up through magic.

Stories involving witchcraft are a good example of how *Nkhani Zam'maboma* both built on widely shared knowledge among its public and carried allusions congenial to further elaboration by those who claimed to know more. The knowledge required to interpret details was unevenly distributed, much as *Nkhani Zam'maboma* broadcast incidents and notions that had not been discussed in public arenas before. The next chapter will discuss the feature the program shared with many oral genres, namely the way in which even generally accessed genres can entertain meanings and allusions whose interpretation requires specialist knowledge, based on the principle that "transparent, perspicacious texts are felt to be dull, even worthless" (Barber 2009: 10). For this chapter, the task is to understand how the mention of witchcraft in some of these stories engaged the ethnographer's imagination with allusions that were not always relevant to their public.

By the end of the twentieth century, witchcraft, particularly in African settings, had returned to anthropology as a topic through which to explore popular experiences of economic, political, and religious transformations. The thesis about the "modernity of witchcraft" (Geschiere 1997) appealed to many students of Africa beyond anthropology for its propensity to do two things at the same time. On the one hand, it declared Africans equally modern as their Western counterparts. On the other hand, it claimed to reveal how modernity took culturally and historically specific forms in different parts of the world, with witchcraft a particularly potent discourse on contemporary politics and economy in Africa. Although I had published a critique of tautologies and unwarranted assumptions in this emerging literature (Englund 1996b), I was also intrigued by the frequency with which concerns about witchcraft were expressed during my various research projects in Malaŵi. Witchcraft stories on *Nkhani Zam'maboma* seemed an excellent opportunity to explore further the specifics of an African public arena.

My initial sense of what mattered was not determined simply by recent currents in scholarship but also by listeners' and editors' apparently similar interest in witchcraft stories. I was often told how new and exciting it was to hear about witchcraft on the radio—nothing like *Nkhani Zam'maboma* had existed during Banda's autocratic regime.[3] Contagious as it was, excitement among listeners and editors was inevitably filtered through the particular anthropological categories and assumptions I brought to bear on studying this program. The idea that witchcraft was a popular discourse that was an alternative to more technocratic or sociological explanations trivialized the range of discursive resources at listeners' and editors' disposal and the many allusions stories mentioning witchcraft made. It took me a long time to realize that an anthropological interest in witchcraft, particularly when it conflated witchcraft with the occult, confined rather than enriched my understanding of the way in which *Nkhani Zam'maboma* addressed a public that reflected on the abuse of power. For one thing, as is discussed in more detail in the next chapter, only a third of the stories mentioned witchcraft, whether directly or indirectly. A primary interest in witchcraft stories would have ignored the majority of contributions to *Nkhani Zam'maboma* and obscured the ethos and impact it had.

Witchcraft was, in point of fact, often merely an element in far-reaching reflections on power and injustice. When I played back the graveyard story to villagers and township dwellers in 2006, virtually everyone drew my attention to the former speaker of parliament Sam Mpasu. He had recently become embroiled in a similar incident in Machinga District in Southern Malaŵi.[4] Also a former cabinet minister and, at the time of the incident, the spokesman for the former president Muluzi, Mpasu was found sitting on a tomb late one afternoon in the company of a healer. Irate villagers blocked Mpasu's escape from the graveyard, and after hiding for two hours, he had reportedly offered them money in an effort to leave the scene. They had, however, called the police, who

arrested the politician. Released on bail, Mpasu denied in subsequent statements and interviews that the incident had anything to do with witchcraft. He
explained that he had taken a wrong path while on his way to a friend's house.
The real reason for the conflict, he said, was the attempt by the new ruling party
to destroy his political career.

My interlocutors in villages and the township had not seen the press reports on this incident, and their knowledge was based on rumors that had
spread across the country. Yet they were able both to add detail and to arrive
at far-reaching conclusions about governance in Malawi. No one doubted that
Mpasu's motives had been sinister. It was common knowledge that his political career was in the doldrums after he had lost his parliamentary seat in
the 2004 general elections and his boss, the former president Muluzi, had lost
favor with the incoming president Mutharika. Villagers and township dwellers
saw Mpasu's graveyard visit as an instance of the general procedure by which
some secured success at work, as described in the graveyard story broadcast by
Nkhani Zam'maboma. Mpasu was preparing for the 2009 presidential elections
at a time when it was still unclear who would be his party's candidate. Virtually everyone pointed out to me that it was not by accident that Mpasu visited
a graveyard in Machinga, Muluzi's home district hundreds of miles away from
Mpasu's own home in Ntcheu. Mpasu wanted to harm Muluzi and his family,
who were rumored to contemplate fielding Muluzi's son, or Muluzi himself,
as the party's presidential candidate.[5] That Mpasu would turn against his own
boss was entirely plausible to villagers and township dwellers, accustomed as
they were to observing baffling maneuvers among Malawi's political class. The
country's transition to multiparty democracy had heralded an era of constantly
shifting loyalties, the malleable alliances between parties and among individual
politicians often forged without their constituents' knowledge or consent (Englund 2002b).

Although, as will be seen in part 2, the editors of *Nkhani Zam'maboma* did
not broadcast stories that involved politicians, listeners' imaginations were not
restrained by such a policy. In fact, both editors and listeners cherished the
program precisely because of the perspectives it opened up on the abuse of
power in Malawi and beyond, decades of deceptive broadcasting on the MBC
having taught everyone the art of critical listenership. Local stories could, and
frequently did, gather national and transnational dimensions as listeners debated their resonance with what politicians were said to be doing with their
Malawian and foreign accomplices, whether business partners or aid donors
(compare Englund 2006: 190–192). The interest in witchcraft could appear to-

gether with resolutely meritocratic ideas, such as when those who had caught a glimpse of the then British prime minister Tony Blair in the print media would report to others that youths (*achinyamata*) had attained high offices in other countries, their ascension to power based on education (*maphunziro*) rather than occult schemes. The excitement about witchcraft on the radio was invariably a reaction *against* the occult, nourishing the imagination of alternatives to its immoral methods.

To the extent that anthropology may be restrained by the category of the occult in its descriptive work, human rights activists are not alone in their difficulties to envision alternatives. As such, before the revelatory powers of anthropology are allowed to raise hopes too high, this chapter uses the category of the occult to examine anthropology's own limitations in recognizing alternatives. At the same time, anthropology's limitations are best countered by ethnographic fieldwork, a sense of alternatives produced not so much by conceptual refinement as by the claims of the ethnographer's interlocutors. This chapter begins by exploring broadcasters' aspirations and frustrations in light of the MBC's troubled history described in chapter 1. The quest for alternatives in the newsroom challenges not only anthropology's representation of the occult as the quintessential African alternative but also assumptions among aid donors and human rights activists about the fallacies of public service at the MBC. The fascination with witchcraft stories in Malaŵi's media requires analysis, but only after this description of the MBC journalists' commitment to public service. By thus situating witchcraft stories within a wider set of journalistic concerns, this chapter is able to reclaim anthropology, not least against the pronouncements by some African intellectuals, as the study of intellectual and pragmatic alternatives to prevailing policy and activist orthodoxies, such as the freedom-focused human rights regime.

Serving the Government of the Day, Every Day

As journalists at the MBC frequently discover, others are only too eager to advise them on how to conduct their professional duties. Their colleagues in Malaŵian media, for example, shift between biting criticism and brotherly counsel.[6] "Our brothers and sisters," a Malaŵian magazine appealed to journalists at the MBC in 2008, "open up and serve the public and not politicians."[7] "It's high time," it added, "you started acting professionally so that you win back the trust of the people you have disappointed because of 'too much politicking.'" Aid agencies sponsoring Malaŵi's democratic experiment have been equally confident about the MBC's shortcomings. In 2000, the Danish governmental agency criticized the MBC for providing "top-down information from government to the citizens, with little room for alternative viewpoints and little dialogue with end users."[8] In 1994, a visiting European Union delegate set the tone for criticism by observing that programs on the MBC were "boring."[9] Urging the MBC journalists to become "inquisitive and analytical," the delegate advised them to "tackle critically topical issues."

A lack of linguistic skills may explain the failure of expatriate aid donors to notice how "alternative viewpoints" have been broadcast on the MBC in the midst of the misinformation they have rightly condemned. The kind of advice given above, whether by Malaŵians or foreigners, has itself arisen from a particular view of journalism that is at odds with the professional ethos of many editors and reporters in the MBC's newsroom. By calling for inquisitive and analytical reporting, these advisers have assumed that serving the government has represented a pitiable surrender to political interference. The idiom of "serving the government of the day" that I heard, in English, time and again during my fieldwork with MBC journalists was entirely compatible with their personal qualms about the parties and politicians that ran the affairs of the government. It was as though the journalists were themselves responsible for maintaining the timeless legitimacy of the state. News beginning with a reference to the government or the state president were, therefore, evocations of institutions and authorities that were supposed to embrace all Malaŵians. This ethos of journalism resembles the "who-leads" that Jennifer Hasty (2005: 49–55; 2006: 78–84) identifies as a key feature of state media in Jerry Rawlings's Ghana. As the leading paragraph in a newspaper item, the who-lead begins with a quote from an authoritative personality rather than with an event. "Meaning," Hasty explains, "is not objectively embedded in an event and uncovered by the autonomous individual" (2006: 85). Whereas an event-focused news narrative highlights conflict and novelty, who-leads "emphasize cooperation, legitimate authority, and redemptive development" (Hasty 2006: 85).

Crucial to MBC journalists' own sense of professionalism has been a separation between partisanship, on the one hand, and dedication to legitimate authority and redemptive development, on the other. Those journalists, including the editors of *Nkhani Zam'maboma*, who have withstood successive regimes have inevitably had to exercise some form of self-censorship, but their dedication came to be challenged, paradoxically, most directly by a rejuvenation of public broadcasting after Mutharika's capture of the government. In early 2007, a new director general and his deputy were appointed, the former's long experience in journalism contrasting with the latter's youthfulness and lack of background in the field. A former moderator of Malawitalk, an internet discussion forum, Bright Malopa had little else to show for in the field of media and communications, even his credentials in marketing, his apparent profession, attracting some controversy in Malaŵi's print media.[10] He had, however, spent several years in the United Kingdom and brought to the MBC a new rhetoric of public-service broadcasting. Malopa designed new programs, some based on investigative journalism, others on humor. Although his attempts at a fresh start were welcomed at the MBC, particularly by those in junior positions whom he promoted while sending certain directors on extended leave, it soon became clear to many in the newsroom that sycophancy at the top had merely changed rhetorics.

While claiming to hold politicians accountable through investigative journalism and satire, the new programs focused on opposition politicians. *Mpungwepungwe Pandale* (Pandemonium in Politics) fulfilled its mandate of investigative journalism by pursuing rumors and allegations regarding Muluzi's regime, such as the apparent suicide of his economic adviser. *Makiyolobasi*[11] combined actors' voices with excerpts from Muluzi's and other opposition leaders' speeches, the background sound of raucous laughter creating the impression of a live audience. Malopa described the program as a political cartoon, a genre familiar to newspaper-reading Malaŵians, but many both inside and outside the MBC were troubled by the way opposition leaders' words were given a new context to make them sound idiotic. When other radio stations, Muluzi's own Joy Radio at the helm, retaliated with a similar program format, now targeting government ministers, concerns with hate speech and intolerance deepened among Malaŵian media analysts, human rights activists, and religious leaders. The Catholic bishops, for example, noted in their 2008 pastoral letter that these programs contributed to "political intolerance and the demonisation of certain individuals in our society."[12] Various other initiatives under Malopa's leadership continued in the same vein, however, including the re-broadcast of Muluzi's speeches in which he had, as the state president, made exorbitant promises to his subjects. *Constituency Barometer* also sought to expose current opposition parliamentarians' disregard of their constituents.

In his conversations with me, Malopa argued that programs such as *Mpungwepungwe Pandale* did for the national level what *Nkhani Zam'maboma* did for the local level—they both held authorities to account. Yet his view, unaware of Malaŵians' capacity to make critical inferences across different levels, seemed to be as much out of touch as a comment by the United Democratic Front's secretary general. The latter was quoted as saying that the new programs took "advantage of the illiterate masses who [were] unable to differentiate propaganda from development and entertainment messages."[13] Such condescension was rare in the newsroom, as was journalists' acclaim for the kind of partisan public service that Malopa had introduced, much as he claimed to be inspired by the fierce approach to politicians on the BBC. The castigation of dissidents and the opposition had certainly been a part of MBC journalists' remit throughout the different regimes, but for those with few prospects of, or little interest in, favors from politicians, it never became a source of professional pride. The broadcast of positive news, the mainstay of the MBC's news bulletins, was their calling. The constant evocation of government was a civil servant's way of swearing allegiance to the timeless legitimacy of the state and its transcendental project of development. While keeping their heads down, and while privately admitting preference for Mutharika's technocracy over Muluzi's populism, many in the newsroom felt "shame" (*manyazi*) over the new programs. In their view, the ridicule heaped on opposition leaders by *Makiyolobasi* was often "nonsense" (*zachabechabe*) and made leaders look "despicable" (*onyozeka*).[14]

During my fieldwork, a sense of public service prevailed despite mounting financial difficulties. Those who had joined the broadcasting house during Banda's era maintained entrenched habits of service even when they were not strictly required. Not only technicians but also some journalists and librarians would forsake their day off whenever the state president's public appearance somewhere in the country on a Sunday had to be broadcast live. Some of them would sit in suits by their desks, ostensibly idle but in their demeanor the very custodians of the state. Younger journalists also found opportunities to experience their belonging to an institution that outlived any particular incumbent in political office. Because their houses were scattered in Blantyre's townships, some of them were, particularly when working on a night shift, given a lift to the broadcasting headquarters by one of the few remaining four-wheel drives at the MBC. When they cruised into villages in these vehicles to perform assignments, they were received with the respect (*ulemu*) that many Malaŵians thought the work of government (*ntchito ya boma*) deserved. With two exceptions, no one in the newsroom owned a car, and the journalists' houses I visited in townships were sparsely furnished and never equipped with television sets. The newsroom had the only television available at the MBC for viewing by its rank and file. The continuous broadcast of BBC or Sky News channels attracted viewers also from other departments. This exposure to images from foreign countries contrasted with the poverty of the journalists' homes.

Fear and Loathing in the Newsroom

Boma, "government" or "state," could thus be the object of journalists' dedication, and it was their duty to broadcast the commitment of its elected representatives to the redemptive project of development.[15] Such a view on dedication, if not vocation, is important to bear in mind against the reduction of
state journalists to passive vessels of state propaganda, a reduction that Hasty
(2006: 90) has also criticized. Pushing the argument further, Dominic Boyer
(2003) has described censorship in the German Democratic Republic as an
intellectual practice. Noting how unusual it is to find accounts of censorship
from practitioners' rather than victims' point of view, Boyer (2003: 513) observes that censors working for authoritarian regimes are often depicted as
functionaries rather than intellectuals (see also Hultin 2007). In this regard,
the branding of MBC journalists as "slavish apparatchiks" (ARTICLE 19 n.d.:
13) is a case in point.

However, while they were involved in knowledge production rather than
mere propaganda, and while their commitment was more often to the timeless
legitimacy of the state than to any incumbent of political office, MBC journalists were by no means universally content with the conditions of their work.
Dedication to public duty was tempered by the delay or non-payment of salaries, particularly after the parliament had declined to endorse a budget for
the MBC (see chapter 1). The period also saw the coming of the new management mentioned above, whose rhetoric of business practice cast a shadow of
retrenchment over a historically secure employment. At the same time, financial difficulties hampered retrenchment through retirement. The broadcasting
house was reported to owe millions of kwacha to employees whose retirement
packages it had not been able to pay.[16]

Other frustrations among the rank and file were long-standing. They concerned the inequality of income within the organization, the allocation of assignments, procedures for promotion, and pressures from politicians. In line
with the practice in governmental and non-governmental organizations in
Malaŵi, the payment of allowances for various expenses represented a substantial addition to the basic salary, in some cases more than doubling it. However, those with the lowest salaries were also the least able to access allowances.
While a housing allowance and, from the late 1990s onward, a mobile telephone
allowance were paid to every reporter and editor in the newsroom, the allowances to which the management were entitled aroused both resentment and
ridicule. Not only were the controllers, deputy director general, and director

general able to enjoy allowances for a car, cook, gardener, electricity, water, and their children's education; they were also able to claim a pet allowance to buy food for dogs and cats, a particularly outrageous perk from the viewpoint of those whose income never seemed enough to meet all the obligations that their status as civil servants entailed. In 2008, it was revealed that the controllers' 100 percent raise in basic salary was coupled with an increase in their allowances whose combined amount far exceeded the new basic salary itself.[17] During the same period, the word went around in the newsroom that the top management were cashing their security allowances despite using guards employed at the broadcasting headquarters to look after their residences. "We don't say anything," a reporter commented to me with a sarcastic smile.

The habit of not saying anything had been molded by bitter experiences. The wave of strike action that swept over the rest of civil service in the 1990s (see Anders 2009) also reached the MBC. In 1998, three hundred employees at the MBC went on strike for three days over pay, but thirteen of them were dismissed in its aftermath (ARTICLE 19 2000: 14). Among the dismissed were journalists who had not even participated in the strike. The use of dismissal and its threat has been an efficient method to discipline journalists who have shown an inclination for balanced reporting. For example, four senior journalists were dismissed soon after the 1999 general elections, in spite of the respect they had acquired among independent observers for their work (ARTICLE 19 2000: 67). The United Democratic Front's Task Force inside the MBC, mentioned in chapter 1, created a particularly distrustful ambiance in the newsroom, the meteoric rise of its key figure from a reporter to the controller of news to deputy director general a demoralizing tale of sycophancy securing promotion.[18] Reporting assignments have similarly been subject to party-political considerations, with the most coveted presidential functions, such as trips to foreign countries, available only to those whose dedication to serve the government has been expressed through unambiguous loyalty to the incumbent.

Opportunities for further training have been elusive and, when they have arisen, scarcely relevant to the work in the newsroom. Some donor agencies have offered occasional short-term courses on topics such as HIV/AIDS and children's rights, but reporters and editors, most of whom did not have formal qualifications in journalism, yearned for studies at a diploma or degree level.[19] The fees charged for journalism training in Malaŵian institutions were beyond their means.[20] Under these circumstances, many in the newsroom were more concerned about retaining their positions than demonstrating ambition. In their conversations with me, reporters and editors often listed employment in an international organization or the establishment of their own radio station as the most desired next step in their careers. Yet they were aware that international organizations were not likely to recruit persons who were seen to have served the government too closely. Nor was capital for founding a radio station available to most employees at the MBC, despite the inspiring example of the Zodiak Broadcasting Station, which had been launched by a former MBC journalist. Those who had some capital tended to be involved in the ownership of internet cafes and advertising companies. The vast majority, however, supplemented their income with ventures similar to the ones that most low- and middle-ranking civil servants in Malaŵi pursued: keeping chickens in the backyard, and paying others to cultivate land or to trade in secondhand clothes and other cheap goods.

Politicians' interference with the work of the newsroom exacerbated the sense of dissatisfaction with the MBC among its own journalists. Although successive ministers of information in Muluzi's and Mutharika's administrations made ample use of their direct telephone line to the controller of news, and all of them expected to be able to make pronouncements on the radio as and when they pleased, senior employees recalled even more intimidating practices during Banda's regime. Officials from the Malaŵi Congress Party (MCP), then the only party, would arrive unannounced in the newsroom to instruct journalists not only on what to have in the news bulletin but also in what order items were to appear. They could even try to write news themselves, tossing an unfinished text to an editor with the injunction to "write it up well" (*mulembe bwinobwino*). What would normally be accommodated within journalists' dedication to serving the government could become an unlivable contradiction when it attacked their personal convictions. A senior MBC employee, detailing his experiences for the first time to anyone other than his priest, provided me with a particularly harrowing account of the contradiction between his Catholicism and the MCP's fierce reaction against the Catholic bishops' Lenten letter in 1992.

Before the letter had been read out in Catholic churches, this employee, who was a Chicheŵa newsreader at the time, had been moved by the pope's visit to Malaŵi in 1989. In addition to what the visit had meant to a devout Catholic like himself, he, along with many Malaŵians, had been astonished by Banda's submissive attitude to the pope, whose hand Banda had kissed. This unprecedented display of humility had prepared the newsreader for the candid assessment of Malaŵi's governance and economy in the 1992 letter. However, instead of receiving the message with the same humility he had displayed in

1989, Banda and his lackeys launched a hostile campaign against the bishops, with some overexcited MCP members even suggesting their murder (Schof-feleers 1999: 132–136). News bulletins on the MBC became a central means by which this hostility was expressed, and this newsreader, himself elated by the contents of the letter, found himself reading one such hostile piece of news in the evening bulletin. He felt physically sick when he finished his shift, but he knew he would have to read the same piece the following morning. He de-liberately missed the car that collected him for work and arrived at the MBC three minutes past the hour to find that someone else had stepped in to read the news. He announced his intent to take sick leave the same morning, and together with the vacation he had not taken before, the absence turned out to be two months.

As soon as he had returned to the MBC, he was made to read a news bul-letin in which the first three items were all insulting (*kunyoza*) to the bishops. He jumped (*kulumphalumpha*) over the most offensive parts and put together other parts to make the news sound coherent. When he left the solitude of his recording cubicle, he was certain that he would face instant dismissal. No one seemed to have noticed, however, and he was able to continue his surreptitious ways until he was asked to read out a commentary (*ndemanga*). It was an attack on the bishops that required the reader to have a suitable tone of rage (*ukali*) in his voice. He had neither the strength nor the desire to read it, and at the last minute his insistence made a colleague read the commentary. As a conse-quence, he had to appear before a disciplinary committee whose chairperson proposed either demotion or dismissal. The newsreader's argument that he had been left alone to prepare the news bulletin that evening prompted an enquiry into why this had happened and deflected attention from his handling of the commentary. The newsreader told me that his priest had been the only one to hear about his maneuvers. The priest had commended him on acting accord-ing to his conscience.

"We do not tell each other" (*sitiuzana*), this broadcaster answered when I asked whether the bishops' letter had created space within the MBC to ex-press discontent with politicians. His present tense was telling, indicating that even decades of working together in the same institution did not ensure enough confidence to share political opinions with colleagues. The UDF Task Force in the late 1990s undoubtedly only increased the need to be on one's guard. How-ever, my observations, admittedly made after the threatening presence of the Task Force had subsided, also indicated that long-standing colleagues did find ways of sharing sensitive views, if only tacitly or jokingly. For example, many would pass by the MBC library to read newspapers, and their news prompted engagement in arguments about various events in the country.

A particularly revealing example occurred in 2008, when an editor walked into the newsroom with the breaking news that ammunition had been found at the parliamentary secretariat. His colleagues were at first astonished by the news, but their mood changed quickly into good-humored skepticism. The discovery was made when the leader of the opposition was embroiled in a controversy with the parliamentary secretariat over his use of its money for visiting his wife at a South African hospital. Before they had heard what an MBC reporter, based in Lilongwe where the secretariat was located, would say later in the news bulletin, these journalists in the newsroom made the connection and laughed at its implausible inference. One of them said, "I am doubtful" (*ndiku-kaika*), while someone else asked why workers at the secretariat had found the ammunition at this precise moment when they were there every day. The implication was that the ammunition had been planted to tarnish further the opposition politician's reputation. Before it evaporated, the issue was reported in the print media, but no mention was made of the opposition leader.[21] By contrast, the MBC's report dwelled on seemingly suspicious political motives. The exchange in the newsroom showed that the MBC's own journalists found it difficult to believe such a partisan report.

A Fusion of Life-worlds

What the above description of journalists' grievances at the MBC indicates is that the procedures and institutions of liberal democracy have had limited impact on the internal affairs of public broadcasters. Resort to strike action to ameliorate poor pay has exposed journalists and other employees to retribution by the management. The pursuit of freedom of expression in order to provide balanced reporting has cost some broadcasters their jobs. Cautionary tales have been numerous enough to make, as in the above example from the period of the democratic transition, rank-and-file journalists adopt weapons of the weak (Scott 1985), such as absenteeism and covert tactics of noncompliance. It would be wrong, however, to portray them as being locked into acts of resistance on a perpetual basis. Their pride in professionalism needs to be taken seriously, their dedication to public broadcasting inseparable from actual opportunities to apply certain skills and standards. The evocations of the timeless legitimacy of the state were one such opportunity, *Nkhani Zam'maboma* was another. The import of this program lies not only in its popularity. Precisely because its apparently nonpolitical profile tended to avert the attention of the MBC's management, media analysts, human rights activists, and aid donors, *Nkhani Zam'maboma* gave its editors considerable leeway to pursue *their* vision of public-service broadcasting.

The entrenched habits of presenting news defuse any threat of the MBC becoming a mere conduit for stories that are in global circulation, a prospect some analysts have called "McDonaldised, standardised or routinised news" (Nyamnjoh 2005a: 51). The universality of journalism's aims and practices is likewise an assumption in need of some rethinking (see Bishara 2006; Hasty 2006; Ståhlberg 2006; Wahl-Jorgensen 2010). *Nkhani Zam'maboma* indicates how diverse practices obtain even within the same newsroom. Its popularity has introduced somewhat comparable initiatives in other broadcasting and print media in Malaŵi, such as the weekly program *Zochitika Padziko Lapansi* (Happenings in the World) on the Zodiak Broadcasting Station, the *Newsmongers* column in *Pride Magazine,* and the *Kambaangamwala* column in *Malaŵi News,* whose motto reads, "Strange and interesting news happening in this and foreign countries."[22] Common to these initiatives is their blend of local human-interest stories with quirky news obtained from international agencies. The absence of the gutter press makes them somewhat out of the ordinary in Malaŵi, but their contents and editorial policies are different from *Nkhani Zam'maboma.* They do not invite listeners or readers to contribute stories, nor does their lighthearted and truncated treatment of issues bear much resemblance to the webs of allusions that stories on *Nkhani Zam'maboma* weave.

Rather than isolating it as the program's key feature, the broadcasting of witchcraft stories must be viewed within the complex of grievances and professionalism this chapter has begun to identify among its editors. As the subsequent chapters will show in more detail, editors considered *Nkhani Zam'maboma* as a crucial aspect of their public service, perhaps even more so than the official news bulletins they also edited. The grievances described above, and the relatively modest standards of living among editors, facilitated a certain commitment to the rural and urban poor as the public of their public service. In this regard, the MBC's newsroom was a qualitatively different workplace from many aid agencies and human rights NGOs that also considered the poor as the subjects of their efforts. Even when they were modestly paid themselves, human rights activists shared with many development professionals in Malaŵi a set of aspirations and lifestyles that set them apart from the people they defined as their beneficiaries (Englund 2006: 85–95; Swidler and Watkins 2009). Starting with their preference for Chicheŵa and other Malaŵian languages in both professional and everyday communication, as opposed to the use of English in NGOs and aid agencies, journalists in the MBC's newsroom did not assert a cleavage between themselves and their public. On the contrary, many of them felt that their professionalism entailed close contact with the public, whether in beer halls or township churches, in order to know the news that circulated among them. It was because the editors' life-world was so similar to the life-world of its listeners that witchcraft featured in *Nkhani Zam'maboma*.

Although scholars working in Africa have noted the popularity of witch-craft stories in the mass media, they have rarely studied them in the context of specific journalistic aspirations and practices. While witchcraft is not a new preoccupation in Africa, its recent appearance as a topic in public arenas has been associated with, among other things, the growth of Pentecostal and charismatic Christianity in many countries (see, e.g., Englund 2007b; Hackett 1998; Meyer 2004). Pentecostalism is by no means the only (or even the most important) influence in this regard, but its attacks on witchcraft, often infused with concerns over Satanism, have come to shape public discourse through its adherents' use of the electronic and print media (see also chapter 8). Anthropologists, as mentioned, have generally considered mass-mediated witchcraft stories as an indication of African modernities, the collapse of the dichotomy between "tradition" (witchcraft) and "modern" (mass media) taken as evidence of modernity's culturally specific forms. Misty Bastian's close readings of witch-craft stories in the Nigerian popular press, for example, have discovered in them insights into "urban African life at the beginning of the twenty-first century; expressions of alienation; desire and fragmented social relations in contemporary Nigeria; representations of masculinity under conditions of late capitalism" (2001: 72). "Witchcraft becomes," she has written elsewhere, also with reference to witchcraft idioms in the Nigerian popular press, "a medium for describing the complexities of Nigerian urban and rural relations for Nigerians themselves" (1993: 133).

As Bastian puts it, contemporary anthropologists understand witchcraft idioms as *a* rather than *the* medium for Africans' reflections on the way their world is. Yet this qualification does not bypass the privileged standpoint from which the anthropologist supplies explanatory sociological and historical detail to contextualize such popular reflections. In other words, rather than exploring how African subjects themselves contextualize witchcraft stories—how those stories assume significance in a conceptual and material universe that necessarily exceeds the scope of witchcraft itself—these anthropologists tend to subscribe to a division of intellectual labor by which African subjects think in terms of witchcraft while their anthropological interpreters think in terms of sociology and history.[23] The problem is nowhere as acute as in the study of mass-mediated witchcraft stories. Without analyzing the objectives of those who report and edit such stories, anthropologists risk making witchcraft look like the African discourse par excellence.[24]

Witches in the News

As mentioned, only a third of the stories broadcast on *Nkhani Zam'maboma* made a reference to witchcraft. Yet from the late 1990s onward, a visiting anthropologist determined to uncover the modernity of witchcraft would have been forgiven for thinking that the Malaŵian mass media was saturated with witchcraft stories. Although the MBC carried its witchcraft stories mainly on *Nkhani Zam'maboma,* other mainstream media such as Television Malaŵi and the biggest dailies *The Nation* and *The Daily Times* included such stories in their coverage of national news. The veracity of these stories was rarely, if ever, a subject of journalistic inquiries. Instead, a whole range of incidents came to be reported through the topic of witchcraft. For example, Sam Mpasu, mentioned at the beginning of this chapter, was not the only political leader to be embroiled in a controversy over witchcraft. Muluzi had adopted orphaned children during his presidency, but after his tenure he was reported to have sent some of them back to the orphanage because of their witchcraft.[25] After some newspapers had carried the story that a man suspected of theft had changed into a hyena, a lion, a leopard, and a snake while in prison, several politicians were reported to have tried to contact him for the potent substances he possessed.[26] The parliament has discussed related issues, such as the alleged rise of Satanism in the country.[27]

The involvement of legislators in these discussions has often brought to the fore the incompatibility between law and witchcraft, in Malaŵi as in many other African countries (see Geschiere 2006; Hund 2004). The Witchcraft Act of 1901 has been the only legal framework for considering witchcraft in Malaŵi, but like other such pieces of colonial legislation in Africa, it has outlawed witchcraft accusation rather than the practice of witchcraft (see Evans-Pritchard 1931).[28] A considerable number of newspaper reports have publicized attacks in which victims' body parts, particularly genitalia, have been removed for occult purposes; others have reported on the efforts of the police to protect suspected witches against angry neighbors.[29] While the biggest human rights NGOs have been quick to condemn the outbursts of violence against suspected witches as "mob justice" (see Englund 2006: 180–185), some local organizations promoting children's rights have demanded the inclusion of a clause on witchcraft in the constitution.[30] Popular calls for a new witchcraft law have, at least thus far, received little support in Malawi's mass media, journalists often highlighting the problems with evidence that such a law would encounter.[31]

Witchcraft stories have an undeniable market value in attracting popular interest in a competitive media environment. Yet to view their appeal solely in marketing terms would obscure not only the reasons for the public's interest in these stories but also journalists' own fascination with them. In a rare attempt to situate mass-mediated stories of mythic or magical figures in journalists' own aspirations and concerns, Lesley Fordred-Green (2000) suggests that journalistic conventions came to be revised during the transition to democracy in South Africa. While stories about spiritual beings would appear as the "laugh-of-the-day" in newspapers before the transition, they moved to the pages of serious news when new racial and cultural politics swept across the country. Rather than simply inverting South Africa's black and white binary, as though the change in newspapers signaled their Africanization in culturalist terms, Fordred-Green argues that the change was symptomatic, at least during a brief transitional period, of a broader discontent with a positivist epistemology that had guided journalistic conventions. What the ambiguities and contradictions of spirit stories brought out clearly was the need for a more complex view of power in general. They expressed discontent with superficial changes by which the white elite was substituted for a small black elite. In a similar vein, it is no accident that witchcraft stories began to appear in Malawi's media in tandem with deepening concerns over the nature and direction of the country's democratization.

Much as authoritarian practices prevailed at the MBC, *Nkhani Zam'maboma* offered a program format within which journalists could join their public to reflect on the ambiguities of power and inequality. Although witchcraft stories were an indicative rather than the cardinal aspect of such space for reflection, their inclusion was a particularly clear demonstration of journalists' occupation of the same life-world as their public. Absent was the condescension that some human rights activists showed toward so-called mob justice. Absent, too, was any condemnation of "tradition" and "backwardness" that journalists working for the state media in China have been observed to broadcast (see Anagnost 1997; Fong 2007). Malawian journalists understood law and witchcraft to be incompatible not because law was thought to be inherently superior but because their epistemologies were distinct. The verification of witchcraft and other stories was a central concern among the editors of *Nkhani Zam'maboma*, as chapter 6 will detail, but the reality of witchcraft was beyond doubt. At the same time, the ambiguities of these stories included the possibility that witchcraft itself was a domain of mere trickery. When competing over news about witches, journalists could suspect each other of fabricated reporting.

An example comes from the print media in 2005. Both the *Nation* and *Pride Magazine* reported that a man flying a witchcraft aircraft had crash-landed in one of Blantyre's townships.[32] The aircraft, as is common in such incidents, looked like an ordinary basket, known as *lichero*, but it could accommodate in its small space several passengers because of its magical properties. The man had been flying his new aircraft without passengers from Mozambique to his home district of Machinga when, as the *Nation* reported, its "computers went dead" and he found himself on top of an iron-roofed house. He was firmly stuck to the roof, so much so that the iron sheets would have been disconnected from the roof if the man had been removed by force. Instead, a specialist healer was called to remove him, and the police were needed to protect the pilot against an enormous crowd that had gathered to watch the proceedings. The owners of the house explained that they had used medicine to fortify their house against approaching witches, hence the crash landing when the witch was flying over the house.

Both publications reported the incident in a matter-of-fact style and drew on interviews with the alleged witch, the police, the owners of the house, and various eyewitnesses. When I interviewed the reporters, the one working for the *Nation* accused his colleague in *Pride Magazine* of staging a picture of the man on the rooftop. The *Nation* reporter claimed to have been the first journalist on the scene, but even he managed to take a picture of the man when he was already in a police car (see figures 3.1 and 3.2). The colleague in *Pride Magazine*, he asserted, had paid the police to bring the alleged witch back to the rooftop for pictures. This colleague vehemently denied the charge, pointing out that he lived in the same township where the incident had taken place and could therefore be on the scene within a short time. Neither of them had any doubts that the incident had taken place as described in their reports. Yet this shared conviction could itself be a basis for disputes about fundamental

Fig. 3.1. The alleged witch photographed on the rooftop. Courtesy of *Pride Magazine*.

Fig. 3.2. The alleged witch on the *Nation*'s front page.

issues, such as journalistic ethics. Far from foreclosing argument and doubt, reporting about witchcraft could be one arena within which to cultivate skepticism.

This propensity to evoke ambiguity and argument was a key feature of witchcraft stories on *Nkhani Zam'maboma*. Its editors were aware that the reality of witchcraft was denied by many white people and even some of their fellow Malawians. The way in which these stories threw into relief a politics of knowledge was evident in an incident an editor described to me. A young priest, fresh from the seminary, had been stationed to lead the Catholic church the editor attended. The priest made it clear right from the beginning that witchcraft did not exist (*ufiti kulibe*), and he delivered sermons on this topic with considerable passion. Soon an owl (*kadzidzi*) established a base on the rooftop of the priest's house and would wake the priest up at night, only to disappear with daylight. The priest tried to chase it away by throwing stones at it, and when this did not help, he started to pray at night whenever the owl woke him up. He also suggested that some in his congregation were trying his faith. Things took a more serious turn when the priest started to find himself naked in a graveyard at night. He had gone to sleep in his own bed but woke up in the graveyard at sunrise. Because his house was located nearby, he was able to sneak back a few times without anyone noticing, but his luck ended when he was spotted doing so. The congregation now spoke openly about his strange behavior, and the priest announced his departure in a sermon that accused the congregation of "making me sleep in the graveyard" (*mukundigonetsa kumanda*). The congregation was incensed by this accusation of witchcraft, expecting the priest to have asked for its assistance.[33]

Just like the stories broadcast on *Nkhani Zam'maboma*, the editor's story was as much about conceit and injustice as bizarre details. Although the priest was in a privileged position to condemn his congregation's convictions, painful experiences taught him that he was subject to powers beyond his comprehension. Similar trajectories by which injustice unraveled found expression in *Nkhani Zam'maboma* even when the stories were not about witches, as the next chapter shows. Yet the capacity of witchcraft stories to reveal conceit and ambiguity lay in the very multiplicity of witchcraft itself, a rich Chichewa vocabulary enabling a sense in which morally neutral and protective practices belonged to the same complex of meaning as occult machinations.[34] Three themes seemed to dominate the witchcraft stories in my sample—the crash landings of witchcraft aircraft; the use of rats, hyenas, and other animals as witchcraft technology to steal property and money; and the bewitching of children by adults—but a key source of ambiguity was the thin line that often separated protective and occult technology, with healers' (*asing'anga*) expertise in both a particularly potent example of this ambiguity. Not only would it be wrong, therefore, to represent all witchcraft stories as shocking narratives about the occult. It is also essential to attend to the allusions they evoked among both journalists and their public, recognizing that seemingly small issues took on large proportions when, as in the controversy over Mpasu mentioned at the beginning of this chapter, an illicit graveyard visit became an occasion to reflect on governance.

Alternatives and Alterities

"The legacy—and burden—of anthropology in Africa," Jemima Pierre writes, "is its historical construction of African Otherness that has served to mark the continent in ways that are unparalleled elsewhere" (2006: 47). A hallmark of such anthropology, she goes on to proclaim, is its "treatment of African phenomena as always already exceptional and (not so implicitly) *racially* distinct" (Pierre 2006: 47; emphasis in original). This verdict recognizes no exceptions to the appetite for exceptionalism in the history of anthropology in Africa, and it refuses to see any substantial significance in the shift, accomplished long ago, from racial to cultural difference in the anthropology she criticizes. African exceptionalism comes to the fore already in anthropologists' choices of subject matter, such as when they focus on witchcraft or corruption (Pierre 2006: 52–54). This line of criticism, though coming in Pierre's case from the particular vantage point of African American Studies in the United States, finds resonance among some African intellectuals. Its parameters range from the innocuous, if simplistic, assertion that anthropology is "the study of the insider by the outsider, for the consumption of those who share the culture of the anthropologist" (Thiong'o 2005: 160) to the vitriolic accusation that all anthropology is irredeemably racist (Mafeje 1998). Somewhere between these positions lies the serious intellectual issue of whether any study of otherness or alterity is condemned to repeat the alleged defect of anthropology in Africa, its adoption of a "Western vernacular for alien Africa" (Onwudiwe 2001: 217).

It is, of course, a measure of how bitterly polarized these criticisms are that they never seem to engage with the many complex ways in which Western scholars have addressed the issue of alterity, from hermeneutic philosophy (Ricoeur 1992) to contemporary anthropology (Strathern 1988; Wagner 1981). Nor do they take much notice of anthropologists' own disputes over the utility of the culture concept and its relation to the concept of race (see, e.g., Kuper 1999; Stolcke 1995).[35] Max Gluckman (1975), for example, identified a disturbing affinity between the abstract theorizing of cultural difference in some Euro-American universities and the justification of separate development in apartheid South Africa in cultural terms. Indeed, appeals to cultural difference in the study of politics are now most likely to be voiced by non-anthropologists (see, e.g., Chabal and Daloz 2005; Harrison and Huntington 2000). Anthropologists' observations on ritualized violence in Liberian civil conflict, for instance, are seized by a historian to support the claim that "Liberians believe" in a spirit world that ultimately controls their prospects for stability and leadership (see Ellis 1999: 308–309; Moran 2006: 36). A recent collection of essays on witchcraft in Africa, moreover, is said to have an advantage over other similar volumes because its African contributors bring to bear "an acuteness of observation" usually lacking in non-Africans' writings on the topic (ter Haar 2007: 3). What is left unremarked is these Africans' status as professors of theology and religious studies, thereby begging the difficult question of why their insights should be any more authentic than those of anthropologists, African or not, who are engaged in long-term fieldwork.

The issue of alterity requires consideration in the pursuit of alternative ideas of equality and human rights, especially if the talk about witchcraft appears to be one aspect of those alternatives. In Pierre's (2006) argument, alterity equals exceptionalism, and she appears to leave no scope for alterity in the condition of equality she clearly strives for. In this regard, it is instructive to explore how some anthropologists themselves seek to erase alterity from their purview. Pierre (2006: 52) counters anthropologists' insistence on the modernity of witchcraft by claiming that it merely represents a defensive reaction to the old problem of exoticization. Here again she misses the mark, insofar as Jean and John Comaroff, whom she cites, are driven by a rather more uncompromising project to deliver anthropology from its association with the study of alterity. Not unlike their concept of lawfare mentioned in the previous chapter, "occult economies" is a notion that collapses difference into one planetary predicament, "a response to a world gone awry" (Comaroff and Comaroff 2000: 316; see also Comaroff and Comaroff 1999). Pyramid saving schemes and stock markets address the same quandaries as witchcraft and ritual murder. Pierre need not worry that the othering of Africa is at issue, for the Comaroffs are not constrained by the modesty of representing only one continent. Occult economies, despite the diversity of their methods, have enticed people to embrace the "millennial moment" of making money out of nothing everywhere, whether "in post-Soviet Central Europe or postcolonial Africa, in Thatcherite Britain or the neoliberal United States, in a China edging toward capitalism or neo-Pentecostal Latin America" (Comaroff and Comaroff 2000: 316–317).

The erasure of alterity spells the end of alternatives, analytically as well as pragmatically. Observable discourses and practices, however diverse, become derivative phenomena, responses to "a world gone awry." Anthropology's claim to studying alternatives gets diluted, because fieldwork can only uncover further instances of what scholars already know. In this regard, it is ironic that the Comaroffs recognize "the epistemic importance of critical distance," based on a refusal to take "the ideological tropes and surface forms of the culture of neoliberalism . . . as analytic constructs" (2000: 335).[36] Very little in their method suggests that critical distance could be the prerogative of anyone other than the scholar. Here the anthropological study of witchcraft does have a reputable tradition of enquiry to uphold, its openness to compare and juxtapose knowledge practices in academia and witchcraft initiated by E. E. Evans-Pritchard (1937) and sustained by further reflections on the notions of (ir)rationality and belief, among others, that present themselves all too easily as analytical categories (see, e.g., Ashforth 2005: 111–130; Kapferer 2002; Sanders 2008).[37] Harry West's (2005; 2007) work in northernMozambique is a recent illustration. He reports that he shares with his Mozambican interlocutors "the urge to somehow get outside" of the world of witchcraft, "to move beyond it in order to gain perspective on it" (West 2007: 80). This shared concern in knowledge practices introduces a productive parallel between anthropology and the convolutions of witchcraft talk. In the life-world he shared during fieldwork, "every maneuver was the starting point for countermaneuver, every spin the stuff of counterspin, every interpretative vision the object of subsequent (re)visionings" (West 2007: 84). Reflexivity was, patently, intrinsic to the knowledge practice that talk about witchcraft elucidated.

The merit of anthropological notions of alterity, once they are dissociated from cultural/racial difference, is that the alternatives they suggest are never absolute, as if alterity threw human beings into separate, incommensurable worlds. Alterity can offer intellectual resources to engage issues that are not within its orbit. The stories of injustice on *Nkhani Zam'maboma*, for example, afford critical distance toward the prevailing human rights regime while having the potential of enriching the concept of human rights. By the same token, the anthropological and journalistic ways of representing the world can converge (compare Malkki 1997; Hasty 2010; Ståhlberg 2006), such as when both become committed to working against the occult, one by de-emphasizing its importance as a topic for anthropology and the other by broadcasting witch-craft stories as merely one node in complex webs of allusions.[38] Moreover, the celebration of witchcraft as a knowledge practice carries the risk of disregard-ing the violence that sometimes attends it (see Pratten 2007). Anthropologists may unwittingly entrench this aspect of witchcraft, if they do not consider its tangible and institutional ramifications (compare Green 2005).[39] The associa-tion of alterity with cultural difference is the obstacle here, though for other reasons than what anthropology's critics claim. Whereas cultural difference is for some contemporary anthropologists "a happy story about plurality" (Fer-guson 2006: 192), about the equality of modernities in cultural terms, alterity can also be produced by exclusion and marginalization. Anthropology fulfills its mandate to pursue alternatives not simply by representing marginalized voices, as though they could not speak for themselves, but by exploring rea-sons for their marginalization no less than the challenge they pose to received wisdom.

PART 2

The Ethos of Equality

4

A Nameless Genre

Newsreading as Storytelling

"A man who works in an Asian's store in Limbe in Blantyre is said to have made his children drink beer when he did not have money to feed the children."[1] This headline introduced a story about destitution that epitomizes many of the themes and rhetorical devices in *Nkhani Zam'maboma*. The man was said to live in a particular neighborhood in Ndirande, a township in Limbe's twin city Blantyre, and his troubles came to a head when the Asian boss failed to pay his salary. Tired of poverty, his wife abandoned him, leaving behind children crying from hunger. Unable to find food in the house, the man went to look for leavings of *masese,* opaque homemade beer, in the cartons drinkers had thrown away. He returned to give the beer to the children as if it was porridge, with the result that the children became drunk.

Just as the stories involving witchcraft carried allusions to various other issues, so too did this story evoke a range of themes, amenable to further expansion by listeners all too familiar with the hardship and injustice it depicted. It illustrated the thin line separating ordinary poverty from destitution. When listening to it with villagers in Dedza District and migrants in Chinsapo Township, I began to realize how a single story could evoke a range of grievances and reflections among its public. Some listeners in the township would describe their own experiences of employers skipping the payment of salary. Others gave further examples of the arbitrary and exploitative labor conditions in the enterprises owned by the merchant class of South Asian extraction.[2] They described workers being locked up to prevent them from taking a break, the rejection of their requests to attend funerals, unexplained deductions taken from salaries. The domestic trouble mentioned in the broadcast story sounded familiar to listeners in both rural and urban settings, the ideal of the man-as-provider and the woman-as-housewife crushed under the weight of poverty. Although the act of giving beer to hungry children was the detail that made this story out of the ordinary, the entire scene it conveyed was at variance with the carefully cultivated image of a nation enjoying the fruits of development in the MBC's official news bulletins.

The stories prompted by *Nkhani Zam'maboma*, imaginative and told with considerable skill in language, could themselves have appeared on the program, but listeners rarely mentioned such a prospect when they embarked on their own reflections. Personal predicaments were foremost in their minds, evoked by the personal stories heard on the program. The connections they made between the stories they heard and their own experiences were inevitably selective and expanded on particular themes in broadcast stories. Lenadi Mlauzi in Dedza District, a man in his early thirties with young children, started to reflect on poor parenting rather than work conditions and Asian bosses. Having known Mlauzi for several years, I was not surprised that his thoughts turned to the tragic family of his wife's sister. As relatively successful farmers living among his wife's impoverished kin, his own family had often borne the brunt of misfortune among their neighbors. Notorious for beer drinking and crop thefts, the sister-in-law had recently died when we listened to my recording of the above story. Her husband, the last among a string of men who had fathered her children, had predeceased her by only some months, and I had been away when Mlauzi had adopted one of their orphaned children (*ana amasiye*). It was the story about this child that preoccupied him when we stopped listening to the account about a destitute father buying beer for hungry children.

The young boy had slept in the same room with Mlauzi's own son, but the orphan would often wake everyone up in the house with his crying. When asked why he cried, he would say that people had come to take him to practice witchcraft (*ufiti*). The observation that all doors were closed had not soothed the distraught boy, who had pointed at the corners by the roof in his room as the witches' entrance. After repeated incidents, Mlauzi and his wife had taken the boy to a healer who had made incisions on his body for protective substances and had also provided Mlauzi with medicine to protect his house. The nocturnal crying did not subside, however, and fearing that the boy might start teaching their own children witchcraft, they sent him to another relative living in a different village. Mlauzi said they had not heard about the orphan since.

The threat of witchcraft was merely an aspect of the tragedy reckless parenting had unleashed. Mlauzi traced the boy's troubles to his mistreatment by his parents rather than to any unconnected witchcraft attack. He felt that the late parents had been preparing their children for a fate similar to their own: premature death after a life of drunkenness and stealing. Their neglect of the children had resulted in little or no schooling, with the second grade in primary school the highest achievement in the family. Mlauzi assumed that the boy's talk about witchcraft had been inspired by his mother, who herself had been suspected of witchcraft. The boy had also attracted attention for his habit of walking long distances alone, claiming to be on his way to funerals in faraway villages. The children in the story broadcast by *Nkhani Zam'maboma*, Mlauzi observed, shared the same dim prospects with the children of his sister-in-law. Although the tragedy in the broadcast story was inflicted more by the employer than the father's own behavior, Mlauzi predicted that the father's children would also end up as orphans deprived of schooling and good health. "Poverty brings many problems" (*umphaẁi umabweretsa mavuto ambiri*), he concluded, making poverty the link between the two stories' perspective on parenting.

Listeners' reflections on the stories they heard on *Nkhani Zam'maboma* could therefore take different directions according to their own circumstances. Personal stories on the program prompted other personal stories. However, this proliferation of stories about particular lives by no means resulted in a cacophony of unconnected voices. *Nkhani Zam'maboma* addressed a public with recognizable characteristics and suggested a particular set of narrative conventions to generate stories about listeners' own lives. The aim of this chapter is to outline the key ways in which *Nkhani Zam'maboma* accomplished these effects. The chapter begins by discussing the program's origins, modes of presentation, and the way it summoned a public that downplayed many of the political, regional, ethnic, religious, and linguistic divisions Malaẁians otherwise recognized within their body politic. Its success in doing so depended not only on its entertaining contents and the spread of its stories across different districts and regions. A sense of appropriate ways of delivering those stories was also crucial to its success, raising the complicated question of how its status as a news program intersected with the genres of verbal arts. The elucidation of sometimes bizarre or surprising details was not provided within the program, and the chapter proceeds to explore how its moral imagination of authority was compatible with a certain democratization of interpretation. Finally, an overview of the major themes on the program briefly describes several stories that were broadcast.

From Development to Misdemeanors

When it was first broadcast in 1998, *Nkhani Zam'maboma* emerged in the context of three trends in Malaŵian public life: the liberalization of the airwaves; the decentralization of local government; and participatory development. The immediate motivation was the search for programs for the newly established Radio Two, and the idea for *Nkhani Zam'maboma* originated from the newsroom rather than the management. News editors had proposed to solicit local accounts of development, stories of successful projects that made development such a legitimate preoccupation in the main news bulletin. The reference to districts (*maboma*) in the title of the program accorded with the desire, expressed by Malaŵi's foreign donors and apparently shared by the new democratic government, to devolve power to district assemblies.[3] This value placed on the local level was an instance of a more general trend in Malaŵi and elsewhere to exhort poor people's participation in development projects. The expectation at the MBC was that *Nkhani Zam'maboma* would give inspiring examples of how participatory development operated in practice. To the editors' surprise, however, the local stories they started to receive often made no mention of "development" (*chitukuko*) and dwelled, instead, on the misdemeanors of various local notables, such as chiefs, religious leaders, and teachers. The broadcasting of such stories only stimulated more stories in the same vein, with the result that stories about development came to be confined to another new program, the biweekly *Nkhani Za Ku Malaŵi* (News from Malaŵi), its contributions often obtained from development organizations themselves.[4]

The editing of *Nkhani Zam'maboma* was located in the Department of News and Current Affairs, and its editors also participated in preparing the regular news bulletins in Chicheŵa. The presentation of the program mimicked closely the format of news bulletins. *Nkhani Zam'maboma* began with the reader's announcement of his or her name, followed by the routine of reading out the day's headlines, typically prefaced by the phrase, "First hear its headlines" (*poyamba imvani mitu yake*). The headlines were repeated at the end, typically with the statement, "To finish *Nkhani Zam'maboma,* hear again its headlines" (*pomaliza Nkhani Zam'maboma imvaninso mitu yake*). Each broadcast usually had a sponsor, whose name was mentioned in the middle of the program, as in "You are listening to *Nkhani Zam'maboma* which is brought to you by [the sponsor's name]" (*mukumvera Nkhani Zam'maboma zomwe anakupatsirani ndi*). The sponsor's jingle was played immediately before and after the program. It was the popularity, rather than the contents, of *Nkhani Zam'maboma* that attracted sponsors, which have included the National Bank of Malaŵi and various companies advertising, among other things, cooking oil, soap, and paint. The contents did attract one sponsor, namely the Anti-Corruption Bureau, one of the institutions established by the new constitution to safeguard good governance. For a brief period, it publicized its agenda in conjunction with *Nkhani Zam'maboma.*

After its initial success on Radio Two, *Nkhani Zam'maboma* also came to be included on Radio One, with the ten-minute program broadcast every evening at 7:30 PM on Radio Two and at 9 PM on Radio One. The ten-minute slot usually accommodated between six and ten stories, and three or four of them were selected for the headlines. The diversity of themes was sustained by another constant in the way each story was presented. The stories always began with a mention of where the incident had taken place, with the names of the village, chiefdom, and district given for rural locations and the names of the city and its township or other residential area provided for urban ones. As a consequence, the information was often specific enough for locals to assume who the protagonists were, attaching, as described later, an important disciplinary element to *Nkhani Zam'maboma.* However, the mention of personal names was carefully avoided after early broadcasts had drawn complaints, in some cases even libel actions, from irate listeners against the MBC. The subtle combination of anonymity and local knowledge, together with the reader's matter-of-fact tone, ensured that most listeners experienced *Nkhani Zam'maboma* as a news program, albeit a rather more engaging one than the official news bulletin on the MBC. Many villagers and township dwellers who had never sent stories to the program told me that the MBC's own reporters (*atolankhani;* literally, "those who pick up stories") collected the stories. The assumption was that the MBC had, as would befit the national broadcaster, a nationwide network of reporters who kept an eye on events wherever they happened. This assumption added to the effect that *Nkhani Zam'maboma* had on its public's imagination of a nation that, despite the localism of each story, was subject to comparable incidents of abuse and injustice the length and breadth of the country.

Unity within Diversity

As my analysis of stories evoking witchcraft indicated in the previous chapter, one motif inevitably led to another, undermining any effort to identify a core to the diversity. By the same token, however, this diversity formed a recognizable genre of mass-mediated storytelling, widely known among Malaẁians even when they did not belong to its regular audience. Although many listeners would single out witchcraft as the key feature of stories on *Nkhani Zam'maboma,* they were also likely to emphasize the resonance with the experiences of deprivation and deception that defined the nation of Malaẁi to them. "We hear many things" (*timamva zambiri*), Malaẁians described the import of *Nkhani Zam'maboma* to me, many of them adding that the things they heard were "what the nation of Malaẁi does" (*zomwe mtundu wa Malaẁi umachita*). In this sense, the diversity of incidents and localities was itself a function of recurrent experiences that enabled the public to imagine a unity that transcended particular incidents and localities.

The avid listeners of *Nkhani Zam'maboma* were often perceptive about the themes that did appear frequently within the considerable diversity and overlap. I was often told that the bulk of its stories revolved around three themes: witchcraft and sorcery; sexual and marital misconduct; and scandals or surprises at funerals. In my sample of 566 stories broadcast in 2003 and 2006, stories that mentioned or alluded to witchcraft or sorcery constituted 31 percent of all stories; stories mentioning sexual and marital misconduct 28 percent; and stories mentioning scandals or surprises at funerals 20 percent. If, however, trouble with money is isolated as a theme, 41 percent of all stories carried it as one of their themes. Trouble with money, and the various other themes that shed light on poverty and injustice as the underlying causes of many reported incidents, may not have been recognized as a separate theme by the public. It was in the drama of witchcraft and adultery, among others, that both the public and the editors found newsworthy perspectives on the moral conditions of everyday life.

Listeners' imagination of the nation was matched by the editors' conviction that the program had a genuinely national audience, an encompassing remit that only a national broadcaster could possess. The apparent localism of each story, in other words, summoned up comparable incidents elsewhere, forming an "imagined community" (B. Anderson 1983) not through nationalist rhetoric but by evoking moral quandaries that cut across, as the experiences of abuse and injustice did, the many divisions that Malaŵians had come to recognize within their body politic. The first decade after the democratic transition saw a heightened sense of regionalism in Malaŵian politics, with the country's three administrative regions each providing a popular base for a different political party (W. Chirwa 1998). Muluzi's presidency also entailed, whether inadvertently or by design, a distinction between his main supporters' identity as Yao and the association of Banda and his henchmen with the Cheŵa. Popular mistrust of Muluzi's Muslim faith also polarized the Christian majority and the Muslim minority, however little Muluzi did in public to cultivate his image as a Muslim. Along with these tendencies to narrow down the grounds for identification existed networks that challenged nationalism by linking persons to places and people beyond the national borders, whether through cross-border kinship and trade (J. Anderson 2006; Englund 2002c) or religious movements (Englund 2003).

In this context, *Nkhani Zam'maboma* had a countervailing effect, its imagination of the nation distinct from the conventional nationalist rhetoric that political leaders still occasionally expressed despite all the divisions they had otherwise managed to manipulate. *Nkhani Zam'maboma* indicates how the imagination of the nation could be intermittent and tied to specific sets of ideas and aspirations that could not be reduced to official rhetoric (see Calhoun 2007). Editors' pride in the program has to be seen in light of this capacity to substitute a sense of unity for all the apparent divisions. Their avoidance of political topics derived from a narrow definition of politics, but the underlying concern about inciting confusion (*chisokonezo*) may not have been dictated merely by self-censorship but also by the editors' sense of unity within divisions. For it was not only party-political affiliations that were never mentioned, ethnic and linguistic labels were equally scarce on *Nkhani Zam'maboma*. Listeners were sometimes able, if they so wished, to infer the ethnic and linguistic context from the location of the story, but editors did nothing to encourage such speculation. The default position of these stories was that the protagonists were Malaŵians, with only foreign identities specified. When whites (*azungu*) and South Asians (*amwenye*) appeared in stories, they rarely did so as protagonists but rather as characters in the background, such as in the story with which this chapter began. Non-Malaŵian African nationalities were also mentioned, their incidence likewise very rare, with only one mention of a Mozambican in my sample.[5]

The use of Chicheŵa on the program came close to accomplishing a one-to-one correspondence between language and nation against the notion, also available to Malaŵians, that Chicheŵa was basically the language of the Cheŵa (compare Barber 2009: 15). However, no one, not even Chiyao- and Chitumbuka-speakers in Chinsapo Township, considered the use of Chicheŵa in *Nkhani Zam'maboma* to be inappropriate. They acknowledged that it was the most suitable language for a broadcast intended for a national audience.[6] Chicheŵa's long-established position as a national and regional lingua franca had prepared them for this opinion, making Malaŵi somewhat different from, for instance, Nigeria, where so-called vernacular broadcasts in the early days of the radio were "incomprehensible to large numbers of listeners who could not understand the main languages of Yoruba, Hausa, or Igbo" (Larkin 2008: 53). In Malaŵi, as elsewhere in Africa, broadcasting has extended the reach and appeal of some African languages at the expense of others. Sociolinguistic surveys in different parts of the country have discovered that Chicheŵa has steadily gained ground in areas where people do not consider themselves Cheŵa.[7]

Neither nationalism nor multiculturalism—the conventional liberal parameters of belonging and citizenship (see Benhabib 2004; Kymlicka 1995)—can explain the ethos by which *Nkhani Zam'maboma* summoned its public. The sense of belonging to a nation that shared the moral predicament of poverty and injustice emerged from both the common language and the way in which a story from one location resonated with experience in another. It was unusual to refer to comparable incidents elsewhere within one story, or to remind listeners of similar events broadcast earlier. However, as an illustration of how regional and ethnic differences could be ignored quite deliberately, consider how one story did make a connection between incidents in entirely different districts. It reported on the discovery of "a body without the private parts and other body parts" (*thupi lopanda ziŵalo zobisika ndi zina*).[8] The incident had taken place in Nkhotakota District, and the story ended by noting that the police in Chiradzulu District had in the previous week arrested a man on the suspicion that "he had killed his sister's child and eaten its flesh" (*adapha mwana wa mchemwali wake ndi kudya nyama yake*). The significance of mentioning the other case was twofold. On the one hand, seemingly unrelated incidents in two ethnically and linguistically different districts, Nkhotakota in the Central Region and Chiradzulu in the Southern Region, were made comparable. On the other hand, most listeners were able to make a stronger connection between the districts than what was reported on this particular occasion. In the early years of the twenty-first century, Chiradzulu had gained considerable notoriety when mutilated bodies, often female ones, missing the genitalia, breasts, and eyes had been found in the bush or fields. While these body parts had long been understood to constitute potent substances for witches' lethal trade, the unsolved atrocities in Chiradzulu became widely known in Malaŵi through print media and rumor. The connection between the two districts in this story extended beyond what was said, the earlier atrocities in Chiradzulu, rather than the reported act of cannibalism, akin to the discovery in Nkhotakota.

Cross-references between locations and incidents were rare, in other words, but even when they occurred, the public was often already knowledgeable about comparable incidents elsewhere. The ease with which the public made such connections was also aided by a measure of compatibility between the spatial distribution of stories and Malaŵi's population. Whereas the national population census found in 2008 that 15 percent of Malaŵians lived in urban and 85 percent in rural areas (National Statistical Office 2010: 9), in my sample of 566 stories broadcast in 2003 and 2006, 26 percent originated from urban areas and 74 percent from rural locations (see table 4.1.). While not identical to the census figures, this distribution indicates consistency with them, particularly if the higher rate of radio ownership in urban areas is taken into account.[9] The spatial distribution of popular topics accorded with this pattern, with 21 percent of stories about witchcraft/sorcery coming from urban areas and 79 percent from rural Malaŵi, and 26 percent of stories about marital and sexual misconduct coming from urban and 74 percent from rural areas. The regional distribution of stories was less consistent with the results of the 2008 population census, virtually unchanged from the censuses of 1987 and 1998, that 45 percent lived in the Southern Region, 42 percent in the Central Region, and 13 percent in the Northern Region (National Statistical Office 2010: 8; see table 4.1).[10] That 65 percent of stories in my sample came from the Southern Region is partly explained by the location of the MBC's headquarters in the southern city of Blantyre. The editors and other MBC personnel at the headquarters occasionally received stories from their own acquaintances and from persons who hand-delivered their letters.

Editors expressed some surprise at my finding on the predominance of the Southern Region in their broadcasts, because they abhorred any suggestion of bias. They explained that they did not have the time and means to monitor the actual frequency of submissions from different parts of the country. They did,

Table 4.1. The Spatial Distribution of Stories

Rural Areas	74 %	Southern Region	65 %
Urban Areas	26 %	Central Region	29 %
Total	100 %	Northern Region	6 %
		Total	100 %

however, try to include stories from all the regions in each broadcast. What the above figures obscure are the ways in which different places could play host to similar events and practices, just as a story from one place could resonate with experiences in another place. The rural-urban contrast is a particularly apposite example of a potentially misleading spatial distinction. Although some stories on *Nkhani Zam'maboma* highlighted the quintessentially urban problems of employment and consumption, most stories that took place in cities, like the impoverished majority who experienced them, highlighted the rural-urban divide as a continuum rather than a contrast. Nothing in the following story from Ndirande, a populous township in Blantyre city, made it incompatible with rural experiences.[11]

A child was reported to have fallen ill but was cured in a hospital. After returning home, another child had told him that "he would have eaten him" (*akanamudya*). The listeners of *Nkhani Zam'maboma* did not need to be told that such a threat alluded to witchcraft, the child's illness thereby acquiring a sinister dimension. The child relayed the threat to his parents, who then questioned the other child's parents. Because they professed ignorance about the matter, the concerned parents took it to their chief. He suggested that "it is best to go to a healer/diviner so that he tells them the truth" (*kuli bwino kuti apite kwa sing'anga kuti awauze zoona*). The story concluded by describing how the car they had taken broke down and "the journey to the healer ended there" (*ulendo wa ku sing'angako unathera pomwepo*).

The allusions and courses of action in this story bound them to no particular location in Malaŵi, least of all to one or the other in the rural-urban division. Townships in Malaŵian cities were overseen by chiefs (*mafumu*) and headmen (*nyakwaŵa*), some of whom were in their position as representatives of the villages that preexisted urban growth, while others had been elected by township dwellers themselves. Similar expectations informed their and their rural counterparts' work, a life-world that also involved healers operating in both urban and rural areas, kept in business by, among other things, witches' facility to inflict harm in cities no less than in villages. Funerals also linked urban residents to their rural areas of origin. This continuous life-world, while certainly susceptible to rhetorical assertions of the rural-urban divide, wove together economic, spiritual, and moral imperatives. Few Malaŵians could afford to sustain themselves in cities without recourse, however intermittent, to land and other assets in the village, just as urban incomes supported funerals, weddings, and school fees in rural areas (Englund 2002a).

Traces of Genres

As a recognizable genre, stories on *Nkhani Zam'maboma* adhered to certain narrative conventions, based on a sense of the appropriate way to deliver their contents (compare Furniss 1996: 15–17). Identifying those conventions is not an easy task, however. In general terms, listeners would describe stories variously as strange (*zodabwitsa*), scary (*zochititsa mantha*), funny (*zoseketsa*), and educative or informative (*zophunzitsa*). The same characteristics of course applied to a number of other genres in listeners' life-worlds, from popular songs to church sermons, and the specific components of *Nkhani Zam'maboma*'s distinctiveness have to be understood in relation to how it had absorbed elements of other genres. Also crucial to listeners' appreciation of *Nkhani Zam'maboma* as a genre was their enjoyment of the language it deployed. No other program on the radio quite matched its pithy, idiomatic, and proverbial Chicheŵa. The sharply different responses its stories could evoke among listeners, ranging from horror to humor, owed much to editors' choice of particular expressions, words, and proverbs, not all of which were in frequent use in everyday, conversational Chicheŵa.

The uses of language are best outlined in the next chapter on editorial procedures, but when exploring the program as a distinct "aural genre" (see Gunner 2000), it has to be admitted from the outset that its success was based on an ingenious adaptation of several preexisting genres. Primary among them was the genre of news, with both editors and listeners, as mentioned, insisting that *Nkhani Zam'maboma* was a news program. The conventions of its presentation described above left little room for ambiguity in this regard, and yet its contents no less than its language were strikingly different from the news bulletins on Malaŵi's airwaves. The term *nkhani* in its title helped to produce this versatile genre. Although used for "news" among Malaŵi's Chicheŵa broadcasters, *nkhani* also means "stories" and has been used by several Chicheŵa novelists and playwrights to describe their texts (see S. Chimombo 1988: 24–25). Conversely, however, *nkhani* does not define a genre and is often replaced by more specific concepts in discussions about oral and written literature, such as *mwambi* (proverb), *nthano* (fictional narrative), *nyimbo* (song), *sewero* (play), *ndakatulo* (poem), *mbiri* (history, biography), and *ndagi* (riddle).[12] *Nkhani Zam'maboma* had created a genre without a name.

Oral and written literature in Chicheŵa was another important influence on the program's narrative conventions. Newsreading became a form of storytelling when the text included features from oral narratives such as *chomwe chinachititsa dzaye kuti njovu ithyoke mnyanga*, "the thing that made a hard wild fruit fall to break the elephant's tusk." It introduced the root cause for the incident being described and was an expression borrowed from situations of storytelling around fire after dark or at beer parties. When asked, editors showed familiarity with Chicheŵa literature, but I never saw them consulting it during their work. It seemed that much of the familiarity derived from their schooldays, and, among the verbal arts, popular songs and drama appeared to have a more active presence in their lives than the written literature. The news format also entailed obvious differences between *Nkhani Zam'maboma* and Malaŵian creative writing as genres. Newsreading did not allow for renditions of dialogue, although protagonists' direct citation was possible. The perspective stories gave on incidents was often that of the downtrodden, but the actual voice in which stories were presented was never that of the protagonists, with only the third-person pronouns deployed. It was in the contents of *Nkhani Zam'maboma* that the most feasible parallel with Malaŵian fiction could be discerned. The broad trend in Chicheŵa fiction for the past one hundred years has been the exploration of morality (see Moto 2001).[13] Whether morality tales inevitably lead to moralizing or didacticism requires a separate discussion in the next chapter on editing. However, John Gwengwe, one of the most prominent writers when Malaŵi gained independence and well known for his works in the newsroom, often prefaced his books with allusions to an ethos that suited *Nkhani Zam'maboma*. Far from suggesting that elders had completed their moral education, he insisted on the capacity of his stories to educate "child, adult, chief, and slave alike" (*mwana, wamkulu, mfumu kaya kapolo*; Gwengwe 1965: 5).

Listening to popular radio drama on the MBC had been a favorite pastime among many editors during their schooldays. One immediate parallel between *Nkhani Zam'maboma* and the popular radio shows of the 1980s and early 1990s, such as *Kapalepale* and *Pa Majiga*,[14] was the contemporary character of their stories as opposed to the folkloric or historical settings of some

Chicheŵa literature and drama. These radio shows shared with the subsequent *Nkhani Zam'maboma* a keen eye for conflicts arising from material problems and, of course, a strong moral perspective on them. Although they came to be replaced by radio drama that various governmental and non-governmental sponsors harnessed to broadcast specific messages, these pioneering plays already were clear about the lessons they wanted to give to their audience (Kerr 1995: 178). The pattern by which their plays moved from the description of conflict to judgment and resolution was not replicated by *Nkhani Zam'maboma*. Its moral argument operated in a more subtle register, with some ambiguity allowed for resolutions and some space retained for different listeners' different skills to interpret stories. Paradoxically in this regard, another contrast was between the improvisation in the radio plays and the carefully scripted stories in *Nkhani Zam'maboma*. The difference was between drama and news as genres—the person who read out the stories was rarely their co-author in the way that actors in radio plays participated in generating dialogue. Finally, although these radio plays were located in peri-urban settings, stories broadcast on *Nkhani Zam'maboma* covered a wider range of places, with the majority of stories depicting, as has been seen, rural locations.

The question of location touches on another aspect of genres than form and content: addressivity (Barber 2007: 138–139; see also Bakhtin 1986). While much was new about the form and contents of the news broadcast by *Nkhani Zam'maboma*, the public it addressed shared familiar matrilineal features. Although it is open to argument whether "matrilineal kinship" properly describes the complexity produced by many decades of migration, intermarriage, and colonial and postcolonial policies, similar ideas of the family have prevailed in the Southern and Central Regions, cutting across ethnic and linguistic divides much as Chicheŵa has done.[15] Crucial to these ideas has been the kin group of sisters known as *mbumba*, whose representative or guardian (*nkhoswe*) on formal occasions is their mother's brother (*malume*). This simple principle already suggests considerable variation in practice, if only because the groups of sisters often encompass the daughters of women who were themselves sisters, thereby opening up the position of guardianship to a potentially unwieldy number of aspirants. Although the association of land tenure with matrilineal values appears to be resilient in rural Malaŵi (Jul-Larsen and Mvula 2009), the principle by which all men except the chief move to live with their wives' kin is much less prevalent in practice. A man's access to land elsewhere than in his wife's village, or his business engagements, can result in his taking her with him, the woman known as *chitengwa,* a term based on the passive voice of the verb *kutenga,* to take.

Kinship was only one aspect of the knowledge *Nkhani Zam'maboma*'s public was expected to possess. Other aspects had to do especially with the constitution of different kinds of authority, from chiefs to healers to preachers. Important for understanding how the program addressed its public as a whole is the realization that these apparently stable, largely rural features of life by no means set up an idealized village community. Precisely because they depicted conflicts against the background of this assumed knowledge about relationships, stories constantly created an impression of relationships brought under strain by poverty and injustice. The criticism leveled at the radio drama discussed above, namely that it "offered gratifying pseudo-solutions by imposing a traditional system of rural moral values on a modern urbanized society governed by a wage economy" (Kerr 1995: 179), would be too harsh in this case.[16] Stories on *Nkhani Zam'maboma* invited reflections on power and authority rather than merely affirming a traditional way of life. The difficulty in assigning a name to this genre is a function of its novelty, not just of the complex ways in which it borrowed from existing genres. As a result, the public it addressed was also new, because new genres take shape when new audiences are addressed, or old audiences are addressed in new ways. The expectations that the public brings to bear are what lend recognition to the new genre. In other words, "emergent genres and emergent constituencies come into being in response to each other" (Barber 2007: 138).

As a new kind of public, the listeners of *Nkhani Zam'maboma* were able to imagine a nation of comparable subjects, downtrodden and impoverished, achieving moments of equality with their superiors, moments when claims and disciplinary effects could be thrust on them. The radio has been instrumental in producing such new constituencies in Africa, perhaps less through the participatory agendas of community radio stations than by transforming preexisting genres. Previously excluded or unnoticed performers, for example, have achieved unprecedented success when their songs have become new genres mediated by radio or television (see Diawara 1997; Durán 1995). To the extent that *Nkhani Zam'maboma*'s success in summoning a new public derived from a creative, if largely unintended, mixture of genres, it illustrates the broad historical trend by which adaptive genres have been key to artistic and moral innovation in Africa and elsewhere (Finnegan 2007: 182). An illustration from the world of artistic production is the influence Hausa films have drawn from oral and written literature (Adamu 2002; Furniss 2005). Within the compara-tive study of genres, the specific interest of *Nkhani Zam'maboma* is its primary status as a news program. How different genres of news summon their publics has been a question neglected by those who have otherwise called for new per-spectives on audiences in the anthropology of media (see Peterson 2010: 171). Ethnography on *Nkhani Zam'maboma* shows how a new genre of news gener-ates a new kind of public, in this case a debating, reflexive public distinct from the docile public of the MBC's official news bulletin.

All Is Not Revealed

The subtle interplay between anonymity on the airwaves and local knowledge was merely one aspect of the differences in interpretative capacities among the public of *Nkhani Zam'maboma*. For all its novelty as a genre that was ac-cessible to Malaŵians irrespective of gender, age, religion, and ethnicity, the program owed its success partly to the surprising and puzzling observations it broadcast. Expressed in a pithy and idiomatic language, those observations often required elucidation that was not forthcoming within the program itself. *Nkhani Zam'maboma* therefore advanced the interpersonal nature of radio lis-tening in Malaŵi by creating opportunities to consult and to clarify. However, the clarification of meaning entailed its own ambiguities, ranging from suspi-cions that the commentator's knowledge of witchcraft was rather too intimate to doubts over who should share the knowledge. With the exception of the pro-gram's Christian critics discussed in chapter 8, listeners generally cherished these ambiguities even as they sought clarification. Their inclination was an-other instance of its resonance with other genres of verbal arts in Malaŵi and elsewhere in Africa. For interpretations to be based on knowledge, they had to be the prerogative of particular persons, mirroring the hierarchies of relation-ships within which stories were situated (see Barber 2009: 9).

One novelty of *Nkhani Zam'maboma* derived from the way it had not au-thorized anyone in particular to supply interpretations. Just as it opened up the airwaves for voicing grievances about different kinds of authority, so too was it possible to have several interpretations of the same incident. No one had mo-nopolized the elucidation of the new genre. As an illustration, consider three different listener responses to a story whose details were as cryptic as they were captivating. The headline announced, "A giant male rat that had three charms hanging from its neck died when it failed to enter a healer's compound."[17] The rat, which had tried to enter the compound when the healer was away digging for medical plants, had begun to tremble before it fainted. The healer found a large crowd of people outside his/her compound watching the rat, which he/she proceeded to kill with his/her medicine. The healer asked the village headman to be present for an autopsy. Inside the rat were needles, foam from a mattress, hair of a child and a white person, and a rag. When he/she mixed the items with medicine before burning them, the healer effectively cursed the person who had sent the rat. Soon afterward a couple came to see him to ask him to stop the witchcraft, because they had heard that he had killed the rat. The story ended by saying that the healer had ordered the couple to pay the one who was ill either one goat or five chickens.

Apart from the meaning of the items found inside the rat, the connection between the rat, the healer, the couple, and affliction was not made explicit by the broadcast. A Pentecostal pastor in Chinsapo Township offered an elaborate interpretation when I listened to the story with him. Having been introduced to some of the knowledge in healing and the *gule wamkulu* secret society as a Cheŵa growing up in Lilongwe District, the pastor used his old knowledge in his new life to expound on the ways of witches and other satanic forces. The interpretation of stories broadcast on *Nkhani Zam'maboma* was one of his favorite activities, much as he joined the program's other Christian critics in condemning its failure to take the public beyond the dark forces it depicted. The pastor explained that the rat had been sent to kill the healer. The predicament was common among healers whose distinction from witches was often subject to some popular skepticism. Competing for clientele, the pastor observed, healers could deploy lethal methods to eliminate their rivals or they could come under fire from witches. The story did not tell, the pastor pointed out, "whether the protagonists were healers or witches" (*ngati anthu ake anali asing'anga kapena afiti*). The healer's compound had been protected with a stronger medicine than what the rat could withstand, no matter that three pieces of charm were hanging from its neck.[18] The couple in the story were responsible for sending the rat. Following the principle of "evil returns to its origin" (*choipa chitsata mwini*), the couple had fallen ill after the rat had been killed and approached the healer for relief. The healer's words, in the pastor's view, were "give me one goat or five chickens so that I can forgive you" (*mundipatse mbuzi imodzi kapena nkhuku zisanu kuti ndikukhululukireni*).

The pastor readily interpreted the significance of the items the rat had carried inside itself. The needles signified its murderous intent, because no living creature could have needles inside it without dying. *Flexafoam,* as the foam used in mattresses was popularly known in Malaŵi, represented the effort to soften the healer's solid defense. Properly fortified persons, known as *otsirika* (protected) or *okhwima* (ripe, hard), would not be wounded even if they were stabbed with a knife. The pastor explained that the foam was intended to make the healer soft (*ofewa*). He also used the expression *kusukulutsa* (to dilute) to describe how the objective was to "terminate the healer's power" (*kuthetsa mphamvu ya sing'anga*). The hair of a child and a white person served the purpose of fitting many things into a small space. African children and white persons of whatever age were seen to have much hair on their scalps, and their hair was sought after by healers and witches to, among other applications, make magical aircraft accommodate several passengers. Finally, the rag was expected to represent the condition of the healer after the attack: finished off (*akhale wathe*).

All listeners I worked with admitted the possibility of such metonymic connections between objects and the conditions they stood for. The first thing they would say was usually that "the giant rat was not of blood but a made-up one" (*chikhoswe sichinali chamagazi koma chopanga*). However, while the pastor could mesmerize his audience with detailed interpretations of what the different items mentioned in stories stood for, not everyone was equally interested in pursuing such elucidation. Listening to the story in Dedza District with an elderly man, his adult son, and the son's brother-in-law, all smallholder farmers and Roman Catholics, our discussion drifted from the interpretation of details to a critical perspective on deception among some healers. We were at the house of the elderly man, who began to complain about the frequency with which witches' aircraft were reported to crash-land, not only by *Nkhani Zam'maboma* but also through villagers' gossip. He described how some people pretending to be healers would prepare their clients by warning them against leaving the house at night even if they heard suspicious noises. The bogus healer would then throw something heavy on the client's roof at night and place an item signifying witches' aircraft outside the entrance. When the client came to him to ask for help, he would state a large sum of money as his charge. Rather than marveling at the healer's potency in the broadcast story, the man felt inspired to cast a shadow of doubt over the profession of healer, although he stopped short of accusing them all of deception. The younger men, who had actively participated in our conversation on other topics, fell unusually silent when the man expounded on the unscrupulous ways of healers. When he was not present, they explained to me that while it was true that some healers were mere impostors, the threat of afflictions and attacks was real enough for the topic of healing to be broached with some reverence.

This example suggests not only a considerable variety in personal predilections that informed the interpretation of stories on *Nkhani Zam'maboma*. It also alludes to generational tensions that may have made a well-established villager somewhat impatient about ubiquitous healers fueling suspicions. The third example of listener response shows how the issue of healers' powers in the broadcast story could be substituted for a reflection on illicit enrichment among fellow villagers. A middle-aged woman in Dedza District had little to say about the details of the story, shrugging off my queries about the items the rat had been carrying by referring to the generic term *chizimba,* charm. Her interest in the story was the use of a rat as witchcraft technology. She remarked that it was very common to use rats and, to a lesser extent, creatures such as cockroaches, snakes, and ducks to steal property and money from others. A rat may eat all the maize flour (*ufa*) at its victim's house in order to carry it in its stomach to the house of those who had sent it. In this way those who have been lazy (*aulesi*) in the field can avert hunger, whereas hardworking farmers can face food shortages. The woman also recalled stories about male labor migrants using this technology to steal money from their colleagues in the South African mines. One such former migrant, who had allegedly used a snake to steal salaries, was currently the subject of her and many other villagers' disapproval for his adultery and beer drinking. It did not take her long during our conversation to mention this aspect of his past as a further instance of his dubious reputation.

Although the second example indicated generational tensions, this example brought to the fore gendered concerns about injustice and exploitation. The woman, herself an unmarried mother, would often bemoan the heavy workload in her fields, and her view of men was generally dismal, centered on their womanizing and excessive consumption of alcohol. Avoiding the elucidation of its own stories, and not having mandated anyone to provide such elucidation, *Nkhani Zam'maboma* thus opened up discussions and reflections that took its allusions in different directions. Although curious details could get entertaining exegesis from those who claimed specialist knowledge, the life-worlds that stories depicted were often familiar enough to inspire of their own accord reflections on listeners' circumstances. Such reflections were not, however, entirely free from the particular perspective *Nkhani Zam'maboma* imposed on the world. A comment doubting healers' powers took place in the context of urgent problems that did demand the protection and fortification they supplied. More broadly, the moral imagination that identified villains among the figures of authority was not easily ignored in favor of interpretations that defended the powerful. The lack of authority in interpretation was intimately linked to holding all authority accountable.

Dependence and Disappointment

No story in my sample or in the archives I perused mentioned *ufulu wachibad-widwe*, the birth freedom that had become the Chichewa translation for human rights. Nor was the balance between freedom (*ufulu*) and duty (*udindo*) the nub of moral argument, much as politicians and senior civil servants insisted that even the poorest and the least advantaged had to be mindful of their duties instead of merely claiming their rights (Englund 2006: 67–68). When I queried about the lack of the new language on human rights and freedoms on the program, editors dismissed such questions by saying that it belonged to NGOs (*za maNGO zimenezo*; literally, "they are NGOs' things"). A consequence of this dismissal of the new language on human rights and freedoms was the creation of another register for making claims than the one human rights NGOs had publicized. That there was no love lost between editors and human rights activists was unsurprising, but editors appeared more eager to reflect on their relationships with politicians in their confidential conversations with me. Politics, they would emphasize, had no place on the program.

The editors' position rested on the narrow sense of politics as party-political competition and intrigue, resulting in the rejection of stories that referred to such machinations. It is important to realize that their narrow definition of politics was compatible with the broadcast of critical perspectives on authority and power, inevitably inspiring deliberation on politics among listeners. Problems with authority under the conditions of severe poverty were perhaps the single most consistent theme that ran through the specific instances of witchcraft, gender relations, and so on. Without mentioning politicians, *Nkhani Zam'maboma* could address these problems by highlighting misdemeanors among village headmen, teachers, healers, and leaders among both Christians and Muslims. In a country where submission to authority had been required over and again by diverse agencies—from the one-party state to employers to non-governmental organizations—the creation of a public whose docility could not be taken for granted was an achievement. It was, in fact, a subtle achievement, not simply because *Nkhani Zam'maboma* never incited rebellion, but because the program generated a sense of equality as a condition of unequal relationships. The critique of authorities deployed idioms such as disappointment (*kukhumudwa*) to convey not so much discontent with hierarchies as mutual dependence between subjects and their leaders. *Nkhani Zam'maboma* offered an exceptionally accessible medium to voice disappointment as the flip side of dependence.

In spite of the inherited nature of their position, village headmen were expected to merit their power through exemplary conduct, a requirement that often disqualified those who were genealogically predisposed to assume the position but poorly regarded in the general opinion. All of a headman's subjects could be referred to as his or her "children" (*ana*), the evidence for parental virtues of caring and impartiality sought in the conduct of public affairs, such as dispute settlement, the reception of visitors, and representation on local development and administrative committees. In light of these high expectations, stories about misconduct among village headmen were key to the public surveillance of their authority, and *Nkhani Zam'maboma* gave this surveillance an enhanced medium (see also chapter 7).[19] Worldly vice was a common problem in these mass-mediated stories. One of them reported that "a fight erupted between a headman and his younger brother while competing over the headmanship."[20] The headman had married in another village but visited his subjects to hear their disputes. However, villagers preferred his younger brother, who took an interest in the daily affairs of the village. When the fight erupted, villagers urged the headman to "agree" (*kugwirizana*) with his brother. The report ended by noting that the headman "was also scolding himself for his habit of taking bribes" (*akhalanso kudzidzudzula chifukwa cha khalidwe ladyera ndi lolandira ziphuphu*).

A tragicomic incident tarnished this figure of authority in another story that described how "a headman hurt his feet when he fell into a pit latrine while chasing a young man who had taken all his money through gambling."[21] The young man was reported to have denied any wrongdoing, remarking that he "had not invited the headman" to gamble (*sanachite kuitana nyakwawayo*). A breach of headmen's mandate was highlighted in a story that described efforts to sell villagers sites to bury their dead.[22] Although the story referred to the culprit as "a fellow" (*mkulu wina*), it was clear to listeners that only headmen and their elders had authority over village graveyards and that spaces in them were not for sale. The story disclosed that "people in the villages were disappointed" (*anthu am'midziyo anakhumudwa*) and "had no doubt that the fellow was doing it only to get money to solve his own problems" (*sakukaika kuti mku-*

luyo akuchita izi chifukwa chongofuna ndalama zoti athetsere mavuto ake). It was also reported that the village people were "not to imagine doing what the fellow wanted because it was alien to the village" (*sangayerekeze kuchita zimene mkuluyo akufunazo chifukwa ndi zachilendo m'mudziwo*).

The popularity of stories about funerals indicated their status as key events in which authority and subjection were negotiated. The funerals of adults mobilized vast numbers of mourners in both rural and urban areas, many of whom may not have been related to the deceased but who felt close enough to him or her as a colleague or neighbor. A similar affiliation with one of the bereaved also often led to attendance at a funeral. Funerals were, along with some weddings, the only public occasions when people came together regardless of their differences in kinship, ethnicity, religion, gender, and political preferences. The living needed to demonstrate compassion by contributing money, food, firewood, and labor to the proceedings. Reverence for the dead informed funeral proceedings, and the observance of spatial and behavioral rules was sustained by an often implicit fear of reprisals by the deceased.

Some funeral stories on *Nkhani Zam'maboma* described the surprises that the dead could inflict, but the majority of these stories focused on misbehavior among the living. For example, one story carried the headline, "The pastor of a certain church in Nsanje District was ordered to pay M.K.2500 and one goat and a chicken because he did not go to funerals."[23] Striking in this story was of course the offender's identity as a pastor, a servant of God. Funeral stories also described other forms of punishment than monetary compensation. A young man in Mulanje District, for example, was ordered to bury his own grandparent, "because he did not go to other people's funerals" (*chifukwa sapita kumaliro a anthu ena*).[24] After he had toiled in the graveyard for a while, "the village headman felt sorry for him" (*nyakwaŵa yam'mudzimo adamumvera chisoni*) and asked him to pay a penalty so that others would help him. Another man was reported to have been at a beer party during his mother's funeral in Machinga District.[25] He was made to dig his mother's grave, with the result that "he swore he would stop drinking beer and promised to go to funerals" (*ŵanenetsa kuti ŵaleka kumwa moŵa komanso ŵalonjeza kuti azipita kumaliro*).

Offenders were reprimanded not only by village headmen but also by so-called grandchildren (*adzukulu*), who, while not necessarily the actual grandchildren of the deceased, performed important funeral labor, such as digging the grave. In the above-mentioned stories, grandchildren were the ones to initiate the punishment by making public who the offenders were. However, such was the ethos of *Nkhani Zam'maboma* that even these apparent custodians of morality could themselves become villains. For example, one headline stated that "grandchildren in Ntchisi beat badly the bereaved because they had given the grandchildren maize porridge and the relish of green peas instead of meat."[26] The grandchildren were reported to have "sent back maize porridge" (*adabweza nsima*) that had been brought to sustain them during their work in the graveyard. They had argued that a "funeral is a special day that differs from all other days" (*tsiku la maliro limakhala lapadera losiyana ndi masiku ena onse*). When some of the bereaved had regretted the quality of the food, the grandchildren had seized them and begun to beat them up. Others attending the funeral had intervened and bought meat for the grandchildren, "who were very pleased to receive it" (*adalandira mosangalala kwambiri*). The village headman did not, however, approve of this conduct. He demanded that "this bad behavior must end" (*khalidwe loipali litheretu*) and announced that he would "punish the greedy grandchildren" (*ikhaulitsa adzukulu odyerawo*).

Schoolteachers were also expected to be exemplary in their conduct, embodiments as they were of the promise of self-improvement through formal education. For many children from impoverished backgrounds, the profession of schoolteacher represented something to aspire to in order to avoid the tedium of smallholder farming. As such, stories publicizing teachers' misconduct went a long way toward removing them from the pedestal on which they were otherwise placed. A story about schoolchildren witnessing their teacher blind drunk is a case in point.[27] The children had found him lying by the roadside, and when he stood up, they could see that he had urinated in his pants. A laughing crowd of children was reported to have escorted him home, where the teacher was said to remain hiding "because of shame" (*chifukwa cha manyazi*). Moreover, teachers, not unlike village headmen, attracted attention for the squabbles among themselves. A headmistress was reported to have declared at a meeting that "all teachers at the school were witches and ignorant people who did not understand anything."[28] As a consequence, the teachers had refused to go to work, resulting in the headmistress's demotion "because of her bad behavior" (*chifukwa cha khalidwe lake loipa*).

Schoolteachers were often entrusted with other responsibilities than teaching, particularly in rural areas. Two stories from Ntcheu District broadcast on the same day[29] described teachers' mismanagement of relief aid. One headmaster was suspected of keeping maize and soya beans from orphans and giving them only the porridge flour that was included in the relief items. A school committee started to investigate the allegation, further incensed by the refusal of other teachers to work with this errant leader. In another school, the headmaster was said to make pupils pay M.K.10 for the items the school received for free distribution. "He shared," the story reported, "goods with a chief in the area instead of giving them to children."[30] Parents were said "to be asking for help from education officers in the district because they no longer wanted this teacher."[31] Following the liberalization of primary and secondary education in the early 1990s, many schools were run as businesses, their incidents of deception frequently reported on *Nkhani Zam'maboma*. For example, a schoolgirl was said "to complain very much" (*ŵadandaula kwambiri*) because she was not able to write exams after the headmaster in her private school "had eaten her exam money" (*anamudyera ndalama za mayeso*).[32] The headmaster was reported to have given her a "false exam identification number" (*nambala ya bodza ya mayeso*).

As these examples indicate, it was usually, though not exclusively, headmasters and headmistresses who appeared as villains. This pattern accorded with the tendency in *Nkhani Zam'maboma* to single out persons in positions of authority for stories. It might seem tempting to criticize the program for deflecting attention from political leaders, senior civil servants, non-governmental executives, and foreign donors to authorities at the local level. Such criticism appears less plausible, however, when it is accepted that listeners were able to vary the scale and identity of the authority they appraised in their informal deliberations. The story about an anonymous Malaŵian could prompt reflections on national leaders, as described in the previous chapter, with national leaders' business ties to foreigners, pursued at the expense of the poor majority, often the next step in such reflections. The conventional criticism that claims to unveil the truth behind media products will also benefit from a confrontation with the critique of *Nkhani Zam'maboma* advanced by a particular constituency of its public in Malaŵi, namely born-again Christians (see chapter 8).

One more domain of authority that did get mentioned on the program provides more immediate insight into its capacity to nourish moral argument. Employers have long been formidable authorities in Malaŵi, all too often paying meager salaries and subjecting their employees to arbitrary treatment. The introduction of new laws since the 1990s has made only slow progress in labor relations (see Dzimbiri 2002; Englund 2006: 158–169). In this context, *Nkhani Zam'maboma* offered an important outlet for workers' grievances, expressed in idioms that had a wide resonance among its public. For example, one headline stated that "the manager of a firm in Ginnery Corner in Blantyre city is said to maltreat his workers by denying them rest even on big holidays such as 6 July [Malaŵi's independence day]."[33] The story, reporting that he deducted money from the workers' salaries if they did not go to work on public holidays, ended by noting that "people are said to just persevere in this firm" (*anthu akuti akungokhalira kupirira pakampanipo*). Such apparent obedience should not be mistaken for a lack of critical reflection among workers. Just as broadcasting subjects' disappointment with their chiefs could have a disciplinary effect, so too could workers seek to influence their superiors through subtle rather than assertive claims on *Nkhani Zam'maboma*.

The attitude to funerals was a frequent indication of employers' mean ways. Another headline was, "Workers in a well-known firm in Blantyre city were disappointed by the refusal of the firm's superiors to give money to help with the funeral of a worker's mother."[34] Participation in funerals in the village of origin was usually obligatory to urban dwellers, who were pressed by their rural relations to make material contributions from their urban income. As such, the bereaved worker in this story had explained to his superiors that "people in the village rely on him in everything" (*anthu akumudzi amadalira iyeyo pa china chilichonse*), but the superiors refused to give him anything more than transport to the village. His colleagues, who had "sacrificed themselves" (*anadzipereka*) by giving him money, resolved to take the issue to the firm's director in the hope that "the unloving behavior would not continue" (*khalidwe losoẁa chikondi lisapitirize*).

This sense of workers' own moral conduct was an important element of stories about labor relations. One story stated that a "boss" (*bwana*) had "revealed all his cruelty by ruling that a driver in the firm takes unpaid leave because she had given a lift to another person without a permission."[35] The female driver had picked up another woman working in the same firm, as witnessed by the boss who had followed them to the office. He took away her car keys and declared that she would never be allowed to drive again. Other employees were reported to have assumed that "perhaps the woman had refused an affair with the man when he had courted her" (*mwina mayiwo anakana chibwenzi ndi bamboyo atamufunsira*), especially since the firm did not have a policy to prevent drivers from picking up their colleagues. In another story, the worker, also a driver, went a step further by beating up his boss and leaving him by the roadside.[36] They had left the office in Blantyre to visit Zomba some sixty miles away, and the boss had promised to give the driver his daily allowance at their destination. When they were preparing to return to Blantyre, the boss had told the driver that he would get the money once they were back in the office, because "he had paid a debt to someone he had met in Zomba" (*anabweza ngon-*

gole kwa munthu ŵina amene anapezana naye ku Zombako). The explanation infuriated the driver, who stopped the car midway, ordered the boss to step out, gave him a beating, and proceeded on to Blantyre without him. The incident did not surprise his colleagues in the office, who were reported to have pointed out that the driver was new in the firm and unaware of the boss's "habit of harassing drivers" (*khalidwe lake lozunza madalayivala*).

In a country where strike action was rare and trade unions weak, such stories described a relationship between persons in strikingly different positions. Because *Nkhani Zam'maboma* was not explicit about the institutions and laws that supported the democratization of labor relations, its identification of relationship amid the instances of abuse and exploitation tended to be couched in moral terms, as seen above in the woman's assumed refusal of sex with her employer and in the worker's attack on the uncaring boss. A story that did mention the Ombudsman, one of the institutions established by the new constitution, did so at the very end, as if in a footnote. The headline was, "A man who works at a hospital in Karonga District is said to have disappointed people by beating up a patient."[37] The incident had its origin in a setting that was as common as other exploitative labor relations in Malaŵi. A patient who was being discharged stood in a queue to receive medicine to take home, but an officer decided to send him back to the end of the queue. Such an arbitrary display of power was all too common to impoverished Malaŵians in a variety of contexts—from hospitals to post offices, from shops to government departments—where they were expected to wait for attention from members of staff. In this case, the subject did not accept his fate without a protest, resulting in verbal and physical abuse from the officer. Onlookers were reported to have been disturbed by the incident, while "the patient was said to take the story to the chief of the office for hearing people's complaints, Ombudsman."[38] Whatever effect the mention of institutions such as the Ombudsman had, *Nkhani Zam'maboma* was itself a highly popular medium for making grievances public.

Intimate Adversaries

A significant proportion of stories broadcast on *Nkhani Zam'maboma*—28 per cent, as mentioned—revolved around marital and sexual misconduct. Their popularity accords with the observation from a number of African settings that gender has become one of the major fault lines in the process of democratization since the late 1980s (Mama 1997: 69). In Malaŵi, Muluzi's administration launched a gender policy to establish gender equality as one of the rhetorical devices in politicians' speeches. Tangible improvements did ensue, including micro-credit facilities for businesswomen, and the provision of free primary-school education from 1994 was said to benefit girls in particular. Broader attitudinal changes seemed, however, painfully slow to some critics. Banda had styled himself as the Nkhoswe Number 1 of all Malaŵian women, playing on the matrilineal notion of mother's brother as the *nkhoswe* or guardian of the women in his kin group, only to allocate women a role as his adulatory entertainers during public engagements (Mkamanga 2000). The practice was far removed from the influence that adult sisters could exert on their kin groups, and yet it was continued by Banda's "democratic" successor Muluzi, who likewise enlisted large groups of women to dance for him (V. Chirwa 2007: 160). Negative or stereotypical portrayals of women were also found to litter expressions of popular culture, such as literature, written almost exclusively by men, even after the democratic transition (Moto 2001; H. Ross 1998; but see Englund 2004b).

Rather than depicting gender equality as a goal to be pursued, *Nkhani Zam'maboma* offered a platform to remind the sexes of their mutual dependence. To be sure, gender stereotypes exacerbated the effects of inequality among Malaŵians, sometimes perpetuated by the very advertisers who sponsored *Nkhani Zam'maboma* itself. One sponsor, for example, advertised Kazinga cooking oil, its stereotypes based on the idea of women, with strong historical parallels with marketing and advertising in the region, as "maintaining households, satisfying husbands, and raising children" (Burke 1996: 155). In one advertisement broadcast, unusually for a sponsor of *Nkhani Zam'maboma,* in English, a woman visits her friend, with a man heard playing with children in the background.[39] The visitor asks, "How come your husband hangs around all the time these days?" to which the answer is, "You know what, when I discovered Kazinga Superior, I discovered happiness." The woman goes on to explain that "Kazinga Superior is the only way to keep him at home. It is pure refined cooking oil. . . . It is enriched with vitamin A for extra nutrition." The ad ends with a male voice stating, "Kazinga Superior for great family bonding."

The ads of the National Bank of Malaŵi, another frequent sponsor of the program, played on the other side of the gender stereotype, namely male ambition. One began with a short exchange between what appeared to be a husband and wife, with the wife admonishing the man "not to desire the impossible" (*osamakhumbira chosatheka*).[40] The husband's assurance that money would be found was reinforced by another male voice that cut in to ask, "Do you yearn to own a TV, VCR, CD, DVD, sofas, and other modern things?" (*Kodi muku-lakalaka muli ndi TV, VCR, CD, DVD, masofa ndi zina zamakono?*). The voice answered its own question by saying, "Calm down! Go and speak to your own National Bank of Malaŵi, they will help you" (*Inu khalani phe! Kalankhu-leni kubanki lanulanu, National Bank of Malaŵi, akuthandizani*). Further en-ticements were mentioned, such as "doing what the neighbor does" (*kuchita chimene amachita* neighbor), concluding with enthusiastic encouragement to take a loan from the sponsoring bank. For the vast majority of Malaŵians lis-tening to *Nkhani Zam'maboma,* this ad, despite using Chicheŵa, was no more convincing than the one proposing cooking oil as the solution to a husband's absence. TVs, VCRs, CDs, DVDs, and sofas were far removed from the life-worlds of most villagers and township dwellers, as were bank loans that re-quired reputable and well-paid guarantors. Yet both ads reflected gender ste-reotypes that were prevalent in Malaŵi. The stereotypes were challenged by *Nkhani Zam'maboma,* which, far from asserting that women and men were the same, revealed the conditions under which the productive difference between them was made unproductive.

Some stories appeared to support the unequal status quo in gender rela-tions. For example, it might seem that a rather unfortunate cultural practice of silencing women gave rise to the headline that a woman had "startled people by insisting on speaking at a funeral where her mother's brothers and broth-ers were present."[41] The mother's brother, as mentioned, was the conventional guardian of his matrilineal relatives, and his responsibilities included public speaking on his subjects' behalf. The woman in this story broke the conven-tion by "just standing up and starting to explain the history of the deceased who was her grandparent."[42] The story noted that "her behavior is like that" (*makhalidwe ake ndi otere*) and that "even in church she was chosen into an of-fice because of fear toward her" (*ngakhale kutchalichi komwe anamusankha pa udindo chifukwa chomuopa*). When discussing this story with female and male listeners, I realized that its import was twofold and, as such, ambiguous. On the one hand, many listeners commented that a woman could have a formidable public presence that led to her being elected into an office. On the other hand, what the story left unsaid was as important as what it said. Influence and au-thority were not always measured by the extent to which persons were able to speak in public. The same listeners also explained that the matrilineal values underpinning village life did give women opportunities to speak out, the public role played by male relatives subject to women's approval and cooperation. The woman's breach of protocol did not, in other words, indicate the lack of arenas where she could have influenced those entrusted to speak on her behalf.

Most of the stories about marital and sexual misconduct brought material problems to the fore, but fault was found among women as well as men. One headline stated, "A woman is said to astonish people by changing men while looking for wealth."[43] She was reported to have started her marital career with a farmer, but "she chased him away" (*anamuthamangitsa*) and "found a fisher so that she would eat fresh fish" (*anapezana ndi msodzi kuti azidyera matumbi*). Upon the government's restrictions on fishing, the man lost his livelihood and the woman "was confused by another man who seemed to have money at that time" (*anazunguzika ndi mwamuna ŵina yemwe anaoneka ngati ali ndi ndalama pa nthaŵiyo*). Yet another man was said to have followed when this man's money had run out. A different story highlighted somewhat similar issues in the case of a woman with a more secure financial base.[44] She was reported to keep "a secret lover" (*ubwenzi ŵa seli*; literally, a relationship behind), and "what made people dumbfounded was that the woman was enormously fortunate because she was married to one of the richest men in Kasungu District."[45] The story listed the benefits she enjoyed in terms of her diet, the bed on which she slept, and the car she drove. She was reported to have been discovered by her husband committing adultery in his own motel.

In contrast to misogynistic themes that appear in contemporary African discourses (see, e.g., Nyamnjoh 2005b), stories that highlighted female greed and cunning were relatively few on *Nkhani Zam'maboma*. Precisely because the man's conventional role was to ensure the material security of his family, unreasonable behavior among men came under special scrutiny in the program. One story described how a woman's spending of the meager sum of M.K.10 on fried potatoes nearly caused a divorce.[46] Both she and her husband were said to be entrepreneurs, but he had become very angry when he discovered what the wife had done. He was threatening to banish the wife from their house, but "other people helped him with ideas" (*anthu ena anamuthandiza maganizo*), and he was reported "to be still living with the wife" (*akukhalabe ndi mkaziyo*). In another story, it was the wife who was said "to be thinking of ending her marriage because of the greed and cruelty to which her husband subjects her."[47] The husband was reported to interfere with basic household tasks that were the woman's prerogative. For example, the husband helped himself to the wife's maize granary, thereby violating the right that granted, in most of Malaŵi's countryside, every adult woman exclusive access to her granary (see

Englund 1999). "The guy," the story continued, "is said to measure water and flour" (*ndoda akuti imayesa madzi pamodzi ndi ufa ŵake*) in order to receive *nsima,* the staple maize porridge, in the quantity he wanted. Whereas he himself had a "desire for meat" (*nkhuli*), "he also ruled the wife to eat *nsima* only once per day in the afternoon" (*analamulanso mkazi kuti azidya nsima madzulo okha pa tsiku*). The story ended by noting that "now the wife is said to be tired of this behavior and is considering to go to her parents" (*panopa akuti mkazi ŵatopa ndi khalidweli ndipo akuganiza kupita kwa makolo ake*).

Stories broadcast on *Nkhani Zam'maboma* by no means assumed that marriage was the only, or even the principal, domain for negotiating relationships between the sexes. *Ubwenzi* (relationship, affair, friendship) refers to a wide range of arrangements involving material and sexual favors, often specified by *Nkhani Zam'maboma* as *ubwenzi ŵa seli* (secret relationship or, as mentioned, relationship behind), especially when such a relationship existed in the shadows of a publicly recognized marriage. Although the program often highlighted the abusive character of men in these relationships, women could also appear as the initiators of trouble, such as when a woman whose husband was said to be working abroad unsuccessfully "courted a young man" (*anafunsira mnyamata ŵina*).[48] Even after "taking him to watch videos" (*anamutengera kukaonera mavideo*), the young man "refused her" (*anamukana*).

When women were subjected to men's whims, they were not deprived of all capacity to retaliate. An incident between a man working for a firm and a woman working as a teacher in Blantyre city saw the woman taking his ATM card in order to make him comply with her demands.[49] He was to give her the money they had agreed on, and "he was to stop being jealous when he finds her with other men" (*aleke kumuchitira nsanje akamupeza ndi amuna ena*), leaving him to make up excuses when his wife wondered why he could not access his salary. The headline for another incident stated that "a loose woman in Luchenza town stole a fellow's clothes with whom she had agreed that he would give her money for their fornication."[50] The woman had run after him when he had snuck away without paying and, with the aid of someone she had met along the way, stripped the man. "He went ashamed to his house" (*anayenda mwa manyazi popita kunyumba yake*), the story continued, adding that "when we received this story, the woman had not returned the clothes to the fellow" (*pamene tinalandira nkhaniyi mayi anali asanabweze zovalazo kwa mkuluyo*).

Nkhani Zam'maboma had no qualms about mentioning the HIV/AIDS pandemic when broadcasting stories about marital and sexual misconduct. It did so, however, in a very different register from the abundant advice on how to avoid contracting HIV—whether through abstinence or condom use—that politicians, health professionals, popular musicians, and non-governmental and faith-based organizations had spread in Malaŵi since the early 1990s. In accordance with its aversion to delivering didactic messages, *Nkhani Zam'maboma* highlighted poverty as a condition of the pandemic. As such, men's economic position loomed large in the stories that mentioned HIV/AIDS. One headline stated that a man "ended his daughter's marriage by luring her that he will give her wealth and other things, although the father had a venereal disease and the big cough of TB [tuberculosis]."[51] *Nkhani Zam'maboma* often used the Chicheŵa word for AIDS, *edzi,* but the reference in this headline to a venereal disease (*matenda opatsirana;* literally, disease that is given between people) and TB drew on the common Malaŵian understanding that TB often marked the onset of AIDS. The man, reportedly the leader of a road maintenance project, "had begun to eat with his eyes his daughter who had a family of her own" (*anayamba kudyerera pa maso pa mwana wake wamkazi amene analinso pabanja*). "Failing to refuse and challenge her father's words, the daughter did chase her husband away."[52] The father was said to "admit" (*kuvomera*) when he was asked if he had an affair with his daughter. The story's public was left to draw its own conclusions about the combination of incest, wealth differences, and the spread of HIV/AIDS.

Precisely because poverty and injustice distributed moral quandaries so widely in Malaŵi, not all men could appear as shameless exploiters of women's vulnerability. The ideal of romantic love may have suffered a setback in Africa following the general decline of its economies, with mistrust between men and women one consequence of deteriorating material conditions (Ferguson 1999: 187; Simpson 2009: 114; see also Thomas and Cole 2009). However, *Nkhani Zam'maboma* did broadcast heartrending accounts of love (*chikondi*) doomed by poverty, the predicament being not so much a lack of commitment and passion as the circumstances that made them impossible to sustain. "A girl," one headline reported, "is seriously ill after her mother made her drink medicine to abort a pregnancy because she did not want the girl to give birth to a child whose father was poor."[53] The mother was reported to have investigated the father's situation after she had heard about her daughter's pregnancy and, unimpressed, made her drink "herbal medicine" (*mankhwala achitsamba*). Despite her serious illness, the daughter was said to have sworn that "she would continue with the poor one" (*apitirizabe ndi mphawiyo*).

No such commitment to a relationship seemed possible in another story of a similar kind. "A family," the headline said, "ended the relationship of its daughter because the man is poor."[54] After a whole year of courtship, the couple were said to have agreed on a wedding, only to be dismissed by the daughter's family when they realized how poor the bridegroom's family was. As a consequence, the young man's relatives "were following him for the fear that he might kill himself because he loved the girl so much."[55] The young man "did not think he would find another girl like her even if he went around all the corners of this country."[56] Faced with expectations to ensure material security, men no less than women bore the brunt of ill-fated love.

Some editors of *Nkhani Zam'maboma* expressed private concern about mentioning marital and sexual issues on the program. They pointed out to me that the program was broadcast when families were likely to eat dinner together. The timing required, they claimed, special care about the kinds of topics and details that the program could carry. As a measure to keep the listeners tuned to their station, the concern acknowledged a widespread attempt among Malaŵians to cultivate high standards of propriety. Although legislation stipulating that women wear long skirts and men keep their hair short was removed during the democratic transition, women's dress, in particular, continued to attract moral commentary in Malaŵi and elsewhere in the region (Englund 2006: 67; Hansen 2000: 214–220).[57] The commentary fueled controversies over abstinence and condom use in the context of an HIV/AIDS pandemic. When the picture of a woman with a bare thigh appeared in ads marketing condoms in 2003, many Malaŵians condemned the picture, also reproduced on the condom packaging, for depicting a "naked" woman. A story broadcast on *Nkhani Zam'maboma* captured the popular unease by describing a woman beating up a prostitute who had asked her child to read the text on the packaging that had a "picture of a woman who had not dressed well" (*chithunzi cha mkazi amene sanavale bwino*).[58] The woman had sent her child on an errand, but when the child did not return promptly, she had gone outside, only to find a "loose girl" (*mtsikana woyendayenda*)[59] forcing the child to help her read. A fight ensued when the prostitute retaliated against the woman's aggression.

The propensity of *Nkhani Zam'maboma* to broadcast stories involving sex and violence contradicted the claim by some of the editors that they viewed it as a family program. Consider, in relation to the claim about a family program, the headline that a schoolgirl "was confused when it emerged that the man with whom she had agreed to have sex had pierced the condom he wore during the fornication."[60] The girl, a pupil at Standard 7 in a primary school, had consented to sleep with the man for M.K.200, but he "agreed deceitfully" (*anangovomera mwashashalika*) to her demand for a condom and pierced it in secret.[61] Afterward the girl, while fearing that she had caught HIV, was expelled from her school for "bringing the school into disrepute" (*chifukwa chopereka mbiri yoipa yasukuluyo*). Indecency was also striking in the headline, "It is not known where a young man is after people battered him severely for trying to rape his own mother."[62] The mother was said to have found "her own son, a grown-up" (*mwana wawo wamwamuna, wamkulu ndithu*) loitering naked outside her house. When the mother asked him what the problem was, he replied with "very rude words" (*mawu a mwano kwambiri*) and attacked her. The mother's cries alerted others to come and beat the son, who then escaped the crowd, covered in dust and dirt.

Nkhani Zam'maboma was by no means alone in testing the tolerance of obscenity in Malaŵi's public arenas. The popular musician Joseph Nkasa, for example, released a song in 2007 complaining that sexual lust (*nyere*) had resulted in the pregnancy of the girl whose school fees the song's narrator had paid.[63] The public response was to accuse Nkasa of "going explicit," drawing a comment from the Censorship Board that radio stations "must take responsibility" and "watch out for crudely vulgar lyrics."[64] During my fieldwork, although the Censorship Board appeared to have nothing to say about *Nkhani Zam'maboma*, the program's editors were concerned about attracting criticisms of obscenity. They often sought to evade my questions about the contradiction between their image of a family program and the actual content and language of the stories that were broadcast. A common response to my direct quotes from the program was that the stories had been selected by editors who did not work on the program regularly, such as during weekends. However, as discussed in the next chapter, senior editors also had personal predilections that made some more interested than others in stories involving obscene details.

5

Inequality Is Old News

Editors as Authors

Wayilesi yakwanu, "the radio from your place," an editor of *Nkhani Zam'maboma* remarked to me one day when the BBC World Service blared in the newsroom. Before I could think of a response, the editor went on to state that even white people should have a program like *Nkhani Zam'maboma.* "White people also misbehave" (*azungunso amapalamula*), she asserted, making them seem comparable to the Malawian figures of authority whose deceptive appearances made the headlines on *Nkhani Zam'maboma.* Listening to his colleague's comments, another editor of the program concurred with the view that white people, for all their superiority in wealth and education, should also be exposed as liars and adulterers. But he asked me if witchcraft (*ufiti*) existed where I came from. My answer that it did not exist in the same way as in Malawi confirmed the idea he already had about witchcraft and science as the defining domains of Africa and Europe, respectively.[1] After a pause, however, the editor recalled that even white people could adopt Malawian ways, to the extent that a white priest had joined the *gule wamkulu* secret society, an incident that the editor said had been reported on *Nkhani Zam'maboma.*

Impromptu exchanges of views were common between editors and myself during my fieldwork in the newsroom. My interest in *Nkhani Zam'maboma* inspired them to reflect aloud on the nature and purpose of its stories, although they seemed reluctant to attribute an overtly emancipatory agenda to the program. What engaged editors, as in the above conversation, was the scope of their remit to expose abuse and misconduct. The claim that even white people misbehaved contested a legacy of colonial and missionary interventions in Malaŵi, namely the belief that the propensity of white people to find well-paid employment and to live comfortably amid searing poverty somehow bespoke their innate goodness, if not a special relationship with God. Their exposure would have, therefore, been compatible with the ethos of *Nkhani Zam'maboma*, but the other editor's question about witchcraft among the whites raised the issue of the program's belonging to a particular social and historical context. Yet on reflection, as the white priest's example testified, those social and historical boundaries could be transcended, if the outsider submitted to the conditions underlying Malaŵian life-worlds.

Reflections such as these indicated the seriousness with which editors approached *Nkhani Zam'maboma*. The news format was key to the professionalism they identified with. For all its borrowings from other genres, *Nkhani Zam'maboma* was for them an accurate account of reality, a conviction that is so widely held across the world that it is said to make news unique among media forms (see Bird 2010: 5). The editors' pride in the program became apparent to me early on in my fieldwork when I inadvertently referred to the official news bulletin as "real news" (*nkhani zenizeni*). Editors' consternation at the implied notion that stories on *Nkhani Zam'maboma* were somehow less than real began to make it clear to me that the program was cherished and respected among the journalists working in the Department of News and Current Affairs, its editing a coveted task. However, the more time I spent in the newsroom the more apparent it became that editors rarely found an opportunity to discuss the program among themselves. Rather than resulting from a carefully crafted policy, the program owed its specific features to a peculiar relationship between editors and their public. As mentioned in the previous chapter, the early developmentalism of *Nkhani Zam'maboma* quickly evaporated when listeners' letters were allowed to define the concerns to be broadcast. As described in this chapter, editors' habits of revising the language, even the contents, of stories they received in turn generated a particular mass-mediated aural genre to which listeners' contributions sought to adjust.

Although the pace of work in the newsroom left little space for strategic planning, editors were highly conscious about the contents and language of

Nkhani Zam'maboma. Apart from the reflections prompted by the presence of an ethnographer, their sense of the appropriate form and contents in stories was rarely made explicit. One reason was their avoidance of confrontations between colleagues, who may have had different opinions on editorial decisions. Another reason was the several years of experience most editors brought to bear on *Nkhani Zam'maboma,* the decisions on stories and their linguistic features often made so quickly that editors were at a loss to explain them when asked by the ethnographer. The general principle all editors spontaneously emphasized was non-partisanship as a guarantee for objectivity.

After a discussion of the most common editorial interventions to enhance language and narrative style, this chapter presents a close examination of three cases of editorial interventions. Between them, the cases offer insights into editors' decisions to radically alter some stories, to dismiss rejoinders to the stories they have broadcast, and to claim objectivity through a specific kind of non-partisanship. The chapter ends with reflections on the contrast between *Nkhani Zam'maboma,* human rights activism, and the so-called movement of public journalism. The contrast revolves around their different notions of (in)equality, thereby clarifying what ultimately constituted news for the editors of *Nkhani Zam'maboma.*

Creative Editing

The editing of *Nkhani Zam'maboma* took place behind a door with an uninviting sign: "Strictly for Chief Editors. No Noise" (see figure 5.1). Although those most closely involved in editing the program did occupy the room, the sign on its door did not guarantee silence. The newsroom's only computer with internet access was there, and journalists visiting the room would often strike up a conversation with senior editors while waiting for the slow dial-up connection to establish itself. It was usual for *Nkhani Zam'maboma* to be edited under pressure also because its turn came late in the day, after editors had completed their other tasks, such as preparing the news bulletins and commentaries. The timing did not indicate their own priorities—it was merely a function of the program's broadcast in the evening. The stories to be broadcast were usually edited in the same afternoon, and I witnessed occasions when an editor's accumulated tasks made him or her ask a colleague to take over the editing of *Nkhani Zam'maboma* literally in the middle of a sentence.

Despite this often hectic pace of work, the editing of *Nkhani Zam'maboma* was a coveted assignment in the newsroom, associated with seniority. Two or three senior Chicheŵa editors shared the main responsibility for editing

Fig. 5.1. *Nkhani Zam'maboma* was edited in the inner office at the back of the newsroom.

the program, while younger editors and reporters could try their hands at it during weekends. Although everyone at the MBC would insist that its stories were true (*zoona*) and not fabricated (*zopeka*), many talked about its editing in terms of skill (*luso*). Those who had participated in editing compared each other's talents to generate memorable stories, often using the verb for writing (*kulemba*) rather than editing (*kukonza*) to describe the creative work. Few editors doubled as newsreaders, but even those who read *Nkhani Zam'maboma* were often senior presenters and specifically selected for their abilities to imbue their newsreaders' voices with the tone of a storyteller. The association with seniority made the editors of *Nkhani Zam'maboma* feel proud (*onyada*) about the program, a sentiment enhanced by two other considerations. *Nkhani Zam'maboma*, they told me, was an established (*yokhazikika*) program that through its appeal to sponsors "made money for the MBC" (*yopangira ndalama kwa MBC*). Moreover, it was a program that editors thought had effects on the way people behaved. "People are afraid of appearing in *Nkhani Zam'maboma*" (*anthu amaopa kukhala m'Nkhani Zam'maboma*), one editor explained to me.[2]

Beyond the sometimes profound changes editors made on the contents of submitted stories, their interventions also sought to modify the language to improve their expression. Here editors and listeners often echoed each other's appreciation of the language on the program. Apart from adding words such as "many people were surprised" (*anthu ambiri anadabwa*) to amplify a sense of drama in the unfolding story, editors were open about their desire to use idiomatic Chicheŵa (*Chicheŵa chokhuluŵika*), the kind of richly textured and evocative language that was rarely possible on the other programs produced in the Department of News and Current Affairs. Embellishments (*zikometsero*) were key to distinguishing skillful editors from mere novices. Some of the idiomatic expressions had become the program's stock-in-trade and were influenced by the published collections of Malaŵian oral literature that editors had, as mentioned in the previous chapter, read during their schooldays. Commonly used idioms included *kugwira njakata*, "to seize a dilemma," for being dumbfounded by a problem; *kukana kwa mtu wa galu*, "to deny by the head of a dog," and *kutemetsa nkhwangwa pa mwala*, "to hit the rock with an axe," for ardently refusing something; and *mikoko yogona*, "bunches of banana hanging from a tree," for elderly people.

While these idioms could be encountered in everyday spoken Chicheŵa in both rural and urban areas, other expressions were more esoteric and signaled a more specialized skill of storytelling. The use of *chomwe chinachititsa dzaye kuti njovu ithyoke mnyanga*, "the thing that made a hard wild fruit fall to break an elephant's tusk," to pinpoint the cause for an incident often provided a transition from the headline to the narrative. For example, it followed the headline "some were said to be very disappointed with a funeral where the bereaved fought over the deceased's property."[3] The next sentence was, "The thing that made a hard wild fruit fall to break an elephant's tusk in this story was that some among the bereaved wanted the mourners not to put clothes on the deceased when placing him/her into the coffin so that they could take the clothes."[4] The story proceeded to describe the disagreement that ensued among the bereaved and how "many others left disappointed before the burial had taken place."[5]

While *Nkhani Zam'maboma* did not deliver moral lessons through commentary or other forms of didactic expression, the moral standing of protagonists was sometimes conveyed by the editors' choice of words. They preferred a richer vocabulary than what was used by many contributors, substituting common words such as *bambo* (man, father) for more specific and idiomatic expressions. The morals thus conveyed often depended on humor for their effect rather than on solemn condemnation, such as in the vocabulary used by some Christian radio stations (see chapter 8). For example, the mention of the word *ndoda* usually caused a good deal of mirth among listeners. Translated as "guy," it appeared in a story about two men who had been beaten and tied to a tree because they had been drinking the locally brewed spirit *kachasu* instead of attending a funeral. "The two guys are said to have the habit of drinking alcohol every day, but the problem on that day was that the funeral was their own [took place at their home]," the story explained.[6] In a similar way, a man who had attained the status of fatherhood was reduced to a mere boy (*mnyamata*) in the headline, "A boy is said to have been at a loss when the village headman prevented him from burying his child in the village graveyard because he insults the headman whenever he is drunk and also neglects to attend funerals."[7]

Wealthy villains were often called *njonda* or *mpondamakwacha*, neither of which would have been used by the person to refer to him- or herself. The dictionary definition of *njonda* conveys its double meaning as "a rich and well-dressed person" (*munthu wachuma ndiponso wovala bwino*) and "a male person who does clever things to steal from people" (*munthu wamwamuna wochita zinthu zochenjera mobera anthu*; Centre for Language Studies 2000: 263). The word was used alternately with *mbava* (thief) in a story that depicted an elaborate scam to which a tobacco farmer had fallen prey. "The fellow who is a famous tobacco farmer in the area is said to have met the thief who cheated him that he would buy all his tobacco at a good price."[8] The unsuspecting person's delight was evident in the detail that "the farmer is said to have been pleased to kill a chicken for the rich person/thief and to show him a place to sleep at night."[9] After paying the farmer a large sum of money, the thief returned to take more money back through a nonexistent loan scheme for fertilizer and other goods. *Mpondamakwacha*, conveying a person who makes large amounts of the Malaŵian currency kwacha, could also be used interchangeably with *njonda*, such as in a story with the headline, "A rich person (*mpondamakwacha*) who has several shops is ashamed like a sick chicken."[10] It explained that "the rich person/thief (*njonda*) is said to be in the habit of having affairs with his female employees."[11] When a young woman ignored his threat of dismissing her if she married someone else, a further shameful detail came to light. The entrepreneur was reported to have failed to assist his girlfriends materially.

The use of these words and idioms was one of the features that distinguished *Nkhani Zam'maboma* from more conventional news broadcasts, whether on the MBC or other radio stations. Another feature was proverbs (*miyambi*) that editors were keen to add to stories they received. Proverbial expressions were by no means broadcast every evening, but editors explained their use as a way of making listeners contemplate (*kusinkhasinkha*) the meaning of stories. Editors assumed a measure of shared knowledge among the public, because in line with its format, *Nkhani Zam'maboma* did not offer interpretations of proverbs. Although editors often prefaced proverbs with words such as "elders in the past used to say" (*akuluakulu akale adanena*), the situations for which proverbs were deployed were just as contemporary as any stories on the program.[12] For example, a proverb introduced the story, "Elders in the past said, 'This is lovely, this is lovely, the monkey fell on its back.' These words were heard because of what happened [location omitted]. A girl of 16 years who was on Form 1 in secondary school gave birth to twins through operation in a hospital because she had multiple affairs."[13] The next sentence ended this short item: "Even the girl herself is not able to say unequivocally who the father is."[14] The story had been sent to the newsroom without a proverb, but the editor working on it thought that the proverb about a greedy monkey set the right tone for it. The issue, he remarked, was a just reward for reckless behavior. Without the proverb, the twins might have been understood to be the result of multiple sexual intercourses instead of a burden the schoolgirl had inflicted on herself.

Had editors wanted to fix the meaning of stories, they would hardly have chosen to use proverbs to influence listeners' interpretations. When merely cited rather than explained, proverbs could only suggest a direction the interpretation might take, as in a story that used the proverb *mtima wa mnzako m'tsidya lina*, "your friend's heart is on the other side of the river."[15] The story reported that a witch's aircraft had crash-landed near the house of its owner.[16] The pilot was a girl who had been sent by her mother to receive coming-of-age instructions (*malangizo*) from a woman who was active in the women's organization in their church. "Because your friend's heart is on the other side of the river," the story continued, "the mother did not know that her friend was a witch."[17] The mother had begun to suspect that something was wrong when her daughter returned home and "instead of respect spoke to her in a rude way."[18] The situation came to a head when the daughter, driving the aircraft alone for the first time, crash-landed and revealed the source of her knowledge about witchcraft. The proverb had again been inserted by an editor, who explained to me that it helped to clarify the mother's innocence and the need to be on one's guard even with those who pretended to be Christians. He anticipated that the proverb would make listeners contemplate how little they might know about the disposition of those who presented themselves as authorities.

Over the years, listeners' letters had adopted many of the idioms and embellishments that editors appeared to favor. Although problems with language continued to be a major reason for the editors' rejection of stories, I was often struck by how similar many letters were to the stylistic features of broadcast stories. However, editors themselves rarely considered submitted stories suitable for broadcasting without some editorial input. If a submitted story had attempted to use a proverb, its editor was likely to substitute it for the one that he or she regarded more appropriate for the context. It was as if the editors' sense of professionalism required interventions, but they were also aware that their authority in language stood on shaky ground. The Chichewa Board, responsible for standardizing the language during Banda's regime, had been disbanded after the democratic transition, and editors had not begun to consult academics at the University of Malawi in its stead. While regional differences did concern editors, committed as they were to the idea of a national public, uncertainties were resolved on an ad hoc basis through informal consultations within the newsroom. Editors had never, I was told, sat down as a group to discuss whether and how to authorize a particular kind of Chichewa for broadcasting.

Unusually short submissions were not necessarily disadvantaged. On the contrary, their very brevity sometimes seemed to arouse a creative urge in editors, who would casually respond to my queries by saying that "we lengthen stories" (*timakulitsa nkhani*). Short or long, submitted stories were often put aside when the editor began his or her work. After reading a letter, the editor would decide on the most interesting aspect in it before starting to type the story in his or her own words (see figure 5.2). How much of the original text ended up in the final version varied greatly, not only because of the language used but also because of individual editors' own predilections, which affected the choice of stories beyond the editor's particular skill to modify or rewrite them.

As mentioned in the previous chapter, some editors told me that the time of its broadcast made *Nkhani Zam'maboma* a family program. Families would gather for an evening meal when the program was on, and editors did not want to embarrass the parents by broadcasting stories about sex and violence. After observing one editor, however, I noticed that he showed a certain inclination toward obscenity. While editing a story about a madman's sexual attack on a woman at the market, he explained to me that he had substituted the verb *kuwerama* (to stoop down) for *kupolama* (to bend down) in the original to make, in his view, the story less obscene. Yet the broadcast story left little room for ambiguity, describing the woman's short skirt and its effect on the man who had stood behind her. When this editor broadcast a story about a sixty-year-old man having sex with a female goat (*mbuzi yaikazi*) because his wife was absent and his neighbor refused to have intercourse, I confronted him with the notion that *Nkhani Zam'maboma* was a family program. "There are no children these

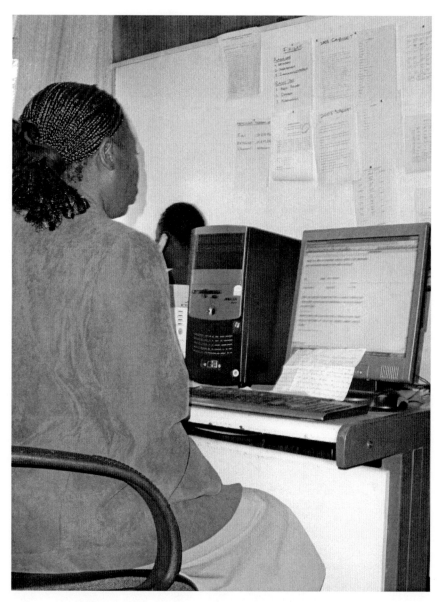

Fig. 5.2. An editor working on a letter to *Nkhani Zam'maboma*.

days" (*kulibe ana masiku ano*), he retorted, as if this was not the first time he had been challenged in this way. Nine-year-old children were taught safe sex in schools to prevent the spread of HIV/AIDS, he claimed, challenging me in turn, "Where should we start from?" (*tiyambire pati?*).

Senior editors were reluctant to assess each other's predilections with me, admitting differences only in the skills they brought to bear on editing stories. Despite their initial denial that they changed much in the stories they received, editors became, as my fieldwork progressed, more forthright than the MBC's management about the creative work on *Nkhani Zam'maboma*. Alluding to the transparency of mass-mediated news, the management would maintain that virtually nothing changed in stories from their initial submission to their broadcast. When a broadcast item was too obviously at variance with the program's broad appeal, senior editors apportioned blame to their inexperienced colleagues, usually the ones working on weekends. Such controversy was rare, however, and was a result of stories about sex and violence rather than more overtly political topics.[19] Party-political stories did arrive in the newsroom, as will be seen below, but their chances of getting broadcast were negligible. For all their creative work and their individual predilections, editors subscribed to a particular form of objectivity. Not only did it spur them to reject party-political items, it also justified radical alterations to submitted stories when their potential for revealing injustice seemed to require it.

Reclaiming Virginity

Apart from lengthening the stories they received, another alteration some editors made on submitted stories was the complete reversal of perspective. For example, one story came to the newsroom in an unmistakably misogynist form and went on air as an account of a woman's tribulations with a husband who wanted to leave her.[20] Its editor, herself a mature woman, did not want to engage in a conversation with me about the reasons for this modification. Shrugging off my observation that the submitted story and the edited version were strikingly different, she swiftly absorbed herself in editing the next story. Some changes, it seemed to me, went so much beyond the application of editorial skill that editors-as-authors preferred to keep them as their own knowledge. This strategy was particularly feasible to senior editors, whose readings of submitted stories were rarely monitored by their colleagues, unless the senior editors themselves requested feedback. In this particular case, the reversal of perspective appeared compatible with the ethos of *Nkhani Zam'maboma* in which the downtrodden's point of view was usually in focus. Moreover, the editor's own marital troubles, which gradually became apparent during fieldwork, must have added a compelling personal impulse to this editorial intervention.

Both versions of the story stated that it had taken place in the Magistrate's Court in Lilongwe.[21] The original text, submitted through e-mail in English, had as its headline, "Worship, the Woman is Polyandrous."[22] It indicated that the husband had brought the case to the court, because he wanted to leave the woman. She retaliated, however, with a battery of accusations, including the demand that he should restore her virginity if he wanted to leave her and that he should cleanse her of AIDS, with which he had allegedly infected her. The woman also pointed out that the husband had lost interest in her because of the stepchildren in their household. "He told me he was tired of caring for step-children," the story quoted the woman as having told the court. Yet every accusation leveled against the husband was countered in a somewhat triumphalist tone by extracts from the husband's defense. "As for AIDS," he was quoted as having said, "I cannot be held responsible, because the woman married three men before me." The story ended with the stern words that the cause of the divorce was "not stepchildren but her ruthlessness and lack of respect for him."

The editor's version made the restoration of virginity the story's main interest and ignored virtually everything else in the original. "People listening to cases in the Lilongwe magistrate's court," the headline stated, "were overtaken by laughter when a mature woman told her husband to restore her virginity if he wanted to end their marriage." Without mentioning the details about stepchildren, AIDS, and previous husbands, the broadcast story went on to set out the husband's claim to divorce, including his lament that he had never had peace in this marriage because of the woman's wordy ways. Here the editor repeated the wife's counter-claim to have her virginity restored if the husband wanted to leave her, and a narrative detail entirely absent in the original came to introduce the story's new ending. The woman was reported to have started to utter obscenities (*zolaula*), describing to the court the state of their matrimonial bedroom. These revelations produced more hilarity in the court, and the editor ended the story by reporting that the husband had insisted that he and the woman should go their separate ways.

Striking in the editor's version was not simply the omission of narrative details but also a radical shift in tone that the reversal of perspective entailed. Although humor was not absent from the original version, the man's predicament in the hands of a treacherous woman was its most apparent theme. The author's bias toward the male protagonist was evident in phrases such as "some tried to think critically and condemned the ex-wife describing her irresponsible." The allegations about the woman's lack of respect and responsibility set the tone for the story, and the author was therefore able to applaud the man for not wasting time "thinking about what he could do for the lady." By contrast, the edited version made the husband look ridiculous, the object of the court's laughter, such as when the woman was said to have disclosed their matrimonial secrets. The allusion to obscenities in the context of the woman's description of their matrimonial bedroom brought the husband's physical performance under scrutiny. Coupled with the demand to have virginity restored, it questioned the balance of power between the sexes that seemed to enable the man to unilaterally end a marriage if the woman was too wordy. By alluding to what was hidden in the darkness of a matrimonial bedroom, and by highlighting the loss of virginity as the woman's predicament, the edited story achieved a reversal of perspective.

The editor admitted that she had no other report on the court case than this submitted story, and working in Blantyre she had few means of, or little interest in, verifying it in Lilongwe. The source was vaguely familiar to her, the author of other recent e-mails in English from the capital city. She had not met him or talked to him, but she knew from his correspondence that he was a salaried person living in the city. Although his use of e-mail and English was unusual among both the sources and listeners of *Nkhani Zam'maboma,* the misogyny of his contribution was likely to resonate among some members of the public. As mentioned in the previous chapter, despite the emergence of misogynist themes in African public arenas, *Nkhani Zam'maboma* eschewed them. The editor's intervention was an example of how this sense of subtlety was achieved in the newsroom by a not-so-subtle modification of contents. Different editors were likely to accord different weight to stories about the relationship between the sexes, but this story was suggestive of equality as a condition of relationships. Assertions of inequality rarely warranted broadcast on *Nkhani Zam'maboma,* not because editors wanted to deny its existence, but because providing an arena for voicing grievances from the downtrodden's point of view was a more interesting source of news. The editor used the word *utsikana* for "virginity," also translated as "girlhood," to indicate the absurdity of making the wife and the husband mutually independent of each other. Writing the story as a mature divorcee herself, she knew only too well that men could carry on marrying young women while their former wives, rarely able to support themselves without any involvement with men, faced an increasingly narrow pool of partners. The moral imperative was not to make women and men identical but to generate a standpoint from which their constitutive obligations, and claims against gendered injustice, could be discerned.

The Truth about Porridge

Whether they had been prompted by editorial high-handedness or not, rejoinders arrived in the newsroom to contest details in broadcast stories. They had few prospects of being aired. *Nkhani Zam'maboma* did not have a slot for corrections or responses, and editors often took "letters of disagreement" (*makalata otsutsa*) as assaults on their own professional authority. "It is not true" (*si zoona*), they would comment when I singled out such letters in the flow of mail the program received every day. Editors were usually satisfied with their own procedures of verification, as described in the next chapter, but broadcasting rejoinders would have done more than cast doubt over the efforts they made to prepare accurate stories. Much as their enthusiasm for *Nkhani Zam'maboma* rested on having the public as the source of its contents, editors hardly considered themselves to be mere ciphers. As editors' authorial aspirations have already indicated, many stories on *Nkhani Zam'maboma* acquired a certain personal quality that rejoinders could only undermine.

Editors' confidence in their own judgment had increased with a change that took place early on in the history of the program. The initial practice of broadcasting the protagonists' personal names sometimes resulted in court cases that also involved the MBC as a source of slander. After discontinuing the practice of broadcasting personal names, editors felt they had little reason to countenance rejoinders. Irate listeners who called the newsroom would often be asked whether they had heard any names mentioned in the stories that had incensed them. Because they had not, an editor was able to ask the further question of why they thought they had been featured in a story. The dissatisfied listener usually lost his or her determination to pursue a corrective when the editor announced that it would involve publicizing his or her name. As will be seen in subsequent chapters, the knowledge about protagonists was often localized, and most listeners preferred to keep it that way rather than having personal identities revealed to the nation.

Editors did not dismiss rejoinders simply because of their own convenience and sense of superiority. This approach was intricately linked to the production of an arena for voicing claims in a world saturated with inequalities. Because most stories highlighted the perspectives of the downtrodden, rejoinders were likely to reassert the order of things that stories precisely sought to question or qualify. Here editors' own sensibilities often assumed precedence over any attempt to establish the facts. One example comes from a story, broadcast with few editorial alterations, and the carefully crafted rejoinder it received.[23] The author of the rejoinder was a primary-school headmaster, who had found his teachers accused in *Nkhani Zam'maboma* of stealing relief porridge meant for pupils and of making pupils work for teachers' benefit. The story was a typical example of how the omission of personal and institutional names could not prevent identification locally. Although it did not mention any teachers by name or even the name of the school, the story was specific enough about the location in a particular district, chiefdom, and village to cause considerable embarrassment. However, the rejoinder included such patronizing assertions of inequality that editors saw no merit in taking it seriously.

The broadcast story took as the main interest the fate of the porridge that schoolchildren in some parts of Malaŵi received as a dietary supplement. Instead of teaching children in the class, teachers in this particular school were said to be preoccupied with the relief porridge. When it was being prepared in the school, the story reported, teachers would come from their houses with plates and wait for it in their office. They would scoop their platefuls before allowing pupils to eat the porridge. The story also asserted that teachers made pupils work for money that teachers kept to themselves. These issues were reported to have disappointed (*kukhumudwa*) parents, who were asking the government officers overseeing education in the district to intervene.

The rejoinder, complete with the school's official stamp, set out in an impeccable handwriting the headmaster's concerns (see figure 5.3). Pointing out that his was the only school in the village whose name had been mentioned, the headmaster disputed the claim that teachers brought their own plates to eat the porridge. He explained that the World Food Program had given the plates that were used in the school to eat the porridge, and it was in accordance with this organization's rules that teachers ate before children to ascertain that the porridge was suitable for children. The rejoinder was longer than the story that had been broadcast, and it included a rebuttal of teachers' alleged use of child labor and reflections on insolence (*mnyozo*), jealousy (*nsanje*), and grudge (*kaduka*) as the author's motivations. Insofar as the story's author was a whistleblower drawing attention to teachers' abuse of their position, the headmaster made the whistleblower's action look irresponsible. The headman reported that the teachers had been so disappointed by the story that they were contemplating a withdrawal from their cooperation with the World Food Program. At a meeting with parents and chiefs, convened five days after the broadcast, the teachers had been asked not to lose their morale over the allegations. The author had merely written "from his or her head" without consulting these leaders who had gathered at the meeting. The headmaster enclosed a letter signed by the "chair lady" of the school's management committee, also reporting on the meeting and confirming that neither the committee nor the chiefs had any knowledge of the alleged abuse.

The editors with whom I discussed this rejoinder ignored the headmaster's closing sentence in which he requested that his refutation of "this fraudulent story" be broadcast. They seized on the headmaster's indirect admission that the teachers did use plates to eat the porridge meant for their pupils. The correction that the plates were not the teachers' own but had been given by the World Food Program caused some mirth among the editors, who retorted that if it was indeed teachers' responsibility to taste the porridge before it was given to children, they could have done so by using spoons instead of whole platefuls of food. This detail confirmed the editors' own sensibilities about the truth of the story, so much so that no one suggested an investigation of the claims in the original and the rejoinder. The headmaster, by contrast, advised the editors to research stories they received, because this author had "merely wanted to damage the reputation of others." Stories that were not researched, the headmaster told the editors, "bring confusion and hatred among people."

My conversations with the editors indicated that the headmaster's comments formed in their view a pattern, a set of dispositions and judgments that were all too familiar to them as assertions of inequality. The teachers who helped themselves to the food that was supposed to enhance their pupils' capacity to learn took their superiority for granted. The editors pointed out to me other instances of such assumed superiority in the headmaster's rejoinder, such as when he speculated that the author's jealousy derived from the teachers' status as the only ones working for the government in the village. Formal education appeared here as the basis for the distinction, an assertion of inequality in the extent of knowledge different persons could claim to possess (see Englund 2006: 89–90). It was only natural, the editors remarked, that such apparently superior beings would associate themselves with leaders in the village. The alleged support from chiefs and some parents did not, therefore, impress the editors, familiar as they were with stories from across the country implicating precisely these custodians of the common good in all manner of misconduct. It was, they thought, in the vested interest of the teachers and their local allies that they were the ones responsible for receiving and administering aid in the village.[24]

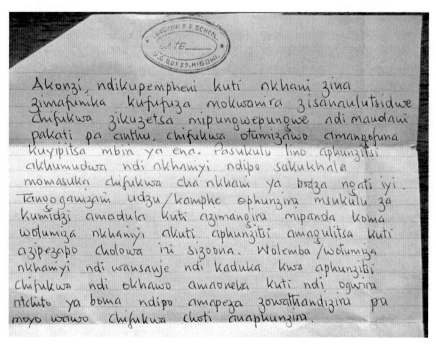

Fig. 5.3. An extract from the headmaster's rejoinder.

The alternative view on justice that informed both the original text and the editors' dismissal of the headmaster's rejoinder did not envision a complete overthrow of the order the headmaster sought to reassert. After all, the broadcast story reported that the abuse it described had caused disappointment among parents. No effort was made to cite or describe children's views on the alleged abuse. In this regard, the story bore little resemblance to those academic and activist perspectives that attach particular value to reproducing children's voices in their desire to advocate children's welfare and rights (see A. James 2007). Rather than using those voices as a rhetorical device, the story assumed the perspective of adults whose obligation it was to care for children. While highlighting teachers' abuse of their obligation, however, it by no means reduced children to mere pawns in a dispute between adults. Children appeared here different but equal in their subjection to obligation. The relief porridge, in point of fact, stood as a potent symbol for this obligation that tied children and adults together. Children's consumption of the porridge would have enhanced their capacity to learn, shifting to them, for its part, the onus of taking schooling seriously. It was their teachers' plunder of the relief porridge that subverted the obligation on which the hierarchical relationship depended.

The editors' views on this controversy illustrate, therefore, what constitutes both alternatives and equality in the ethos of *Nkhani Zam'maboma*. No blueprint of an alternative order animated their broadcast of the story and their dismissal of the rejoinder. The story alluded, rather, to a violation of the order in which obligations made persons mutually dependent. An alternative could thus be discerned within the inequality that the story exposed, and the editors were not inclined to provide ammunition for a discourse on "too much freedom," a conservative critique of the extent to which youths had turned against elders in the new individualistic human rights regime (see Englund 2006: 66–67). Precisely by broadcasting the concern of one set of adults (parents) over the actions of another set (teachers), the story and the editors who endorsed it asserted children as situated in relationships that could not afford the freedom of mutually independent individuals. Neither the humanitarian figures of purity untainted by adult intrigue and politics, nor the abstract and dehistoricized subjects of the rights of the child (Cheney 2007; Stephens 1995; see also Malkki and Martin 2003), children in this story served to remind listeners of equality as a condition of relationships.[25] In this vein, the complaint about the work children performed for teachers did not condemn child labor as such.[26] The contentious issue was due reward for work, denied in this case by the teachers' exclusive claim on the income the children had generated. The headmaster's patronizing comments would have erased what was news about the predicament, namely the teachers' dependence on their pupils.

Serving the Government, Serving the Public

Apart from creatively modifying the contents of received stories and giving rejoinders short shrift, editorial interventions also involved rejecting submitted stories. *Nkhani Zam'maboma* received more stories than it was possible to broadcast, and in many cases the reasons for rejection were obvious enough. The submitted story was either written in such poor language that no editor could discern an interesting angle to it, or it was so clearly motivated by a personal vendetta that no one in the newsroom wanted to proceed with it. It was, however, politics in its narrow sense of *ndale*, party-political intrigue and deceit, that represented the least desirable topic for editors. In my sample of stories, a finding corroborated by my perusal of the program's archives, politicians or parties were virtually never mentioned. An exception was a story that had been broadcast before the presidential and general elections in 2004.[27] It reported that the police had arrested two teachers in a rural area for putting pressure on people not to vote for the United Democratic Front. The story declared that the National Democratic Alliance, then a rival to the ruling party, "had sent the two teachers to sow confusion" (*chinatumiza aphunzitsi awiriwo kukachita zosokonezazo*). A note at the end of the transcript, not read out during the broadcast, revealed its unusual source—the story was a press release from the Ministry of Information.

The editors of *Nkhani Zam'maboma* were usually able to fend off politicians and politically appointed civil servants who wanted to interfere with the program, including the MBC's own management. Although these authorities could, as has been seen, place items in the official news bulletin, they rarely took interest in *Nkhani Zam'maboma*. Editors carefully cultivated a non-political profile for the program and were, as such, able to address a wider range of issues pertaining to inequality and injustice than would have been possible on a program loyal to the ruling party. The youngest of the program's regular editors had joined the MBC in 1995, while the other editors had begun to serve it in the 1970s and 1980s. They had, therefore, seen enough regime change both inside the MBC and in Malaŵi to be wary of expressing their own political preferences. Such wariness, as was seen in chapter 1, had become a part of the institutional culture at the MBC, particularly among those journalists who did not harbor politically motivated promotions. Serving the government, which they defined as their mission, was thus entirely compatible with a sense of serving the public that supplied stories for *Nkhani Zam'maboma*. Non-partisanship, all editors insisted to me in English during my fieldwork, was essential to the program, because only it could guarantee a wide public. "Many people listen to *Nkhani Zam'maboma*" (*anthu ambiri amamvera Nkhani Zam'maboma*), a senior editor pointed out to me, explaining that partisanship would have alienated some listeners. In other words, just as their notion of the government had little to do with the incumbents in political office, so too was their notion of the public one that encompassed, even as it acknowledged, differences within the nation's body politic.

In spite of their success in defending the independence of *Nkhani Zam'maboma* against the management and politicians, the very public that editors cherished did include elements that attempted to get party-political stories on the air.[28] One story submitted in 2008, despite its inelegant presentation, was rather cunning in its appropriation of the imagery and idioms that were seen by many to characterize the program (see figure 5.4).[29] "Makiyolobasi must stop bewitching at night," its headline cried, using the name that the MBC had, in 2007, coined for the former president Muluzi as the main character of *Makiyolobasi*, the new program of what the management called "political cartoons"

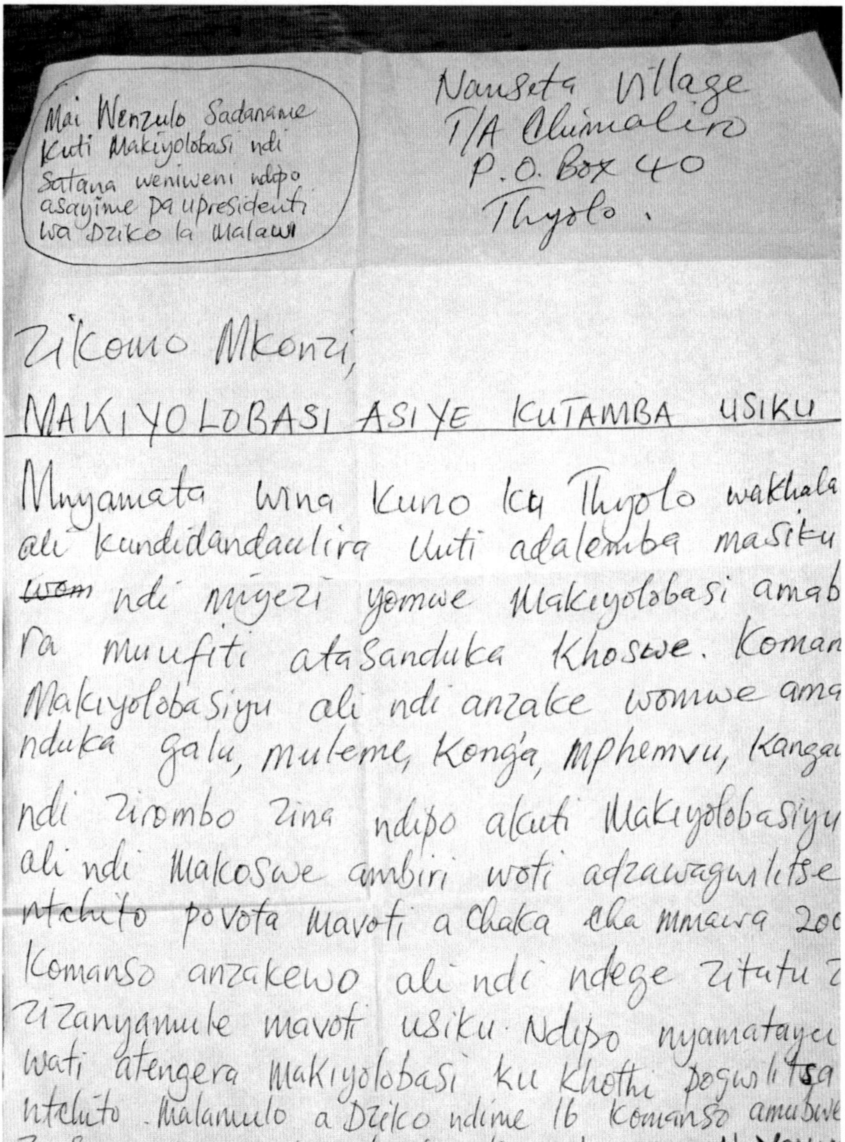

Mai Wenzulo Sadanawe
Kuti Makiyolobasi ndi
Satana weniweni ndipo
asayime pa upresidenti
wa Dziko la Malawi

Nanseta Village
T/A Chimaliro
P.O. Box 40
Thyolo .

Zikomo Mkonzi,

MAKIYOLOBASI ASIYE KUTAMBA USIKU

Mnyamata wina kuno ku Thyolo wakhala
ali kundidandaulira kuti adalemba masiku
~~wam~~ ndi miyezi yomwe Makiyolobasi amab
ra munfiti atasanduka khoswe. Koman
Makiyolobasiyu ali ndi anzake womwe ama
nduka galu, muleme, Konga, Mphemvu, Kangai
ndi zirombo zina ndipo akuti Makiyolobasiyu
ali ndi Makoswe ambiri woti adzawagulitse
ntchito povota mavoti a Chaka Cha mnawa 200
Komanso anzakewo ali ndi ndege zitatu z
uzanyamule mavoti usiku. Ndipo nyamatayu
wati atengera Makiyolobasi ku Khothi pogwilitsa
ntchito. Malamulo a Dziko ndime 16 Komanso amubwe
Zonse wawononga ta ~~wotu~~ sa ake . Ine MC H.YOVIYe

Fig. 5.4. "Makiyolobasi must stop bewitching at night."

(see chapter 3). The story claimed that a young man in Thyolo District had seen Makiyolobasi coming to the area as a rat. Makiyolobasi's companions, moreover, were said to be able to change into dogs, bats, and cockroaches, among other animals, and this shape-shifting was associated with fraud in the coming presidential and parliamentary elections. The story alleged that Makiyolobasi would use a large number of rats during the elections, apparently to steal votes, which would then be transported elsewhere at night by three aircraft. The young man was reported to have warned that he would take Makiyolobasi to court and even return to him the affliction he had caused in others. The story also included a note endorsing what the chair of a women's organization in the ruling party had allegedly said: Makiyolobasi was "a real Satan" who should not be a presidential candidate again.

On the face of it, the story carried themes and allusions that were popularly seen as recurrent features of stories on *Nkhani Zam'maboma*. As has been seen, reports on people changing into rats and cockroaches were common in stories that exposed theft and other forms of illicit wealth creation. The story also effortlessly combined an appeal to the rule of law with the use of Makiyolobasi's sinister methods to return to him the affliction he had inflicted on others.[30] As such, it suggested a condition familiar to many Malawians, whose life-worlds were infused with apparently separate domains, such as law and witchcraft. Above all, the story appeared conducive to the current preferences of the MBC's management and its party-political masters. Not only did it prove that Makiyolobasi had become a household name in Malawi, it also seemed to provide a suitably idiomatic critique of the former president's maneuvers. Based in Thyolo, the current president's home district, its author could also be assumed to be particularly loyal to the current ruling party, if not its official.

An expression of disgust visited the senior editor's face when I observed him reading the letter. Without saying a word, he compressed it in his palms and sent it flying into the nearest garbage container. When I questioned him about his action, he reiterated what I had heard before about non-partisanship. A tone of annoyance colored his voice when he explained that any story showing bias to one or the other politician or political party would divide (*kugaŵa*) the public listening to *Nkhani Zam'maboma*, probably resulting in a diminished listenership. Although he did not discuss the letter or his decision with his colleagues, it was unlikely that he was particularly concerned about a reprisal. He and other editors of *Nkhani Zam'maboma* had already commented on the management's new programs in the newsroom when others were present. At once temperate and caustic, their comments often conveyed thinly veiled relief that the new programs were not the responsibility of the Department of News and Current Affairs. Programs such as *Makiyolobasi*, editors told me, had as their purpose "to damage the reputation of those in opposition" (*kuyipitsa mbiri ya otsutsa boma*). Editors considered the new programs an affront to the professionalism of serving the government and the public. They did not, in other words, participate in the rhetoric that I heard the deputy director general use to justify *Makiyolobasi* as a service to the public. He thought the new programs held Malaŵian politicians accountable through humor and investigative journalism, begging the question of why only opposition politicians were subjected to such treatment. By refusing to allocate time for stories about politicians of any persuasion, the editors of *Nkhani Zam'maboma* signaled a clear break with such expediency and reserved the program for a remarkably wide-ranging exploration of problems with power and authority.

The references to witchcraft, such as the capacity of some human beings to change into animals, did not influence the senior editor's decision to reject the letter. As discussed in more detail in the next chapter, the editors' desire to verify stories did not take issue with the reality of witchcraft. Rather, their procedures of verification assumed that the source of stories lay in personal knowledge, their truth a function of not so much accurate details as the willingness of some persons to present themselves as the source. A similar appreciation of personal knowledge informed the editors' sense of objectivity. However high-handed their interventions might seem, a commitment to the truth (*choona*) was key to their own understanding of their work. The appeal to non-partisanship expressed this objectivity as a need to cultivate and convey the diversity of the program's public. It was, like any public, an imagined public, its composition no less subject to editorial authorship than the very stories it supplied. Partisan voices were excised from this imagined public, as were those perspectives that contradicted the editors' interest in highlighting abuse and injustice. It was ultimately the editors' own personal knowledge of rights and wrongs in their world that determined what constituted news worth broadcasting in *Nkhani Zam'maboma*. Having seen what partisanship could do to journalism and the country, editors served the kinds of government and public their moral imagination invoked.

From Imagined Publics to Public Journalism?

Editorial interventions indicated the editors' sense of ownership of the program, in spite of the official stance that its stories were broadcast in virtually the same form as they were received. The idea of exposure, with its disciplinary effects, was central to the editors' commitment to the program. The appeal of this idea was inseparable from the life-worlds they shared with their listeners, and injustices within the MBC itself made *Nkhani Zam'maboma* all the more precious as an outlet. However, a brief comparison with human rights activism and the movement of public journalism clarifies further what might have been at issue in the editors' engagement with the injustices they broadcast.

After the transition to multiparty democracy, many human rights activists in Malaŵi adopted an approach that built on the entrenched habits of developmentalism. Even if their dissemination of human rights messages deployed the rhetoric of participation, activists announced themselves as the vanguard of a new era, inviting the so-called grassroots to participate in what they had defined as the human rights agenda. By contrast, editors at the MBC found in *Nkhani Zam'maboma* a mode of engagement that arose from an involvement in, rather than a separation from, the life-worlds of Malaŵi's impoverished majority. As such, the idioms and concerns they broadcast needed no participatory rhetoric to be understood, associated as they were with the material and moral quandaries that were at the heart of Malaŵians' preoccupations. Most importantly, *Nkhani Zam'maboma* achieved its status as an alternative to the mainstream talk about human rights and politics precisely because it did not announce itself as an alternative. The impact on the imagination of alternatives was more subtle, more organic, than in those approaches in which activists came as outsiders to assist their assumed beneficiaries.[31]

It follows that the anthropological literature that has examined the use of mass media in activist work may not be especially illuminating in this context. It has described various collaborative projects between anthropologists and disadvantaged populations in which the media, whether by anthropologists or by the local collaborators they have trained, has been harnessed to make claims in public arenas (see, e.g., Ginsburg 1993 and 2002; McLagan 2002; Prins 2002; T. Turner 2002). While this body of scholarly activism has typically found its collaborators among minorities or marginalized groups, *Nkhani Zam'maboma* represented a very different modality of mass-mediated engagement with injustice. Not only did it address the Malaŵian public as a whole, making injustice seem a universal possibility in relationships. It also involved the possibility of imagining a more symbiotic relationship between media professionals and their public than is often the case in collaborative projects between anthropologists and their interlocutors.

By the same token, it may not be accurate to view *Nkhani Zam'maboma* as belonging to the so-called public or civic journalism movement that has spread from the United States during the past decades (see e.g., Glasser 1999; Haas 2007). This movement's historical roots lie in the 1920s, in the contrast between Walter Lippmann's (1922, 1925) elitist, expert-based model of democracy and John Dewey's (1927) argument that journalism could play a pivotal role in bringing about an active, deliberative public. From a 1940s report on a "free and responsible press" (Hutchins Commission 1947) to more recent debates on deliberative democracy (see chapter 2), public journalism has been influenced by a desire to make the public active citizens. For journalists, as one advocate has put it, the injunction has been to engage "citizens as active partners in the newsmaking process" (Iggers 1998: 149), with a view to making journalism more responsive to the actual concerns among its various publics. Discontent with election reporting, among some journalists no less than the public, made public journalism assume the shape of a movement from the late 1980s onward in the United States. Apart from staging voter-candidate encounters and focus group discussions to identify issues that concern the electorate, its initiatives, many localized but some national, have also included special reporting assignments and efforts to facilitate public debates between citizens and experts (see, e.g., Charity 1995; Dinges 2000; Sirianni and Friedland 2001).

While *Nkhani Zam'maboma* hardly fits into public journalism's aspirations, some of the movement's organizing assumptions have already been questioned in academic and journalistic discussions. For example, communitarianism has been noted to hamper the pursuit of public journalism, the assumption that a sense of the common good can evolve through public deliberation (see, e.g., Haas 2007: 34–40; Glasser 1999: 10–12; Schudson 1999: 126–131). Drawing on Nancy Fraser's (1992) critique of the Habermasian ideas of the public sphere, these critics have pointed out how the movement's inadequate theorizing of inequality has resulted in the untenable assumption that citizens occupy a bounded geographical territory and are therefore potentially united by shared interests and values. Underlying this assumption is a distorted theory of the public, leading one critic to declare that "communities are not publics" (Schudson 1999: 131). While some have argued that public journalism's search for a common ground actually narrows rather than widens the range of public discourse (Corrigan 1999: 172), others have taken the unusual step of asking what public journalism might actually look like if it was viewed from outside of the Euro-American context.[32] The findings have not, however, been altogether reassuring. Surveying instances of public journalism in Africa, Asia, and South America, Tanni Haas noted that "one would expect the participating news organizations to have assumed a much more activist, journalistic stance, including by focusing attention on problems of particular concern to the most marginalized segments of the citizenry" (2007: 127).

The reason for Haas's disappointment was too close a resemblance between American and non-American public-journalism initiatives, a condition that could be explained by the source of their funding. For Malaŵi, Haas (2007: 125) mentioned radio listening clubs as examples of public journalism. As an aspect of the so-called community radio, listening clubs have, as was seen in chapter 1, presented few actual challenges to gendered and technocratic biases in Malaŵi's public life. Perhaps a better example of public journalism in a Malaŵian context occurred when the Zodiak Broadcasting Station renovated a rural health clinic as a response to rural poverty.[33] However, a deeper problem may lie in the very association of public journalism with activist and developmentalist interventions. Haas assumed that by "working directly with nongovernmental organizations" (2007: 127), journalists outside Euro-American contexts could have achieved more innovative forms of public journalism. Yet it was precisely by making such a sharp break from the entrenched habits of human rights NGOs that *Nkhani Zam'maboma* engaged the moral imagination of its editors and listeners. Rather than posing as the vanguard leading the public away from ignorance and human rights violations, editors saw a continuity between their life-world and that of their imagined public, neither of which was exempted from the scandals of poverty and injustice.

The specific character of *Nkhani Zam'maboma* appears even more clearly if it is contrasted with the refined public journalism that some critics have proposed. Haas urged journalists to "help citizens reflect on their different, and potentially conflicting, concerns" (2007: 37). Journalists could do so "by making salient social inequalities the very subject matter (or focal point) of public deliberation" (Haas 2007: 37). While this proposal appears to be an improvement over the communitarianism of earlier public journalism, its sense of what requires revelation—what ought to make the news—is different from the editors' approach to the stories they received for *Nkhani Zam'maboma*. Haas wrote within a Euro-American mindset in which persons are thought to be born equal, a constitutional and ideological complex that masks the inequalities that public journalists should uncover. By contrast, inequalities permeate Malaŵian life-worlds, from the hierarchies associated with gender and age to the widespread exploitation of workers and children. Here equality as a condition of relationships is a discovery, claims arising from it can become news and a revelation of a different way in which persons might be involved in each other's lives.

It is important to pause on this ethos of equality that insists on a relationship, mutual dependence, between persons. Another perspective on equality gained momentum in Malaŵi after the transition to multiparty democracy, with human rights activists and democratic politicians spreading the news of freedom (*ufulu*) as something everyone was born with. Their emphasis was on rights as the inalienable, defining possessions of autonomous individuals. As news, it was no less startling and engaging than the ethos of equality broadcast on *Nkhani Zam'maboma*. However, the popularity of *Nkhani Zam'maboma*, among both its editors and listeners, can be explained precisely by its more compelling, and more consequential, view on equality as a condition of relationships. Human rights activists and democratic politicians became "pedagogues of progress" in Rancière's (2004: 223) terms, the ones who made equality a goal to be pursued, thereby making it ever more elusive as an aspect of life. By contrast, whether it was a woman demanding her abusive husband to restore her virginity or parents concerned about teachers' plunder of relief food, the perspectives afforded by *Nkhani Zam'maboma* made apparent mutually constitutive obligations between sharply unequal subject positions. At issue was not a communitarian view on obligations as the guarantee of communal harmony. By taking abuse, violation, and conflict as its point of departure, *Nkhani Zam'maboma* made obligations seem as contentious as they were inevitable in human relationships.

6

Stories Become Persons

Producing Knowledge about Injustice

From semi-literates to academics, Malaŵians were generally familiar with *Nkhani Zam'maboma*. Although the regularity with which they followed the program varied greatly, virtually everyone I knew was able to discuss it with me. While many could cite its stories about witchcraft and errant authorities, some were unaware that the sources of those stories lay in letters, telephone calls, faxes, and e-mails from listeners.[1] One university lecturer, for example, explained to me that from time to time some areas would emerge as what he called "hot spots," locations where several incidents took place within a short span of time. Others assumed that the MBC's network of reporters across the country supplied stories. What was remarkable about these perceptions was not so much their lack of accuracy as their expectation that the MBC could alone provide national coverage of localized stories. The expectation bespoke a residual faith in the broadcaster's remit to represent the nation, whatever frustrations these listeners felt over its biased and didactic approach to other programs. In actual fact, in spite of having offices and studios in the three regions of the country, the MBC had no means of gathering stories from villages and townships on a daily basis.[2] The frequent appearance of certain localities was a result of the frequent supply of stories from them.

Many listeners understood that *Nkhani Zam'maboma* did receive its stories from the public, and as the next chapter will show, for some locals a lack of stories from their area indicated pathological tendencies toward secrecy and deception. For the editors of *Nkhani Zam'maboma,* the reliance on the public presented the problem of which sources they should trust. The MBC's inability to use its own journalists to supply stories put the onus on sources themselves to verify them. As mentioned, the early practice of broadcasting personal names ended with the libel cases into which the MBC was dragged. Editors came to regard it essential that every story to be broadcast had a traceable source. In effect, the veracity of stories rested on personal knowledge, not on an investigation of factual elements by editors and other journalists. Even a story with the strangest sequence of events could be broadcast as long as a person stood by it. In the relation between a story and a person, moreover, the source's position as a protagonist, a witness, or an informant passing on reported accounts was less important than the source's identification with the story. For editors, persons and stories constituted each other.

The constitutive import of stories broadcast on *Nkhani Zam'maboma* could, as such, contribute to a source's local prominence. Some sources never sent more than one story, whereas for others editors used the English word "correspondents" to indicate their frequent supply of material for the program. Few of them had ever met the editors of *Nkhani Zam'maboma,* nor was the MBC able to give them monetary or other tangible rewards. As this chapter describes, however, the locally acknowledged position as a source for *Nkhani Zam'maboma* could be intimately linked to a person's overall standing in his or her locality. Correspondents often had unusual occupations or were strangers to the area. Their identification with stories about strange and deplorable conduct was a tightrope stretched between the threat of ostracism and the respect due to those whose prerogative it was to facilitate other people's claims.

The emphasis on free access to information in both conventional liberal journalism and human rights reporting, by contrast, separates information from its sources. Information is assumed to exist as facts and events that are independent of anyone narrating them. By the same token, the well-being of citizens hinges on the extent to which everyone is in the same position to assess those facts and events.[3] While the value of such assumptions for campaigns against repression is self-evident, their insight into actual journalistic practices may be limited. As Hasty has shown for both state (2005: 76–87) and private media (2005: 127–138) in Ghana, sources need to be cultivated for information to flow. Although the challenges the state and private media face in this regard are by no means the same, common to both is journalists' dependence on relationships with those who are able to impart intelligence, labeled variously as knowledge or rumor by others.[4] The way in which the editors of *Nkhani Zam'maboma* conflated information with its source, on the one hand, and practices in human rights reporting, on the other, presents a particularly illuminating contrast. Both drew on testimonies in order to obtain information, but they were driven by different understandings of the relationship between a testimony and an event. Testimony as personal knowledge can, therefore, reveal contrasting notions of personhood and knowledge.

This contrast may appear troubling to many, Malaŵians and non-Malaŵians, who discern in the editorial approach an invitation to supply rumor and gossip as news, accepted for broadcasting as long as someone agrees to act as their source. Yet although listeners questioned whether some stories were true (*zoona*), they rarely did so by doubting the feasibility of the events and actions recounted. Their concern was often remarkably similar to that of editors, namely the reliability of sources.[5] It was, in fact, this convergence of concerns among editors and listeners that made the program exceptional on Malaŵi's airwaves. At the same time, much as this convergence may defuse what observers find troubling in *Nkhani Zam'maboma,* the editorial interventions described in the previous chapter also cast some doubt over their loyalty to the testimonies they received. The doubt can be compounded by the very equality that the ethos of the program seemed to mediate. After all, it comes naturally to social scientists to greet every attempt at alternatives with deep-seated suspicion about new forms of subjection and power.[6] Are not the evocations of equality always pretexts for exercising power in even more insidious ways, beginning, in this instance, with editorial high-handedness? This line of thinking, potentially as prejudicial as it can be revealing, needs to be confronted in light of this chapter's observations on personal knowledge.

Verifying Persons

Some stories arrived in the newsroom with detailed instructions on how to broadcast them. Contributors demanded that personal names be broadcast, whereas others specifically requested that editors withhold any names. Yet others asked the MBC to broadcast a cluster of submitted stories together. Editors rarely paid attention to such requests and were consistent about withholding personal names from stories to be broadcast. Although their creative interventions could bring on air virtually any submitted story, editors were reluctant to consider stories that were too obviously motivated by the author's conflict with particular institutions or persons. One rejected story, for example, had the author as its main protagonist and reported her disappointment with her employer. The author had been forced to call the general emergency number to get transport to a hospital, because her employer refused to provide it. After profusely praising the author's propensity to work hard, the letter ended with the remark that no one from her workplace had come to see her in the hospital. In a similar vein, another rejected story complained that the author's father-in-law was in the habit of chasing his daughter's husbands away when they had economic difficulties. The same was about to happen to the author, the third man to marry the father-in-law's daughter.

Such contributions fulfilled editors' demand for traceable sources, because they did not have any qualms about inserting the author into the story. However, although the predicaments they described may well have provided material for *Nkhani Zam'maboma,* editors were in these cases discouraged by the vengeful tone of the authors. Within its ethos of equality, *Nkhani Zam'maboma* achieved a sense of news precisely by highlighting complexity and unexpected turns of events. In point of fact, many of its stories called for considerable doubt, not as skepticism disengaged from the conditions to which these stories spoke but as an integral aspect of those conditions. Witches, after all, were the greatest tricksters of all, confounding others by turning into animals, by defying the ordinary laws of velocity, or by confining their activities to a few hours at night when others were asleep. At the same time, witchcraft (*ufiti*) and magic (*matsenga*) could also be reduced to mere beliefs (*zikhulupiriro*) and, as such, subjected to ridicule. One broadcast story stated that children had been asked to prepare a chicken for a meal, but it ran away after its head had been cut off.[7] It appeared outside another house where a group of women were talking. The women dispersed in haste, believing that the headless chicken was a sign of misfortune (*malodza*). The children's parents refused to eat the chicken, but the story ended by quoting others who had observed that the incident was "not strange" (*si zachilendo*) and that the parents "were just scared without a reason" (*anangochita mantha zopanda pake*).

Doubt was, however, an underlying theme across the stories broadcast on *Nkhani Zam'maboma,* its ethos calling for constant vigilance against deceptive appearances. The exposure of gullibility did not, therefore, require objectifying witchcraft and magic as mere beliefs, because virtually every aspect of life was subject to the risk of deceit. Conversely, as was seen in chapter 3, witchcraft was usually integral to life-worlds, not a belief abstracted from them. It follows that stories about witches did not stand apart from other stories as a separate category demanding particularly rigorous procedures of verification. Stories that made no mention of witches or magic were liable to the same principle of verification as those that did. A story about a greedy pastor or an adulterous chief, for instance, was potentially as controversial as one about a grandmother bewitching a grandchild. Yet verification, as mentioned, was rarely based on an investigation of the details of a story. Crucially, editors put much weight on the integrity of their source, envisioning veracity as personal knowledge.

Two stories illustrate the criteria by which veracity was established and a decision on broadcasting made. Both describe the use of magic, but only one was accepted. The first story, which was rejected, was about a teenager and his parents in Blantyre District. The teenager did not obey his parents and often slept with his girlfriends away from home. His parents were anxious to improve his habits and found out about a healer in Mozambique. They obtained from him medicine they were instructed to put in the doorway of the boy's hut. When he stepped over the medicine to go out, he would change his habits at once. Unfortunately, the parents did not check whether the boy was inside the hut when they applied the medicine. He was out, and when he came back late at night, he stepped over the medicine as he was entering his hut. The consequence was very different from what the parents wanted—the boy changed into a small antelope called *gwape*. His mother discovered the misfortune in the morning, and the parents decided to return to the healer in Mozambique to ask for assistance. They locked the antelope in the hut, but another child went inside while they were away. Unaware of what had happened, the child was delighted to find the antelope and decided to surprise her parents when they returned from Mozambique. A pot of boiled antelope meat awaited the parents, who could only cry in despair, "You have killed a human being!" (*munapha munthu!*).

This story failed to go on air not because its details were considered fantastic but because its source could not be traced. The editors tried to call the number that the source had given, but no one there recognized the source or the story. The editors' suspicions began to mount when they realized that although the location of the story was not far from where they lived and worked, they had not heard anything about it. Under normal circumstances, stories on *Nkhani Zam'maboma* were local knowledge already before they were broadcast. By contrast, another story that came to the editors' attention at about the same time was accepted despite its equally startling details. Here a man work-ing for a known company in the city of Blantyre was in the habit of spending his lunch hour in the Capital Hotel of Lilongwe city, over 300 miles from Blantyre. He flew the distance in five minutes and always made sure to leave the Capital Hotel at 12:45 in order to be in Blantyre at 12:50, in good time before the lunch hour ended. Weary of his colleagues' skepticism, he once offered to take one of them with him. He advised the colleague to hold tight to the host's collar and to close his eyes. When he asked the colleague to open his eyes, they were in the Capital Hotel, ready to enjoy a good lunch. The two men did this on four days, but on the fifth day the guest made the mistake of opening his eyes while they were flying. He immediately crashed to the ground somewhere in Ntcheu District, midway between Blantyre and Lilongwe. He spent two months in the district hospital of Ntcheu, where a nurse called his company to inform them about their hospitalized employee.

What convinced the editors about this story was the fact that an employee of a known company volunteered the information. A telephone number or an address, and preferably both, had to accompany submissions to *Nkhani Zam'ma-boma,* and if the source of a story could not be traced, its chances of being broadcast were slim. Veracity did not, in other words, inhere in the details of a story that could be ascertained independently of those who presented them-selves as informants. From the editors' point of view, personal knowledge was essential to establishing the credentials of a story. Here is what distinguished the news on *Nkhani Zam'maboma* from both rumors (*mphekesera*) and lies (*mabodza*)—an identifiable source who was usually from the same locality as the protagonists themselves, if not one of them. In most cases, editors did not have resources to do more than check whether the number was for the person mentioned as the source.[8] Yet this procedure of matching stories with specific persons was more than an attempt to find out if the source was a liar. Editors understood personal knowledge to be a function of the source's relationships that editors had neither resources nor any need to trace.

The relational nature of personal knowledge became particularly appar-ent in editors' reflections on why they would ever trace the source after his or her story had been broadcast. A traceable source, editors pointed out to me, was necessary to counter any legal action a story might provoke. Although it never happened during fieldwork, a court case would have, in the editors' view, required the source to account for the details of his or her story. They recog-nized that it would have entailed the source to summon, whether in a further narrative or in person, others who could have corroborated the details. Stories were, in other words, products of particular relational and often localized circumstances. Their sources did not stand apart from them as autonomous individuals carrying out detached observation of events but as persons entangled in the very relationships that gave stories their course. In this regard, it mattered little to editors what, if any, role the source played in the story. Even if the source had obtained it through other people's reports, it was the source's burden to hold those others to account if needed. Too much involvement in a story could, as has been seen, dissuade editors from broadcasting it, such as when the story attempted to do little else than generate sympathy for the source personally.

Testimonial Truth

The editors' principle of verification was, in effect, based on a view that regarded submitted stories as testimonies. Contributors engaged in a testimonial practice in which they stood by their stories as the ones responsible for their veracity and accuracy. Testimonies here were not, however, the individual property of those who delivered them. Because editors did not consider contributors to be lone, detached observers, testimonies were seen to arise from complex relationships informing their generation. The above notes on what this principle of verification indicates about personhood are worth developing further, not least for the perspective they afford on the conundrum of equality in the production of stories for *Nkhani Zam'maboma*. In this regard, the issue of personhood in the program's testimonial practices is profitably contrasted with ideas in the reporting on human rights violations. Beyond the assumptions of objectivity and transparency in human rights monitoring lie the more intriguing deployment of testimonies as sources of insight into violations. The sophistication and criticism of so-called truth commissions, in particular, deserve careful consideration in order to bring out the specific features of testimonial truth in *Nkhani Zam'maboma*.

A training manual on human rights monitoring, published in Malaŵi by a prominent local human rights NGO, indicates how the process of generating information can be represented as taking place outside relationships (CHRR n.d.). In its chapter 7, entitled "Information Gathering," the manual insists that "information should be consistent with material collected from independent sources" (CHRR n.d.: 15). On the basis of on-site visits and interviews, the human rights monitor is expected to arrive at an independent evaluation of the situation, establishing facts after a painstaking and wide-ranging investigation.

Much as the monitor may aim at "developing contacts and establishing a presence in the community" (CHRR n.d.: 12), he or she remains qualitatively independent of any relationship, alone able to traverse the distance between victims, government officials, and NGOs. Indeed, "techniques to corroborate the direct testimony of victims and eyewitnesses" must be applied to mitigate "the perspective or bias of a witness" (CHRR n.d.: 16). In other words, violations occur and can be represented as though they were unaffected by the perspective anyone took on them.

These principles of information gathering have undoubtedly contributed to assisting numerous subjects whose lives have been harmed or ruined by various sorts of violence. Yet although no one expected *Nkhani Zam'maboma* to participate in human rights reporting, its engagement with representing the adverse consequences of poverty and injustice certainly put it on a par with activists' efforts to generate public awareness of violations. The contrast between the two modes of knowledge production is clear already in the origins of the manual quoted above. It has nothing particularly Malawian about it, having been compiled by the NGO on the basis of the training manual produced by the United Nation's High Commissioner for Human Rights.[9] As such, it emerged from a transnational regime of human rights activism whose particular approach to knowledge production and reporting has already been subject to anthropological critique. For example, Colombian activists wishing to address officials in the United States "were instructed to be extremely concise and to present linear narratives focused on specific incidents" (Tate 2007: 121). They were, therefore, "trained in certain kinds of human rights narratives" (Tate 2007: 122), a symptom of a wider difficulty in human rights reporting. Richard Wilson (1997) identified it as decontextualization, the way in which human rights reporting tended to abstract victims from their family and class backgrounds. Such a "universal decontextualized individual" (Wilson 1997: 148) required, in his view, a good amount of anthropological contextualization to convey the richness of subjectivities and the complexity of social relationships.

Marilyn Strathern's (2004: 228–233) response to Wilson's argument seemed to criticize what anthropologists should never question in the first place, namely the value of contextualization itself. Yet Strathern's concern was to recover the complexity of relationships from the status of mere background to which both human rights activists and their anthropological interlocutors had relegated it. What Strathern had in mind was "another order, another perspective altogether" (2004: 231) that relationships provided when juxtaposed with human rights reporting. The juxtaposition was, in effect, between different kinds of description, because rather than simply decontextualizing victims, human rights reporting actually re-described persons. The way in which contextualization has become an issue in human rights reporting lends urgency to Strathern's intervention. The training manual that the Malaŵian NGO had obtained from the United Nations, for example, included an injunction to "understand the context" (CHRR n.d.: 6), said to encompass people, history, governmental structure, culture, customs, language, and so on. Patently, the penchant of anthropologists for contextualization needs to be rethought when the idea of context gets harnessed in this way, "people" themselves becoming a context for the violations activists seek to uncover and document.[10]

This appropriation of critical ideas indicates a productive dynamic between human rights talk and anthropology (see Goodale 2009), and a further challenge is presented by those human rights regimes that have moved from fact-finding to truth-telling as a key mode of exploring and addressing past violations. By drawing on testimonies, they seem to acknowledge that in some situations independent, detached inquiry may not yield as much insight as complex personal narratives do. Yet scholarly critics, notably in the case of South Africa's Truth and Reconciliation Commission, have been swift to point out the effects of genre and convention on this apparently more sophisticated form of human rights reporting.[11] One critical observation concerns the perpetuation of inequalities within the commission's egalitarian predilections. All hearings adhered to a common structure and the principle of equal opportunity to be heard, but in practice witnesses were bound to have unequal narrative skills in relation to the conditions and requirements of the emerging genre (Blommaert et al. 2007: 40). Such unrecognized differences in communicative competence made commissioners disqualify aspects of some testimonies as meaningless or trivial, narrowing down what could be officially heard during the hearings. The problem was compounded by the confines of the roles assigned to some witnesses. Women's testimonies, for example, could go against the grain of what the conventions both inside and outside the commission expected, such as when their experiences went beyond the parameters of motherhood or the individualized victimhood of sexual violation (Ross 2003 and 2007). Testimony was not, as such, "a neutral act" but was made "from positions in which the speaker [was] situated within intersecting and conflicting conventions" (Ross 2007: 103).

Testimony as narrative practice can thus enrich human rights reporting and yet be constrained by its pragmatic, moral, and legal imperatives. In a broader intellectual framework, testimonies and other narratives are co-authored by the speaker and those involved in his or her life, not best understood as finished products (see Ricoeur 1991). Anthropologists have long been interested in exploring how persons are constituted by narratives (Ochs and Capps 2001). Treating both written and oral configurations of words as texts, Karin Barber has recently argued that "texts do not need to be (apparently) descriptive or (apparently) confessional to yield insights into personhood. They yield such insights above all because they help to *constitute* personhood, and because they shed light on *how* it is constituted through their use of language" (2007: 107; emphases in original). Dissociating her argument from the view that human relationships exist only as or in texts, Barber points out how the operations of "word culture" no less than "material culture" can constitute persons.[12] Editors' verification of stories submitted to *Nkhani Zam'maboma* appeared to admit as much, each story understood to be a co-authored text of intersecting lives outside the editors' own purview.

The practice of testimonial truth in *Nkhani Zam'maboma* should not be confused with the ideas of participation and collaboration, so central to current trends in journalism that is committed to social justice. Those experiments with community radio in rural Africa, for example, that have subscribed to the methods and tenets of Participatory Rural Appraisal have inevitably become entangled in managing "two bodies of knowledge" (Ilboudo 2000: 57)—of scientists and technocrats on one hand, and of peasants, on the other. When "a margin of imprecision" (Ilboudo 2000: 57) has been attributed to the knowledge of peasants, an implicit hierarchy between the orders of knowledge has been signaled within the rhetoric of participation and collaboration.[13] The editors of *Nkhani Zam'maboma* may not have been forthright about their own authorial aspirations, but they never denied hierarchical difference in their views on verification. Testimonial truth as personal knowledge assumed a gap between editors and their sources. Like stringers supplying Hindi newspapers in India with local stories (see Rao 2010; Ståhlberg 2002), regular contributors to *Nkhani Zam'maboma* could enjoy the status of indispensable conduits of information among both editors and locals. Though not paid like these stringers, they could become vital nodes in the networks that generated the program's public.

Becoming a Correspondent

Regular contributors, whom editors called correspondents, were persons who often had a particular license to supply stories to *Nkhani Zam'maboma*. The very regularity with which they sent stories to the MBC marked them out in the localities where they lived. Although personal names were not mentioned in the broadcast stories, locals usually had little trouble figuring out who the protagonists were. The same applied to correspondents, who rarely even attempted to keep their identities secret, hoping thereby to gain access to more stories. Being a correspondent for *Nkhani Zam'maboma* was, therefore, an ambiguous condition, a position from which to expose other people's scandals and to gain some local renown as an associate of a popular and respected national radio program. This ambiguity was key to the way in which submissions to *Nkhani Zam'maboma* constituted correspondents as persons. Their output of stories made it unlikely that they were themselves protagonists, but their contributions put them into somewhat different relationships with editors and locals. For editors, by reporting on incidents involving others, they became a part of the stories as the guarantors of their veracity and accuracy. For locals, the ambiguity of their position was more acute, imbued variously with truth-telling and backbiting.

Such ambiguity befitted those whose standing in the locality was out of the ordinary. Many correspondents during fieldwork were relative strangers in the areas where they lived, brought there by their work as schoolteachers, farm managers, agricultural advisers, and so on. While some correspondents appeared to be in a more transitory state than others, common to all to whom I spoke was a commitment to a form of accurate reporting that would spare them the experience of shame (*manyazi*). They feared complaints reaching the MBC, which would have jeopardized their chances of getting more stories on the air. The fear of shame influenced their dealings with both editors and locals. Stories had to be public enough locally for them to venture to write them down. Many correspondents claimed to investigate (*kufufuza*) stories before sending them to the MBC. By doing so they also generated a local audience for themselves that would defuse any charge of betrayal or deception unleashed by protagonists. The generation of such an audience could also be instrumental to qualifying their status as strangers with truth-telling, thereby allowing for an expansion of their relationships and, as a concomitant, their personhood.

Because I consider a correspondent's local situation more closely later in this chapter, it is instructive to discuss here the ways in which the relationships between correspondents and editors could also have mutually constitutive aspects. Editors could not offer a firm definition of the criteria, beyond the perceived regularity of submissions, by which they called some contributors correspondents. However, correspondents had different patterns and paces of submission that made some quiescent for a while and others very active for a relatively short period. While no one had stayed with the program from its inception in 1998, some correspondents had been sending stories for years, whereas the majority of them appeared to carry on with this work for only a few weeks or months. The status of a correspondent was not formalized by the MBC and involved, as mentioned, no official remuneration or other tangible benefits. The reward was, however, often apparent in correspondents' imagination of their own status, such as when a farm manager living in Kasungu District added to his handwritten stories the letterhead "Mtunthama News" to indicate the area where they came from. It was as though he had proceeded a step further from the status of a correspondent to that of a news agency.

Many correspondents established some familiarity with particular editors without ever meeting them in person. Some sent their photographs to the newsroom, but many correspondents also had access to mobile telephones, which they used to communicate with editors even when they had no stories to deliver.[14] Each correspondent tended to have a specific editor whom they contacted. It was revealing to observe how the demeanor of editors differed when they received a telephone call from an unknown source and from a correspondent familiar to them. Although new callers received a curt response focused on the details of a story, correspondents' calls often prompted good-humored exchange of gossip and personal news. They would share information on problems (*mavuto*) in each other's lives, and occasionally an understanding would emerge that one or the other was in need of some material assistance. The editor was almost invariably the recipient of such assistance. For example, I witnessed how one editor bemoaned to a correspondent his financial difficulties to arrange transport for his daughter to return home from her boarding school. After this telephone call and some subsequent text messages, the correspondent, a businessman living far away from both the editor and his daughter's school, sent M.K.2000 (U.S.$14) into the editor's bank account. Both confirmed to me after a few weeks that the editor had paid the amount back to the correspondent.

Such gestures were known as assistance (*chithandizo*) in the newsroom, never subject to intimations of bribes (*ziphuphu*) taking place to secure stories on the air. They were material aspects of the everyday familiarity that characterized a range of relationships in which both editors and correspondents were involved. Correspondents were aware of the MBC's financial crises, including the delays in the payment of salaries, and as people with some earnings, they could often be in a better financial position than editors. Although the gestures of assistance indicated a measure of compassion in the relationship, they did not seem to influence editorial decisions. Nor did most correspondents expect that they would—they understood the editors' duty to broadcast stories from different parts of the country, and their conversations with editors often nuanced their insights into the making of the program. Editors and correspondents were entangled in "multiplex associations" (see Gluckman 1965: 173) in which broadcasting was only one element in increasingly personal exchanges.

Editors reserved to themselves the prerogative to revise correspondents' stories, as they did with any stories submitted to *Nkhani Zam'maboma*. This, too, seemed to arouse little consternation among correspondents, largely because in their cases editorial interventions were seldom as radical as those described in the previous chapter. Indeed, for a person to become a regular contributor, he or she had to embrace key aspects of the ethos and linguistic conventions of *Nkhani Zam'maboma*. This observation is all the more significant when it is recognized that correspondents were by no means the poorest of the people who submitted stories, some of whom, editors suspected, were prevented by the cost of postage to become regular contributors. Despite their access to mobile telephones, correspondents were not affluent either, located as they often were in deprived rural areas. Yet their regular income and relative newness also set them apart from locals, a condition that could have given rise to patronizing views. As has been seen, teaching and other occupations correspondents had were not universally conducive to the ethos of *Nkhani Zam'maboma*. Correspondents were, like editors themselves, those who went against the grain of their apparent advantage in a country beset by severe poverty and facilitated, for their part, the imagination of alternatives to the status quo.

The Growth of a Correspondent

The personal knowledge on which submissions to *Nkhani Zam'maboma* depended cannot be adequately understood through the generalities mentioned thus far. While correspondents tended to stand out from others in their localities, the precise ways in which their association with *Nkhani Zam'maboma* shaped their local standing were diverse, influenced by correspondents' differences in employment, age, gender, and affinal and other ties in the areas from where they supplied stories. A comprehensive investigation of this diversity would have required me to travel the length and breadth of the country, because correspondents were located in several districts across Malaŵi's three regions. Interested in various other aspects of the program's production and reception, I could do no more than conduct interviews with correspondents by telephone and observe in some detail the daily activities of one of them. The reason why I chose to work with a correspondent living in Mchinji District in the Central Region bordering Zambia, several hundred miles from the MBC's newsroom in Blantyre, was his friendship with the editor who had also become my closest companion in the newsroom. His circumstances and aspirations provide one perspective on the manifold local and trans-local relationships in which the supply of stories was embedded.

Born James Umar in 1964 in Machinga District, he became Imran Umar in 1979 after undergoing the *jando* circumcision ritual customarily associated with the Yao. Being a Yao and a Muslim was central to his identity in Mkanda, a rural trading center in Mchinji where he had settled hundreds of miles from Machinga. He had adopted the title *shehe* (sheikh) and described himself as a teacher (*mphunzitsi*) in the small Muslim community of Chiyao-speaking traders and businessmen in Mkanda.[15] The poverty of his accommodation contrasted with the meticulous attention he paid to his own appearance, donning either a Muslim costume or smart clothes desired by most Malawian youths (see figures 6.1 and 6.2). When proudly walking in his Muslim gown and cap, he cut a striking figure in Mkanda, situated as it was in the heartland of Chewa and Nsenga smallholders and tobacco growers, the vast majority of whom swore allegiance to Christianity or the male secret society *gule wamkulu*. Umar had been sending stories from Mkanda to *Nkhani Zam'maboma* for over a year when I met him in 2008. His association with the program contributed to a complex set of local, national, and international pursuits he was involved in.

When I asked him when he had settled in Mkanda, he first gave the year, 1995, and then, without further prompting, added, "eleventh of November." His recollection of the actual date thirteen years later was consistent with his ambiguous standing in the area, at once a highly visible participant in its affairs and self-consciously different from its majority. Mkanda was not, however, the first destination in his migrant's career. In the mid-1980s, he spent a year in a secondary school in Southern Malawi where he was from, but he attributed it to his parents' early demise that he had no means of continuing the secular form of education. Instead, he found an opportunity for further studies in the Blantyre Islamic School that was funded and managed largely by Muslims of South Asian extraction. After graduation, he left Southern Malawi to work for the Lilongwe Islamic Movement as an itinerant teacher of Islam and an assistant in the movement's charitable projects. His first base in this capacity was in Salima District, followed by a stint in Nkhotakhota District, both along the

Fig. 6.1. Imran Umar outside his house.

Fig. 6.2. Imran Umar on Mkanda's main street.

shores of Lake Malaŵi, where most Chiyao-speakers in the Central Region live. It was in Nkhotakhota where he found his wife, and it had remained his only marriage when I met him. For reasons I could not verify, he decided to leave the Lilongwe Islamic Movement and continue independently as an Islamic teacher. Through earlier migrants from Machinga, he found in Mkanda a small mosque needing a leader, but his ambitions soon led him to develop multiple commitments related to political, charitable, and business activities.

Umar arrived in Mkanda when Malaŵi had been under Muluzi's rule for some eighteen months. A Yao Muslim from Machinga like Umar himself, Muluzi rarely emphasized the religious factor in his quest for wealth and power, but it was evident that he and his United Democratic Front enjoyed widespread support among the Yao populations of the Central and Southern Regions.[16] In the sharply divided political landscape, especially during Muluzi's two terms in office, vast areas of the Central Region appeared to be the strongholds of the Malaŵi Congress Party, previously the only party in the one-party state and then the main opposition party. Inroads into these strongholds were as desirable as they were difficult for both the United Democratic Front and the

Democratic Progressive Party, its successor as the ruling party after Mutharika became president in 2004.[17] Umar told me that he had acted as the United Democratic Front's link to Mkanda and had, among other things, received money "to buy people" (*kugula anthu*). He sounded proud when he explained that was exactly what he had done with the money, giving it to locals to encourage their support for the ruling party rather than embezzling it for his own purposes, such as buying iron sheets to replace the grass-thatched roof of the house he rented. This experience initiated a pattern by which he has sought to carve out a niche for himself in Mkanda as a contact with the government (*boma*). When Muluzi fell out with the incoming Christian president Mutharika, Umar thought that religious leaders (*atsogoleri achipembedzo*) were comparable to civil servants and chiefs. They were all supposed, in his own English expression, "to serve the government of today."[18]

Once while visiting Umar, I witnessed a car bearing the Malaŵi government license plate stopping at his house. The two casually dressed men who stepped out of it had come from Blantyre under instructions from Mutharika's office. They wanted to find out if enough interest could be garnered in the area for a well-attended public meeting with the president. The new ruling party's virtual absence from the area had made Umar a go-between, and he escorted the officials to the headquarters of the Traditional Authority responsible for the area. He had earlier shown me two letters he had received from Mutharika, both rather formulaic responses to the letters of congratulations Umar had sent him first on the occasion of Mutharika's nomination as a presidential candidate and then after his election victory in 2004. Umar's continued desire to be associated with the government made it necessary to distance himself from Muluzi, and it appears that the local network of United Democratic Front supporters evaporated with his shifting allegiances. For Umar himself, however, expediency did not drive his actions. His rhetoric of serving the government was similar to what the editors of *Nkhani Zam'maboma* expressed, but Umar faced the added challenge of negotiating a potentially hostile local scene. His comment that the area's long-serving Malaŵi Congress Party parliamentarian was a "good person" (*munthu wabwino*) was both diplomatic and an acknowledgment of popular support for the opposition. His approach to the Traditional Authority and other chiefs in the area was equally deferential, earning him some local recognition as a link to the inevitable institution of *boma*.

Umar was, therefore, a stranger in a double sense, a Muslim Yao in a predominantly Christian Cheŵa/Nsenga area and a servant of the government in an opposition stronghold. It was clear that his Muslim identity informed much of his engagement with various commitments, and shortly before the end of Muluzi's regime in 2004 he had officially registered his own faith-based organization called the Islamic Dawah Propagation Association.[19] It was in his capacity as the association's chairman that he had sent the letters to Mutharika. The establishment of the association had clearly consolidated his presence in Mkanda beyond his teachings and leadership at the local mosque, backed by the group's nine trustees appointed by Umar from the Muslim community in Mkanda and the wider Mchinji District. The animosity between Muluzi and Mutharika did, however, influence the way in which he portrayed the purpose of his association. While it had been formed when Muslims were still seen to run the government in Malaŵi, by 2008 it had become, among other things, a means to counter the "Muslim threat," whether in Malaŵi's own affairs or more internationally.[20] One of the first things Umar said to me when we met concerned his commitment to further dialogue between Muslims and Christians. Explaining Europe's affluence as a result of its natives' fear of God, he seemed to assume that I would be particularly taken with such an agenda to defuse religious tension and, moreover, impressed by this Muslim's respect for the religiosity of the continent where I came from. Although I duly received the bank account details for his association, a perusal of its constitution suggested that Umar's decision to use the association to seek reconciliation was rather recent. Written before the Christian president had replaced the Muslim, the first three objectives mentioned in the constitution all focused on the promotion of Islam.[21] Nowhere in the document was Christianity or religious tolerance mentioned.

Umar's initial reaction to my presence, changing into a more multifaceted interaction as time went on, illustrated both his situational interests and his aspiration to create contacts far beyond Mkanda. Trans-local relationships could be facilitated by local visibility, such as when the manager of a fuel company in Malaŵi invited Umar with him to Mecca in 2007, along with other Muslims from different parts of rural Malaŵi. Umar's participation in the *hajj* was his first journey outside Malaŵi, and he described to me in considerable detail the process by which he had obtained his first passport in Lilongwe and then a Saudi Arabian visa from Lusaka in Zambia, crowned by his first experience of air travel when he flew to Saudi Arabia through Nairobi and Dubai. He bought his most cherished gown during this trip, its golden color adding to the air of wealth and authority. Whatever blessings his host attained through this act of generosity, it also testified to Umar's own success as an independent Muslim leader. His involvement in local affairs was key to achieving the good fortune of international travel, because it was through his prominence in Mkanda, backed by his own association, that Muslims elsewhere recognized him as a leader and teacher. Contributions to *Nkhani Zam'maboma* and the visits of foreigners such as myself were other means by which he keenly sought to expand his social world beyond the locality where he had settled. It would be too cynical to view greed and calculation as the motivations for these attempts. Rather, at issue was the development of Umar's own self, a complex entwining of local and trans-local relationships ensuring recognition for his name and reputation.

The stories he supplied for *Nkhani Zam'maboma* played a specific role in this relational growth of Umar as a person. He described to me his delight at being the source (*gwelo*) of stories through which "the whole country" (*dziko lonse*) heard about Mkanda. This remote rural trading center, in other words, became a subject of national attention through Umar's mediating efforts. Trans-local recognition operated, as mentioned, the other way around too, such as when his association with *Nkhani Zam'maboma* brought him local prominence as a servant of public broadcasting. It is revealing that he became a correspondent after Muluzi's regime had ended. When the Muslim involvement in government diminished, it left a vacuum that his identification with the MBC's public service partially filled. At the same time, as has been seen, Umar was able to represent his religious association as an agent of interfaith dialogue. He told me that even if people of different faiths argued (*amanenana*) elsewhere, Mchinji District would be known for its tranquility and tolerance, thereby again indicating how he pursued his local aspirations with an eye to generating a trans-local reputation. His cooperation with local notables should not, however, obscure his involvement in many mundane and charitable activities in Mkanda, many of which enabled him to gather stories for *Nkhani Zam'maboma*. Having himself been the recipient of charity, he said, he wanted to give to the poor and disadvantaged whatever little he had. As a consequence, and despite the attention he paid to his personal appearance, he continued to live in a grass-thatched house amid iron-roofed ones thirteen years after his arrival in Mkanda.

By the time I worked with him, Umar's local reputation had grown to the extent that people would arrive with stories at his house or mosque. While the topics accorded with the trends noted in chapter 4, Umar had introduced his own methods of verification. He explained to me that the MBC had never received complaints from Mkanda, and he attributed this state of affairs to his determination to supply only true stories. One method, important especially when he did not know the person who had brought the story, was to make him or her sign the piece of paper on which it was written. Umar attributed even more significance to public knowledge about the incidents that stories reported. The weekly market of agricultural products and secondhand clothes was not only his main setting for obtaining stories, it was also the principal context in which he could test their veracity. Moving through the crowd he would ask different persons whether they had heard about the incidents others had told him about. Different versions of a story could emerge, and his propensity to decide on one coherent version was often similar to the interventions editors made at the MBC. Yet the most important issue to Umar was whether a story had enough public resonance at all. He gave me a hypothetical example of a couple fighting in the dead of night with only Umar hearing them. The reason why he would not send such a story to the MBC was not that domestic disputes were uninteresting. The reason was the lack of a local audience to endorse the story.

While Umar aspired to discover a local audience for his stories, his work as a correspondent also entailed a relationship beyond his various sources and collaborators in Mkanda. A youthful editor at the MBC had become a friend, and his enthusiasm partly ensured Umar's continuing supply of stories. Complaining that letters took too long to arrive, Umar communicated his stories through his mobile telephone. His favorite editor had been one of the first to receive them when he started to call the MBC, and by the time of my stay in Mkanda, he had long used the editor's personal mobile number instead of calling the newsroom's telephone. I observed in both Mkanda and Blantyre that they talked to each other virtually every day, in spite of weeks sometimes passing by without Umar having any stories to deliver. Although never meeting in person, they addressed each other as brothers (*achimwene*), shared jokes and family news, and Umar would occasionally send a money order to the cash-strapped editor. The friendship was another indication of how *Nkhani Zam'maboma* could mediate new relationships. Umar and the editor did not have a common first language, ethnic identity, district of origin, or religion, and yet their involvement with the program generated such conviviality that these differences paled into insignificance. The friendship was, however, merely one facet in the multiplex associations in which Umar's work as a correspondent was embedded. The personal connection diverged from Umar's highly public commitments to Islam and the government. At once both contradictory and cross-cutting, these relationships and the obligations they entailed were all indispensable to accomplishing Umar's particular position as a stranger in Mkanda. For their part, stories for *Nkhani Zam'maboma* contributed to Umar's growth as a person within multiple relationships.

Inequality Unveiled?

Does the program whose ethos is to reveal equality conceal inequality in the procedures of its own production? Some of the observations in this and the previous chapter would seem to justify an answer in the affirmative. Editors not only reserved to themselves the right to decide on whether submitted stories were to be broadcast, they could also make high-handed interventions to rewrite their contents. The management's view on news, including the stories broadcast on *Nkhani Zam'maboma,* as transparent reports on events obscured the actual process by which editors decided on what could go on the air. While editorial bias was evident in the contents of the official newscasts, their interventions were less apparent in *Nkhani Zam'maboma.* Yet the very idioms that gave the program its folksy flavor were carefully chosen and inserted by editors themselves. Moreover, by deciding on what kind of testimonial truth was acceptable, they also set the conventions within which the veracity of stories was determined.

It would be wrong to bring description to a halt after these observations have been made. This chapter has gone beyond the description of editorial interventions to consider the aspirations and conditions informing regular contributions to the program. Correspondents' situations were diverse, but a common trait was their position as relative strangers in the areas from where they supplied stories. Some correspondents had enough access to cash to make them financially more secure than many editors. By thus continuing description, it is possible to qualify the unequal features of production with a sense in which contributors and editors were both variously dominant and subordinate in their relationship. Obligations emerged the more they had to do with each other, with both having to offer what the other desired. The relationship was not, however, equal in any formal sense, as if editors and correspondents were engaged in a reciprocal exchange of favors. A tacit understanding of editorial prerogatives usually underlay the relationship. Yet by associating veracity with testimonial truth, editors also acknowledged their dependence on the listeners who supplied stories. As personal knowledge, the details of a story were always embedded in circumstances beyond the editors' knowledge and control. While they could alter the contents of some stories, their acceptance of many others with minor or no revisions submitted them to the authority of their contributors.

To the extent that an alternative notion of equality begins to emerge through these observations, one obstacle to its proper elucidation may lie in the very questions social science teaches its critical students to pose, such as the one with which this section began. Unmasking or unveiling as a social scientific procedure may foreclose intellectual and pragmatic possibilities if it is heeded as a matter of routine. Varieties of Marxism had entrenched this procedure before the Foucauldian turn in anthropology and related disciplines, its unmasking of power debunked by Sahlins as "the latest incarnation of anthropology's incurable functionalism" (1993: 15). Whereas biological needs or economic interests had previously explained away a whole world of human complexity, power had now become "the intellectual black hole into which all kinds of cultural contents [got] sucked" (Sahlins 1993: 15). Yet precisely because these acerbic remarks do no justice to the many innovative uses of Michel Foucault's (and Karl Marx's) ideas in anthropology, the problem they suggest extends beyond the influence of particular theorists. One facet of the problem is the division of intellectual labor that unmasking proposes.[22] It is not simply that the subjects of a study lack a properly emancipatory discourse to unmask their circumstances to themselves. Even when they do have a discourse on demystifying the operations of those who dominate them, it more often than not turns out to be in the social scientific analysis yet another form of mystification.

It is, as mentioned in chapter 2, this unequal division of intellectual labor that lies at the heart of Rancière's (2004) critique of Bourdieu's sociology, among a host of other European theorists. Both Rancière and Bourdieu are concerned with the exclusive status that intellectual work has assumed, but they arrive at diametrically opposed positions. For Rancière, alternative discourses with emancipatory effects are not absent among the dominated, but they are largely inaudible in the division of intellectual labor that obtains in their world. While it may be true that Rancière has confused causes and consequences in Bourdieu's perspective—for the latter, the lack of capacity to formulate a genuine alternative is a consequence and not a cause of domination (see Nordmann 2006: 98–100)—Bourdieu has said enough to assert his sociology as a science out of reach of those whose deprivation it theorizes. "The sociologist's misfortune," Bourdieu maintains, is that "the people who have the technical means of appropriating what he says have no wish to appropriate it," adding that "those who would have an interest in appropriating it do not have the instruments for appropriation (theoretical culture, etc.)" (1993: 23).

Against such exclusiveness arises Rancière's exploration of "the transgressive appropriation of an intellectual equality whose privilege others have reserved for themselves" (2004: 223; see also Rancière 1991). Writing, for example, pre-occupied many mid-nineteenth-century French workers (Rancière 1989), as it did subordinated Africans in colonial situations (see Barber 2006).

Writing is not, of course, the only medium of transgressive intellectual work. Sharing stories in a Malaŵian market place, and sending them to the public radio through a mobile telephone, can also sustain reflection and debate on issues that academics, politicians, and activists might regard as belonging to their orbit. The following chapter on the reception of stories on *Nkhani Zam'maboma* also shows how the work of reflection and debate did not end with a broadcast but was further animated by stories from elsewhere than the listener's own locality. This perspective on reception is necessary, among other things, to indicate the program's place in the lives of those who did not send their stories to the newsroom. In fact, editors and correspondents may have appeared in this and the previous chapters as somewhat atypical of the Malaŵian poor who enjoyed *Nkhani Zam'maboma*. Yet its lack of a didactic tone, its deliverance from a patronizing posture, indicated the extent to which editors and correspondents, however salaried and educated they were, shared the predicament with their public. Few of them were shielded from the effects of severe poverty and inequality, not only as subjects to the claims and demands others made on them, but also in their own vulnerability to the vagaries of an unequal political economy.

PART 3

The Aesthetic of Claims

7

Cries and Whispers

Shaming without Naming

When I discussed *Nkhani Zam'maboma* with people I had known for over a decade in Dedza District, many would add to their reflections a sober comment on the area's invisibility in the program.[1] The villages in their chiefdom did not seem to feature in the stories broadcast on *Nkhani Zam'maboma*, an observation corroborated by the absence of incidents in this area from my sample of stories. No one who made such a comment thought it warranted complacency. Rather than indicating the area's exceptional record in avoiding scandals, the lack of its stories on the radio, I was told, arose from villagers' problematic tendency to "keep secrets" (*kusunga zinsinsi*). Stories about misconduct and abuse did circulate locally, but their failure to reach the national radio bespoke a widely shared fear (*mantha*) of publicizing unsavory incidents. I heard stories and witnessed events that could have provided material for *Nkhani Zam'maboma*, and villagers were able to give further examples of similarities between their experiences and those reported on the program. Not only were witches' aircraft seen to crash-land here as elsewhere, many less spectacular incidents could also have appeared on *Nkhani Zam'maboma*. For instance, some villagers told me, in hushed voices, about the widespread sexual abuse of female children, often by their own kinsmen.

That the example of sexual abuse was itself inspired by the appearance of the topic on *Nkhani Zam'maboma* highlights intricacies in villagers' self-criticism. Much as their area seemed absent, its violations and injustices could become topics of conversation and reflection through stories from elsewhere. At the same time, the absence itself was conducive to reflections that questioned entrenched habits not only among those who abused but among those who remained their silent witnesses. An additional layer of complexity, as a case study in this chapter will detail, was produced by the perceived prevalence of stories from a neighboring chiefdom on *Nkhani Zam'maboma*. While it could support the assertions of "our" moral superiority over "their" frequent failures, more often the tenor of reflection was dismay at how similar chiefdoms could be so different in their approach to making abuse and injustice public. The deliberations of impoverished villagers on a headman's misconduct were nurtured by a report on *Nkhani Zam'maboma* on a similar predicament in the neighboring chiefdom.

These mediations—reflections on one's own situation prompted by stories from elsewhere—kept villagers as avid listeners of *Nkhani Zam'maboma*. After the launching of Radio Maria, few villagers appeared to favor the MBC otherwise in this predominantly Roman Catholic area. Certainly their thirst for news was quenched by Radio Maria and, from 2005 onward, the Zodiak Broadcasting Station rather than by the MBC. As the intricacies outlined above indicate, however, reception—the conventional counterpart of production in media studies—was not a matter of individual listeners' preferences and interpretations. Spitulnik (2000: 144–147; 2002: 338–339) has argued that reception should be viewed within the relationships that constitute listeners' lives, not as an ego-centric practice. This socio-centric approach has informed ethnographic work on television and film viewing as embedded in historical, political, and cultural processes that render suspect the notion of a passive and uniform audience (see, e.g., Abu-Lughod 2005; Dickey 1993; Mankekar 1999). The status of *Nkhani Zam'maboma* as a news program raises the question of how genre influences listeners' co-authorship of mass-mediated stories. Those who never supplied the program with stories could nonetheless contribute to the significance and effect it acquired in particular relationships. A key feature that attracted them, one that distinguished *Nkhani Zam'maboma* from other news programs in Malaŵian media, was the moral imagination it nourished. The evaluation of conduct arose from existing repertoires of knowledge, not from a didactic mode of delivering stories. The relation between morality, genre, and the aesthetic of claim-making is central to this chapter's exploration of the program's disciplinary effect.

In Dedza District, radio listening was rarely confined within domestic interiors. Moreover, as elsewhere, reception was shaped by specific technological and material conditions. The ownership of a receiver was subject to the vicissitudes of poverty, not only because of frequent requests to lend or share it, but also because of the relatively high cost of batteries in an area where villagers had no electricity in their homes. Many tried to find ways of conserving battery energy, whether by tying together a string of used batteries or by minimally recharging them, while better-off villagers deployed old car batteries.[2] One consequence of playing the radio, even inside one's house, was often to make others appear, keen to share the programs one was listening to. Having the radio on outside the house often resulted in an impromptu gathering of young and old, women and men (see figure 7.1). While such occasions could be revealing for the unparalleled way in which diverse participants felt able to comment on issues raised by the programs, these gatherings could also place a burden on hosts to provide food to those who attended (see also Kasoma 2002: 182–183; Vokes 2007: 814). *Nkhani Zam'maboma* was particularly affected by this prospect, broadcast as it was when villagers usually had their main meal that for many tended to be, especially during the lean period, their only meal.

Because it was broadcast at 7:30 and 9:00 PM, well after darkness had fallen, *Nkhani Zam'maboma* was rarely listened to outdoors. Although some youths gathered to listen to it around a fire on the outskirts of villages, it was most often consumed in homes. Its timing was, however, conducive to including large numbers of villagers in its public, many of whom stayed in their fields from dawn till dusk.[3] Those who did not have receivers in their own homes might come to specifically listen to its ten-minute broadcast, their acceptance or refusal of food depending on the particular configuration of personal debts within which they found themselves. While listenership was rarely confined to the nuclear family, a measure of intimacy often characterized the groups who listened to *Nkhani Zam'maboma*. Its timing was late by villagers' standards, and those who paid visits at these hours tended to be close neighbors or kin. Intimacy facilitated critical reflections on the controversies heard on the program, but those reflections were by no means restricted to the moment of listening to it. Particularly compelling stories were recounted days after they had been broadcast to those who had missed them, at beer parties and funerals, in marketplaces, and while visiting. This sharing of stories, often accompanied

Fig. 7.1. Listening to the radio in Dedza District.

by further reflections, generated the disciplinary effect that will be explored in this chapter. Even when claims were cryptic, or voiced in the intimacy between persons who trusted each other, the very presence of *Nkhani Zam'maboma* made it possible for popular disaffection to find a powerful outlet.

Making Moral Models Explicit

The didacticism that observers have noted as permeating African arts and journalism (see, e.g., Barber 2000: 418; Furniss 1996: 10; Newell 2002: 2–3) was peripheral to *Nkhani Zam'maboma*. It offered no commentary on the stories it broadcast, its ethos cultivated doubt and ambiguity, it had not authorized anyone to interpret its contents, and it cited rather than explained proverbs. Yet it was clear from both editors' and listeners' interest in the program that it sustained a vibrant moral discourse. Its mediation of equality rested on its provision of an arena in which the claims and perspectives of the downtrodden could be presented. One result was the doubt it encouraged about the integrity of various kinds of authorities, widespread deception and fallibility calling for constant vigilance. Because no egalitarian vision was projected into the distant future, equality was an aspect of the here and now, the expectation of improved conduct giving some hope for the near future. The moral imperative, as articulated in editors' and listeners' reflections rather than in the stories themselves, was to treat everyone with respect, a respect that revealed mutual dependence between sharply unequal subject positions.[4]

The evaluation of conduct, and the disciplinary effect it had, raises the question of how *Nkhani Zam'maboma* nourished the moral imagination without succumbing to didacticism. The editorial interventions have already become apparent, such as the choice of words to convey specific moral qualities among protagonists. Listeners' conviction that stories educate (*kuphunzitsa*) is also relevant in this regard. It alludes to a diversity of ways in which the idiom of education enters the consumption of media products. Certainly, no connection to schooling was suggested, unlike among those Tanzanians who have been reported to write out the lyrics of popular songs they find in newspapers (Weiss 2009: 190–191).[5] Rather, stories were educative in the sense of informing listeners about the range and extent of abuse in their world. It is not simply because *Nkhani Zam'maboma* addressed a public with shared background knowledge that didactic messages were redundant. The doubt and ambiguity it conveyed asked less for the affirmation of customary duties than for debate and deliberation on the specific examples of human conduct. The shared background knowledge was about a myriad of everyday problems and institutions, so sophisticated that the teaching of customs or rules (*miyambo*) by the program would have been not only tedious but subversive of learning genuinely novel things about the world.[6] Examples multiplied just as the stories themselves did in listeners' deliberations. Even if a moral model of appropriate conduct between authorities and subjects informed stories, as examples of human foibles and virtues they were not replicated but retold and re-enacted in diverse circumstances. After all, it is hardly plausible to expect a moral model to be exhausted by a single example (see Barber 2000: 398).

How to make the tacit moral model explicit was not a problem for editors and listeners. It is a problem for the ethnographer who is inclined to bring the anthropological and philosophical distinction between moral rules and ethical practice to bear on this case. One way to circumvent this tiresome distinction, which always threatens to become an unbridgeable dichotomy, is by de-emphasizing the role of rules in moral conduct in favor of a notion of exemplary morality in which precepts take the form of exemplars (see Humphrey 1997). The interest here is the way in which moral precepts may emanate from exemplars that are highly personal, tied to the specific relationships between authorities and subjects, mentors and followers. The figure of the Reasonable Man, as identified by Max Gluckman (1955) in the juridical contexts of Southern and Central Africa, embodies a key aspect of such a moral model by constantly adjusting explicit rules while passing judgments on personal crises.[7] The public of *Nkhani Zam'maboma* knew that authorities such as village headmen and religious leaders were supposed to be caring and reasonable. Its stories could not be news if they merely reiterated what everyone knew already. It was the range of incidents and situations that captured the attention of listeners, the specific and personal instances of injustice inspiring debate on other examples of moral conduct and its inversions.

In this regard, a choice between the Foucault-inspired emphasis on the techniques of the self and earlier anthropological insights into gossip and scandal as tools of social control may not be productive. The difference between these bodies of scholarship is apparent when a distinction is made between internal and external sources of discipline, between the formation of self-regulating subjects and the awareness of a critical public evaluating one's conduct. *Nkhani Zam'maboma* encompassed both modalities of moral disposition, if only because it was not one of those media formats that have appeared in different parts of the world to intensify a certain preoccupation with the self (see Matza 2009). To be sure, the program's capacity to deter people from undesirable action involved them in monitoring their own conduct, and the unvoiced in-junction granted them a certain freedom to choose between different courses of action.[8] At the same time, a sense of externally generated social control also informed the relationships that *Nkhani Zam'maboma* helped to constitute.

The concept of social control, as associated with Gluckman (1963), among others, has often been misunderstood to put too much emphasis on rule-governed behavior, with an abstract and unchanging society as the assumed source of those rules and norms (see, e.g., Howell 1997: 7).[9] Yet if social control is decoupled from the concept of society as a mechanism regulating indi-vidual behavior (see Strathern 1985: 112–113), a perspective on a public that re-flects on shifting relationships of variable scales can be achieved. Gluckman alluded to the way in which genres summon their publics by arguing that "gos-siping is a duty of membership of the group" (1963: 313). The reflections that sto-ries broadcast on *Nkhani Zam'maboma* inspired, whether within the confines of a domestic unit or in public places, were constitutive of relationships that changed as circumstances changed. Transposed to the scale of mass-mediated stories, such gossiping took place as a genre whose characteristics Gluckman's focus on small-scale groups could not anticipate. Crucial was the awareness of a public that transcended the relationships one's gossiping helped to generate.

The Aesthetic of Using Few Words

Much else than the underlying moral model was left tacit in *Nkhani Zam'ma-boma,* as the ethnography on editorial procedures has shown. The very claims that its stories contained and inspired were not always particularly outspoken and direct. Here the background knowledge shared by the program's public needs to be explored further. Villagers' complaints about their habit of keeping secrets appear to be at variance with the value placed on silence in Chichewa public culture. Proverbs advise caution with words, such as in *chalowa m'khutu chayanza malo,* "What has entered the ear has found a place." A Malawian exe-gesis states that "what a person hears cannot be taken out, hence it is wise to be careful while speaking and to fear mistakes" (Chakanza 2000: 40).[10] Similar sentiments have been expressed in Chichewa literature and journalism. In his preface to a collection of short stories in the 1960s, John Gwengwe (1964) ex-plained his intent as an effort to give a sense of storytelling to those youths who no longer had the opportunity to spend much time in the company of elders. However, he immediately added that elders' exegesis of their stories was often concise: "Instead of saying many words, they merely said one word, maybe two, perhaps three" (Gwengwe 1964: 5).[11] More recently, Willie Zingani (2004), in a short story entitled "Lilime Limalakwa" (language/tongue makes mistakes), has highlighted the potential for error when using many words. "War is to quarrel," he points out, "it starts because of people who talk too much, who are foul-mouthed" (Zingani 2004: 6).[12] In a newspaper column, paradoxically entitled *Zakukhosi* (literally, "from the throat"; idiomatically, "straight talking"), the author observes that "when you talk much, you also err a lot. Elders therefore told the proverb that when you travel don't leave the lips behind."[13] "Sometimes being quiet says many words."[14]

These sentiments parallel what some philosophers have said about African propensities to avoid conflict and argument. Kwame Anthony Appiah, for example, has stressed the need to accommodate conflicting views among those "who are bound to each other as neighbors for life" (1992: 129–130). Kwasi Wiredu, in turn, has drawn attention to the flimsy "speech and dissent rights" (1990: 259) among certain social categories, such as youths and women, making the negotiation of consensus the prerogative of adult males. While quite plausibly highlighting the importance attached to negotiation and accommodation—and the multiple exclusions that inhere in such processes—these philosophical generalizations fall short of illuminating the actual intricacies of claim-making in particular African settings. Where silence itself can "say many words," the need is to attend to the specific and variable aesthetics of claims.

Two radically different intellectual projects—one a historical-ethnographic account of Southern African oral genres and the other a conceptual exploration of anthropology's knowledge practices—have used the term "aesthetic" in ways that deliver it from its Romantic connotations. Detaching "aesthetic" from the belief in beauty as an end in itself, Leroy Vail and Landeg White (1991: 79) argued for an earlier sense in which it had denoted common sets of assumptions among artists and their audiences about creative work. Extending the scope of aesthetic from artistic to academic production, Marilyn Strathern's use of the concept drew on "the persuasiveness of form, the elicitation of a sense of appropriateness" (1991: 10). In other words, aesthetic—from African oral literature to academics' conceptual schemes—is the form that the various artifacts of human creativity have to take in order to have an effect. Several genres can be encompassed by a single aesthetic, whereas different kinds of claims can emanate from strikingly different aesthetics.

The concept of aesthetic makes it possible to discern alternative procedures of claim-making within the apparent drive toward consensus and accommodation. Not all claims need to be assertive in tone in order to have an effect, and it is in this regard that the silence of *Nkhani Zam'maboma* on particular villages in Dedza gave rise to claims in a double sense. On the one hand, it called for critical reflections on why the area should be so absent from the program. On the other hand, precisely by keeping their reflections intimate, villagers' silence in public was ominous to those whom they criticized, villagers' whispers having the potential of becoming mass-mediated cries. Here also lies a contrast to another aesthetic of claims whose emergence in Malaŵi coincided with the launching of *Nkhani Zam'maboma*. Democratic politicians and human rights activists swore their commitment to the constitutional freedom of expression by, among other things, telling the populace that they were individuals carrying inalienable rights. Rather than seeking ways to make claims that acknowledged subjects' obligations toward each other, these politicians and activists called for contentious claims, based on an aesthetic that sought to make grievances explicit. The appeal of such an aesthetic among would-be claimants themselves was doubtful, as this chapter will indicate. Moreover, despite resulting in effective claims in the legal sphere, particularly when mobilized to garner recognition for women's rights, activists' aesthetic was all too often restricted to rhetorical assertions rather than sparking pragmatic interventions. Instead of advocacy, activists defined civic education as their mode of engaging with the poor, thereby leaving their subjects without a proper institutional support for confronting those who had caused their injury (see Englund 2006: 99–122).

What the diversity of ways of making claims suggests is a diversity of genres and aesthetics at villagers' disposal. From a comparative point of view, Africans' alleged commitment to accommodation and consensus is at best an overstatement. Verbal abuse in public, often associated with particular kinds of kin and ritual relationships (Irvine 1993; Parkin 1980), is only one instance within a wider set of genres through which political authority, for example, has been praised, blamed, invoked, and evaluated (Apter 2007: 12–13). Southern and Central Africa, in particular, is renowned for its contentious poetic traditions, whose common aesthetic has been discerned in spite of scholars' tendency to associate particular genres with particular ethnic groups, such as "Shona harvesting songs, Bemba praise songs, Chewa pounding songs, and so on" (Vail and White 1991: 41). A key aspect of their common aesthetic is a special license, variously attributed to specific poets or to social categories engaged in particular tasks, to criticize the figures of authority such as chiefs and male householders. This common aesthetic has inspired Andrew Apter to develop "a general model of critical agency" (2007: 32) in which, among other things, the conventional division between speaker, message, and receiver needs to be supplanted with a subtler sense of shifting subject positions. Praise poems, for example, have combined praise with critique, at once speaking on behalf of the chief to highlight his or her legitimate authority and on behalf of the chief's subjects who evaluate his or her performance (Apter 2007: 48). A distinction between the authority of high office and the variably performed power of its incumbent is thus crucial to this model. However, a somewhat similar distinction applies to the one licensed to praise and criticize. The "freedom of expression" (Vail and White 1991: 43) in Southern and Central African poetic traditions has been linked to the aesthetic itself rather than to the person using it, to the performance rather than to the performer (Vail and White 1991: 56–57). As such, the aesthetic has not been the prerogative of exceptional individuals, but a particular medium associated with specific contexts of delivery.

However much praise poetry in chiefly courts may have served as a paradigmatic case, a wide variety of performances is, therefore, possible to accommodate within this common aesthetic. In fact, poetic license has applied to other contexts than to royal praises in much of postcolonial Malaŵi. Apart from Ngoni Paramount Chiefs, anything resembling royal praises has been rare, and for the vast majority of villagers in the country other kinds of songs have sustained the aesthetic of critique and evaluation. For example, songs composed and performed by women while pounding maize or millet have provided insights into discordant gender relations during a famine (Vaughan 1987: 30–37). Even under autocratic conditions, women's songs have made allusions to the abuse of power by postcolonial political leaders (White 1987: 245–246). In Dedza District, this poetic tradition lives on especially in women's dances known as *chimtali,* usually performed at weddings and beer parties, whose merriment is enhanced by songs depicting a range of concerns from domestic and sexual problems to politics. Popular music spread by audio cassettes, compact discs, and the radio has become perhaps the most significant aspect of this poetic license, particularly after the transition to multiparty democracy. Where the engagement with social and political critique by more literary poets and writers has been hampered by linguistic, institutional, and personal reasons, popular musicians have acquired increasing public recognition (Chirambo 2002; Lwanda 2008).[15]

The shared aesthetic of several oral genres does not, however, exhaust the Southern and Central African modes of making claims in public arenas. Public deliberation has been another discursive register, most notably attached to the institution of chieftaincy. The most sophisticated examples come from Botswana, where age-set assemblies and chiefdom councils have long been convened to address public disputes, taxation issues, and the need for collective work (see, e.g., Schapera 1938; 1965). *Kgotla,* a representative forum of chiefs and headmen, has gained particular renown for its generation of consensus and shared decisions through careful deliberation (Comaroff 1975). The freedom of speech on this forum has been molded by a history of popular restraint on chiefly power, with "over-mighty chiefs . . . expelled, assassinated, or deserted by their subjects" (Iliffe 2005: 150). However, to the extent that *kgotla* has promoted the values of democratic deliberation, it has also highlighted its exclusions and limitations. Not only can consensus be partial and women and youths excluded from the deliberation; transposing *kgotla* to an instrument of the postcolonial state has raised questions of Tswana chiefs' legitimacy to represent Botswana's ethnic minorities (Durham 2002: 161). The pursuit of consensus has, therefore, given way to counter-claims about exclusion and difference when the institutions and values of postcolonial nation-building have come under scrutiny.

Although hardly comparable to *kgotla* in its significance to national public culture, *bwalo* has represented in Malaŵi the principal medium of deliberation. Among so-called traditional authorities, each level in the hierarchy from village headmen to chiefs has its own *bwalo*.[16] It is a concept that denotes both the physical location for hearing disputes and the assembly of councilors (*nyakwaŵa*) who assist the headman or chief to reach a decision. Disputes heard at *bwalo* typically concern land and domestic affairs, whereas criminal cases are often referred to the police and magistrate's courts. The practice of collective decision-making, with its search for consensus, is sustained not only by this assembly but also by the way in which litigants usually speak through their representatives. In Dedza District, these representatives are called *ankhoswe* (guardians), matrilateral male relatives who are expected to solve disputes among themselves before bringing them to *bwalo*. Discussions at *bwalo* ought to be unhurried and balanced lest the headman or chief stands accused of incompetence or partiality. As a forum for making claims, *bwalo* is an instance of villagers keeping an eye on multiple obligations while expressing their views. The litigant does not address the assembly as an individual, and his or her guardian is expected to speak on behalf of the relationships in which the litigant is embedded. In other words, claims are made on litigants even as they hope to make claims of their own. The aesthetic may not be the same as what was identified above for various oral genres—the consensus-seeking *bwalo* contrasts with contentious songs—but deliberation in this case is no less informed by shifting subject positions and the awareness of what harm carelessness with words can bring.

Local Notoriety, National Anonymity

Although the above discussion suggests that several genres can be accommodated within one aesthetic of poetic license, it is clear that some genres of claim-making fit uneasily in it. *Nkhani Zam'maboma* introduced an aesthetic that was as new as the assertive claim-making promoted by some human rights activists. Despite the use of idiomatic Chichewa familiar to some listeners from textbooks they had read in school, stories on *Nkhani Zam'maboma* were not tales (*nthano*) but news (*nkhani*). The events it reported were expected to be not only contemporary but quite literally true, whatever doubts may have been expressed about this or that detail. Yet the greatest challenge for understanding these stories as a new genre with an aesthetic of its own is the medium of their distribution. Localized as they may seem, stories did more than constitute a local public arena in which kin and neighbors settled their scores with little regard for a national public (see Werbner 2004: 143–144). The medium was inseparable from the effects stories were thought to have, and what got on air acquired meaning from the understanding that it was heard by millions of Malawians.

One aspect of the new genre was that it gave, in principle, everyone the tools for making grievances public. Gone was the need to speak through a representative, and gone, too, was the imperative to reconcile conflicting viewpoints. Although the cost of postage may have prevented some villagers in Dedza from writing to the MBC, they could cite few other practical reasons for the absence of their stories. Contributions to the program presupposed some degree of literacy or access to a telephone, but few villagers unable to read and write in Dedza were so deprived of contact with the literate that they would not have found anyone to write a letter on their behalf. And because villagers were unaware of the sometimes profound editing that went into preparing the program, skills at allusive and gnomic expressions did not appear to be required. On the contrary, precisely by being able to complete or add to broadcast stories, villagers gained a sense of becoming their co-authors, with similar stories to tell.[17]

Just as editors did not attribute an overtly emancipatory agenda to their work, however, so too did villagers reject my suggestion that *Nkhani Zam'maboma* represented a revolutionary program to uproot hierarchies. What was contested was the conduct of particular persons in specific situations. As such, the real sinister side of *Nkhani Zam'maboma* might be assumed to inhere in this attention to persons rather than institutions. By making persons seem responsible for the perpetuation of injustice, the program might be seen to have incited violence and intolerance against them without addressing the root causes. This line of thinking, as has already been seen, is hard to avoid in social science and contrasts with Malaŵian critiques of *Nkhani Zam'maboma*, as the next chapter will show. However, the disciplinary effect of the stories that were broadcast was an issue that was not imposed on the ethnographer simply by the pressure felt in social science to unmask power relations. Fear (*mantha*) and shame (*manyazi*) were frequently cited by both editors and villagers as the main effects of the claims made on the program.

Such effects were very much a result of listeners' co-authorship of the stories that went on the air. The tacit moral model left it to listeners to infer the possible or right courses of action. Because many stories made no mention of a closure or resolution in the incidents they described, it is instructive to consider the general patterns by which stories ended. It has already become apparent that the idiom of being disappointed (*kukhumudwa*) was common on *Nkhani Zam'maboma*. In contrast to anger (*mkwiyo*) and hatred (*udani*), disappointment allowed for an ambiguous response to misconduct, often requiring the miscreant to correct his or her behavior without an overt demand to do so. For example, one story reported that "a woman walked her head bent down because people had revealed that she was a witch."[18] As was seen in chapter 3, witchcraft stories fused into other stories in their tendency to cultivate ambiguity, if only by suggesting that widely shared suspicion rather than violent reprisal constituted enough reason for people to check their conduct. Another story described how after an aircraft carrying witches to their "annual big meeting" (*msonkhano waukulu wapachaka*) had crash-landed, people in the village "were just keenly watching each other to see who were walking as though they had injured themselves such that they might have been among the people on that journey."[19] As the story's ending, the image of villagers watching each other was an effective way of conveying ambiguity that defused the possibility of direct verbal or physical attacks.

Some transgressions did incite violence or its threat, but when depicting such scenarios, stories on *Nkhani Zam'maboma* often introduced other modes of intervention by highlighting alternative perspectives. A grandmother, for example, was reported to have been found naked close to a crossroads at night, and after she had been taken home, her son had "shouted very much" (*ana-*

kalipa kwambiri) and had wanted to beat her up for "causing people shame in the village" (*chifukwa chochititsa manyazi kwa anthu pa mudzipo*).[20] His relatives had prevented him from doing so, but the village headman was reported to have warned the grandmother that if she did it again, he "would not hesitate to chase her away from the village" (*sichitira mwina koma kumuthamangitsa m'mudzimo*). The different courses of action suggested by this story indicated, in other words, different perspectives on the incident, from the son's threat of violence to his relatives' rejection of it to the village headman's warning. It was clear that both the son and the headman saw the incident, with its allusions of witchcraft, as more than a domestic problem. Yet the other relatives' rejection of violence suggested ambiguity in the response to it, whereas the headman could do no more than issue a warning of ostracism.

The headman's warning as the story's final element accorded with a pattern in some stories to end with a reference to customary ways of policing misconduct and solving disputes. However, as has been seen, authorities such as village headmen were by no means infallible custodians of virtue. One story drew attention to a headman's unreasonable ruling by reporting that a woman had undressed in public to demand that the headman "does not make her pay a fine of M.K.200" (*asamulipiritse chindapusa cha 200 kwacha*).[21] The woman had been found trespassing on the site where the male secret society *gule wamkulu* was preparing for a funeral ceremony. After hearing the headman's ruling, she had torn her clothes off and cried that "she was a poor person who was not able to find that money" (*iye ndi mphawi ndipo sangathe kupeza ndalamazo*). The story ended by noting that "many people deplored the headman because of his cruelty toward the woman" (*anthu ambiri anadzudzula nyakwawayo chifukwa choonetsa nkhanza kwa mayiwo*). The headman's customary penalty appeared as a greater infringement than the woman's violation of the customary expectation to avoid the site where *gule wamkulu* was being prepared.

Between them, the above examples give a sense of the ways in which stories reporting on transgression and misconduct ended. Whether the result was shame among the culprits and wider sets of relationships in which they were located, a threat of violence or ostracism, or a criticism of customary rulings, stories did not generally convey such indignation that would have warranted violent retribution or persecution. At the same time, although multiple perspectives undermined the endorsement of any single course of action, transgression was often striking enough to be the actual news in a story. In this regard, more significant than the suggested action was the very act of broadcasting those transgressions to a national public. Villagers in Dedza District supported the MBC's practice of omitting personal names from the stories it broadcast, but the popularity of *Nkhani Zam'maboma* ensured that even unnamed miscreants could feel shame. For many villagers as for editors, one effect of the program was to deter people from misbehaving in ways that would attract its attention. The extent to which *Nkhani Zam'maboma* had entered the everyday deliberation on proper conduct was evident in a pastor's comment after his expulsion from his congregation had been announced. "Today *Nkhani Zam'maboma* will have enough stories," he was reported to have said in response to the litany of grievances that had led to his expulsion.[22]

Villagers' emphasis on the preventive impact of *Nkhani Zam'maboma* indicated that the program could actually defuse the specter of violence in controversial events. By the same token, the misconduct that did get broadcast could also intensify shame and disappointment rather than incite violence precisely because it had been made public to the nation as a whole. Here villagers' preference for maintaining the protagonists' anonymity introduced important limits to their desire to take transgressors to task. They shared editors' understanding that most stories on *Nkhani Zam'maboma* were in local circulation by the time they went on the air, but the broadcast of personal names would have considerably increased the scale of claims and accusations. Nation-wide notoriety, I was told, would have damaged the prospects of making a new beginning anywhere in the country. In extreme cases, the miscreant could be ostracized from his or her area, but villagers opposed a complete elimination of the opportunity to seek new sets of relationships elsewhere. The inclination to keep personal identities as local knowledge asserted a certain commitment to civility amid all the disappointments and violations that were the stuff of gossiping. Villagers' insistence on an exit option resonated with the historical observation that Southern and Central Africans have been frontierspeople, periodically ejected out from pre-colonial and colonial polities to found new political entities elsewhere (Kopytoff 1987). A twenty-first-century equivalent is, for example, a Pentecostal pastor who hears his scandal publicized on the national radio and decides to move elsewhere to re-establish himself and his congregation.

From Controversy to Comeback

The scarcity of stories from the area in Dedza District where I work might be assumed to have given *Nkhani Zam'maboma* the status of entertainment rather than an instrument of discipline and social control. In point of fact, while the program certainly entertained villagers, the very absence of their villages from its broadcasts only accentuated the internal and external modes of discipline. On August 1, 2003, for example, villagers' ears pricked up at the mention of their neighboring chiefdom on *Nkhani Zam'maboma.* According to this story, both incest and child abuse had taken place in a village headman's house. The headman was having sex with his daughter when his wife returned home from their garden one morning. A fight erupted, with the result that the headman had to collect his belongings and leave the house.[23] The story emphasized the presence of a wider public beyond the domestic flare-up by reporting that "people in the area are very disappointed with what the headman did with his daughter."[24] It was not only because of its location in the neighboring chiefdom that villagers took a special interest in this story. The citizens of Kabudula village also had long-standing grievances over their former headman, known here as Gama, who had likewise been implicated in incidents involving incest and other forms of illicit sex. The story was broadcast, moreover, at a time when he was making a comeback as the Group Village Headman for his area, a position one rung above the headman in the hierarchy of so-called traditional authorities (see note 16).

Although the story provoked reflections, mentioned earlier, on the extent of child abuse in the area, it was Gama's conduct that animated villagers' conversations wherever they came together, from weddings to funerals, from beer parties to church gatherings, from markets to homes. I had grown accustomed to having Gama as a topic of conversation already during my first period of fieldwork in 1992–1993, when he had cut a charismatic, confident, and controversial figure in the area's affairs. He had not ascended to headmanship because of genealogy, having been born into a family that did not supply headmen for the village. The actual headman of Kabudula had, however, taken a liking to Gama, who had gradually assumed all the practical and ceremonial duties of a headman, while the *de jure* headman kept a store outside the village and only rarely became involved in its affairs.[25] Gama himself was a relatively affluent villager, whose years as a labor migrant in South Africa in the 1970s and 1980s had generated enough wealth to invest in cattle and a spacious iron-roofed house in the village. His prominence in local affairs derived from his involvement in various public arenas, not least as an elder of the Church of the Central African Presbyterian (CCAP), the biggest church in Kabudula. He had also befriended other headmen in the area and its long-serving member of parliament, who had, among other things, given him a bicycle as a gift.

The story broadcast in 2003 struck a chord with villagers' present concerns, but those concerns had, of course, taken shape over a long period of time. In this regard, Gama's case shows how stories broadcast on *Nkhani Zam'maboma* could resonate not only across different locations but also with experiences that had started before the contemporary moment and therefore constituted it. Although Gama appeared controversial already in the early 1990s in his immodest and occasionally autocratic ways, the fallout with his subjects took place toward the end of the decade. It had been preceded by increasingly unreasonable conduct of the headman's *bwalo*, untoward behavior as a church elder, and alleged sexual exploits, all topics of intense gossiping among villagers. Suspicions of witchcraft added urgency to this gossiping and eventually raised such a prospect of popular discontent that other village notables decided to replace him with a different, more likable person. Although the recent past was the focus of villagers' gossiping, they would sometimes recall dubious details from Gama's more distant past. He was, among other things, alleged to have used magic (*matsenga*) to enrich himself in South Africa. He had, villagers told each other, sent a snake to steal his fellow workers' money.

While villagers appeared able to tolerate Gama's immodesty, it was his alleged breach of the church elder's mandate that commenced his downfall. Toward the late 1990s, an area by the main road, formally within the territory of Kabudula village, became a bustling marketplace whose central attraction, drawing patrons from far and wide, was several simultaneous beer parties. Although non-Presbyterian headmen in the chiefdom were entitled to a free gourd of beer when it was brewed for sale in their territory, Kabudula villagers were dismayed to discover that Gama had begun to demand similar gifts from the owners of the parties at the marketplace. He denied that he consumed the beer and claimed to store it in his house to entertain visitors, especially headmen from other villages. Even more damaging to his reputation was villagers' gossip about his promiscuity. Pregnancies among unmarried young women were seen to have become more common than before, and gossip implicated Gama as the father of their children. In some cases, he was thought to have impregnated schoolgirls and his own relatives. The women's secrecy about their partners, and the denials by the men some of them did name, were all grist for the mill of villagers' gossiping. They exchanged stories about Gama's nocturnal excursions, claiming that he was sneaking around in the village "like a hyena" (*ngati fisi*), wearing only a pair of shorts in order to disappear into the darkness.

Deliberation on Gama's private vice was inseparable from villagers' criticism of his public performance. His conduct of the headman's *bwalo* to hear disputes was a particularly contentious issue. He had begun to impose fines far heftier than what villagers considered reasonable. He had also become more rigid in enforcing his self-made rules about the way in which people had to behave at *bwalo*. Seated on a chair, Gama ordered his subjects sitting on grass in front of him to adopt extreme gestures of deference. Men, for example, were expected to maintain the same posture of bended knees throughout hearings, and an attempt to light a cigarette, or even the wave of a hand to remove an ant from one's body, could result in an instant fine. Gama's diabolical nature was confirmed when fresh fish was discovered at *bwalo*. He had placed them in the grass, villagers concluded, to attract ants so that he could collect more fines from his tormented subjects.

These grievances had caused such discontent in the village by the dawn of the new millennium that certain male elders, who served as Gama's councilors at *bwalo*, persuaded the *de jure* headman to preside over the public nomination of Gama's replacement. It was clear that the elders were motivated by the fear of reprisals against Gama, a prospect significantly exacerbated by the intensification of witchcraft discourse in villagers' gossiping. When some of the unmarried women's young children died, it appeared plausible to villagers that Gama had killed them for his occult purposes. His alleged hyena-like behavior at night, coupled with his nudity, also drew on familiar witchcraft imagery.

The *de jure* headman reluctantly accepted to convene the meeting to select Gama's replacement, but Gama's friendship with him appeared to continue intact. Gama became, however, humble and inconspicuous in public life, having also been stripped of his status as a church elder. He did not relinquish involvement in public affairs entirely and used his wealth to entice a group of young men in his neighborhood to regard him as the chairman of their vigilante group known as Inkatha, its name derived from Zulu to convey fearless warriorhood.[26] During the 2001–2002 food crisis, he staged outside his house public beatings of people caught stealing crops in gardens. These brutal displays were partly condoned by popular sentiment that tended to sanction harsh treatment of thieves, a sentiment made all the more acute by the failure of harvest in many households. However, many villagers also showed some understanding toward the thieves' plight, particularly if they were elderly people, and complicated public outrage with criticism of Gama's interventions, arguing that he should have ordered the thieves to work for others instead of physically harming them. In fact, Gama's best chance of making a comeback in public life lay in his friendship with several headmen in nearby villages and with their chief. It was this friendship, lubricated by Gama's generosity with beer, that soon paved the way for his ascension to the position of a Group Village Headman. The comeback, causing consternation in Kabudula village, took place around the time when *Nkhani Zam'maboma* broadcast the above-mentioned story about a headman's incestuous affair in the neighboring chiefdom.

The Uses of Silence

The higher they are in the hierarchy of traditional authorities, the less dependent are incumbents on support from their subjects. While the appointment of Paramount Chiefs and Senior Chiefs invariably involves endorsement by the central government, Group Village Headmen are those intermediary authorities who often owe their positions more to their peers and superiors in the hierarchy than to their subjects. Much as they may still occupy an in-between position in the political organization—at once answerable to their own people, to their superiors in the traditional hierarchy, and to various levels of governmental institutions—the foundational observations in the anthropological literature on Southern and Central African chiefs and headmen may seem somewhat unrealistic when applied to contemporary circumstances (see Gluckman et al. 1949). Anticipating what historians came to see as polities based on the accumulation of people rather than on the control of arable land (see, e.g., Alpers 1969; Kopytoff and Miers 1977), Audrey Richards observed for the Bemba in Zambia that "the headman's prime difficulty was in fact to persuade relatives to join him or if they had already done so to persuade these kinsmen not to leave him" (1956: 38). Isaac Schapera reported a particularly pithy proverb among the Tswana: "A chief is a chief by grace of his tribe" (1937: 184).

What these observations emphasized was performance in office, the constant evaluation of incumbents against the standards of the authority they were supposed to embody. Villagers' gossiping and some of the oral genres mentioned earlier in this chapter suggest that subjects' capacity to monitor and influence headmen's performance had not been entirely lost to colonial and postcolonial impositions.[27] However, Gama's comeback also shows how ascension to office without villagers' consent did not necessarily eradicate a sense of obligation between the incumbent and his subjects. A new mode of evaluation had become available to villagers, based on a new genre of expressing discontent. *Nkhani Zam'maboma* had introduced a means by which Gama could be made to monitor his own conduct, with or without discontent being voiced in public.

Although Gama did not refer to *Nkhani Zam'maboma* in public, its stories did seem to affect his conduct. He had a radio powered by a car battery in his house, and several neighbors would often gather there in the evenings to listen to it. Gama's house had welcomed them throughout the years of his increas-

ingly controversial behavior, but his hospitality appeared to have deepened together with his humility after he had been deposed. However, while visitors
were now treated to food as a matter of routine, many of his neighbors commented to me how Gama seemed to avoid *Nkhani Zam'maboma*. The program
had been a regular item of entertainment at his house before his downfall, but
afterward he would keep his radio tuned to a different station when the time
for it was approaching and would only reluctantly switch to the MBC if his visitors insisted on it. He would often leave the room for much of the ten-minute
broadcast and remain quiet when his visitors discussed the stories.

Silence played an important role in both Gama's attempts to regain authority and villagers' monitoring of his conduct. After years of blunt talking,
Gama did not choose his words with care only when *Nkhani Zam'maboma*
was discussed. His return to the status of a church elder presupposed participation in numerous church services and meetings as a humble and quiet con-
gregant who never spoke in public unless asked to do so. Outside the formal
and public arenas of village life, the subdued air he had about him drew comments from villagers when he was not present. Although casual encounters
with him would still involve some joking interspersed with customary greetings, particularly those who were not his kin or affines felt that his use of dis-
respectful expressions, such as the second-person singular pronoun *iwe*, had
decreased. Compassion at funerals and generous gift-giving in weddings were
the other obvious instances of his attempts to change popular perceptions of
him, especially noticeable for the silence he maintained in public during those
occasions. While no funeral or wedding in Kabudula village had proceeded
without a speech by Gama before his downfall, his period of repentance was
marked by his complete withdrawal from public speech-making.

These changes in personal conduct ensured that Gama never had to use
the exit option mentioned above. Yet villagers' gossiping may not have had its
impact without the popularity of *Nkhani Zam'maboma*. Here silence on the
radio spoke volumes, because it was, from Gama's point of view, an ominous
silence, a constant threat of exposure that could have made the exit option inevitable. As such, much as some villagers bemoaned the lack of stories from
this area on the program, many others also rejected it as a medium to publi-
cize Gama's misdemeanors. The reason was their fear of escalating a village-
based conflict into a rupture within the chiefdom. What would it mean, these
villagers asked themselves, to have Kabudula mentioned on the national radio
as a village where the daughters of several families were alleged to have been
subject to the headman's sexual exploits? What would it entail for the village's

standing among other villages, whose headmen could have been seen by their subjects to carry some of Gama's guilt because of their association with him? The fear of escalation concerned not only the village's reputation as a moral entity but also, inseparably, its access to relief and development aid in the area. To the extent that this access was mediated by traditional authorities, a scandal tainting the reputations of Gama's peers and superiors would not have augured well for Kabudula. They could have retaliated by withholding aid from Kabudula or by turning the officials of local government against it. The silence on the radio was, therefore, both an attempt to keep the discontent confined to those most immediately affected by the scandal and a threat of future exposure. Here the limits to revealing scandals were set as much by the local configurations of power as by the avoidance of notoriety at the national level.

The Disciplinary Effect of Silent Claims

The suppression of dissent under Banda's regime may have made it difficult for scholars and human rights activists to appreciate the variety of genres and aesthetics Malaŵians have had at their disposal to criticize and reflect on the abuse of power. Titles such as *Where Silence Rules* (Africa Watch 1990) and *Suffering in Silence* (Mkamanga 2000) have conveyed the stifling conditions of postcolonial autocracy. Yet an exclusive focus on the silencing practices of the state may attribute undue weight to the significance of speaking out in public. Some claims can only be properly heard if they are subtle, expressed in muted voices and an allusive language.[28] The strategic uses of silence, moreover, are themselves intimately linked to claim-making in settings where people are as mindful of hierarchies as they are capable of imagining equality as a condition of relationships. Some of the genres mentioned in this chapter, from praise poems to pounding songs, have perfected cryptic and allusive standpoints on human relationships. Together with a long-standing capacity, emanating in response to the mass-mediated misinformation before and after the democratic transition, to see in news stories more than meets the eye, such genres paved the way for the reception of *Nkhani Zam'maboma*. It was reception deeply embedded in the relationships of everyday life, from the sharing of the listening experience to the co-authorship of stories in a variety of public and intimate encounters.

The novelty of *Nkhani Zam'maboma* as a genre owes much to its mass-mediated status, but it is also important to recognize the specific historical juncture at which it became established on Malaŵi's airwaves. It coincided not only with the liberalization of the airwaves but also with the rapid rise of new claims in public arenas, largely articulated by politicians and human rights activists as assertions about individual freedoms. As has been seen, *Nkhani Zam'maboma* presented a rather more complex view of inequalities provoking the imagination of equality, but its commitment to exposure and revelation, if only within the limits imposed by anonymity, did signal a new genre in Malaŵian deliberations on poverty and injustice. In this regard, the study of its reception in an area that was not a frequent supplier of stories has a special contribution to make.

My fieldwork in Dedza District helped me to understand how the local popularity of *Nkhani Zam'maboma* did not necessarily translate into the submission of stories. The absence of people eager to act as correspondents may have been an anomaly, because the area did have its share of strangers in teachers and agricultural extension workers who, as was seen in the previous chapter, tended to crowd the program's pool of regular contributors. What is significant here is the way in which the stories heard on the radio got inserted into villagers' relationships even when the radio made no mention of their locality. Editors emphasized fear and shame as the program's effects on its listeners, but when seen within the relationships of a particular locality, those effects, and the public's interest in the program, were shaped by an aesthetic of claims that did not always need words in order to be heard. The sometimes ambiguous endings of the broadcast stories were matched by the continuing contestation of Gama's public role in Kabudula village. The lack of a closure or resolution in villagers' tribulations with him was not, however, merely a function of how local politics operated. *Nkhani Zam'maboma* had an effective local presence that was likely to have defused the specter of a more confrontational approach to Gama's misdemeanors. Listening to the program had generated a form of public silence that, containing as it did a public secret, influenced personal conduct. By withholding their grievances from the radio, villagers also subscribed to a liberal sense of civility that prevented the conflict's escalation beyond the confines of their village.

Much as villagers' gossiping—drawing on, for example, the customary norms of sexual propriety—represented a source of social control over Gama's behavior, his formation as a self-regulating subject required more than conformity with externally imposed norms. The aesthetic of claims against him enlisted him in a far more subtle manner in his own subjection. The local circulation of gossip was amplified by the ominous silence about his failings on the radio, a predicament that made him adopt the conduct of a subject rather than a leader. The cynical view that sees in Gama's change of heart only strategic conformity with norms would lose sight of the personal turmoil it involved, from being deprived of the headmanship to facing the sinner's plight in the church. Through his subjection, villagers were able, in the context of mass-mediated stories about errant authorities, to generate a sense of equality with Gama without voicing overtly emancipatory claims or seeking to negate the moral order of headmen and their subjects. By the same token, *Nkhani Zam'maboma* as an institution in its own right may well keep Gama on his guard even in the new position of Group Village Headman, however much he owes it to his superiors in the hierarchy of local authorities.

8

Christian Critics

An Illiberal Public?

As one facet of the liberalization that gathered momentum at the turn of the millennium, *Nkhani Zam'maboma* invites consideration of whether liberal values and procedures have any purchase on the moral imagination in a country like Malaŵi. Questioning the extent to which politicians and human rights activists were the most consequential participants in new public arenas, this book has sought to demonstrate that African-language claims mediated by the radio can yield insights into the broader issues of rights and obligations under the conditions of poverty and inequality. By thus including in the purview both the broadcasters and listeners of a popular radio program, this book shares an intellectual affinity with various attempts to go beyond Habermas's notion of the public sphere (see chapter 2). Concepts such as counter-publics (Hirschkind 2006) and the parallel public sphere (S. Dewey 2009), in particular, might seem congenial to the project here to show that much else has been taking place in public than the endless bickering between politicians and activists over freedoms and responsibilities in the governance of Malaŵi. However, although much of this recent ethnographic and conceptual work is wary of imputing models of resistance to the alternatives it has discerned, the tendency to assume a measure of duality between the dominant and subordinate public arenas has not been repeated in this book. It was difficult to identify any emancipatory agenda in *Nkhani Zam'maboma,* because both its editors and listeners appeared to take for granted the institutions whose incumbents the program described. The idea of resistance has also been undermined by the editors' commitment to serving the government.

The editors' subservience to Malaŵi's successive governments can easily be criticized for working against their best interests, both professionally by curtailing the scope of their journalism and, especially during the budget crisis under Mutharika's first administration, financially. A similar faith in institutions in the stories they broadcast on *Nkhani Zam'maboma* would seem to warrant a further criticism. The social-scientific quest for unmasking power relations would take issue with the attribution of blame to persons rather than to the undemocratic institutions they embody. Moreover, by refusing to mention politicians, and by presenting each story as a localized affair, *Nkhani Zam'maboma* can be criticized for depriving its listeners of tools for understanding how power is constituted at the national and transnational levels. Its localized stories can also be admonished for harking back to an idealized village life in which kinship obligations bind persons together and local institutions such as the village headmanship continue, at least in principle, to serve their subjects.[1]

These are important criticisms, and it would be unfortunate if the tenor of this book was thought to lend unqualified support for *Nkhani Zam'maboma.* Precisely because the project here is more descriptive than normative, criticisms are just as much subject to analysis as are the contents and effects of the program. The criticism that *Nkhani Zam'maboma* turns its listeners' gaze inward to focus on their localities has already been countered by insights into the public's capacity to shift the scale of their deliberations on misconduct and abuse. The long years of autocratic rule had created a "knowledgeable community" (Barber 1997: 8; Gunner 2000: 228; Lekgoathi 2009: 577) that saw in news more than met the eye and used apparently localized and innocuous stories as allegories for the abuse of power at much higher levels. An African-language critique of power may arise from seeing enough attempts at regime change and institutional reform rather than from a fundamentally conservative disposition.

The editors and listeners of *Nkhani Zam'maboma* may have had sound historical reasons for their lack of interest in institutional reform, not least after the much-touted transition to democracy that had brought few tangible improvements in their well-being. Their desire to hold the incumbents of public office to account represented a different mode of political thought and action, one whose merits and demerits vis-à-vis the conventions of liberal democracy, as they were marketed to Malaŵians, would be the subject of a more normative account than can be given here. At any rate, this interest in evaluating performance in office suggests that the editors' pride in *Nkhani Zam'maboma* and their commitment to serving the government were not entirely disparate dispositions. For them, the government was an institutional complex that outlived the politicians who ran its affairs and, with its transcendental project of development, possessed legitimacy in a way that its mortal officials did not. In a similar vein, localized institutions such as the village headmanship were as respected as their incumbents were subjected to constant evaluation. It was because the overt evaluation of ruling politicians was so risky that stories on *Nkhani Zam'maboma* became allegorical outlets for the editors' professional and personal grievances.

Rather than embarking on an exogeneous critique of *Nkhani Zam'maboma* before its ethos and historical context are fully understood, the analyst will do well to explore how Malaŵians themselves criticized the program. As has been seen, the editors' concern over verification was matched by their public's capacity to question whether some details were true or not. Although this doubt, widespread among both educated and semi-literate listeners, rarely took issue with the feasibility of topics such as witchcraft, it kept everyone attentive not only to the contents of the program but also to the ethics of its overall purpose. As was discussed in the previous chapter, the popular appreciation of exit options indicated the public's awareness of the damage the program might do to the reputations of those whose misconduct it publicized.

Most listeners in Dedza District and Chinsapo Township had been exposed to human rights talk, its increasing audibility in Malaŵi's public arenas having coincided with the rising popularity of *Nkhani Zam'maboma*. Although both addressed questions of injustice and violation, few listeners suggested a connection between human rights talk and *Nkhani Zam'maboma*. Few were, in point of fact, particularly inclined to deploy human rights talk in their everyday lives, associated as it was either with controversial changes in gender and generational obligations or with the rhetoric of individual freedoms among politicians and civil-society activists. Conversely, as has been seen, few politicians or human rights activists saw reason to comment on *Nkhani Zam'maboma*. In this regard, although it did not announce itself as such, *Nkhani Zam'maboma* represented an alternative to human rights talk. It was an alternative from without, whereas those Malaẅians who criticized the program tended to present an alternative from within its own ethos.

The most explicit and consistent critics of *Nkhani Zam'maboma* during fieldwork were born-again Christians. Many avid listeners of the program, and even some journalists in the newsroom, were themselves born-again Christians, but common to the Pentecostals I had come to know well in Chinsapo Township in Lilongwe was a certain frustration about the program's lack of inspirational content.[2] It could, I was told, weaken (*kufooketsa*) people when they heard about bad behavior among the men and women of God. Stories on *Nkhani Zam'maboma* showed "what people were doing" (*zimene akuchita*) but not "what they were not doing" (*zimene sakuchita*). By failing to broadcast stories about personal salvation, the program did not harness in full its transformative potential.

These born-again Christians' criticism appeared to acknowledge only one aspect of the program's disciplinary effect mentioned in the previous chapter. They recognized that its stories could serve the function of social control by deterring people from misbehaving, but they were less convinced of its capacity to transform persons into self-regulating subjects. Here they had other products of the broadcast media to contrast with *Nkhani Zam'maboma*. As was seen in chapter 1, nine of the sixteen radio stations in Malaẅi in 2006 had a religious profile, and the broadcasts of five stations had an Evangelical and Pentecostal orientation.[3] In this chapter, I compare a popular Chicheẅa program on one of them, Transworld Radio, with *Nkhani Zam'maboma* in order to explore what born-again critics considered a more plausible form of engaging the problem of worldly vice.

As a testimonial program, *Ndamasulidwa* (I Was Released) had more than formal similarities with *Nkhani Zam'maboma,* such as the exposure of misconduct, because human relationships, and the obligations they entailed, provided in both programs idioms for expressing violation and abuse. The inclination of the testimonies to also discover, with God's guidance, salvation in and through those obligations indicated that critics were not so much radically outside of the world of *Nkhani Zam'maboma* as seeking alternatives within it. A central question to be explored is whether the Christian program summoned an illiberal public in contrast to the liberal public of *Nkhani Zam'maboma.* The question draws attention to the boundary between liberal and illiberal dispositions, and in certain respects the boundary seemed clear enough. Unlike the inclusive ethos of *Nkhani Zam'maboma,* the Christian testimonials were broadcast with their editors' direct appeals to the public to change their lives in specific ways. "What are you waiting for?" (*mukudikira chiyani?*), the presenter would often ask after the testimonial, admonishing listeners to get prepared for the Christ's second coming by refraining from immoral activities while embracing the practice of praying and regular attendance at church. In contrast to the cross-cutting ethnic, religious, and other ties imagined in the ethos of *Nkhani Zam'maboma*, the Christian program delineated a distinct constituency of blessed people (*anthu odalitsika*) that others were urged to join. It is not obvious, however, that this emphasis on exclusiveness marked the program out as illiberal. The critics of liberalism have long pointed out its exclusionary politics, evident in the demands of citizenship liberal nation-states inflict on migrants and asylum seekers (Benhabib 2004; see also Arendt 1951). Toward the end of this chapter, the comparison between alternatives within and alternatives without discusses the extent to which liberal and illiberal dispositions may share certain features.

Before this comparison, it is necessary to know more about the presence of Christianity in the MBC's newsroom and Chinsapo Township. My account provides only qualified support for those critiques of the Habermasian public sphere that have highlighted the continuing public presence of religion in the era of electronic and digital media (see, e.g., Meyer and Moors 2006). Against the assumption that religion becomes increasingly privatized as the mass-mediated circulation of images and ideas proceeds on a planetary scale, scholars have disclosed the roles religion plays in public culture in various parts of the world. For Africa, they have demonstrated how religious broadcasts mediate new publics often in tension with the secular claims of the state (Hirschkind 2006), how commercial and religious aspirations can be linked (Schulz 2006), how the local and transnational media participate in managing religious diversity (Hackett 2006), and, particularly in relation to Pentecostalism, how charismatic leadership benefits from the use of electronic media (De Witte 2003). However, while most of these themes could be examined in Malaŵian contexts, they are not central to the objectives of this chapter. On the one hand, MBC journalists' religious convictions were almost as carefully guarded against public exposure as were their political opinions. On the other hand, township Pentecostals did not engage with the broadcast media as its producers but as its public and did not, as their familiarity with *Nkhani Zam'maboma* indicated, confine their media consumption to a few specifically religious programs. Publics, it is worth recalling, are neither communities nor corporate groups, and it is possible for the same person to belong to multiple publics. The most ardent Christian critics of *Nkhani Zam'maboma*, however, were hardly receptive to its ethos. Taken together, these observations situate born-again Christianity and the critique it inspired in the range of relationships in which both MBC journalists and their Christian critics pursued their lives.

Religion in the Newsroom

A microcosm of Malaŵi's religious diversity awaited the observant visitor to the MBC's newsroom during my fieldwork. The visitor had to be observant, because few religious symbols were on display. Apart from two Muslim women conspicuously dressed in headscarves, women and men in the newsroom wore clothes, many of them secondhand, whose formal style was common to Malaŵian office workers. A long beard could suggest a man's Apostolic commitments, whereas Roman Catholics appeared to often wear their rosaries under their clothes. I never witnessed proselytization in the newsroom, although some journalists were Pentecostals. The editors responsible for *Nkhani Zam'maboma* were all Christians: members of the Roman Catholic Church, the Church of Christ, the Jehovah's Witnesses, and the Seventh-Day Adventists. This diversity of denominations was remarkable in light of the amicable working relations among the team. It seemed that not only were religious symbols usually invisible in the newsroom but editors also preferred to keep their denominational convictions to themselves.

The cooperation between the members of the Church of Christ and the Jehovah's Witnesses was particularly unlikely if Christian identities were assumed to define persons' being in the world. As an African-instituted church, the Church of Christ was somewhat eclectic in its adoption of practices and doctrines, using the Presbyterian hymn book while allowing the consumption of alcohol in contradistinction to the Presbyterian doctrine. The Jehovah's Witnesses, on the other hand, were far less ambiguous in their condemnation of alcohol, and their attempts to distance themselves from the state had resulted in persecution in Banda's Malaŵi (Africa Watch 1990: 64–67). It was, therefore, somewhat surprising to find a Jehovah's Witness in the newsroom swearing the same commitment to serving the government as everyone else. This editor, like many others in the newsroom, had a past of involvement in various Christian denominations, including Pentecostalism in this case, and the current religious affiliation was often as much a function of marriages and other relationships as of doctrinal reasons. The editor's involvement in the Jehovah's Witnesses was by no means a frivolous pastime, if only because other adherents raised concerns over *Nkhani Zam'maboma*. It was not uncommon, however, for civil servants to be Jehovah's Witnesses after the democratic transition, and the editor negotiated personal and professional commitments with the ingenuity that the middle-class status, however precarious, allowed for. Regular white-collar employment was precisely what many Christians in Malaŵi regardless of denomination took as a sign of being blessed.

The sense of work (*ntchito*) as professionalism served to moderate the editors' expression of religious and political preferences both inside and outside the newsroom without, however, becoming a simple assertion of secularism. A Jehovah's Witness and a member of the Church of Christ could be close colleagues when they shared little else of their lives than their professional commitment to serving the government through public broadcasting. Religion was, for the most part, avoided as a topic of conversation in the newsroom, along with politics and ethnicity. Some editors privately suspected their colleagues of using rather too much discretion in editing stories about religious characters, but it was also clear that no journalist in the newsroom viewed *Nkhani Zam'maboma* as antithetical to Christian values. When I reported to them what some Pentecostals in Chinsapo Township had said about it, born-again journalists would retort by saying that persons had been weak (*ofooka*) already before hearing stories on *Nkhani Zam'maboma*, if those stories were supposed to have a detrimental effect on their faith. Asked about the neutral tone with which some stories were told about healers (*asing'anga*)—a diverse group of practitioners categorically condemned by Pentecostals—these journalists would point out that healers' associations paid taxes to the government and were therefore legitimate. A sense of public-service broadcasting could, in other words, qualify some of the convictions that these journalists' Christian lives involved otherwise.

Journalists' Christian orientation could, at specific junctures, contradict their work for the MBC, as was described in chapter 3 for the Catholic newsreader during the democratic transition in the early 1990s. However, frustrations over the partisan content of their work were countered by the capacity of *Nkhani Zam'maboma* to highlight abuse and injustice without tailoring stories to the requirements of the ruling party. In their efforts to broadcast the perspectives of the downtrodden, editors had an opportunity to mold news according to a morality that owed as much to Christian teachings as to so-called indigenous kinship principles. Their Christian values could not be made explicit in the programs that the Department of News and Current Affairs produced, and nothing in the newsroom suggested that its editors and reporters had any qualms about the secular inclination of public broadcasting. Christian morals found expression on *Nkhani Zam'maboma* not as a means to proselytize listeners but as editors' sensibilities of what constituted violation and scandal.

Crucial to this expression of Christian morals was the way in which editors had not defined themselves first and foremost as Christians in their approach to news. In other words, while their moral imagination could draw on Christian idioms, it rarely made its debt to Christianity explicit. MBC journalists were usually lay members of their congregations, and their long and sometimes irregular working hours made it difficult for them to assume positions of responsibility in churches they attended. They were, however, in demand for such positions because of their status as relatively educated and formally employed professionals. Some journalists in the newsroom did serve on church committees in the townships where they lived, while some Pentecostals would spend the lunch break at prayer meetings in town and be asked to play a public role there. Whether or not they had such public presence in their churches, journalists in the newsroom did not admit a rupture between their work and their Christianity. It was a Christianity of the actively proselytizing sort that was shunned in the newsroom, but such a sentiment was by no means a declaration of secularism. Rather, as mentioned, it was in the very practice of editing *Nkhani Zam'maboma* that Christianity as an element of editors' moral imagination imparted its taken-for-granted influence.

Pastors in the News

Pentecostal pastors (*abusa*) and church elders (*akulu ampingo*) in Chinsapo Township were rather more forthright about their Christian predilections than journalists in the MBC's newsroom. The difference between them lay more in the extent to which they made those predilections public than in any compartmentalization of religion and other aspects of life. Just as MBC journalists pursued their apparently secular profession as persons shaped by Christian morals, so too were Pentecostals in Chinsapo entangled in relationships that went beyond their congregational lives. With the exception of those few pastors whose churches had well-established transnational links, most Pentecostal pastors in the township depended on small-scale trading, farming, and carpentry for their living (see Englund 2003 and 2007b). Their housing standards in a township where most households lacked access to electricity and piped water were identical to those of their neighbors, many of whom belonged to other churches or were Muslims or members of the *gule wamkulu* secret society.[4] Such proximity, coupled with a need among traders to cultivate extensive networks of information and customers, required peaceful co-existence and made proselytization a skill to be applied in the appropriate contexts.[5] Some Pentecostals in Chinsapo did spend considerable amounts of time every day in praying and Bible study and often participated in so-called crusades and fellowships at weekends. In their keenness to deplore what they considered negative views on Christianity on *Nkhani Zam'maboma*, they differed from other Christians in both Chinsapo Township and Dedza District. Catholic and Presbyterian villagers in Dedza, for example, rarely suggested to me that stories about misbehaving church leaders were a concern to them.

Stories on *Nkhani Zam'maboma* could not be accused of singling out particular denominations, because the editorial principle of anonymity extended to churches. Although born-again Christians were sometimes mentioned, usually the only clue to the protagonist's denomination was whether the story used the term pastor (*mbusa*) or priest (*wansembe*)—in itself a rather inconsequential distinction, because a whole range of Protestant, Evangelical, and Pentecostal leaders could come under the category of *mbusa*. More significant than the denomination appeared to be church leaders' propensity to be embroiled in the same predicament of poverty and inequality as everyone else. One headline, for example, stated that "the pastor of a church in Chileka in Blantyre District is said to have sworn that he will remove from the church each and every Christian who does not share with him the free food [relief aid] that people in the area receive."[6] The pastor, who was said to be "the headman's child" (*mwana wa nyakwawa*), had warned that he would "expel from the village" (*amuchotsa m'mudzimo*) anyone who was removed from the church. The story reported that the reason for this behavior was that the pastor "did not receive goods although he had registered his name as an orphan with the intent of receiving those free items."[7] The members of his church were reported to have refused to share relief aid with the pastor, because "they did not see sufficient reason to do so."[8]

Rather than overseeing a just distribution of relief aid, the pastor here was beset by greed that had made him register for the aid under a pretext and, when it failed, threaten to use his influence as a leader in the church and village to punish those who did not share their aid with him. Such transgressions involving material wealth and well-being were common in stories that implicated pastors. Another story reported that Christians in a particular church "were very disappointed about what their new pastor was doing."[9] "Among other things" (*mwa zina*), the story explained, the pastor had stated that "he would remove from the church everyone who did not give tithe and that they should not give silver money [coins] but paper money [banknotes]."[10] Moreover, the pastor had ordered that "Christians must collect money every week to buy fuel for his motorbike."[11] Just as the pastor in the previous story had done nothing to act as a trusted leader when relief aid was delivered, so too in this story was the pastor as a servant of God turned into an avaricious person preying on his impoverished Christians.

When hearing such stories on the radio, Pentecostal pastors in Chinsapo were not, however, only incensed by the discouragement they might spread among the members of their congregations. Although these pastors did have an alternative radio program to use as an example of what Christian reporting should accomplish, *Nkhani Zam'maboma* also held their attention for the way in which its stories could be deployed to define their own principles. At the same time, more was at issue than deploring ungodly behavior in order to draw praise for one's own righteousness. Inserted into the everyday contestation of Christian lives, stories about pastors on *Nkhani Zam'maboma* could become matters of divergent interpretations among pastors themselves. For example, the above story about a pastor demanding money also reported that "the pastor preached in English and gave verses from the Quran."[12] Preaching in English was almost universally condemned by pastors in Chinsapo, most of whom lacked fluency in that language and yet were exposed to its use in various prayer meetings in the capital despite the obvious capacity of everyone present to understand Chicheŵa. The use of English, these pastors concurred, amplified the impression that the pastor in the story was a conceited person.[13] By contrast, they disagreed about the use of the Quran, with some maintaining that it was acceptable to cite it for comparison with the Bible, whereas others insisted that everything worth saying was in the Bible and therefore no other book should be used as a basis for sermons. "The Bible is enough, it is holy, there is nothing that can add to it" (*Baibulo ndi lokwanira, lopatulika, palibe lina lowonjezera*), one pastor explained to me after we had listened to the above-mentioned story. Another pastor rejected the use of the Quran on the grounds that it might provoke violence (*chipoloŵe*). He thought that the comparison between the two books should be confined to the moments when, for example, a pastor taught the Bible to a Muslim within the privacy of a home.

While debating the methods of spreading the Gospel, Pentecostal pastors in Chinsapo commonly recognized that *Nkhani Zam'maboma* was accurate in its depiction of ungodly pastors not only as alienated from their congregations by greed but also as all too entangled in the vices and immorality of the people around them. Stories about pastors' dealings with healers, magic, and witchcraft did not surprise these pastors. Healers, as mentioned, were categorically condemned by Pentecostals, but their involvement with pastors indicated the thin line that sometimes separated the apparent adversaries. "The pastor of a church," one headline announced, "astonished people when a healer came to his doorstep to remind him of the medicine he had taken."[14] The purpose of the medicine had been to enable the pastor "to finish with the Christians who disagreed with his conduct" (*athane ndi Akhristu amene amatsutsana ndi zochita zake*).[15] This was one of the frequent stories implicating pastors in practices they otherwise condemned, and Pentecostal pastors in Chinsapo were able to add similar stories from their own experiences with dubious servants of God. The pursuit of a successful career as a pastor could entail the manipulation of murky medicine, such as when medicine was sought to make the pastor's voice sound like a lion's roar, or when the pastor placed in his church similar medicine to the one used by shopkeepers to multiply the people flocking to them. Pastors and other Christians who told me these stories invariably ended them by observing how the success of such manipulations would be short-lived, their result some misfortune that the failure to trust God would unleash.

Another side of the stories depicting pastors in the life-worlds of healers, magic, and witchcraft was their frequent exposure to them even if they stayed loyal to God. Their Christians could try their hands in forbidden medicine, such as when a man was reported to have used magic to see his fellow worshippers naked even though they had dressed well.[16] "The man was said to do this magic in the church," the story ended, "to punish the pastor of the church who did not agree with the man."[17] The problematic relationships in which pastors were embedded found particularly striking instances in stories that drew attention to their own families. One story reported that after a witches' aircraft had crash-landed and a healer had been summoned to sprinkle (*kuŵaza*) medicine on it, "from the aircraft emerged a pastor's son along with other people."[18] The pastors listening to this story in Chinsapo had no doubt that the pastor, although absent in the group of witches that had been traveling, was himself a witch. Their conclusion—assuming that if one person in a family was a witch, then others were too—was at variance with stories, also frequent on *Nkhani Zam'maboma*, about children being taken to learn witchcraft at night without their guardians knowing about it. The pastors to whom I put this observation were able to accept that in some families children were being bewitched regardless of their parents' habits, but they seemed to find the mention of a pastor's son too compelling to ignore. For them, the ambiguity of this mention was less interesting than the opportunity it gave to further elucidate some pastors' involvement in ungodly practices. They would point out that much as healers might appear in pastors' lives not only as sources of condemned medicine but also as the ones who revealed witches, they could not end witchcraft—only the second birth in Christ could.

The talk about rupture and radical personal change did not, in other words, deny the reality of one continuous world. It evoked, sometimes with the help of stories broadcast on *Nkhani Zam'maboma*, a world in which born-again Christians were entangled in multiple relationships, not all of which they had chosen themselves. These relationships entailed hostility as well as obligations, but crucial to Chinsapo Pentecostals' understanding of a continuous world was their inclination to see in their predicament universal features. In contrast to the demonization of tradition and culture suggested by some studies of Pentecostalism in Africa (see, e.g., Meyer 1998; van Dijk 1995), Pentecostals I worked with in Chinsapo insisted that stories on *Nkhani Zam'maboma* did not describe a culture (*chikhalidwe*). They acknowledged that, if backed by Christian programs on the radio, my interest in *Nkhani Zam'maboma* could give me examples to teach (*kuphunzitsa*) proper conduct once I returned to where I had come from.

This perspective on the universality of the incidents and themes depicted on *Nkhani Zam'maboma* had a parallel in editors' thoughts on the resonance of its stories beyond Malaŵi, as mentioned in chapter 5. More parallels and continuities are identified below in the discussion of the program that Pentecostals in Chinsapo saw as an alternative to *Nkhani Zam'maboma*. However, the objective is not to repudiate what its born-again critics took as evidence of a different program. The felt disjuncture between the programs illustrates how some alternatives emerge within one continuous world.

Relationships That Save

Transworld Radio, which was founded in the United States in 1952, was the first Evangelical station to reach Malaŵi. Broadcasting in local languages has always been central to Transworld Radio's mission, and it began its Chicheŵa broadcasts from Swaziland in the 1980s and acquired an FM license from the Malaŵi government in 2000 (Wendland 2005: 43). Its staff have long been Malaŵians, and during my fieldwork they contrasted their station with the African Bible College Radio, whose programs were almost exclusively in English and often imported from the United States. In addition to a range of locally produced news, music, youth, and drama programs, Transworld Radio had achieved particular popularity among Christians in Chinsapo, virtually irrespective of denomination, through a program called *Ndamasulidwa*. A weekly program of testimonies, its title derived from the passive tense of the verb *kumasula*, "to set free" or "to release." The literal translation "I was released" summons up the unchaining of the subject from the confines of his or her previous life. The passive tense is significant, because it draws attention to the limits of the subject's own choices. God works through human relationships that constitute and, during the second birth, *reconstitute* the subject.

During my fieldwork in the Lilongwe studio, the program's emphasis on personal transformation was often unclear to those listeners who came to deliver their testimonies.[19] The editors of *Ndamasulidwa* had to explain time and again that they sought not so much accounts about God's miracles as testimonies on the many ways in which God saved people from their misfortunes and misdemeanors. "Thanking God" (*kuthokoza Mulungu*) had to emerge from the contrast between the old life and new. The experience of becoming a born-again did not have to be recent, and some testimonies were delivered by listeners who had been pastors for several years. An immediate parallel to *Nkhani Zam'maboma* was the concerns driving editorial discretion, not least because of the fifteen-minute slot that *Ndamasulidwa* had. Most guests had far more to say than what could be broadcast, and while some testimonies were compelling enough to warrant broadcast in two fifteen-minute parts, editors often cut the material down to what they considered to be the essence of God's work in a particular case.

Editors' own born-again sensibilities were crucial to their editorial input. No one at Transworld Radio expressed doubt over the veracity of the testimonies they broadcast, however fantastic their details might have seemed to those who had not experienced the second birth. No less than in the MBC's newsroom, however, verification was an issue to editors, who tended to treat every new testimony with some initial skepticism. The reason was the false motives that could draw people to the studio, some seeking instant fame, others driven by the hatred of other religions or by a desire to take revenge on their enemies. In such cases, editors had no qualms about rejecting the testimony even if its narrator claimed to be a born-again Christian. More complicated were the situations in which editors found the narrated events plausible but regarded the narrator a lapsed Christian. He or she may have experienced what the testimony said, but something in the person's current demeanor told editors that he or she was a backslider. Such impressions could also result in rejecting the testimony, whatever its merits were otherwise. Editors rarely had the opportunity to investigate their guests' background and relied therefore on their sensibilities as born-again Christians.

The knowledge that was presented and evaluated was intensely personal for both editors and their guests, and what was personal was always a function of the specific relationships that constituted persons. For born-again Christians who delivered their testimonies on *Ndamasulidwa*, relationships were an inescapable feature of life, rarely entirely optional, and sometimes not simply constraining but outright harmful, even lethal. Yet precisely because they were inescapable, relationships both destroyed and saved. Finding Jesus was itself a function of being subject to the right kinds of relationships, and the urge to expand the scope of brothers- and sisters-in-Christ sustained the sense of salvation promised by the second birth. Insofar as relationships could have a radically different moral and spiritual content, the relationships that produced the born-again condition were, for Malawian Pentecostals, their main sources of trust in an otherwise hostile and troubled world (see Englund 2007b).

Many testimonies on *Ndamasulidwa* described violent acts, some of them occult, others more obviously physical. A testimony by the victim of domestic abuse showed how the two kinds of violence, occult and physical, could be defeated by spiritual warfare in and through human relationships. Mayi Lazima had not realized that her husband was a witch (*mfiti*) until a pastor explained it to her. Her suffering at the hands of an abusive husband was long-standing, one contentious issue being her inclination to attend a church. The husband tried to forbid her from going there, and once, two days before Christmas Day, he attacked her at night with the apparent intent to kill her. He hit her head with a hammer several times until she managed to escape into the night, bleeding and terrorized. A resident in a township, Lazima ran to the house of the pastor whose church she had attended. The pastor received her and began fiery prayers, while she vomited and felt ill. The husband found her at the pastor's house, and when the pastor offered to pray for his sake too, he insulted the pastor and dragged the woman back to their house. He locked her outside the house, but she was too scared to run away again.

On Christmas Day, the pastor came to pray for her and, because the husband was away, persuaded her to come to the church. During the festivities at the church, another pastor, a stranger to Lazima, explained to her that the husband was a witch who had wanted to kill her in order to have human flesh to bring to the witches' feast (*phwando*) at Christmas. Afterward Lazima pleaded with her maternal uncle (*malume*) to take her back to her village of origin. The uncle obliged but also recommended that she leave the church. She refused to do so and, upon her return to town, resumed worshipping in the same church, now separated from her husband. Describing the physical injuries she had suffered, she concluded that "Jesus protects me" (*Yesu amanditeteza*), evident, among other things, in her being cured without the services of any healers. Moreover, although her marriage with the abusive husband ended, she stated that "God had given me another family" (*Mulungu anandipatsa banja lina*). It was an answer to her persistent prayers, and her testimony ended with the reassuring message that her current husband attended the church with her.

Another testimony, delivered by Mateyu Phiri, a former soldier who had become a pastor, showed how a marriage could be the very foundation upon which the second birth was erected. This testimony, broadcast in two parts, was exceptionally detailed in its depiction of the relationships that had shaped the person's journey in life. They involved, among other things, the death of his mother when he was only two years old and his adoption by an unrelated, childless old woman in the village. Phiri's father was working in Johannesburg and sent remittances to his maternal uncle, who used the money for his own children's benefit. After an eventful childhood and youth, which included excellent performance in school against all odds, Phiri settled in a township of Lilongwe and was eventually admitted into the Malaŵi Army. His wife became a born-again Christian, who would pray aloud when he returned home from his drinking sprees. At one point he decided to send her back to her home village, because he had found another woman whom he wanted to marry. The wife did not stay in the bus where he had left her and returned to look for him in beer parties in the township. She resumed living in the same house with him.

Around the same time a funeral occurred at the army barracks, and the wife took the lead there to pray and preach. Phiri's colleagues were aware of his wayward habits, but one of his superiors was especially surprised to realize that his wife was a committed Christian. The superior reprimanded him for being a loser while his wife was an exemplary Christian. These words, Phiri said, "touched me deeply" (*anandikhudza kwambiri*), and he cried all night afterward. While crying in the bedroom and saying things such as "what I am doing is evil" (*zimene ndikupanga ndi zoipa*), the wife prayed aloud in the next room. When he eventually emerged to see her, she started to pray for him and asked him to raise his arm. "She made me receive Jesus" (*anandilandiritsa Yesu*), he disclosed.

The testimony continued by describing Phiri's spiritual growth, involving praying on a mountain and, above all, a series of miracles that demonstrated to him his calling to become a pastor. Once, for example, he passed by a funeral among people he did not know in a different residential area in Lilongwe and decided to stop there. To his surprise he was asked to pray, and without even knowing what he was doing, he ordered the corpse to wake up. Wake up it did, the first of his miracles that also saw, among other things, a lame woman in the township standing up and walking after he had prayed for her. Particularly triumphant was the experience he had in his village of origin. His uncle had remained hostile to him ever since he had lost his mother, and he reported in his testimony that this uncle had become angry when he had heard of his new life as a born-again Christian. Phiri had no doubt that the uncle tried to harm him through magic, and when one of his children fell ill while he was visiting the village, he summoned his relatives for a prayer session. The child got healed, and several in his family professed a desire to receive Jesus. Phiri's uncle, on the other hand, was soon killed by lightning. "People at home now know Jesus" (*panopa anthu a kwathu amadziwa Yesu*), Phiri added with some pride.

These two testimonies serve as examples of what most testimonies accomplished as narratives. They narrated events and processes from the viewpoint of the subject's relationships, asserting his or her immersion in the world of human relationships as a precondition for receiving Jesus. Although some testimonies did include depictions of solitary moments of revelation, typically while praying on a mountain or hearing God's voice in the privacy of one's bedroom, the veracity and consequences of these personal spiritual experiences could only be realized in and through human relationships. The above testimonies also indicate how some relationships brought tribulations rather than protection and delight. Some relationships, moreover, had to end for the Holy Spirit to achieve its aims, such as when Mayi Lazima had to sever the relationship with her abusive husband, or when the uncle's death appeared to pave the way for the extended family's baptism in the Holy Spirit in the second example. The manner of his demise, struck by lightning, had obvious spiritual and occult resonances for Malaŵian listeners. Lightning is associated not only with divine intervention but also with witchcraft, its use a long-standing device to defuse occult attacks. According to the principle "evil goes back to its origin" (*choipa chitsata mwini*), the witch's attack returns to him or her in the form of a lightning strike.

Equally clear, however, was the status of relationships as the evidence, indeed as the vehicles, of positive transformations. Lazima's self-realization as a born-again Christian was inseparable from finding another family (*banja lina*) and a husband who shared her spiritual commitment. Phiri, whose second birth presupposed submission to his wife's capacity to mediate the transformation, grew in the Spirit both by performing miracles and also by expanding the scope of his spiritual kinship to include his worldly kin in the village of origin. In neither case was the objective to decrease the extent to which the subject had obligations toward other people. Nor were diabolical relationships a sociologically fixed category.[20] One spouse could be a witch and another a fellow born-again, while one matrilineal relative could embody evil and others the triumph of salvation. The actual quality of a relationship was contingent on the particular existential situation in which the subject found him- or herself.

As these examples illustrate, three considerations were particularly salient to the ways in which the Christian critics of *Nkhani Zam'maboma* in Chinsapo saw an alternative in *Ndamasulidwa*. First, they cherished its depiction of born-again Christians' capacity to live without subjection to the dubious powers of healers and all the immoral manipulations and aspirations it was known to entail. Second, by thus going beyond the descriptions of what people did, as in *Nkhani Zam'maboma*, *Ndamasulidwa* conveyed both the need and the means for a radical personal transformation. What was the purpose of broadcasting scandals, Christian critics in Chinsapo would ask me, if the story did not show how another life was possible? Third, although the testimonies broadcast on *Ndamasulidwa* were a familiar genre for those who attended so-called crusades, Christian fellowships, and Pentecostal church meetings, Christian critics in Chinsapo thought that their mass-mediated nature amplified them to challenge or displace less desirable programs on the radio. Yet precisely by so closely linking their praise for *Ndamasulidwa* to their criticism of *Nkhani Zam'maboma*, these critics demonstrated how an alternative moral imagination was in part conditioned by its contender. Born-again Christians' adversarial rhetoric—proceeding through categorical distinctions—might be understood to always require a rather forceful notion of what it promises to leave behind. However, the kind of alternative that Christian critics in Chinsapo expressed takes us beyond this simplistic view to a more nuanced look at both their Christianity and the very nature of moral, political, and spiritual alternatives.

Alternatives within and Alternatives without

Affinities between *Nkhani Zam'maboma* and *Ndamasulidwa* extended from editorial practices to program contents. Just as the editors of *Nkhani Zam'maboma* thought they were affirming the veracity of stories when they vetted the credentials of those who had submitted them, so too were the editors of *Ndamasulidwa* prepared to accept the personal knowledge of testimonials if the narrating person appeared to be a genuine born-again. This parallel in the procedures of verification bespoke a broader affinity between the life-worlds in which journalism on the MBC and Transworld Radio was embedded. The incidents depicted on *Nkhani Zam'maboma* and *Ndamasulidwa* could have taken place in the journalists' life-worlds no less than in those of their listeners, and the editors of both programs did not, therefore, assert themselves as pedagogues detached from those whose stories they broadcast. The most revealing parallel between the programs was the emphasis their contents gave to human relationships in shaping their eventful stories. Obligations appeared in both instances as the stuff that made persons, and whether obligations were honored or disregarded gave insight into the person's moral and spiritual outlook. To the extent that both programs used narratives as testimonies, moreover, they were informed by the common assumption that testimonies conveyed relational rather than individual circumstances.

Alternative as difference was, nevertheless, more obvious than these continuities between the two programs. The aesthetic of claims, for example, seemed to be radically different. Although *Nkhani Zam'maboma* treasured anonymity, *Ndamasulidwa* encouraged speaking out in one's own name. Among the listeners of these programs, the capacity of *Nkhani Zam'maboma* to mediate allusive, even silent claims contrasted with the spirited and apparently direct ways of holding people to account that *Ndamasulidwa* urged. Differences also obtained between the editors of the two programs. MBC editors' tendency to keep their Christian convictions to themselves arose from their particular commitment to public-service broadcasting, whereas journalists at Transworld Radio were explicit about deploying their own born-again sensibilities to verify testimonies offered to *Ndamasulidwa*. *Nkhani Zam'maboma* broadcast scandals involving pastors in the same spirit as it exposed other figures of authority. No domain of relationships was identified as a shelter against deception and abuse. *Ndamasulidwa*, by contrast, was as exclusive about who constituted its public as it was expansive in its desire to recruit more members.

Another challenge to the identification of parallels between the two programs comes with a disciplinary controversy. Anthropology, it has been argued, is so loyal to the principle of cultural continuity that it has portrayed even Christianity as a thin veneer imposed on enduring cultural patterns (see Robbins 2007). The radical personal transformation that many forms of Christian conversion have promised is, therefore, diluted to suit anthropology's investment in the models of time and belief that emphasize continuity. As regards the radically transformative potential of Christianity, however, it would be wrong to suggest that the idea of a second birth has been an exclusively Christian notion in Malaŵian thought and practice. Perspectives on initiations and other ritual life have repeatedly put forward ideas that emphasize discontinuity in a person's acquisition of new attributes and responsibilities. A popular Chicheŵa novel, for example, explains that "when leaving their hideout, initiates must be changed people, new people, people who know tradition" (*anamwaliwo pochoka kusimbako akhale atasinthika, ali anthu atsopano, anthu amwambo*) (Manyeka 1990: 47). In a similar vein, the installation ceremonies of new chiefs and headmen have involved symbolically killing the existing person to pave the way for his rebirth in the new position (see, e.g., Mitchell 1956: 122).

What these examples indicate are more complex ideas of convention and discontinuity than the juxtaposition between cultural continuity and Christianity's ruptures seems to suggest. The way in which "knowing tradition" signals being "new people" admits rupture in the life-journeys of particular persons, but just as new chiefs and headmen become new persons by embracing what is understood to be a timeless set of dispositions and obligations, so too are initiates made new people by their submission to convention. The patterns of personal conduct are expected to change completely, not by individual volition but by entering a new constellation of relationships that entails new demands and responsibilities. It is difficult to see how born-again Christianity could dispense with this general interplay between convention and discontinuity. At once a radical personal transformation and mediated by recurrent signs and techniques of submission to the Holy Spirit, the second birth introduces discontinuity through conventional means.

The hope that both the editors and listeners of *Nkhani Zam'maboma* expressed for it to "change the conduct" (*kusintha khalidwe*) among those who had violated a sense of justice and morality situated the program in a similar set of aspirations as *Ndamasulidwa*. What Christian critics argued when contrasting the two programs was that *Nkhani Zam'maboma* did not go far enough to specify the methods and consequences of radical personal transformation. They rejected *Nkhani Zam'maboma*'s propensity to leave it for the listener to infer the right courses of action and demanded a more didactic approach to broadcasting. In this regard, *Ndamasulidwa* seemed to repeat in an extreme form the apparent tendency, discussed in the previous chapter, for *Nkhani Zam'maboma* to support personal rather than institutional reform. Here a reaction against Pentecostalism more generally would seem to be pertinent. Despairing of the apparent shift in African Christianity from social teachings to the issues of personal salvation and prosperity, Paul Gifford remarked that "any transformation possible through purely personal effort must be extremely limited" (1998: 348). Gifford's call for structural and immediate changes in Africa's political economies subscribed to a common policy preference for institutional reform.

The condemnation of born-again Christians' discourse on obligations and injustices, particularly when it arises from a generalized view of what Pentecostalism propagates in contemporary Africa, may too quickly turn description into a critique. Testimonies broadcast on *Ndamasulidwa* were not simple instances of the Prosperity Gospel, because the victory or success they proclaimed was often gained against challenges such as marital discontent, witchcraft, disease, hunger, and unemployment. Both the challenges and the success had a material element, but delivered by impoverished rural and peri-urban Christians, testimonies on *Ndamasulidwa* were not boastful reports on an individual's acquisition of consumer goods.[21] To dismiss these testimonies on the basis of how Pentecostalism might appear elsewhere is to overlook their actual contribution to public debates on poverty and obligation (see Englund 2007b). It would also obscure the way in which mass-mediated claims, whether explicitly Christian or not, can themselves challenge the notion that Africa lacks effective institutions to hold authorities to account.

Ultimately the affinities and discrepancies between *Nkhani Zam'maboma* and *Ndamasulidwa* turn on the question of how alternatives are best envisioned. The question is particularly vexing when studying the nature and prospects of liberal reform. Do alternatives to liberalism require a temporal and ideological rupture, or are they emergent properties in the very complex they seem to challenge? The relationship that did exist between the two programs suggests the latter line of analysis. As was seen in chapter 3, *Nkhani Zam'maboma* had inspired human-interest formats elsewhere in Malaŵi's electronic and print media, but their somewhat frivolous ethos had fewer similarities with *Nkhani Zam'maboma* than had the media product its critics considered to be its alternative. Precisely by evoking *Nkhani Zam'maboma* as a foil for highlighting the contributions of *Ndamasulidwa*, Christian critics betrayed the affinity between the alternatives. As alternatives from within, the two programs extended each other's potential by addressing comparable issues in their different registers of mass-mediated storytelling. The born-again ethos of *Ndamasulidwa* was present *within* the apparently secular and public-service ethos of its more widely followed rival.

Human rights talk and *Nkhani Zam'maboma* were, by contrast, alternatives from without. Both summoned publics which were in certain respects liberal, and yet sustained strikingly different aesthetics of claims. The critical distance between their aesthetics was rarely, if ever, bridged by Malaŵians, and therefore *Nkhani Zam'maboma* affords a perspective on human rights from outside of the many disputes and revisions the concept has generated. This sense of alternatives is, therefore, itself an alternative to the alternatives within, and it enriches Malaŵian, and broader African, disputes over the concept of human rights that have tended to be unduly constrained by versions of the juxtaposition between Western individualism and African communalism. The perspective offered here questions the view that the incongruity between human rights talk, as it was introduced to Malaŵians, and *Nkhani Zam'maboma* inevitably represented a contrast between liberal and illiberal dispositions. At the same time, it may seem ominous to some that the Christian program of testimonials shared more with *Nkhani Zam'maboma* than did human rights talk, the quintessentially liberal discourse. Bearing in mind the violence inherent in some liberal projects to redeem and to punish (Asad 2003: 60), however, the sources of civility, obligation, and equality outside the vanguardism of human rights talk appear less inauspicious. The challenge *Nkhani Zam'maboma* presents to comparative study is not so much whether liberal predilections should be rejected or accepted as what their influence is on both the ethnographer and his or her interlocutors. It remains to bring together the key observations in this book to see how the conceptual alternatives arising from this ethnography— "equality" being the principal among them—respond to that challenge.

9

Beyond the Parity Principle

The first article of the Universal Declaration of Human Rights states that "all human beings are born free and equal in dignity and rights." While the Second World War had attached new urgency to the definition and implementation of human rights, the 1990s wave of liberalization in Africa and elsewhere revived this project in the context of crumbling autocracies and widespread poverty. Much as its principled attention to *all* human beings could inspire fresh political, economic, and legal challenges to the status quo, the discourse on human rights was often highly selective in practice. Of the first article's emphasis on freedom and equality, only the idea of freedom came to inform the public interventions by Malaŵi's human rights activists and democratic politicians. As has been seen, the very concept of human rights was translated into Chicheŵa through the concept of freedom.

It would be futile, however, to expect that a conceptual shift from freedom to equality would by itself rectify the neglect of social and economic rights that the emphasis on political and civil liberties has seemed to reinforce. As central concepts in liberal political and moral theory, freedom and equality have been shown to carry multiple meanings and open up potentially contradictory possibilities. Feminist theorists, for example, have argued that once decoupled from its association with personal autonomy and self-rule, "freedom" can prompt questions of how social relations and institutions both enable and constrain subjects (Hirschmann 2003: 35–39; see also Friedman 2003). Such questions become particularly contentious when they no longer assume a categorical distinction between the subject's desires and socially prescribed conduct, or that submission to external authority necessarily subverts the subject's potentiality (Mahmood 2005: 31). As for "equality," some philosophers have at least since Rousseau recognized how the apparent neutrality of formal equality can consolidate existing inequalities by denying differences in situations, resources, and needs (Hirschmann 2003: 223–224). Moreover, equality comes with variable complexions and goals, with the demand for one type of equality (such as equal rights) inconsistent with the demand for another type (such as the equality of incomes) (Sen 1992).

The recognition and elaboration of such contradictions by liberal theorists makes it difficult to dismiss the ideas of freedom and equality as mere ploys to perpetuate inequalities. The reflexivity of the best minds in liberal theory has clear anthropological resonances. As Nancy Hirschmann puts it, "Liberal theory has all sorts of assumptions—the priority of liberty, the primacy of rights, the doctrine of individualism—built into it so deeply that we hardly see them as assumptions anymore but rather consider them a definition of the world" (1992: 26). "It is remarkably difficult," Quentin Skinner comments, "to avoid falling under the spell of our own intellectual heritage" (1998: 116). One way of resisting this spell and to expose implicit assumptions is by reaching beyond the canonical works of liberal theory. According to Skinner, "equipped with a broader sense of possibility, we can stand back from the intellectual commitments we have inherited and ask ourselves in a new spirit of enquiry what we should think of them" (1998: 117).

Whereas liberal theorists can achieve "a broader sense of possibility" by excavating the vast repository of Western philosophy and theology, anthropology—and the study of Africa more broadly—often substitutes textual analysis for fieldwork.[1] Such a move, as this book has shown, is by no means incompatible with the analysis of texts, whether written or oral. Fieldwork becomes necessary when it is recognized that those texts that are most readily available to analysts, such as the documents and statements produced by human rights NGOs, co-exist with a range of African-language genres that require linguistic competence and ethnographic investigation in order to be understood. With the shift of focus from one set of texts to another can come a profound change in perspective. Directed by the preferences of impoverished villagers and township dwellers, the ethnographer can discover a whole world of claims and moral debate in African-language media. The journalists editing the MBC's *Nkhani Zam'maboma* were no dissidents—if they were, they would not have been working for the public broadcaster—but through their own tribulations they experienced some of the injustices they read about in the letters from their public. Two observations sum up the change of perspective from NGOs' and politicians' human rights talk to claims expressed in an African language. First, the program's aversion to vanguardism and didactic tone contrasted with the idea in much Malaŵian activism that human rights needed to be introduced to the masses by experts. Second, by evading the attention of both human rights activists and the MBC's politically appointed management, *Nkhani Zam'maboma* mediated an alternative debate on injustice.

The Liberalism of the Chicheŵa Radio

Liberal reformers are often certain about the conditions they wish to transform. The consequent paradox is well known: the permissive and inclusive ethos of liberalism is subverted by the determination, even violence, of liberal reform. From natural rights to nationalism to the war on terror—and to the prescriptive democratization of African polities along the way—liberal reform has always involved fighting demons. Commenting on how the imagery of nature has been evoked for different purposes during the history of liberal thought, Talal Asad notes: "Violence required by the cultivation of enlightenment is . . . distinguished from the violence of the dark jungle" (2003: 60). Whereas early liberalism bared its radical intents by declaring existing inequalities unnatural, more contemporary varieties have represented nature as a darkness that threatens to overwhelm the enlightenment liberal reform has achieved. Addressing injustices in the history of liberalism—such as the political exclusion of women, the propertyless, and colonial subjects—"can be re-described as the gradual extension of liberalism's incomplete project of universal emancipation" (Asad 2003: 59).

Scholars and activists do not cast out the spell of liberalism simply by recognizing its paradoxes and violence. Their debt to liberal thought needs to be explored, especially when an ill-defined notion of equality spurs their engagement with the world. To this end, this book has asked how this intellectual and moral debt appears when it is confronted with insights into an unexpected domain. *Nkhani Zam'maboma* was compatible with liberal predilections for at least four reasons. First, its origins lay in the liberalization of Malaŵi's airwaves and political life. Liberal reform was not, in other words, extraneous to it but its very condition of existence. Second, *Nkhani Zam'maboma* transformed the paternalism of public broadcasting by providing an arena that was widely accessible for Malaŵians to voice their grievances. This inclusive ethos was achieved by the editors' decision to broadcast stories from all corners of the country and to avoid ethnic, religious, and political bias in their selection of stories. Third, the public thus addressed was a debating, reflexive public, its civility and tolerance apparent in the way stories often ended with the prospect of temporary ostracism or shame rather than violent retribution. Fourth, although no egalitarian vision was implied, *Nkhani Zam'maboma* mediated the imagination of equality by facilitating claims for mutual dependence between sharply unequal subject positions.

Among the "family resemblances" (Gray 2000: 20–21) that constitute the diversity of liberal thought, *Nkhani Zam'maboma* assumed its rightful place as a medium that addressed a particular kind of liberal public, distinct from the more conventional liberal public of human rights talk. But is this attempt to prove the liberal credentials of *Nkhani Zam'maboma* merely another instance of making African achievements acceptable to Western sensibilities? Is not liberalism, like nationalism (Chatterjee 1986), a derivative discourse within which the true subjects of history are always Europeans and North Americans, the rest of the world left to emulate their standards and achievements? Engaging as they are, these critical questions may fail to notice how the discovery of a liberal public is here a result of ethnographic investigation rather than of political or ethical preferences. The ethnography of *Nkhani Zam'maboma* confronts mainstream political and moral thought because the program itself was a part of the mainstream, in its nationwide reach and popularity comparable to the influence of human rights talk in a country that was in the throes of political and economic liberalization. Resisting the temptation to reduce the ethos and impact of the program to a culturally peculiar set of concerns is also to sever the link to liberalism's usual alternatives, such as communitarianism and various illiberal persuasions.

Nothing in the above should suggest that the conventions of liberal thought and reform can remain intact when confronted with this ethnography. A key interest of the preceding chapters has been to identify both conceptual and pragmatic challenges to prevailing liberal ideas. For example, it surely runs counter to much liberal reform in Africa to represent the MBC as involved in producing a liberal public. Accused of being mired in political bias and self-censorship, its journalists have had few sympathizers among the agents of liberalization in Malaŵi. This categorical condemnation has, however, been blind to journalistic aspirations within the MBC, thereby losing sight of *Nkhani Zam'maboma* as a particular kind of liberal institution in the new Malaŵi. The principle by which everyone, regardless of age, gender, and other markers of hierarchy, was able to submit stories was unprecedented among Chicheŵa verbal arts. Although editorial preferences prevented certain kinds of stories from getting on the air and substantially altered others, their interventions were themselves informed by the program's particular ethos of equality. *Nkhani Zam'maboma* had become an institution precisely by presenting an alternative to the common patterns of communication by which employers always had the last word in disputes with their employees, NGOs spread the new gospel of human rights without pausing to listen to its assumed recipients, and politicians engaged in intrigues without consulting their constituents. Editorial interventions arose from the editors' own, muted grievances and envisioned a different public, if only by silencing certain voices.

Critics of the Habermasian public sphere, as was seen in chapter 2, would not be surprised to notice such exclusionary practices in the apparently liberal and inclusive medium. At the same time, those critics' efforts to develop more nuanced perspectives on democratic deliberation would benefit from attention to the ways in which *Nkhani Zam'maboma* summoned its public. From the listeners' point of view, it was the program's status as an institution that could make explicit claims redundant. Silent claims were effective when everybody knew that the radio could make them public. Unlike the deliberations of the bourgeois-rational public in Habermas's scheme, the debate and reflection among the public of *Nkhani Zam'maboma* took place within an aesthetic that accommodated allusive language and outright silence as much as it did vibrant moral argument. The most direct association this book has with the critics of the Habermasian public sphere is in their move away from the idea of a singular public. Human rights talk summoned its own public of mutually independent individuals making contentious claims for their constitutional freedoms. The interest in juxtaposing different publics is not only the demonstration of different aesthetics informing their claims. It is also the contrast between the reforming zeal of human rights talk, however confined to political and civil rights it was in this case, and the endorsement of existing hierarchies in *Nkhani Zam'maboma*. This contrast has revolved around two different concepts of equality.

Equality as a Goal and a Condition

The alternative to human rights talk in *Nkhani Zam'maboma,* never elevated to the status of an explicit policy, took the idea of equality beyond its familiar parity principle. Whatever its internal contradictions and multiple meanings, the concept of equality, it will be recalled from chapter 2, arose in English as a term of measurement, still apparent in the image of justice as a matter of balance. The parity principle does not accept difference and hierarchy, whereas the stories broadcast on *Nkhani Zam'maboma* presumed that claims addressing the wealthy and the powerful could be effective precisely when they left difference and hierarchy intact. This alternative ethos of equality may seem counterintuitive, or even a contemptible assault on worthy causes such as equal pay, but the interest here is to consider the possibility of equality in the absence of an egalitarian ideology. The Chicheŵa word for "being equal," *kufanana,* is loyal to the parity principle through its connotations of being the same, commensurate, and identical. Not only was the word absent from the claims broadcast on *Nkhani Zam'maboma;* editors and listeners told me that its connotations would have been inappropriate there. Their concern was whether the poor had access to credit and agricultural inputs and, above all, whether those capable of assisting them acknowledged a relationship between the poor and themselves. Another way of describing this ethos of equality is by saying that subjects are motivated less by the idea of rights than by the idea of obligations. Here obligation presupposes neither acts of charity by the well-off nor overt rebellion by the poor. It presupposes mutually constitutive dependence.

Anthropologists have reported egalitarian sentiments and practices in hierarchical relationships no less than hierarchical tendencies in egalitarian relationships (see, e.g., Gulbrandsen 1991; Parry 1974; Shipton 2007). In view of such complexity, the objective cannot be cultural translation, as if equality assumed different meanings in different cultures. Rather, this book has explored how African-language claims made under the conditions of severe poverty contest and qualify the notion of equality that is based on the parity principle. At the same time, as mentioned in chapter 2, it is anthropology that has done little to dispense with cultural translation in its approach to equality. In Louis Dumont's (1980; 1986) foundational work on hierarchy and equality, the two notions have represented two civilizations, with Western individualism all too inevitably taken as the model of equality (see Rio and Smedal 2009: 27–34). It has, therefore, remained difficult for anthropologists to discuss equality anywhere else than in the shadow of individualism, no matter how sophisticated liberal political and moral theory has become in the meantime.

Among anthropological efforts to move beyond this impasse, it has been pointed out that individualism tends to entail competition that actually presupposes and promotes inequality (Béteille 1986). It has also been suggested that Western egalitarianism is not "a cohesive ideology but a conundrum" that produces through its contradictions disagreement (Fardon 1990: 579). To these insights this book adds the possibility that the claims broadcast on *Nkhani Zam'maboma* can deliver equality from the shadows of individualism to open up a brighter prospect of comparison. These claims enable us to consider equality as a condition of human relationships, as an ethos rather than a policy, as an obligation to be realized in particular situations rather than an ever-elusive goal to be pursued. A reformist vanguard paving the way for a more egalitarian future would undermine equality as the very possibility of making claims in the here and now. A question for comparison is how, and to what extent, constitutive obligations are claimed under different historical and institutional circumstances.

Between African Alternatives and Liberal Cosmopolitanism

The association between equality and obligation advanced here provides a corrective to both African exceptionalism and liberal cosmopolitanism.[2] The positive accounts of African alternatives often offer little more than a mirror image of what they seek to challenge. As such, the interventions that highlight the idea of rights appropriate to African circumstances often do so with recourse to the idea of obligation or duty. In the African concept of human rights, for example, "the extreme individualism of current human rights norms is tempered by the individual's obligation to society" (Mutua 2002: 80). It is, within the parameters of the individual-society distinction, a short step from the individual's duty in African alternatives to the individual's choice in liberal cosmopolitanism. World poverty may well demand a consideration of the obligations that moneyed cosmopolitans in the North have toward the distant poor, but such a consideration is typically a matter of moral contemplation in which personal ethics assumes a pride of place. Although the variations in liberal cosmopolitans' views on "duty allocation" (Kreide 2007: 157) are substantial, ranging from direct personal involvement (e.g., Singer 2009) to an awareness of institutional and transnational factors (e.g., Pogge 2002), little dispute appears to complicate the conclusion that liberal cosmopolitans are "as individuals responsible for doing what [they] believe will be effective in alleviating and preventing severe poverty" (Wenar 2007: 274). Obligations as duties and responsibilities thereby loom large in perspectives on both African alternatives and liberal cosmopolitanism, and so does the individual, whether as subsumed under the imperatives of an abstract society or as the ethical subject making choices within no less abstract political and economic structures. Not unlike the academic discussions about equality, both perspectives operate under the shadow of individualism.

One way of leaving the shadow in this instance is by distinguishing relationship from connection. Liberal cosmopolitanism envisions a connection between the poor and the well-off on the basis of their shared humanity, the global framework of production and consumption, or the threat posed by severe poverty to the security of the affluent world. Missing is the possibility that obligation is a corollary of a relationship constituting subjects instead of merely connecting them as pre-social individuals.[3] In the story with which chapter 2 began, for example, the white master's Malawian servant did not draw on abstract medical ethics when he felt offended by the master's obligation to a dog. It was the work he had rendered for the master that made him, in his own view, a more worthy recipient of assistance than the master's dog. In a similar vein, despite their anonymity, the stories broadcast on *Nkhani Zam'maboma* always depicted *specific* relationships, not generic social categories. Existing hierarchies were their taken-for-granted standpoint, indeed the implicit justification for claims when persons were seen to neglect their obligations. And yet, the program's particular form of social control was at variance with the individual's submission to an abstract society assumed in some perspectives on African exceptionalism. The tenor of these stories was to show how moral conduct among authorities such as chiefs and religious leaders was not guaranteed by customary norms but had to be achieved time and again within the contingencies of poverty and injustice. In other words, to the extent that the stories delivered lessons, they encouraged caution with abstraction, with even the highest custodians of the moral order susceptible to worldly vice.

Surely, it may be retorted, *Nkhani Zam'maboma* was a program that reduced the structural problems of unequal wealth creation and distribution to the level of individuals—it made those problems seem particular and localized. In response, it must be reiterated that the program was not a forum for making and implementing policies. As such, it neither subverted policy-making nor succumbed to its standards of evaluation. At issue was the moral imagination informing and shaping the experience of injustice under the conditions of severe poverty. The values of transparency and accountability—so central to the current rhetoric of policy-making in Africa—did not find an exact counterpart in the program's complex mix of exposure and allusion. *Nkhani Zam'maboma* had emerged within a tradition of critical listenership molded by the long years of autocracy, a tradition by which the public had become accustomed to adding detail to the news it heard on the radio, to assess what the news did and did not say, and to draw links between ostensibly separate events and persons. A key consequence for the moral imagination was the public's capacity to proceed from an apparently localized story to a critique of national politics, such as when an anonymous woman's visit to the graveyard prompted reflections on national leaders' maneuvers (chapter 3). Implicit in this capacity to see in the stories more than met the eye was the ease with which the program's rural and peri-urban public shifted the scale of their reflections on moral authority. National leaders' ties to donors and business partners beyond Malaŵi's borders were often a part of the critique, the transnational scale of injustice explaining some of the causes of poverty.

Despite this ingenuity of the moral imagination, it might still be objected that *Nkhani Zam'maboma* did not offer a systematic insight into the causes and origins of injustice. Precisely by attaching so much significance to moral conduct, the objection might go on to contend, its stories did sustain a personalized ethics that actually was not noticeably different from the one among liberal cosmopolitans. As was argued in the previous chapter, however, rather than producing an exogeneous critique—an intervention that comes all too easily to social scientists—we can profitably explore how Malaŵians themselves criticized the program. The import of the indigenous critique is to show how the apparently personalized discourse *Nkhani Zam'maboma* inspired was itself an institution in Malaŵi, widely known and influential even if not always endorsed. In other words, the landscape of editors, correspondents, listeners, and critics that this book has mapped delineated an institution for imagining and voicing grievances over poverty and injustice. By the same token, personal failings were judged to be such against the moral precepts attributed to particular institutions. Claims about persons presupposed the strength of institutions, not that they were weak.

Against the oft-heard lament about Africa's lack of democratic and developmental institutions, the case of *Nkhani Zam'maboma* asks us to look harder for African-language resources to imagine equality and justice. At issue is not an argument against strengthening the conventional institutions of liberal democracy, but the key conclusion of this book is methodological rather than technocratic. Insofar as some of the most consequential alternatives to Africa's ills are unplanned, as the format and contents of *Nkhani Zam'maboma* initially were, scholars and other analysts will do well to allow alternatives to their own assumptions to arise from the process of investigation itself. In this book, for example, anthropology's investment in the occult as the quintessential African alternative has been modified by a consideration of the range of issues that animates the moral imagination. In a similar vein, the dismissal of MBC journalists as passive vessels of state propaganda has been tempered by an appreciation of both their grievances and their subtle ways of producing an alternative to the status quo.

The rejuvenation of human rights talk requires a similar methodology for the exploration of alternatives. Rights struggles waged in opposition to the dominant paradigm of rights and privileges typically mirror the power structure they seek to challenge (see, e.g., Brown 1995). Such struggles can be consequential, but they are unlikely to open up the concept of human rights to other kinds of pragmatic and intellectual possibilities. A preliminary step is to move away from the notion that human rights are primarily a legal construct (Wilson 2007) and to examine what the moral imagination within the conditions of abuse and injustice would suggest if it was *not* subsumed under the encompassing remit of human rights. It might, as it has in this book, become more difficult to accept the view, expressed by Paul Rabinow among others, that "currently no secular counterdiscourse exists that has anything like the legitimacy, power, and potential for successful expansion that the human rights discourse does" (2003: 25). The lack of effective and plausible alternatives to human rights talk is a problem mainly to academics whose critique is not complicated by fieldwork. As for others, a genre of claim-making whose public runs into millions of people may well rejuvenate human rights talk from without. Just because the claims are seemingly localized and expressed in an African language, they should not escape the attention of those who count among the human rights values the ideas of equality and freedom.

Appendix 1

Presidential News

Main news on the MBC's Chicheŵa news bulletin, February 2, 2003, followed by translation.

Pulezidenti wa dziko lino Dr Bakili Muluzi ŵati sadzalola nduna iliyonse yo-sakhulupirika kugwira ntchito m'boma lake. Polankhula pamsonkhano omwe ana-chititsa dzulo kwa Chinsapo One m'dera lakuzambwe mumzinda wa Lilongwe, Pulezidenti Muluzi anati akufuna nduna zomwe zili ndi chidwi chotumikira chi-pani ndi boma. Pulezidenti Muluzi anafotokoza kuti cholinga cha boma la UDF ndi kutumikira anthu osati kugwiritsa ntchito maudindo pazofuna zawo. Mtso-goleri wa dziko linoyu anati boma lake lili ndi mfundo zambiri monga zoleme-keza ufulu wachibadwidwe wa anthu, kulimbikitsa ufulu wa demokalase ndi ku-limbana ndi umphaŵi. Dr Muluzi anati ichi n'chifukwa chake sagwirizana ndi zomakangana pa ndale zomwe anthu ena amachita. Pulezidenti Muluzi anati ndi cholinga cha boma lake kupezera anthu zofuna zawo pa ntchito ya chitukuko. Iye anakumbutsa anthu kuti pa nthaŵi ya ulamuliro wa boma lakale aMalaŵi ank-awapondereza ndipo analibe mwayi wogwira ntchito za bizinesi ngakhale wogu-litsa zinthu m'mphepete mwa misewu ya m'mizinda ndi m'matawuni. Dr Muluzi ananenetsa kuti ndi chipani cha UDF chokha chomwe chingalimbikitse mfundo za boma la demokalase ndi kukweza miyoyo ya anthu. Dr Muluzi ananenetsa kuti palibe chifukwa chomapatula amayi ndi achinyamata monga momwe zinkakhalira zinthu pa nthaŵi ya ulamuliro wa boma la chipani cha MCP.

The president of this country Dr. Bakili Muluzi says that he will not allow any untrustworthy minister to work in his government. Speaking at a meet-ing he had yesterday in Chinsapo One in the west of Lilongwe city, President Muluzi said he wants ministers to be keen to serve the party and the government. President Muluzi explained that the objective of the UDF government is to serve people and not to use public positions for personal gain. The leader of this country said his government has many objectives such as to honor people's birth-freedom, to strengthen democratic freedom, and to fight poverty. Dr. Muluzi said that this is the reason why he does not agree with political bickering as practiced by some other people. President Muluzi said it is the aim of his government to help people to have what they need in order to work for development. He reminded people that during the rule of the previous government, Malawians were oppressed and had no opportunity to do business or sell goods along the roads in cities and towns. Dr. Muluzi emphasized that the UDF is the only party that can strengthen the objectives of democratic governance and raise the standards of living. Dr. Muluzi insisted that there is no reason to exclude women and youths as was the case during the rule of the MCP government.

Appendix 2

Graveyard Visit

A story broadcast on *Nkhani Zam'maboma* on July 25, 2003, followed by translation.

Mayi ŵina wa m'mudzi mwa [location omitted] *akuti anapezeka ali kumanda masanasana dzuwa likuswa mtengo. Mayiwo amene wangoyamba kumene ntchito pa kampani ina kumzinda wa Blantyre akuti anapezeka atagona pa mitumbira iŵiri ya manda. Anthu atayang'anitsitsa pafupi ndi mayiwo, anapeza kuti panali kathumba momwe munapezeka zinthu monga malezala, singano ndi kabotolo momwe munali magazi. Atamufunsa chomwe amachita kumandako, iye anayankha kuti samadziŵa chomwe amachita ponamizira kuti ataledzera. Anthu ambiri akukhulupirira kuti mayiwo akufuna kukhwimira ntchito imene anayipeza kumene kuti asamuchotse ndiponso akuti akufuna chizimba choti atenthere uvuni ya njerwa zake zomwe akuti akufuna kumangira nyumba ya makono. Mwamuna woyamba wa mayiwo akuti anathawa zochita za ufiti za mayiwo zokhangati zomwezi. Mwamuna amene anakwatiŵa naye mayiwo panopa akuti akumukhwimira kuti asamachoke pa khomopo kuti azingosamalira ŵana cholinga choti iye azipanga zofuna zake.*

A woman from the village of [location omitted] is said to have been in a graveyard in broad daylight. The woman who had recently begun to work for a company in Blantyre city is said to have been discovered when she had fallen asleep on two grave mounds. When people looked carefully around the woman, they noticed that there was a bag which contained things like razor blades, a needle, and a bottle in which was blood. When they asked her what she was doing in the graveyard, she answered that she did not know and lied that she was drunk. Many people believe that the woman wants to protect herself through magic at her new job so that she will not be dismissed, and she is also said to want a charm for heating an oven to burn bricks that she needs for building a modern house. The woman's first husband is said to have escaped her witchcraft of this sort. She is said to have treated with magic the man she is married with now to prevent him from leaving the home so that he would only look after the children while she is doing her own things.

Appendix 3

Drunken Children

A story broadcast on *Nkhani Zam'maboma* on July 19, 2003, followed by translation.

Bambo ŵina yemwe amagwira ntchito pa sitolo ya mwenye ŵina ku Limbe m'mzinda wa Blantyre akuti anamwetsa ana ake masese atasoŵa ndalama yodyetsera anawo. Bamboyo akuti amakhala [location omitted] kutawuni ya Ndirande m'mzinda wa Blantyre. Mwezi wathawu mkuluyu akuti sanalandire malipiro ake a pamwezi pa zifukwa za pakati pa iyeyo ndi bwana wake. Atafika ku nyumba mkuluyu akuti anapeza mkazi ŵake atapita kwawo kamba kotopa ndi umphaŵi. Mayiyo akuti anasiya ana onse amene anabereka ndi mkuluyo ndipo pofika pa nyumbapo bamboyo akuti anaŵapeza anaŵa akungolira ndi njala. Izi zinamuimitsa mutu ndipo anaganiza zosakasaka chakudya. Pochoka pa khomopo mkuluyu anatenga poto ndi kuloŵera kumalo ena kumene amagulitsa mowa wa masese. Atafika kumaloko bamboyo akuti anatolera mapakete a masese omwe anthu anataya ndi kuyamba kukhuthulira masese otsalira mu potomo. Poto litadzadza mkuluyu anabwerera kunyumba yake ndi kuŵiritsa masesewo. Ataŵira bamboyo akuti anamwetsa anawo omwe anaganiza kuti ndi mphala. Atamwa masesewa anaŵa akuti analedzera kwambiri ndipo mkulu anaŵanyamula ndi kuŵagoneka. Pakadali pano akuti bamboyo anaima mutu ndipo ŵasiya kupita ku ntchito.

A man who works in an Asian's store in Limbe in Blantyre city is said to have made his children drink beer when he did not have money to feed the children. The man is said to live in [location omitted] in Ndirande Township in Blantyre city. The fellow is said to not have received his monthly salary last month for reasons between him and his boss. When he came home, the fellow is said to have found that his wife had left for her home because she had become tired of poverty. The woman is said to have left all the children she had given birth to with the fellow, and after reaching the house, the man is said to have found the children crying from hunger. It puzzled him, and he decided to look for food. He left the house with a cooking pot and went to a place where people sold homemade opaque beer. When he arrived there, he is said to have picked up cartons of beer which people had thrown away and started to empty the remaining beer into the cooking pot. When the pot was full, the fellow returned to his house to boil the beer. After it had boiled, the man is said to have given it to his children who had thought it was porridge. When they had drunk the beer, the children are said to have become very drunk, and the fellow carried them to sleep. As of now the man is said to be at a loss and has stopped going to work.

Appendix 4

Giant Rat

A story broadcast on *Nkhani Zam'maboma* on July 15, 2003, followed by translation.

Chikhoswe chachikulu champhongo chimene chinali ndi mphinjiri zitatu m'khosi mwake akuti chafa chitalephera kulowa m'mpanda kwa sing'anga ŵina [location omitted]. Sing'anga akuti anachoka kunyumba kwakeko chama half past five m'maŵa kukakumba mankhwala kuphiri. Ali kumeneko chikhoswecho chinafuna kuti chilowe kunyumba kwakeko, koma chinangoyamba kujenjemera mpaka khangati chakomoka. Pamene sing'anga anafika kunyumba anapeza anthu atadzadza kukaona chikhoswecho. Iye sanalankhule ndi munthu koma anangolowa m'nyumba kukasiya mankhwala amene anakumbawo ndipo kutuluka ndi mankhwala ophera amene anaŵaza chikhoswecho mpaka kutsirizika. Ataitanitsa nyakwaŵa ya m'mudzimo sing'anga akuti anang'amba chikhoswecho ndipo mkati mwake anapeza masingano, flexafoam, tsitsi la mwana ndi la mzungu kudzanso nsanza. Sing'anga anatentha zinthu zonsezo atasakaniza mankhwala ndipo analonjeza kuti munthu amene anatuma chikhoswecho aona. Pasanathe masiku mkulu ŵina ndi mkazi wake akuti anapita kwa sing'angayo kukamupempha aŵachotse ufiti popeza kuti anamva kuti anapha chikhoswe kunyumba kwakeko. Sing'anga analamula anthuwo kuti amene akudwala kuti alipire mbuzi imodzi kapena nkhuku zisanu.

A giant male rat that had three charms hanging from its neck died when it failed to enter a healer's compound [location omitted]. The healer is said to have left his/her house at about half past five in the morning to dig for medicine in a mountain. When she/he was there, the giant rat wanted to enter his/her house, but it just started to tremble until it collapsed. When the healer reached home, she/he found the place full of people looking at the giant rat. He/she did not speak to anyone but merely entered the house to leave the medicine she/he had dug and came out with lethal medicine that he/she sprinkled on the giant rat until it died. After asking the village headman to be present, the healer is said to have torn open the giant rat and found inside it needles, foam from a mattress, the hair of a child and a white person as well as a rag. The healer burnt all of them after mixing them with medicine and swore that the person who had sent the giant rat would see [would be cursed]. Before many days had passed, a fellow and his wife are said to have gone to the healer to ask her/him to remove witchcraft because they had heard he/she had killed a giant rat at his/her house. The healer ordered the couple to pay the one who was ill either one goat or five chickens.

Appendix 5

Reclaiming Virginity

Unedited version of a story broadcast on *Nkhani Zam'maboma* on July 11, 2008. The transcription is a copy of the original sent to the MBC, and no attempt has been made to amend its spelling and grammar.

"Worship, the Woman is Polyandrous!"

A woman speaking at the First-Grade Magistrate's Court in Lilongwe demanded her husband to restore her virginity and cleanse her of AIDS if he wanted to leave her. But some tried to think critically and condemned the ex-wife describing her irresponsible.

Magistrate Kachama made the situation even worse when he said: "The woman is saying you are still her husband. And that if you want to leave her, you should restore her virginity and cleanse her of AIDS, which she claims, you infected her. What are you going to say?"

The husband did not waste time thinking about what he could do for the lady. He just hit the nail on its head saying: "I don't want this woman. As for AIDS, I cannot be responsible because the woman married three times before me."

She alleged that her husband had also dumped her simply because she had stepchildren. "He told me he was tired of caring for stepchildren," she explained. But the husband denies the allegation arguing the cause of the breakage is not the stepchildren but her ruthlessness and lack of respect for him.

The broadcast version of the story, followed by translation. The transcription is a copy of the text prepared by an editor at the MBC, and no attempt has been made to amend its spelling and grammar.

Anthu omwe amamvera milandu kukhoti la Magistrate ku Lilongwe anagwa ndi phwete mayi wina wachikhulire atauza mwamuna wake kuti amubwezere utsikana wake ngati afuna kumusiya ukwati. Mwamuna akuti anapita kukhotiko ndi cholinga chofuna kuthetsa banjalo ati chifukwa mayiwo ndi wamkamwa kwambiri. Pozenga mlanduwo mwamunayo anafotokoza kuti chiyambire pomwe anakwatira mkaziyo sanakhalepo pamtendere. Mwamuna anati pachifukwachi waimika manja kuti banja lithe, koma mkazi anagwedeza mutu wake kuti sizitheka ndipo ngati mwamunayo amuwumirira kuti banja lithe amubwezere utsikana wake. Pamenepo mkaziyo akuti anayamba kulankhula zolaula zomwe zimachitika kuchipinda ndi bamboyo pogona usiku ndipo anthu m'khotilo anafa ndi phwete. Koma bamboyo watemetsabe nkhwangwa yake pamwala powuza mkaziyo kuti ayendere yake.

People listening to cases in the Lilongwe magistrate's court were overtaken by laughter when a mature woman told her husband to restore her virginity if he wanted to end their marriage. The husband is said to have gone to the court to end the marriage because the wife was too talkative. Stating the case, the husband explained that right from the start of the marriage he had not had any peace. The husband said that he had given up and the family should end, but the wife had refused and had said that if he demanded the family to end, he should restore her virginity. Then the wife was said to have told obscenities about what happened in the bedroom with the man, and people in the court collapsed with laughter. However, the man still insists that the wife goes away.

Appendix 6

The Truth about Porridge

A story broadcast on *Nkhani Zam'maboma* on June 14, 2008, followed by translation. The transcription is a copy of the text prepared by an editor at the MBC, and no attempt has been made to amend its spelling and grammar.

Anthu okhala dela la [location omitted] *adadandaula kwambiri ndi khalidwe lomwe akuchita aphunzitsi a pasukulu ina kumeneko ati pomatangwanika ndi phala lomwe limaphikidwa pasukulupo m'malo mophunzitsa ana m'kalasi. Amene watitumiza nkhaniyi wati pasukulupo pamaphikidwa phala lomwe ndi imodzi mwa ndondomeko ya boma kuti ana adzilimbikira maphunziro. Koma chodabwitsa n'chakuti aphunzitsi pasukulupo akumabwera ndi mbale pochoka kwawo, akatero akuti akumakhala muofesi kudikilira kuti phala lipse, nthawiyi akuti ana amangopatsidwa ntchito monga kukadula senjele zomwe akuti aphunzitsiwo akumagulitsa kuti apezepo cholowa. Izi akuti zakhumudwitsa kwambiri makolo awana omwe ali pasukulupo. Ndipo apempha oona zamaphunziro m'bomalo kuti achitepo kanthu.*

People living in the area of [location omitted] complain very much about what teachers in a school are doing by busying themselves with porridge that is cooked in the school instead of teaching children in the class. The one who sent us this news says that the porridge that is cooked in the school is a part of the government's policy to strengthen children's studies. However, what is surprising is that the teachers in this school come with plates from their homes and wait in the office for the porridge to be ready, while children are given work such as cutting grass that the teachers sell to find some income. This is said to have disappointed very much the parents of the children who are in the school. They have therefore asked those monitoring education in the district to do something.

Two rejoinders, followed by translations. The transcriptions are copies of the originals sent to the MBC, and no attempt has been made to amend their spelling and grammar.

Kutsutsa nkhani yomwe munaulutsa pawailesi ya MBC pa 14 Juni 2008

Ine mphunzitsi wamkulu wapasukulu ya [name omitted] *yokhayo* [location omitted] *ndalemba kalatali pofuna kutsutsapo pankhani yomwe munaulutsa loweruka madzulo pa 14 Juni 2008.*

Nkhani yoti aphunzitsi amatenga mbale kuchoka nazo kwawo kumakadikilirira phala ya soya siyoona. A WFP anapereka mbale zomwe timagwiritsa ntchito kulandirira phala. Chomwe ndikudziwa ine ndi choti lamulo la WFP pa phalali ndi loti ana asanadye, aphunzitsi ayambe alidya pofuna kutsimikizira kuti liri bwino ndipo ana adye. Choncho poona kuti mbale zimapita kwa aphunzitsi kukadya ena sakondwera nazo kapena.

Choncho wotumiza nkhaniyi wangokhala ndi mtima wa mnyozo ndi wosakonda anthu a m'delali. Cholinga chake ndi choti ife tikayipidwa ndi izi tiyimitse kubwera kwa phala. Izi sizoyenera komanso ngati pali ogwira ntchito, mphunzitsi amayesetsa kuti tiyi yekha amwe. Phala sinkhani yoti mphunzitsi atsusuke nalo.

Akonzi, ndikupempheni kuti nkhani zina zimafunika kufufuza mokwanira zisanatulutsidwe chifukwa zikuzetsa mipungwepungwe ndi maudani pakati pa anthu, chifukwa otumizawo amangofuna kuyipitsa mbiri ya ena. Pasukulu lino aphunzitsi akhumudwa ndi nkhaniyi ndipo sakukhala momasuka chifukwa cha nkhani ya bodza ngati iyi. Tangoganizani udzu ophunzira m'sukulu za kumidzi amadula kuti azimangira mipanda koma wotumiza nkhaniyi akuti aphunzitsi amagulitsa kuti apezapo cholowa sizoona. Wolemba/wotumiza nkhaniyi ndi wansanje ndi kaduka kwa aphunzitsi chifukwa ndi okhawo amaoneka kuti ndi ogwira ntchito ya boma ndi amapeza zothandizira pa moyo wawo chifukwa choti anaphunzira.

Tinayitanitsa msonkhano wa makolo pa 19 Juni 2008 ndipo iwo anali odabwa ndi okhumudwa ndi nkhani yomwe iwo samayembekezera. Aphunzitsi anawapempha kuti ndi bwino aleke kusayina mafomu kuti aWFP asiye kubweretsa phalali ndikuti tizingogwira ntchito yomwe tinalembetsedwa. Makolo ndi mafumu anati-

pempha kuti tisakhumudwe ndi izi zimene wotumizayo sanawauze atsogoleriwo koma ndi za mutu wake. Munthuyu ndiwoti afuna ayipitse mbiri ya sukulu lino ndi mafumu omwe amatumiza ana awo pasukulu lino.

Ndidzakhala wokondwa mutaulutsa zakutsutsa kwanga pankhani ya bod-zayi pofuna kuti dziko limve zoona zenizeni ndi kuchotsa mnyozo wa anthu pank-haniyi.

Refutation of the news you broadcast on the MBC on June 14, 2008

I am the headmaster of the school of [name omitted] that is the only school in [location omitted]. I wrote this letter to refute the news you broadcast on the Saturday evening of June 14, 2008.

The news that teachers take plates from their homes to wait for the por-ridge of soya is not true. The WFP gave the plates that are used to receive the porridge. What I know is that the WFP's rule is that before children have eaten, teachers should eat to confirm that the porridge is good for the children to eat. Therefore some perhaps were not pleased to see that the plates go for the teach-ers to eat.

The one who sent the news is just insolent and unloving toward the people in this area. His/her intent is that when we get annoyed by it we will stop the delivery of the porridge. This is not appropriate, and as someone in em-ployment, the teacher tries to have tea to drink. Porridge is not something the teacher would crave for.

Editor, some news need to be researched enough before they are broad-cast, because they bring confusion and hatred among people as the sender merely wants to damage the reputation of others. In this school the teachers are disappointed with this news and they are not feeling at ease because of this fraudulent story. Students in rural schools cut grass to make fences, but the sender of this news says that teachers sell it to find income but it is not true. The author/sender of the news is jealous and has a grudge, because teachers are the only ones who are seen to work for the government and they can help themselves because they had education.

We convened a meeting with parents on June 19, 2008, and they were sur-prised and disappointed about the unexpected news. They asked the teach-ers not to sign forms to stop the WFP's delivery of porridge so that we would only do the work we have been employed to do. Parents and chiefs asked us not to be disappointed, and the sender did not tell these things to the leaders but they are from his or her head. The person is someone who wants to damage the reputation of this school and of the chiefs who send their own children to this school.

I shall be pleased if you broadcast my refutation of this fraudulent news for the country to hear the real truth and for the insolence against people to disappear.

Kukamblana za nkhani ya mphala yomwe inatuluka mu nknani za maboma
Tinaitanitsa msonkhano wa makolo omwe ali ndi ana pasukulupo pamodzi ndi mafumu. Tinakambirana zokhudza nkhaniyi, ndipo makolo anali odandaula ndi nkhaniyi. Ndipo ife akomiti ndi mafumu tinali wokhumudwa chifukwa sitina-wonepo zimenezi zikuchitika pasukulupo. Choncho anthu onse anapepetsa kwa aphunzitsi onse ndipo afumu anapempha anthu onse kuti zimenezi zisazachiti-kenso.

Concerning the news about porridge that was broadcast in *Nkhani Zam'maboma*

We called a meeting with parents who have children in this school together with the chiefs. We discussed the news, and the parents complained about this news. We as the committee and the chiefs were disappointed because we had not seen these things happening in this school. Therefore everyone apologized to all the teachers and the chiefs urged everyone that these things should not happen again.

Appendix 7

"Makiyolobasi Must Stop Bewitching at Night"

A story submitted to *Nkhani Zam'maboma* but rejected in 2008, followed by translation. The transcription is a copy of the original sent to the MBC, and no attempt has been made to amend its spelling and grammar.

Mai Wenzulo sadaname kuti Makiyolobasi ndi satana weniweni ndipo asayime pa upresidenti padziko la Malawi

Zikomo Mkonzi

Makiyolobasi asiye kutamba usiku

Mnyamata wina kuno ku Thyolo wakhala ali kudandaulira kuti adalemba masiku ndi miyezi yomwe Makiyolobasi amabwera muufiti atasanduka khoswe. Komanso Makiyolobasiyu ali ndi anzake womwe amasanduka galu, muleme, mphemvu, kangaude ndi zilombo zina ndipo akuti Makiyolobasiyu ali ndi makoswe ambiri woti adzawagwirilitse ntchito povota mavoti a chaka cha m'mawa 2009. Komanso anzakewo ali ndi ndege zitatu zoti zizanyamule mavoti usiku. Ndipo mnyamatayu wati atengera Makiyolobasi kukhoti pogwiritsa malamulo a Dziko ndime 16 komanso amubwezere zonse wawononga pamatenda ake.

Mrs. Wenzulo did not lie when saying that Makiyolobasi is the real Satan and he should not be again a presidential candidate in Malawi

Dear Editor

Makiyolobasi must stop bewitching at night

A young man here in Thyolo is complaining that he has been counting the days and months when Makiyolobasi comes through witchcraft after changing into a rat. Makiyolobasi also has his friends who change into a dog, bat, cockroach, spider and other animals, and he says Makiyolobasi has lots of rats that he will use during the elections next year in 2009. His friends also have three aircraft that will pick up votes at night. The young man also says he will take Makiyolobasi to court using chapter 16 of the constitution, and he will also return to him everything he destroyed through his illness.

Notes

Introduction

1. For a short moment before the English voice-over began, Banda's words in Chicheŵa could be heard on the BBC radio on October 26, 2006.

2. Quoted in "Madonna Takes a New Baby Home," posted on the allAfrica.com website on October 13, 2006, and in "Calls for Review of Law in Wake of Madonna Adoption," posted on the allAfrica.com website on October 17, 2006.

3. For anthropological perspectives on transnational adoption, see Howell 2006 and 2009, and on parenting and fostering, see Goody 1982.

4. For example, "Father Now Backs Madonna Adoption," posted on the BBC News website on October 26, 2006.

5. "Madonna Adoption Plea Postponed," posted on the BBC News website on March 30, 2009.

6. "Madonna Tries to Adopt Second Child," posted on the allAfrica.com website on March 30, 2009.

7. The "hyperprivileging" (Barber and Furniss 2006: 4) of English in Africa has been evident in its status as the language of colonial power and now as the language of global communications. However, the appeal for taking African-language oral, written, and aural genres seriously does not deny the creative uses of English by Africans, not all of whom have been members of intellectual elites (Barber and Furniss 2006: 3). It does draw our attention to the overwhelming importance of Chicheŵa as the medium of everyday communication in Malaŵi, where the vast majority are not able to use English.

8. The issues that the Law Commission chose to focus on included the death penalty, marriage rights, children's rights, the right to education, the rights of arrested and detained persons, and political rights relating to party funding (Mbazira 2007: 221). Some of these issues bore obvious relevance to socioeconomic rights, but it is remarkable that the balance between political and civil rights and socioeconomic rights did not itself become a focus of review.

9. When the United Nations Development Programme published its first human development report on Malaŵi in 2001, it announced that 65 percent of the population were poor (UNDP 2001). "Poverty" was defined as the condition of living below the minimum per capita daily cost of basic needs. While the poor faced difficulties in meeting their food and nonfood requirements throughout the annual cycle, the sub-category of "ultra-poor," 29 percent of the total population, could not meet all their food requirements throughout the year. Among Malaŵi's three administrative regions, nearly 68 percent of the population in the Southern

Region lived in poverty, while the figure for the Central and Northern Regions was about 63 percent.

10. A new national land policy was approved by the government in 2002, but controversies and continuing consultations have delayed its implementation. Rather than focusing on the estate question, the policy proposes to increase the security of land tenure by turning the so-called customary land into private land, thereby going against the grain of evidence from elsewhere in Africa that individual titling alone rarely increases security and productivity (see Paul Kishindo 2004; Peters 2009; Peters and Kambewa 2007).

11. Among anthropology's recent metaphors for globalization, I prefer "friction" (Tsing 2005) to "vernacularization" (Merry 2006). Whereas vernacularization assumes that some agents, such as human rights activists, translate global or universal principles to meet the demands of particular situations, friction dissolves more decisively any lingering global-local distinction by insisting that what appears to be universal is always an artifact of particular and unequal interconnections. As such, African-language claims broadcast on Malaẇi's public radio, for example, are not intrinsically more local or parochial—or more "vernacular"—than the claims made in human rights talk. The question is how those wielding political and technocratic power come to regard some claims as having global purchase, while others are considered local.

12. Not all Malaẇians call the language Chicheẇa, with Chinyanja also a common name. The official name had been changed from Chinyanja to Chicheẇa by the Malaẇi Congress Party in 1968. The new government attempted to revert to the old name in the 1990s, but the popular use of the name Chicheẇa made the attempt unsuccessful. The language is often known as Chinyanja or Nyanja in Malaẇi's neighboring countries.

13. An intellectual affinity with Bruno Latour's (2005) recent call for tracing contingent associations should be noted. Max Gluckman ([1961] 2006: 20) contemplated abandoning the concept of society altogether in favor of analytical tools such as "social fields." His insights into "multiplex associations" (1965: 173), along with Meyer Fortes's (1949) analysis of cross-cutting ties beyond clans, represent early attempts in the anthropology of Africa to conceptualize human relationships without abstracting a society into which the individual needs to be socialized.

14. "Seemingly," because their preference for civic education as a key activity has done little to make human rights activists advocates of poor people's claims.

15. Impetus for fresh debates among liberal theorists has come from the perceived pluralism of established liberal democracies. Ethnic, religious, and linguistic diversity has raised doubts about classic liberal concepts of universal values, most notably, within the liberal tradition itself, in communitarian critiques (see Sandel 1982). Forging a way beyond communitarianism and libertarianism, a great number of liberal theorists have offered various revisions that seek to address so-called multiculturalism (for overviews, see Gray 2000; Kymlicka 1995). Though not intended as a contribution to debates on multiculturalism, it is in this intellectual climate of liberal revisionism'that my discussion of equality and obligation has to be understood.

16. As will become clear later in this book, the disparaging label of "state broadcasters" is inaccurate because of both the legal change that has made the MBC a public-service broadcaster and the particular ethos among its rank-and-file journalists.

17. For a discussion of near and distant future, see Guyer 2007. The argument there about the decline of near future in popular and technocratic imaginings may share the problem mentioned earlier with regard to studies of globalization in Africa. The everyday conduct of personal relationships appears to receive relatively little emphasis in these perspectives. The prac-

tical struggles attending that conduct in many cases of contemporary Africa are too readily interpreted to feed a presentism against which the various fantasies of globalization, from evangelical Christianity to human rights activism, provide a vision for the distant future. It must be conceded, however, that the temporal horizons of contemporary Africans can vary greatly, with a palpable loss of future apparent in some instances (see, e.g., Niehaus 2007). What the present study seeks to achieve is a more nuanced standpoint from which such differences can be discussed.

18. The reference to Cornelius Castoriadis's (1997) thought does not imply its wholesale adoption for the purposes of this book. His celebration of the imagination rests on an unfortunate faith in personal autonomy, now defended against conformism that has all but eliminated the "historical creation of autonomy and . . . a new type of being capable of calling into question the very laws of its existence" (Castoriadis 1997: 18).

1. Rights and Wrongs on the Radio

1. The date of the broadcast was August 28, 2006.

2. The Chicheŵa word *boma* is used for both "government" and "state," as in the translation of this headline, broadcast in the Chicheŵa bulletin on the same day: *Boma lati likudzipereka pa ntchito yotukula midzi.*

3. As the book goes to press, *Nkhani Zam'maboma* remains popular, and many of the observations reported in this book describe the present situation. I use the past tense, however, in recognition of the research having taken place during the first decade of the twenty-first century.

4. The other two stations were the national broadcasting corporations of Zambia and Rhodesia, the latter becoming the Zimbabwe Broadcasting Corporation after Zimbabwe's independence in 1980.

5. Reith, of course, pronounced his vision for public broadcasting from a particular, paternalistic class position, with a mixture of Victorian ideals of social reform, nationalism, and a middle-class taste for the arts (see Born 2004: 26–31). Yet his vision also drew on what had been a radical tradition of advocating the freedom of expression.

6. In this regard, it is no wonder that little evidence supports Robert Fortner's identification of an "evangelistic component" in the BBC, based on the principle that "what worked at home ought to work throughout the empire as well" (2005: 30).

7. Richard Carver, who authored both the Africa Watch (1990) report on the Banda era and the ARTICLE 19 report on the Muluzi era (n.d.), used in both the example of Cecilia Kadzamira's speech to a regional conference of the United Nations held in Malaŵi in 1985. The Official Hostess, who was widely thought of as Banda's wife despite his apparently unmarried and puritan ways, had remarked that "man cannot live without a woman." The print journalists who had duly reported her words were arrested, as was the MBC journalist who had protested their treatment.

8. Radio Two came to be broadcast in the FM mode, whereas Radio One had been broadcast as an AM station.

9. The seven languages were English, Chicheŵa, Chitumbuka, Chiyao, Chilomwe, Chitonga, and Chisena. This development qualified the role of Chicheŵa as the sole African language recognized by the state. Although Chicheŵa remained the national and regional lingua franca, the expectation was in the late 1990s that the use of other languages would gradually extend to other radio programs than news bulletins and that a policy of mother-tongue instruction would be enforced in primary schools (see, e.g., Centre for Language Studies n.d. b; Pfaffe

2000). The official commitment to multilingualism, also backed by Malaŵi's democratic constitution, has suffered from a lack of political will to implement it (see Pascal Kishindo 1998). For more on Malaŵian languages, see chapter 4.

10. Page 14 in Malawi Broadcasting Corporation 1998.

11. As described in chapter 3, the castigation of the Catholic bishops posed particular problems to those journalists at the MBC who were themselves Catholics. When the tidal wave of reformism grew too high to ignore, Banda used the MBC to suggest that multipartyism would mean war.

12. Based on information obtained from the Malaŵi Communications Regulatory Authority (MACRA) in 2006.

13. By 2006, MACRA had licensed three private television channels, but they had not become operational. In 2007, Joy Television would have become Malaŵi's second television channel had MACRA not intervened to uproot its transmitters. It did so on the grounds that the owners of Joy Television did not have an appropriate license to hold a dual ownership. As will be seen below, Joy Radio became the target of MACRA's interventions. See "Malaŵi: Radio Station Resumes Broadcasting Following Suspension of Its Licence," Media Institute of Southern Africa, press release, October 22, 2008.

14. Aleke Banda, no relation to Kamuzu Banda, became a prominent politician and minister in the one-party regime but fell out with the Life-President. After his detention, he emerged as a leading politician in the United Democratic Front and subsequently formed another political party, the People's Progressive Movement. His involvement in the print media continued with the *Nation,* Malaŵi's leading daily, owned by his family.

15. The ownership of the *Daily Times* has been complex, changing hands from the Malaŵi Congress Party, the only party during Banda's regime, to the new government. Its contents have reflected these changes, although the newspaper has more recently offered relatively balanced reporting. The *Nation,* despite its ownership by a politician (see the previous note), has enjoyed a measure of editorial independence.

16. The 1998 Population and Housing Census, which did not ask the respondents to read any statement to ascertain their literacy, reported the literacy rate of 64 percent for everyone aged fifteen years or older, with 75 per cent of adult males and 54 percent of adult females considered literate (National Statistical Office 2002: 52). Another survey carried out by the National Statistical Office in 2002 did test the respondents by asking them to read a sentence in either Chicheŵa, Chitumbuka, or English (National Statistical Office 2003: 22). The literacy rate was 79 percent for adult males and 49 percent for adult women, with notable differences between urban and rural areas. Gender, age, and rural-urban differences are also significant in the levels of educational attainment. While 14 percent of adults in urban areas had never attended school in 2002, the figure was 34 percent in rural areas, albeit only 12 percent had never attended school in the northern districts (National Statistical Office 2003: 19–21). Twenty-four percent of the respondents had completed secondary school in urban areas, but only 4 percent had done so in rural areas. Only 6 percent had pursued education beyond the secondary level in urban areas, while 0.4 percent had done so in rural areas. These findings suggest, among other things, low levels of English proficiency in Malaŵi. However, as has been discussed elsewhere, despite only 0.2 percent of the population giving English as their most commonly used language (National Statistical Office 2002: 33), the status attached to it far exceeds its actual usefulness in Malaŵi (see, e.g., Englund 2006: 91–93; Mtenje 2002).

17. These surveys, now out of date, could not investigate a pluralist broadcasting environment, but they include the kind of detail—such as data not only on households possessing radios but also on households without a radio but whose members listen to *other* households'

radios—that has long since ceased to be available on Malaŵi (see, e.g., National Statistical Office 1971 and 1972).

18. "Kaliati Threatens to Close 4 Radios," *Nation,* April 12, 2007.

19. "MACRA Directive Irks UDF, Radios," *Nation,* April 11, 2007; "Court Rules against MACRA on Live Broadcasts," *Nation,* April 20, 2007.

20. "Politicians Should Not Own Radios—Kaliati," *Nation,* June 8, 2008.

21. "MACRA Takes Joy Off Air," *Nation on Sunday,* October 19, 2008; "Malaŵi: Radio Station Resumes Broadcasting Following Suspension of Its Licence," Media Institute of Southern Africa, press release, October 22, 2008.

22. Press statement from the State House broadcast on the MBC, July 9, 2008.

23. "Immigration Pounces on Joy Radio," *Nation on Sunday,* July 13, 2008.

24. It was unclear who the audience of these reports was, because they did not circulate beyond MACRA's own offices. Their findings also seemed implausible, such as in the report entitled *43rd Week Positive and Negative News from 15th to 21st August, 2006,* which singled out the MBC and Television Malaŵi as the only broadcasters that did not broadcast any negative news at all.

25. "No Money for MBC, TVM, Mana," *Nation,* June 8, 2008.

26. "Kaliati Tells MBC, TVM to Be Professional," *Nation,* April 13, 2007.

27. "MBC Financial Woes Worsen," *Nation,* February 2, 2008; "The Funding of MBC, TVM: What Next?" *Sunday Times,* July 13, 2008.

28. "Sheriffs Impound MBC Boss's Vehicle," *Nation,* February 13, 2008.

29. "MBC Bosses Get 100% Salary Raise," *Weekend Nation,* July 26–27, 2008.

30. "Government Funds MBC, TVM," *Nation,* March 3, 2007.

31. Technology is an issue that many employees at the MBC feel proves their relative poverty when compared to private radio stations. When I started my research at the MBC in 2001, magnetic tapes were still in use to record programs, and much of the music played was from vinyl records. The donations of secondhand computers and mixers had substituted compact discs for tapes by 2008, but digital technology remained a distant prospect, correspondents sending their inputs through telephone. On the other hand, the size of the MBC's operations could be used to explain its superiority over private stations. While many private stations, an MBC engineer told me, could operate with two computers and a mixer, the MBC's several studios made the shift to digital technology rather more demanding.

32. "Zodiak Brings Another Innovation," *Malaŵi News,* August 26–September 1, 2006.

33. In Malaŵi, the transition to multipartyism heralded a period of intense regionalism, with the main parties dividing the country's three administrative regions between them during the first decade of multiparty democracy (W. Chirwa 1998). For a perspective on presidential paternalism as an aspect of African nation-building, see Schatzberg 2002. For an argument that insists on the continuing force of nationalism in the contemporary world, see Calhoun 2007.

34. The inaugural lecture on linguistics, entitled "The Role of Language in National Development: The Case for Local Languages," was delivered by Alfred Mtenje in 2002, and the inaugural lecture on English literature, entitled "Malaŵian English Literature in Culture and Development," was delivered by Brighton Uledi-Kamanga in 2008.

35. For perspectives on the various ways in which "participation" can be conceptualized and operationalized, see Cooke and Kothari 2001 and Hickey and Mohan 2004.

36. Story Workshop was founded by an expatriate to educate the public through drama. Subsequently under Malaŵian management, it has produced numerous plays on topics relating to the HIV/AIDS pandemic and food security.

37. Broadcast on Transworld Radio, September 5, 2006.

38. *Inu muli pantchito, mumalandira mwezi ukatha ndi mumathandiza ana anu, nanga ineyo?*

39. *Osamagulitsa nokha bwanji? Sukulu imachulukitsa mwayi woti azimayi akhale odzidalira pa okha pa chuma komanso pa ntchito zina.*

2. Obligations to Dogs

1. Broadcast date, September 1, 2006.

2. The verb *kuzoloẁera*, "to be used to something," summons the end or absence of "fear" (*mantha*) (see Centre for Language Studies 2000: 366). The goats in this story did not, therefore, display mere familiarity with people but also the unnatural trait of lacking fear in encounters with them.

3. Physical distance appears significant to those who point out that it is in the modern world where the cost of reaching the distant poor has become low. As F. M. Kamm (2004: 63) has commented, this claim may unwittingly reinforce the view that nearness does indeed matter in moral considerations.

4. For a subtle argument on moral individuation that highlights the importance of the distinction between self and other, see Benhabib 1993.

5. Some feminist theorists have more decisively reclaimed key liberal notions such as equality, freedom, and autonomy for perspectives that appreciate obligations and dependence in the human condition (see, e.g., Hirschmann 1992 and 2003; Mackenzie and Stoljar 2000).

6. Original as it is, Rancière's concept of equality has been criticized for producing "an inconsequential account of democracy" in which the effects of equality are "unabashedly sporadic and intermittent" (Hallward 2009: 157, 152). As my distancing of the perspective in this book from anarchism will also indicate, the challenge posed by my ethnography is to understand the nature and effects of equality within the hierarchical orders Malawians seem to uphold.

7. The choice of what factors to highlight in the unmasking of inequality is itself an artifact of a particular moment. Writing about Muslim women in Egypt after the 9/11 terrorist attacks, Lila Abu-Lughod (2002) moved from her earlier interest in the unmasking of inequality in communal life (Abu-Lughod 1986) to an argument about the historical and contemporary involvement of Western powers in producing injustice in this society. Following Mahmood 2001, she began to ask whether the desire for emancipation and rights, so central to the United States government's justification for military intervention, was merely one among many desires among women in the Middle East.

8. Even when they deploy the concept of culture, liberal theorists, such as Will Kymlicka (1995), rarely find it necessary to explore what anthropologists have said about it. A rare instance of a liberal philosopher quoting an anthropologist is a negative one—Nussbaum's (2000: 56–58) attack on Veena Das, who had, in an unpublished paper, questioned this liberal's "very intuitive idea" (Nussbaum 2000: 56) of each person as end. Elsewhere Nussbaum recalls her encounter with "an elegant French anthropologist" (1995: 64), whose mindless relativism, as Nussbaum describes it, did seem to bring the discipline into disrepute.

9. According to Richard Fardon (1990), anthropologists have also maintained the value of equality in their representations of their own field-based knowledge production without attending to the actual arguments that are intrinsic to the idea of equality.

10. Although presented as a continental comparison, Berman's (2004) argument owes a good deal to his long research experience in Kenya, particularly by stressing the pathological effects of ethnicity and by lamenting a lack of inter-ethnic public arenas.

11. For a critique of Afropessimism, see Zeleza 2003.

12. In Mozambique, for example, the post-independence experiment was as much modernist as socialist. The ruling Marxist-Leninist vanguard party condemned what it called obscurantism, including chiefly authority, bridewealth, the use of medicinal substances, the consultation of diviners, and the supplication of ancestral spirits (see, e.g., West 2005: 176–177).

13. For recent reassessments of the socialist experiments in Africa, see Pitcher and Askew 2006 and Schneider 2007.

14. As Didier Fassin (2007: 250–251) has discussed, however, the South African public discourse on the African Renaissance and the concomitant evocations of *ubuntu* did not result in a homogenous view. Assertions of an essentially African identity co-existed, and sometimes combined, with calls for an engagement with the wider world.

15. The propensity of African states to pay lip service to collective rights became clear, for example, during negotiations over the United Nations Declaration on the Rights of Indigenous Peoples (Oldham and Frank 2008: 6–7; see also Pelican 2009). In 2006, a group of African countries issued a range of objections against the draft declaration. The objections were rebutted by the African Commission on Human and Peoples' Rights of the African Union, but the African countries proceeded with a set of amendments in 2007, including the provision that every country would have the prerogative to define who constitutes indigenous people. Most of the amendments were rejected.

16. Jenkins's (2006) own argument arises from his vision of a convergence between corporate media and new participatory media in the North.

17. While defending methodological eclecticism as a feature of ethnography, S. Elizabeth Bird (2003: 7) appeals to anthropologists' own qualms about holism and the demarcation of a field to justify relatively short periods of fieldwork and reliance on the ethnographer's prior familiarity with media products. Such research may well pass for ethnography in media studies, but it is not difficult to envision projects, such as the one this book is based on, that do require time-consuming efforts to learn languages and to participate in people's lives beyond their encounters with the mass media.

18. Broadcast on February 2, 2003. See appendix 1 for a transcription and translation.

19. A tension between democratic aspirations and professional prerogatives has also characterized the movement of public journalism, as discussed in chapter 5.

3. Against the Occult

1. Broadcast on July 25, 2003. For a transcription and translation, see appendix 2.

2. Healers (*asing'anga*) are experts on protective medicine and the ways of witches. As such, they are also often feared of being able to inflict harm on others through magic, a suspicion that has motivated their condemnation as Satanists by some Christian movements, particularly Pentecostals. In practice, *asing'anga* are a diverse group of experts who continue to heal various illnesses and ailments in both rural and urban areas, some of them mimicking biomedicine in their clinics while others are self-conscious traditionalists. An extensive command of medical botany often characterizes the most successful healers (see Morris 1996).

3. Although one aspect that distinguished Banda's regime from the neighboring countries' pursuit of African socialism was the official approval rather than condemnation of tradition, witchcraft had no place in its idealized view of customs and village-based institutions. The view was not only idealized but also Chewaized, transplanting Banda's admiration for some Chewa customs to the level of national culture (see Vail and White 1989).

4. This story was reported in the print media. For example, "Mpasu Found in a Graveyard, Arrested," *Nation*, March 13, 2006; "Mpasu's Graveyard Case Fails to Start," *Nation*, April 20,

2006; "Mpasu Case: Court to Visit Graveyard," *Nation*, June 25, 2006; "The Machinga Grave-yard Saga: Mpasu's Tragedy," *Pride*, July/August 2006; "'I Gave Mpasu Charms': Witchdoctor Hadji Tells the Untold Story," *Pride*, July/August 2006.

5. The former president was endorsed by his party as its presidential candidate for the 2009 elections, but a constitutional dispute over his eligibility made him enter an alliance with an-other opposition party. As for Mpasu, he was found guilty of trespassing, but the verdict came in 2009 when he had already begun serving a six-year sentence for a corrupt deal in educa-tional materials struck during his time as the minister of education. See "Mpasu Found Guilty in Graveyard Case," *Nation*, February 22, 2009. As is discussed later in this chapter, Malawi's laws do not recognize the practice of witchcraft as an offense.

6. See, for example, the two opposing viewpoints in "The Funding of MBC, TVM: What Next?" *Sunday Times*, July 13, 2008.

7. "Open Letter to TVM and MBC," *Pride*, March/April 2008.

8. "Consultation Mission Report on Danish Support for the Restructuring of the Malawi Broadcasting Corporation," Danish Ministry of Foreign Affairs, 2000.

9. Quoted in ARTICLE 19 2003: 15.

10. For example, "MBC Boss Says Namisa 'Laughable,'" *Daily Times*, January 23, 2007. The author of this article had unsuccessfully tried to ascertain the institutions where Malopa had obtained his qualifications in marketing and business management. A few days earlier, Ma-lopa had remarked on Malawitalk that "journalistic theories and article scribbling experiences" were less relevant to running a media house than "best business practices" (posted on Mala-witalk on January 18, 2007).

11. My informants did not agree on the origin and meaning of the term *Makiyolobasi*. While Malopa himself told me that it was derived from the word "micro-bus" and referred to the crowding of a small space with lots of things, many in villages and at the MBC thought it referred to a person with dubious characteristics. They understood the person to be Muluzi.

12. "Taking Responsibility for Our Future: Together towards the 2009 Elections," Catholic Bishops' Pastoral Letter of May 11, 2008.

13. "UDF, Kamlepo to take MBC to Task over New Programme," *Nation*, August 24, 2007.

14. Many villagers and township dwellers shared these sentiments, although many of them admitted listening to *Makiyolobasi*. Another tension introduced by this program at the MBC derived from Malopa's decision to start selling its episodes on compact discs through the broad-caster's business department. Many journalists felt that other programs, particularly *Nkhani Zam'maboma*, would have deserved such treatment more than *Makiyolobasi*.

15. The common rhetorical use of *boma* even in rural Malawi indicates rather different ex-pectations than what has been reported for some other parts of Africa (see, e.g., Jones 2009). However poorly they have been served by the government, rural Malawians have continued to deploy *boma* as one relevant category in the local configurations of power and authority.

16. "Tension at MBC over Restructuring," *Nation*, March 22, 2007.

17. "MBC Bosses Get 100% Salary Raise," *Weekend Nation*, July 26–27, 2008.

18. After Mutharika became president, her meteoric rise came to an abrupt end when she was unceremoniously transferred to an inconspicuous position in the Ministry of Foreign Af-fairs.

19. After professional courses in journalism had been introduced in Malawi, the MBC began to offer attachments to students and recent graduates, but their prospects for securing permanent posts there were poor. Many among senior MBC journalists were school teachers by training, but diversity in educational background had increased in the 1990s. Reporters and

editors included persons with a background in accounting and agricultural extension work. When the MBC was still able to recruit new journalists, the tests they had to take examined their knowledge of current affairs rather than the specifics of their previous training.

20. In 2008, the fee for a one-term course in journalism was about M.K.20,000 (U.S.$143), the equivalent of a month's salary among junior reporters.

21. "Police Examine City Centre Ammunition," *Nation,* July 14, 2008.

22. *Nkhani mwachidule zodabwitsa komanso zochititsa chidwi zochitika m'dziko muno komanso kunja kwa dziko lino.*

23. The beginning of this argument can be found in Englund 2007a, where I suggest that the propensity of witchcraft to mediate the imagination makes it a non-topic, never sufficient in itself to constitute the subject of analysis. The problem with this argument is, of course, its apparent affiliation with those sociological and historical perspectives that always end up explaining witchcraft away. Description is, however, both a more modest and more demanding intellectual operation than explanation (compare Latour 2005). By describing the ways in which witchcraft contextualizes and gets itself contextualized, the anthropologist attends to its life-worlds without prejudging what the unit of analysis is.

24. Although Bastian (1993) gives an overview of what else is covered in the Nigerian popular press, it is striking that her analysis of a particular newspaper editorial does not involve conversations with its author.

25. "Of Ghosts and Presidents," *Nation,* April 4, 2005; "Muluzi's Adopted Daughter Back to Orphanage," *Nation,* November 14, 2006.

26. "Politicians Queue for Divason Muti," *Nation,* July 29, 2006.

27. "House Discusses Satanism," *Nation,* October 21, 2005.

28. Section 4 of the Witchcraft Act states that "any person who, otherwise than laying information before a court, police officer, a chief, or other proper authority, accuses any person of being a witch or with practising witchcraft or names or indicates any person as being a witch or wizard shall be liable to a fine of 25 pounds and to imprisonment for five years." Some magistrates have, however, convicted witches, using its Section 5, which outlaws witchcraft confessions: "Any person who by his statements or actions represents himself to be a wizard or witch or as having or exercising the power of witchcraft shall be liable to a fine of 50 pounds and to imprisonment for ten years." See also "Court Throws Out Witchcraft Charge," *Nation,* September 29, 2007.

29. Among others, "Police, Army Arrest Hundreds," *Nation,* April 27, 2005; "Boy Claims He Was Abducted for Sacrifice," *Nation,* January 26, 2006; "Police Save Witchcraft Suspects in Lilongwe," *Nation,* April 13, 2007.

30. "Young Persons Act Bill to Fight Child Superstition," *Chronicle,* August 28–September 3, 2006.

31. "Enacting a Witchcraft Law a Tricky Issue," *Nation,* October 19, 2006; "Why a Policy on Witchcraft Is Difficult to Formulate," *Daily Times,* December 18, 2006.

32. "Police Rescue Man after 'Plane' Crash," *Nation,* July 29, 2005; "Witchcraft at Work," *Pride,* October 2005; "Wizard Convicted," *Pride,* January/February 2006.

33. This story included motifs that are associated with witches far beyond Malaŵi, such as visits to graveyards outside burial ceremonies, nocturnal incidents, nakedness, and the involvement of an owl.

34. *Ufiti,* the concept that has been translated in this chapter as "witchcraft," is therefore only one among many Chicheŵa concepts belonging to the realm of witchcraft, sorcery, magic, and healing. Although it is the most common concept for the sinister connotations of "witch-

craft," it co-exists with concepts that depict protective rather than harmful practices (see Englund 1996b and 2007a; Marwick 1965).

35. Nor do they, it might be added, take much notice of how anthropology has established itself as one of the social and human sciences in Africa (see, e.g., Ntarangwi et al. 2006).

36. Such claims to step outside the "culture of neoliberalism" became common in anthropology at the dawn of the new millennium. According to one statistic, while fewer than 10 percent of the articles published in the journals *American Ethnologist* and *Cultural Anthropology* used the term "neoliberal" during the decade until 2002, 35 percent of the articles in these journals used it over the four years from 2002 to 2005 (Kipnis 2007: 383). Just as their critiques of inequality had often failed to define the concept of equality informing the critiques, anthropologists writing about neoliberalism had little to say about the possible impact of liberal predilections on their own thought. I share David Williams's opinion that talk about neoliberalism lets liberalism "off the hook" (2008: 6), but I attempt to convey rather more complexity than his assault on liberalism seems to allow for. Neoliberalism is best considered only one among the many strands of liberal thought and practice (see also Ferguson 2009).

37. In this regard, the suggestion that the term "occult" should be substituted for "religion" in comparative scholarship still seems to assume too much about the domain within which moral debate is to be analyzed (see ter Haar and Ellis 2009).

38. On replication in the knowledge practices of anthropologists and their interlocutors, see Miyazaki 2004. The differences between anthropology and the ethical and epistemological principles taught in schools of journalism are of course well known, including journalists' avoidance of rapport with their sources in the name of objectivity (Bird 2010: 5).

39. To put the point differently, the actual consequences of witchcraft in Africa are so diverse that to regard it either as a knowledge practice or an institution inciting violence and hatred is to foreclose ethnographic research. As such, the webs of allusions that witchcraft stories, among others, weave in *Nkhani Zam'maboma* would not warrant Maia Green's comment from a different context: witchcraft turns "people's gaze inwards to their own community rather than outwards to the content of policy processes which produce poverty and vulnerability" (2005: 260; see also Englund 2007a).

4. A Nameless Genre

1. Broadcast on July 19, 2003. See appendix 3 for a transcription and translation.

2. Migrants from India and Pakistan came to Malaŵi during the colonial period and, as elsewhere in the region, established themselves as shopkeepers and service providers. The term *amwenye* was originally used for the first Malaŵians to come into contact with Islam through Arab traders before the arrival of Europeans (Bone 2000: 13). It now refers to persons of South Asian extraction, many of whom are naturalized Malaŵians. The term would not be used for the Chinese, known as *maChaina* in Chicheŵa, who are the other notable Asian population in Malaŵi.

3. Local councils that had served Banda's one-party regime were abolished after the democratic transition in 1994, but the local elections in the new multiparty framework were held only in 2000. District, town, and city councilors served for five years, but new local elections were postponed at least until 2010 by the central government. In the meantime, district affairs have been run, as before the move toward decentralization, by district commissioners and local-government civil servants.

4. *Nkhani Za Ku Malaŵi* was discontinued shortly after it had been launched. Editors in the newsroom explained its demise as the result of a general lack of interest in it.

5. Broadcast on September 22, 2003, this story depicted a Mozambican committing adultery. Mozambique appeared, such as in a story broadcast on November 26, 2003, as a place where potent medicine could be procured.

6. However, the suggestion that Chicheŵa should be granted an official status as the national language, as put forward during the process of constitutional review, troubled them as it did many Malaŵian academics. Their fear was that such a status would undermine whatever modest recognition other African languages had begun to receive in democratic Malaŵi. For a comparative perspective on African languages in the media, see Mazrui 2009.

7. While the Central Region has long been an overwhelmingly Chicheŵa-speaking area, the other two regions have been linguistically more diverse. However, sociolinguistic surveys conducted in the late 1990s revealed a consistent pattern. Comparing the results with those of the 1966 population census, the researchers concluded that Chicheŵa was "gaining ground" in the Southern Chiyao-speaking areas, with 95 percent of the respondents speaking both Chiyao and Chicheŵa (Centre for Language Studies n.d. a: 9). The situation for the other major Southern languages was described in identical terms: "Chicheŵa has permeated every fabric of Lomwe society thereby making Lomwe societies bilingual/multilingual" (Centre for Language Studies n.d. a: 66) and "Chicheŵa has permeated every fabric of Sena society thereby making Sena societies bilingual/multilingual" (Centre for Language Studies n.d. a: 81). In the Northern Region, Chitumbuka has retained a strong position, but the researchers remarked that "one cannot realistically talk of a Chitumbuka-speaking area that has not felt the impact of Chicheŵa" (Centre for Language Studies n.d. a: 51). This impact was evident, among other things, in student respondents' preference for Chicheŵa rather than Chitumbuka as a medium of instruction. They saw Chicheŵa opening up better prospects for employment and further study than their first language.

8. Broadcast on August 28, 2006. *Ziŵalo zobisika* literally means "hidden body parts." It is similar to the notion of "private parts" that is commonly used by English-speaking Malaŵians.

9. According to the 1987 population census, 11 percent lived in urban areas (National Statistical Office 2002: 10). It should be noted that 11 percent of the total population in 1998 lived in the four main urban areas that were defined as urban Malaŵi in my sample (Blantyre-Limbe, Lilongwe, Mzuzu, and Zomba). According to both the 1998 and 2008 national censuses, only 3 percent lived in other municipalities (National Statistical Office 2010: 8). The 2008 national census indicates that the proportion of the population in these four towns was 12 percent of the total population, with Lilongwe and Mzuzu registering the intercensal annual growth rate of over 4 percent and Blantyre and Zomba 3 percent or less (National Statistical Office 2010: 3).

10. During the period of fieldwork for this book, the country was divided into twenty-eight districts, with thirteen districts in the Southern, nine in the Central, and six in the Northern Regions.

11. Broadcast on July 28, 2003.

12. Lest these categories are thought to lend themselves to neat typologies, see the subtle discussions in M. Chimombo 1988: 13–31 and Ngoma and Nkhoma 2002.

13. One of the pioneering Chicheŵa novels was *Nthondo*, written by Samuel Ntara. In 1933 it won the first prize in a writing competition organized by the International Institute of African Languages and Culture in London and was published in English under the title *Man of Africa*.

14. Both titles referred to personal names.

15. For anthropological and historical perspectives on matrilineal kinship in Malaŵi and the wider region, see Chanock 1985 and Peters 1997. Important to keep in mind here is that *Nkhani Zam'maboma* assumed the existence of matrilineal features much as many Malaŵians

did, with little regard to how rural life had been affected by missionary and colonial policies favoring men and, more recently, by the scarcity of arable land (see also Peters 2002; Peters and Kambewa 2007). Although prevalent in the Southern and Central Regions, the appeal to matrilineal principles is also common in parts of the Northern Region, particularly among Chitonga-speakers. For a perspective on whether the practice of kinship in rural Malaŵi should be analyzed in cognatic rather than matrilineal terms, see Englund 2002c: 55–57.

16. It might have been too harsh even in the case of the radio drama, particularly because it was not supported by research on reception.

17. Broadcast on July 15, 2003. See appendix 4 for a transcription and a translation.

18. *Mphinjiri* is a type of charm that is attached to a string and worn around the neck, especially by young children. That the rat had three instead of the regular one *mphinjiri*, coupled with the rat's enormous size, indicated that much effort had gone into making it potent. Its subsequent demise served, of course, to underline the healer's even greater potency.

19. Most stories about headmen on *Nkhani Zam'maboma* referred to them with the term *nyakwaŵa*, whose connotations were less specific than those of *mfumu*, the more common word for chief or headman. *Nyakwaŵa* could refer to persons belonging to the headman's entourage of advisers as well as to the headman him- or herself. *Mfumu* referred less ambiguously to the actual incumbent and was therefore avoided by the editors, who wanted to prevent the identification of protagonists.

20. *Mkangano akuti udabuka mpakati pa nyakwaŵa ina ndi mng'ono wake polimbirana unyakwaŵa.* Broadcast on September 3, 2003.

21. *Nyakwaŵa ina yavulala miyendo itagwera mu chimbudzi pamene inathamangira mnyamata ŵina amene anamudyera ndalama zonse zimene anali nazo pa juga ya ŵachiona ndani.* Broadcast on September 14, 2003.

22. Broadcast on September 21, 2003.

23. *Mbusa wa mpingo ŵina kuboma la Nsanje analamula kuti alipire MK2500 ndi mbuzi imodzi ndi nkhuku imodzi chifukwa choti sapita kumaliro.* Broadcast on July 22, 2003.

24. Broadcast on September 2, 2003.

25. Broadcast on July 22, 2003.

26. *Adzukulu ena am'dela la Nchisi adamenya kwambiri amafedwa chifukwa choti adaŵapatsa nsima ndi ndiŵo ya khobwe m'malo mwa nyama.* Broadcast on July 20, 2003.

27. Broadcast on July 12, 2003.

28. *Aphunzitsi onse apasukulupo ndi afiti otamba komanso ndi mbuli zosazindikira chilichonse.* Broadcast on September 15, 2003.

29. November 22, 2003.

30. *Akumagaŵana zinthu ndi mfumu ina yakudelalo m'malo mopatsa ana.*

31. *Akumapemphanso akulu azamaphunziro m'bomalo kuti athandize chifukwa safunanso mphunzitsiyo.*

32. Broadcast on September 23, 2003.

33. *Mkulu wa kampani ina ku Ginnery Corner m'mzinda wa Blantyre akuti akuvutitsa ogwira ntchito ake powakaniza kuti asapume pakakhala tchuthi ngakhale chachikulu ngati 6 Julayi.* Broadcast on July 11, 2003. Ginnery Corner is a commercial area in Blantyre.

34. *Anthu ogwira ntchito pa kampani ina yotchuka m'mzinda wa Blantyre anakhumudwa ndi zomwe anachita akuluakulu a pa kampaniyi pokana kupereka ndalama kwa mkulu ŵina zokathandiza pa maliro a mayi wake.* Broadcast on September 1, 2006.

35. *Anaonetsa nkhanza zake zonse poyera polamula dalayivala ŵina pa kampaniyo kuti apite ku tchuthi chosalipira chifukwa chonyamula munthu ŵina popanda chilolezo.* Broadcast on September 24, 2003.

36. Broadcast on July 15, 2003.

37. *Mkulu ŵina amene amagwira ntchito pa chipatala china muboma la Karonga akuti ana-khumudwitsa anthu chifukwa chomenya munthu wodwala.* Broadcast on September 30, 2003.

38. *Wodwalayo akuti akadandaula nkhaniyi kwa mkulu wa muofisi ya zomva madandaulo a anthu, Ombudsman.*

39. Broadcast on July 9, 2003.

40. Broadcast on September 1, 2006.

41. *Ŵadodometsa anthu polimbikira kuti alankhule pa maliro amalume ndi achimwene ake ali pomwepo.* Broadcast on July 24, 2003.

42. *Amayi anangoimirira ndi kuyamba kulongosola mbiri ya malemu amene anali gogo wake.*

43. *Mayi ŵina akuti akudabwitsa anthu chifukwa m'mene amasinthira amuna pofuna chuma.* Broadcast on July 22, 2003.

44. Broadcast on September 12, 2003.

45. *Chomwe anthu anaima nacho mitu kwambiri ndi choti mayiwo anali ndi mwayi waukulu chifukwa choti anakwatiŵa ndi m'modzi mwa anthu okhupuka kwambiri kuboma la Kasungu.*

46. Broadcast on July 29, 2003.

47. *Akuganiza zothetsa banja lake chifukwa cha umbombo ndi nkhanza zomwe mwamuna wake akumuchitira.* Broadcast on September 16, 2003.

48. Broadcast on July 21, 2003.

49. Broadcast on July 24, 2003.

50. *Mayi ŵina woyendayenda m'tawuni ya Luchenza ŵalanda zovala za mkulu amene ana-gwirizana naye kuti amupatse ndalama awiriwo akachita zadama.* Broadcast on September 27, 2003.

51. *Anathetsa banja la mwana wake wamkazi pomunyengerera kuti ati amupatsa chuma ndi zinthu zina pamene bamboyo ali ndi matenda opatsirana ndi chifuŵa chachikulu cha TB.* Broadcast on September 4, 2006.

52. *Polephera kukana ndi kutsutsa mawu a bambo wakeyo anathamangitsadi mwamuna wakeyo.*

53. *Mtsikana ŵina akudwala mwakayakaya mayi wake atamumwetsa mankhwala kuti achotse pakati ati chifukwa choti sakufuna kuti mtsikana abwereke mwana amene bambo wake ndi mphaŵi.* Broadcast on November 23, 2003.

54. *Banja lina lathetsa chibwenzi cha mwana wamkazi chifukwa choti mwamuna ndi wosauka.* Broadcast on September 9, 2003.

55. *Akumamulondalonda poopa kuti mwina angadziiphe chifukwa choti anamukonda kwambiri mtsikanayo.*

56. *Saganizanso kuti angapeze mtsikana ŵina wofanana naye ngakhale atazungulira m'madela onse m'dziko muno.*

57. The women's dress promoted by Malaŵi's first regime as traditional costume was modeled on a white mission employee's design of a housemaid's uniform from the turn of the twentieth century (Vail and White 1991: 294).

58. Broadcast on July 9, 2003.

59. *Mtsikana woyendayenda* can be translated as "loose girl," because the verb *kuyenda-yenda*, frequently used for "prostitutes" (*mahule*), refers to moving or walking about without a clear destination.

60. *Wasokonezeka m'mutu atatulukira kuti mwamuna amene anagwirizana kuti achita naye zadama anaboola chishango chomwe anavala pamene anachita naye chisembwerecho.*

61. Piercing the condom appears consistent with the view, reported from Africa and elsewhere, that male condoms reduce male pleasure and a man's sense of conquering his female

partner. In addition, semen deposited in a condom is a disconcerting prospect for some men in extramarital affairs. Writing about Zambia, Anthony Simpson explains that "some men feared that their semen might be used in love potions to lure them away from their wives, or even in witchcraft attacks against them" (2009: 140).

62. *Mnyamata ẁina sakudziẁika komwe walowera anthu atamukuntha kodetsa nkhaẁa chifukwa chofuna kugwirira mayi wake wobereka.* Broadcast on July 20, 2003.

63. Released in 2007 on the audio cassette entitled *Mizimu* by Joseph Nkasa.

64. "Nkasa Goes Explicit?" *Nation,* June 16, 2007.

5. Inequality Is Old News

1. See Ashforth 2005: 146–148 and West 2005: 237 for popular perspectives on witchcraft as "African science" in South Africa and Mozambique, respectively.

2. The disciplinary effect of *Nkhani Zam'maboma* will be discussed in chapter 7.

3. *Anthu ena akuti akhumudwa kwambiri pamaliro anamafedwa akulimbirana katundu wa malemu maliro asanaike* [the location omitted]. Broadcast on August 1, 2003.

4. *Chomwe chinachititsa dzaye kuti njovu ithyoke mnyanga pankhaniyi ndi choti ena mwa anamafedwawa amafuna kuti omwalira asamuveke zovala pomuika mu bokosi kuti atenge zovalazo.*

5. *Ena ambiri anachoka chokhumudwa maliro asanaike.*

6. *Ndoda ziẁirizi akuti zili ndi chizoloẁezi choledzera mowa tsiku ndi tsiku koma chomwe chinavuta pa tsikuli chinali choti maliroẁa anali awo omwe.* Broadcast on September 18, 2003.

7. *Mnyamata wina akuti anasoẁa chochita nyakwaẁa itakaniza kuti asaike mwana wake m'manda m'mudzimo* [location omitted] *chifukwa choti amaitukwana akangoledzera moẁa komanso akuti sayenda maliro.* Broadcast on August 1, 2003. The story went on to describe how he had brought the corpse of his child to the police, who had sent him back home. The presenter noted that the story did not tell whether the burial had eventually taken place in the village.

8. *Mkuluyo yomwe ndi mlimi wotchuka pa fodya m'delalo akuti anakumana ndi mbavayo yomwe inamunyengerera kuti imugula fodya wake yense pa mtengo wa bwino.* Broadcast on July 26, 2003.

9. *Mwasangalala mlimiyo akuti anaphera njondayo nkhuku ndipo usiku anamuonetsa malo ogona.*

10. *Mpondmakwacha ẁina amene ali ndi sitolo zambiri* [location omitted] *akuyenda mwamanyazi ngati nkhuku yachitopa.* Broadcast on September 18, 2003.

11. *Njondayi akuti ili ndi chizolowezi chochita zibwenzi ndi atsikana ake antchito.*

12. By the same token, the use of idiomatic Chicheẁa did not represent an effort to shield the program from changes in the language. Idioms such as *mpondamakwacha* were so new that they had not been included in the only existing work on Chicheẁa idioms, published in the 1960s (see Nthala 1964). Where the language differed from the everyday uses of Chicheẁa, particularly in urban areas, was in editors' consistent avoidance of English words and expressions, with the phrases used for the time of the day a notable exception.

13. *Akuluakulu a kale adanena kuti 'ichi chakoma, ichi chakoma, pusi adagwa chagada.' Mawuẁa apherezeka chifukwa cha zimene zachitika* [location omitted]. *Msungwana wa zaka 16 amene anali m'fomu 1 ẁachira ndi mpeni kuchipatala komwe anabereka ana a mapasa chifukwa chochulukitsa zibwenzi.* Broadcast on July 21, 2003.

14. *Ngakhale mwini wake akuti sangathe kunena mwatchutchutchu kuti bambo wa mapasa akewo ndi aẁa.*

15. The didactic use of proverbs is of course central to contemporary African public arenas (see Barber 2000: 418).

16. Broadcast on September 1, 2006.

17. *Ndiye poti mtima wa mnzako m'tsidya lina mayiwo samadziwa kuti mnzakeyo ndi mthakati.*

18. *M'malo mwayamba ulemu anayamba kuŵachitira mwano.*

19. No story in my sample or the archives I perused mentioned homosexuality. My research ended before the controversy over Malaŵi's so-called first gay wedding gained international attention in 2009.

20. Broadcast on July 11, 2008.

21. See appendix 5 for a transcription and translation of the two versions.

22. "Worship" is commonly used in Malaŵi to address magistrates.

23. Broadcast on June 14, 2008. See appendix 6 for a transcription and translation of the story and the rejoinder.

24. The headmaster probably sought respect for his school by mentioning that even chiefs sent their children to it. For the editors, however, this detail was another element in a pattern by which the teachers pursued allegiance with local notables rather than with the poorest villagers.

25. A Malaŵian legal scholar, who is explicit about the influence of Christianity on his thinking, has stressed trust rather than contract as the basis of children's rights (see Kamchedzera 1998).

26. For anthropological reflections on the complexity of the controversy over child labor, see Nieuwenhuys 1996.

27. Broadcast on May 2, 2004.

28. Conversely, many listeners were just as aware of the editorial aversion to party-political themes as they were aware of the preferred idioms mentioned above. For example, listeners in Chinsapo Township assumed in 2003 that a story broadcast on *Nkhani Zam'maboma* about a violent conflict there de-emphasized the involvement of Muslims because a Muslim was then the state president (see Englund 2007a: 303–304).

29. See appendix 7 for a transcription and translation.

30. The principle here would have been familiar to many Malaŵians, namely *choipa chitsata mwini*, "evil goes back to its origin."

31. Compare the case of Zulu radio drama in apartheid South Africa. "The censorship of overtly political themes has not meant that what was being produced did not engage with the harsh consequences of apartheid, or with the desire of listeners both to [*sic*] find a medium which would express their suffering and their search for a better life" (Gunner 2000: 231). The uses of language were critical to this alternative public arena: "The ideology of apartheid did not penetrate the language's operation as a carrier of multiple signs and discourses and as a medium for the transformation of consciousness" (Gunner 2000: 228).

32. Another criticism regards public journalism as "a conservative reform movement," in that "it speaks loudly of 'the public' but addresses itself to a professional group without challenging that group's authority" (Schudson 1999: 118–119). Note here a contrast to the thesis of convergence advocated by Jenkins (2006), who sees new media technologies undermining conventional relations between producers and consumers.

33. "Zodiak Celebrate One Year in Style," *Nation*, November 14, 2006.

6. Stories Become Persons

1. The newsroom received on average around twenty stories every day, most of which arrived as handwritten letters. This abundant supply of stories made it unnecessary for the

MBC to specifically solicit contributions from listeners. The rare occasions when it appealed to the public were reminders for listeners to include their names and addresses with the stories they sent.

2. Apart from its headquarters in Blantyre, the MBC has regional studios in Lilongwe and Mzuzu. While the Lilongwe studio is small and covers, in the main, news and reports about parliamentary and presidential affairs in the capital, the Mzuzu studio is larger in order to cater to the greater linguistic diversity in Northern Malawi.

3. Article 19 of the Universal Declaration of Human Rights states, "Everyone has the right to freedom of opinion and expression; this right includes freedom to hold opinions without interference and to seek, receive and impart information and ideas through any media and regardless of frontiers."

4. The cultivation of sources is by no means restricted to journalistic practices in Africa. Foreign correspondents and war reporters in the Euro-American media, among others, depend on relationships that may or may not be acknowledged in their published stories (see, e.g., Hannerz 2004; Pedelty 1995). Ethical issues loom large when collaboration with local journalists is ignored in the final product (see Bishara 2006). Journalists' obligations to the people they work with and report on led Martin Bell (1998) to propose a move from "bystanders' journalism" to "journalism of attachment."

5. The most prominent Malawian critique of *Nkhani Zam'maboma,* as discussed in chapter 8, took issue with a wholly different set of concerns.

6. An example from the anthropology of mass media concerns the alternative views and news expressed by Chinese transnational media (see Yang 2002). Despite acknowledging its capacity to detach "Chinese subjectivity from the state," the anthropologist warns that "even while transnational Chinese subjects have begun to displace state subjects, they immediately face the danger of getting trapped in new and different tentacles of power" (Yang 2002: 205).

7. Broadcast on November 22, 2003.

8. Postal addresses were often taken at face value.

9. The only reference in the NGO's document gives the web address http://www1.umn .edu/humanrts/monitoring, which provided a link to the manual.

10. The similarities between anthropologists and some human rights professionals can be far more complex than this appreciation of context. Critical human rights lawyers, for example, are not so much interested in contextualization as troubled by the very legalism of human rights (Riles 2006). They share, therefore, anthropologists' unease with legal instrumentalism, although the two disciplines encounter it in different ways.

11. I touch here on issues raised by the genre and conventions of testimonies once the commission's hearings had been launched in 1996. The substantial literature that exists on South African experiences has debated much else both before the commission's launching and after the submission of its final report in 1998. An important set of questions revolves around restorative and retributive justice, popular ideas of punishment, and the influence of a religious notion of reconciliation (see e.g., Hamilton 2002; Mamdani 1998; Rotberg and Thompson 2000; Wilson 2001).

12. The use of material objects in constituting human relationships is a classic theme in anthropology, most famously theorized in perspectives on the gift (see Sykes 2005).

13. See note 35 in chapter 1 for references on alternative conceptualizations of participation.

14. Celtel, then Malawi's most popular mobile telephone network, announced that it had one million customers in 2008. Although the use and ownership of mobile telephones was still at a modest level, their increase had been dramatic since 1995, when they were first intro-

duced. Some 6,000 people, as compared to 36,000 fixed-line telephones, were estimated to have mobile telephones in Malaŵi in 1998 (ARTICLE 19 1998: 9–11). The expansion of their use was initially discouraged by high cost and poor coverage. By 2008, much of rural Malaŵi was covered.

15. Yao identity has also historically been linked with trading (see e.g., Alpers 1969).

16. At some 13 percent of the national population, Muslims were a significant minority but did not form a constituency large enough to determine the winner of the presidential elections.

17. Although the Southern Region, as Malaŵi's most populous region, largely decides the elections, the association of the three regions with three political parties, prevalent during most of Muluzi's regime (see W. Chirwa 1998), became complicated by the disarray in the party that was popular in the Northern Region and by Mutharika's own claim to come from the South. In 2009, this regional pattern was subverted by the election victories of Mutharika's party in all the regions.

18. My conversations with Umar were carried in Chicheŵa, a language he had known well since his childhood. He preferred to speak Chiyao with his family and fellow Chiyao-speakers in the area. He occasionally spiced our conversations with rather idiosyncratic English phrases.

19. The term *dawah* is a version of *da'wa,* which one scholar has defined as "a Quranic concept associated primarily with God's call to the prophets and to humanity to believe in the 'true religion,' Islam" (Mahmood 2005: 57–58). For comparative perspectives on *da'wa* and Islamic NGOs in Africa, see Kaag 2007 and Sadouni 2007.

20. Mutharika's regime was careful to avoid the impression of a backlash against Muslims. They continued to feature in political appointments, and the vice president was Cassim Chilumpha, a Muslim originally imposed on Mutharika by Muluzi. However, Chilumpha became a shadowy figure in Mutharika's first government and eventually became embroiled in controversies with him. At the same time, some Muslim organizations in Malaŵi complained that Muslims had been sidelined, while Islamophobia, a long-standing issue in Malaŵi, gathered momentum through rumors and the teachings of some Christian churches.

21. "To disseminate the teachings of Islam through Quran; to promote understanding of Islam; to promote Muslim brotherhood."

22. Recall the discussion of witchcraft as an idiom in chapter 3.

7. Cries and Whispers

1. Dedza is a district in the Central Region, and in this area Chicheŵa is used virtually exclusively by villagers who tend to consider themselves as Ngoni.

2. Wind-up radios have occasionally been distributed in the area, usually by development agencies as tokens of gratitude for participating in their projects.

3. Although it was common to carry the radio to the field, the relatively solitary nature of work did not usually permit a large turnout of listeners. Work parties drawing participants from several households had become relatively rare in the area (see Englund 1999).

4. A somewhat different moral vision documented in the context of Nigerian popular theater emphasizes human potential and the reversal of fortunes (see Barber 2000: 397). The vision is inegalitarian, but it encourages wariness with writing anyone off, because everyone has potential. It has also appeared in Malaŵian literature (see, e.g., Zingani 1984).

5. Comparison of the same genre in different contexts can also raise questions about the variable extent of didacticism. For example, whereas soap operas on the Egyptian public television have carried didactic messages about development (Abu-Lughod 2005), their Nigerian

and Indian counterparts have been described as representing "a space of extravagant action outside of and in contradistinction to state cultural forms" (Larkin 2008: 272).

6. However, see the discussion in Newell (2002: 5) on the ways in which the didacticism and typecasting in African popular fiction can have functions that inspire moral debate among readers.

7. The contrast to the Mongolian case reported by Caroline Humphrey is clear not only in the observation that for Mongols the cultivation of virtues in the self seems to come before the sympathy for others (1997: 33). It is also apparent in her perusal of petitions submitted by serfs in the eighteenth and nineteenth centuries. Applying the notion of "reasonableness" to judgments, she contends that conduct was compared "to a set of unquestioned rules" (Humphrey 1997: 31).

8. A succinct formulation of the Foucauldian principle of discipline and freedom, as developed in a critique of liberal democracy, states that discipline "is not a means of producing terrorized slaves without privacy, but self-managing citizens capable of conducting themselves in freedoms, shaping their newly acquired 'private lives' according to norms of civility, and judging their conduct accordingly" (Rose 1999: 242).

9. For more discussion, see Englund 2008.

10. *Chimene munthu wamva, sangachitulutsenso, choncho n'kofunika kuchenjera polankhula kuopa kupalamula.*

11. *Mwina m'malo mwakunena mau ambirimbiri, amangonena mau amodzi pena aŵiri, kaya atatu.*

12. *Nkhondo ndi kukangana zimayambika chifukwa cha anthu omkamwa, olongolola.*

13. *Pamene ukulankhula kwambiri ndi pamenenso umalakwitsa kwambiri. Ndi chifukwa chake akuluakulu adanena mwambi uja wakuti ukayenda usasiye mulomo.* *Malaŵi News* June 28–July 4, 2008.

14. *Kukhala chete nthawi zina kumalankhula mawu ambiri.*

15. Among the many examples of musicians commenting on current affairs is Joseph Nkasa's influential song "Anamva" ("They Have Heard") that took Muluzi to task for not keeping his promises. Yet popular musicians have also been subject to state patronage in a way that village-based performers are not. Lucius Banda and Billy Kaunda, two of Malaŵi's most popular musicians since the early 1990s, have been embraced by Muluzi and Mutharika, respectively. For comparative perspectives on popular music and the nationalist project in Africa, see Askew 2002; Moorman 2008.

16. The state-recognized hierarchy, largely inherited from the colonial period, is Village Headman, Group Village Headman, Sub-traditional Authority, Traditional Authority, and Paramount Chief. Muluzi added the rank of Senior Chief between Traditional Authority and Paramount Chief. Mutharika, in turn, substantially increased the allowances among all these authorities, albeit after the events described in this chapter.

17. Compare Barber's (2007: 163–168) discussion of how neo-traditional Yoruba media poetry provides materials for its public to co-construct meaning in a way that praise poetry did not.

18. *Mayi ŵina akuti akuyenda mozolika chifukwa choti anamuulula kuti ndi mfiti.* Broadcast on July 28, 2003.

19. *Anthu akungoyang'anitsitsana kuti aone amene aziyenda ngati ovulala kuti mwina akhale m'modzi mwa anthu amene anali mu ulendowo.* Broadcast on September 28, 2003.

20. Broadcast on August 30, 2006. Nudity and crossroads are common themes in Malaŵian witchcraft stories.

21. Broadcast on September 2, 2006. The Chichewa word for the penalty imposed by headmen—*chindapusa*—derives from the expression *ndapusa,* "I made a mistake" or "I was stupid."

22. Broadcast on July 28, 2003.

23. Residence in marriage is usually uxorilocal in this part of Malawi.

24. *Anthu a delalo anakhumudwa kwambiri ndi zomwe wachita nyakwawa ndi mwana wa-wowo.*

25. The actual headman had also given Gama the permission to collect the headman's modest allowance, but Gama's indebtedness to him ensured that a share of the gifts and money Gama received was given to him.

26. Vigilante groups were called Inkatha in many parts of Malawi.

27. The revival of official and popular interest in traditional authorities after the democratic transitions in Africa in the early 1990s has sustained a lively academic debate that has nuanced the negative claims made in Mamdani 1996 (see, e.g., Nyamnjoh 2003; Oomen 2005).

28. Frederick Klaits (2010: 198–202) has described how the members of an Apostolic church in Botswana engaged in a subtle practice of asking that contrasted with bantering requests among non-members.

8. Christian Critics

1. As mentioned in the introduction, contemporary poverty in Malawi suggests a situation in which kinship obligations are increasingly seen as a burden. Beyond the extreme condition of destitution, which may have become more common with decreasing farm sizes, outright landlessness, and unemployment, stories on *Nkhani Zam'maboma* may also be understood to debate whether resource-poor Malawians have much else to count on than their relationships.

2. The condition of "being born again" (*kubadwa mwatsopano*) was by no means the prerogative of Pentecostals in Malawi. Roman Catholics, Anglicans, and even some Presbyterians had established charismatic fellowships in which such an experience was endorsed. This chapter reports, however, on fieldwork among born-again Christians who were Pentecostals.

3. These stations were the Africa Bible College Radio, Calvary Family Church Radio, Channel for All Nations, Living Waters Church Radio, and Transworld Radio. As mentioned, all of the nine religious radio stations had a Christian profile except Radio Islam.

4. Chinsapo had grown on the site of an old Chewa village through migration. Although outnumbered by migrants, those who considered themselves the original Chewa guardians of the land were often staunch supporters of *gule wamkulu,* whose masked characters sometimes attacked uninitiated township dwellers (see Englund 2007a). By the dawn of the new millennium, Chinsapo had about thirty thousand residents.

5. Those who were too obviously zealots ran the risk of frightening potential converts. The most successful pastors appeared to be those who allowed the born-again experience to arise from compassion, such as during funerals and misfortune, or from delight, such as through music and dancing (see Englund 2007b).

6. *Mbusa wina wa mpingo wina ku Chileka boma la Blantyre akuti wanenetsa kuti achotsa m'mpingo mkhristu wina aliyense yemwe samugawira zakudya za ulere zomwe anthu a delali alandira.* Broadcast on November 15, 2003.

7. *Sanalandire katunduyo ngakhale analembetsa dzina lake ngati wamasiye cholinga choti adzalandire nawo za ulerezo.*

8. *Sanaone chifukwa chokwanira chochita zimenezo.*

9. *Ndi okhumudwa kwambiri ndi zimene akuchita mbusa wawo wa tsopano.* Broadcast on July 31, 2003.

10. *Aliyense osapereka chakhumi adzimuchotsa m'mpingo komanso kuti asamapereke ndalama za siliva koma za mapepala.*

11. *Akhristu azisonkha ndalama sabata iliyonse zoti azigulira petulo wa njinga yake ya moto.*

12. *Mbusayo akumalalikira m'Chingelezi komanso kuti akumapereka mavesi a m'buku la Koran.*

13. As already alluded, as a sign of having had some formal education, English is often used by Malaŵian elites and those aspiring to become their members to distinguish themselves from the impoverished masses. The practice involves condescending views on Chicheŵa and other Malaŵian languages (see, e.g., Englund 2006: 91–93; Mtenje 2002).

14. *Mbusa wa mpingo ŵina wadabwitsa anthu pakhomo pake padafika sing'anga kudzakumbutsa za mankhwala amene mbusa anakatenga.* Broadcast on July 16, 2003.

15. The verb *kuthana* refers to finishing off or eliminating someone, often through murder. The story ended by noting that "the person who sent us this story did not explain whether the medicine that the pastor had taken was indeed effective" (*munthu amene anatitumizira nkhaniyi sanafotokoze ngati mankhwala amene anakatenga mbusawo agwiradi ntchito*).

16. Broadcast on November 23, 2003.

17. *Mkuluyo akuti akuchita za matsengazi m'tchalichimo pokhaulitsa mbusa wa tchalichiyi amene samagwirizana ndi mkuluyo.*

18. *Mundegemo munatuluka mwana wa mwamuna wa mbusa wa mpingo ŵina ndi anthu ena.* Broadcast on July 28, 2003.

19. Transworld Radio's main studio was in Lilongwe, but testimonies were also recorded in its second studio in Blantyre. It did not have enough equipment and personnel to record testimonies at its listeners' homes. As a consequence, the majority of testimonies were delivered by people living in Lilongwe and Blantyre, many of whom belonged to the urban and peri-urban poor in areas such as Chinsapo Township. The directions to its two studios were usually given during the program. Because of its nationwide reach, the station occasionally received guests from farther afield who had come to one of the cities to stay with their relatives in order to offer their testimonies to *Ndamasulidwa*. I interviewed editors and observed the making of *Ndamasulidwa* in Lilongwe in 2006, and the examples given here are from the sample of twenty episodes of *Ndamasulidwa* that I obtained. Although undated in the format I received them, they were broadcast in 2005 and 2006, and I use the subjects' names to identify them. Unlike the principle of anonymity on *Nkhani Zam'maboma*, *Ndamasulidwa* usually broadcast the personal names of the subjects delivering testimonies.

20. On both counts—Pentecostals' alleged desire to narrow down their relationships and their tendency to associate diabolical influences with culture and tradition—my analysis here is again at variance with the situations described in Meyer 1998 and van Dijk 1995.

21. By contrast, Gifford (2004: 50–51) found that testimonies in new Ghanaian Pentecostal churches focused on material prosperity, dominated by success with finances, visas, jobs, and marriage.

9. Beyond the Parity Principle

1. Appeals to fieldwork do, however, appear in the recent works of some feminist philosophers, whether to highlight interviews with female activists at a conference (Ackerly 2008) or to provide a single-case illustration of what poverty entails (Nussbaum 2000).

2. I use the phrase "liberal cosmopolitanism" in recognition of appeals to cosmopolitanism in recent philosophical work on world poverty (see, e.g., Appiah 2006; Nussbaum 2000 and 2004; Pogge 2002).

3. The constitutive rather than optional character of obligations separates my perspective from what Wendy James has called "a bourgeois outlook on the niceness of making social relationships" (1998: 17–18).

Bibliography

Abu-Lughod, Lila. 1986. *Veiled Sentiments: Honor and Poetry in a Bedouin Society.* Berkeley: University of California Press.

———. 2002. "Do Muslim Women Really Need Saving? Anthropological Reflections on Cultural Relativism and Its Others." *American Anthropologist* 104 (3): 783–790.

———. 2005. *Dramas of Nationhood: The Politics of Television in Egypt.* Chicago: University of Chicago Press.

Ackerley, Brooke A. 2008. *Universal Rights in a World of Difference.* Cambridge: Cambridge University Press.

Adamu, Yusuf M. 2002. "Between the Word and the Screen: A Historical Perspective on the Hausa Literary Movement and the Home Video Invasion." *Journal of African Cultural Studies* 15 (2): 203–213.

Africa Watch. 1990. *Where Silence Rules: The Suppression of Dissent in Malawi.* New York: Human Rights Watch.

Agamben, Giorgio. 1998. *Homo Sacer: Sovereign Power and Bare Life.* Translated by Daniel Heller-Roazen. Stanford, Calif.: Stanford University Press.

———. 2005. *State of Exception.* Translated by Kevin Attell. Chicago: University of Chicago Press.

Ake, Claude. 2000. *The Feasibility of Democracy in Africa.* Dakar: Council for the Development of Social Science Research in Africa (CODESRIA).

Alpers, Edward A. 1969. "Trade, State, and Society among the Yao in the Nineteenth Century." *Journal of African History* 10 (3): 405–420.

Altheide, David. 1976. *Creating Reality.* Beverly Hills, Calif.: Sage.

Anagnost, Ann. 1997. *National Past-Times: Narrative, Representation, and Power in Modern China.* Durham, N.C.: Duke University Press.

Anders, Gerhard. 2009. *In the Shadow of Good Governance: An Ethnography of Civil Service Reform in Africa.* Leiden: Brill.

Anderson, Benedict. 1983. *Imagined Communities: Reflections on the Origin and Spread of Nationalism.* New York: Verso.

Anderson, Jens A. 2006. "Informal Moves, Informal Markets: International Migrants and Traders from Mzimba District, Malawi." *African Affairs* 105 (July): 375–397.

An-Na'im, Abdullahi A. 2002. Introduction. In *Cultural Transformation and Human Rights in Africa,* ed. Abdullahi A. An-Na'im, 1–11. London: Zed Books.

Appadurai, Arjun. 1988. "Putting Hierarchy in Its Place." *Cultural Anthropology* 3 (1): 36–49.

———. 1996. *Modernity at Large: Cultural Dimensions of Globalization.* Minneapolis: University of Minnesota Press.

Appiah, Kwame Anthony. 1992. *In My Father's House: Africa in the Philosophy of Culture.* Oxford: Oxford University Press.

———. 2006. *Cosmopolitanism: Ethics in a World of Strangers.* New York: W. W. Norton.

Apter, Andrew. 2007. *Beyond Words: Discourse and Critical Agency in Africa.* Chicago: University of Chicago Press.

Arendt, Hannah. 1951. *The Origins of Totalitarianism.* New York: Harcourt Brace Jovanovich.

ARTICLE 19. 1998. *Malawi Communications Reform and Freedom of Expression.* London: ARTICLE 19.

———. 2000. *At the Crossroads: Freedom of Expression in Malawi.* London: ARTICLE 19.

———. 2003. *Memorandum on the Malawi Communications Act 1998.* London: ARTICLE 19.

———. n.d. *"Who Wants to Forget?": Truth and Access to Information about Past Human Rights Violations.* London: ARTICLE 19.

Asad, Talal. 2003. *Formations of the Secular: Christianity, Islam, Modernity.* Stanford, Calif.: Stanford University Press.

Ashford, Elizabeth. 2007. "The Duties Imposed by the Human Right to Basic Necessities." In *Freedom from Poverty as a Human Right: Who Owes What to the Very Poor?* ed. Thomas Pogge, 183–218. Oxford: Oxford University Press.

Ashforth, Adam. 2005. *Witchcraft, Violence, and Democracy in South Africa.* Chicago: University of Chicago Press.

Askew, Kelly M. 2002. *Performing the Nation: Swahili Music and Cultural Politics in Tanzania.* Chicago: University of Chicago Press.

Bakhtin, Mikhail. 1986. *Speech Genres and Other Late Essays.* Translated by Vern W. McGee. Austin: University of Texas Press.

Barber, Karin. 1987. "Popular Arts in Africa." *African Studies Review* 30 (3): 1–78.

———. 1991. *I Could Speak until Tomorrow: Oríkì, Women and the Past in a Yoruba Town.* Edinburgh: Edinburgh University Press for the International African Institute.

———. 1997. Introduction. In *Readings in African Popular Culture,* ed. Karin Barber, 1–12. Bloomington: Indiana University Press.

———. 2000. *The Generation of Plays: Yorùbá Popular Life in Theater.* Bloomington: Indiana University Press.

———. ed., 2006. *Africa's Hidden Histories: Everyday Literacy and Making the Self.* Bloomington: Indiana University Press.

———. 2007. *The Anthropology of Texts, Persons and Publics: Oral and Written Culture in Africa and Beyond.* Cambridge: Cambridge University Press.

———. 2009. "Orality, the Media and New Popular Cultures in Africa." In *Media and Identity in Africa,* ed. Kimani Njogu and John Middleton, 3–18. Edinburgh: Edinburgh University Press for the International African Institute.

Barber, Karin, and Graham Furniss. 2006. "African-Language Writing." *Research in African Literatures* 37 (3): 1–14.

Bastian, Misty L. 1993. "'Bloodhounds Who Have No Friends': Witchcraft and Locality in the Nigerian Popular Press." In *Modernity and Its Malcontents: Ritual and Power in Postcolonial Africa,* ed. Jean Comaroff and John L. Comaroff, 129–166. Chicago: University of Chicago Press.

———. 2001. "Vulture Men, Campus Cultists, and Teenaged Witches: Modern Magics in Nigerian Popular Media." In *Magical Interpretations, Material Realities: Modernity, Witchcraft, and the Occult in Postcolonial Africa,* ed. Henrietta L. Moore and Todd Sanders, 71–96. New York: Routledge.

Bell, Martin. 1998. "The Journalism of Attachment." In *Media Ethics,* ed. Matthew Kiernan, 15–22. New York: Routledge.

Benhabib, Seyla. 1993. *Situating the Self: Gender, Community, and Postmodernism in Contemporary Ethics*. New York: Routledge.

———. 2002. *The Claims of Culture: Equality and Diversity in the Global Era*. Princeton, N.J.: Princeton University Press.

———. 2004. *The Rights of Others: Aliens, Residents, and Citizens*. Cambridge: Cambridge University Press.

Berman, Bruce. 2004. "Ethnicity, Bureaucracy, and Democracy: The Politics of Trust." In *Ethnicity and Democracy in Africa*, ed. Bruce Berman, Dickson Eyoh, and Will Kymlicka, 38–53. Oxford: James Currey.

Béteille, André. 1986. "Individualism and Equality." *Current Anthropology* 27 (2): 121–134.

Bird, S. Elizabeth. 2003. *The Audience in Everyday Life: Living in a Media World*. New York: Routledge.

———. 2010. "The Anthropology of News and Journalism: Why Now?" In *The Anthropology of News and Journalism: Global Perspectives*, ed. S. Elizabeth Bird, 1–18. Bloomington: Indiana University Press.

Bishara, Amahl. 2006. "Local Hands, International News: Palestinian Journalists and the International Media." *Ethnography* 7 (1): 19–46.

Blommaert, Jan, Mary Bock, and Kay McCormick. 2007. "Narrative Inequality in the TRC Hearings: On the Hearability of Hidden Transcripts." In *Discourse and Human Rights Violations*, ed. Christine Anthonissen and Jan Blommaert, 33–63. Amsterdam: John Benjamins.

Boellstorff, Tom. 2008. *Coming of Age in Second Life: An Anthropologist Explores the Virtually Human*. Princeton, N.J.: Princeton University Press.

Bone, David S. 2000. "An Outline History of Islam in Malawi." In *Malawi's Muslims: Historical Perspectives*, ed. David S. Bone, 13–26. Blantyre: Christian Literature Association in Malawi (CLAIM) for Kachere Series.

Born, Georgina. 2004. *Uncertain Vision: Birt, Dyke and the Reinvention of the BBC*. London: Secker and Warburg.

Bornstein, Erica. 2005. *The Spirit of Development: Protestant NGOs, Morality, and Economics in Zimbabwe*. Stanford, Calif.: Stanford University Press.

Bourdieu, Pierre. 1993. *Sociology in Question*. Translated by Richard Nice. London: Sage.

———. 1998. *On Television and Journalism*. Translated by Priscilla Parkhurst Ferguson. Ann Arbor, Mich.: Pluto Press.

Boyer, Dominic. 2003. "Censorship as Vocation: The Institutions, Practices, and Cultural Logic of Media Control in the German Democratic Republic." *Comparative Studies in Society and History* 45 (3): 511–545.

———. 2005. *Spirit and System: Media, Intellectuals, and the Dialectic in Modern German Culture*. Chicago: University of Chicago Press.

———. 2010. "Making (Sense of) News in the Era of Digital Information." In *The Anthropology of News and Journalism: Global Perspectives*, ed. S. Elizabeth Bird, 241–256. Bloomington: Indiana University Press.

Boyer, Dominic, and Ulf Hannerz. 2006. "Introduction: Worlds of Journalism." *Ethnography* 7 (1): 5–17.

Brown, Wendy. 1995. *States of Injury: Power and Freedom in Late Modernity*. Princeton, N.J.: Princeton University Press.

Burke, Timothy. 1996. *Lifebuoy Men, Lux Women: Commodification, Consumption, and Cleanliness in Modern Zimbabwe*. Durham, N.C.: Duke University Press.

Buskens, Ineke, and Anne Wobb, eds. 2009. *African Women and ICTs: Investigating Technology, Gender, and Empowerment*. London: Zed Books.

Calhoun, Craig. 2007. *Nations Matter: Culture, History, and the Cosmopolitan Dream.* New York: Routledge.

Carter, April. 1971. *The Political Theory of Anarchism.* London: Routledge & Kegan Paul.

Castoriadis, Cornelius. 1997. *World in Fragments: Writings on Politics, Society, Psychoanalysis, and the Imagination.* Translated by David Ames Curtis. Stanford, Calif.: Stanford University Press.

Centre for Language Studies. 2000. *Mtanthauziramawu Wa Chinyanja/Chichewa.* Blantyre: Dzuka.

——. n.d. a. *Sociolinguistic Surveys of Four Malawian Languages: With Special Reference to Education.* Zomba: Centre for Language Studies.

——. n.d. b. *Towards a National Language Policy in Education.* Zomba: Centre for Language Studies.

Chabal, Patrick, and Jean-Pascal Daloz. 2005. *Culture Troubles: Politics and the Interpretation of Meaning.* Chicago: University of Chicago Press.

Chakanza, J. C. 2000. *Wisdom of the People: 2000 Chinyanja Proverbs.* Blantyre: Christian Literature Association in Malawi (CLAIM) for Kachere Series.

Chambers, Simone. 2003. "Deliberative Democracy Theory." *Annual Review of Political Science* 6: 307–326.

Chanock, Martin. 1985. *Law, Custom and Social Order: The Colonial Experience in Malawi and Zambia.* Cambridge: Cambridge University Press.

Charity, Arthur. 1995. *Doing Public Journalism.* New York: Guilford Press.

Chatterjee, Partha. 1986. *Nationalist Thought and the Colonial World: A Derivative Discourse?* London: Zed Books.

Cheney, Kristen E. 2007. *Pillars of the Nation: Child Citizens and Ugandan National Development.* Chicago: University of Chicago Press.

Chichewa Board. 1990. *Chichewa Orthography Rules.* Revised Edition. Zomba: Chichewa Board.

Chimombo, Moira. 1998. "Government Journalism: From Totalitarianism to Democracy?" In *Democratization in Malawi: A Stocktaking,* ed. Kings M. Phiri and Kenneth R. Ross, 217–236. Blantyre: Christian Literature Association in Malawi (CLAIM) for Kachere Series.

Chimombo, Steve. 1988. *Malawian Oral Literature: The Aesthetics of Indigenous Arts.* Zomba: Centre for Social Research.

Chimombo, Steve, and Moira Chimombo. 1996. *The Culture of Democracy: Language, Literature, the Arts, and Politics in Malawi, 1992–94.* Zomba: WASI Publications.

Chinsinga, Blessings. 2002. "The Politics of Poverty Alleviation in Malawi: A Critical Review." In *A Democracy of Chameleons: Politics and Culture in the New Malawi,* ed. Harri Englund, 25–42. Uppsala: Nordic Africa Institute.

Chipangula, Eunice Nihero. 2003. *Political Reporting Trends in Malawi: 1980s and 1990s.* Makwasa, Thyolo: Malamulo Publishing House.

Chirambo, Reuben Makayiko. 2002. "'Mzimu wa Soldier': Contemporary Popular Music and Politics in Malawi." In *A Democracy of Chameleons: Politics and Culture in the New Malawi,* ed. Harri Englund, 103–122. Uppsala: Nordic Africa Institute.

Chirwa, Danwood Mzikenge. 2005. "A Full Loaf Is Better than Half: The Constitutional Protection of Economic, Social and Cultural Rights in Malawi." *Journal of African Law* 49 (2): 207–241.

Chirwa, Vera. 2007. *Fearless Fighter: An Autobiography.* London: Zed Books.

Chirwa, Wiseman C. 1998. "Democracy, Ethnicity and Regionalism: The Malawian Experience, 1992–1996." In *Democratization in Malawi: A Stocktaking,* ed. Kings M. Phiri and Kenneth R. Ross, 52–69. Blantyre: Christian Literature Association in Malawi (CLAIM) for Kachere Series.

Chirwa, Wiseman C., E. Kayanula, and Beston Lijenda. 2000. *The Development Broadcasting Unit (DBU), Malawi Broadcasting Corporation: Tracer Study Report on Kanthu n'khama Radio Programme.* Blantyre: Malawi Broadcasting Corporation.

CHRR (Centre for Human Rights and Rehabilitation). n.d. *Training Manual on Human Rights Monitoring.* Lilongwe: Centre for Human Rights and Rehabilitation.

Clark, Samuel. 2007. *Living without Domination: The Possibility of Anarchist Utopia.* Aldershot: Ashgate.

Comaroff, Jean, and John L. Comaroff. 1999. "Occult Economies and the Violence of Abstraction: Notes from the South African Postcolony." *American Ethnologist* 26 (3): 279–301.

———. 2000. "Millennial Capitalism: First Thoughts on a Second Coming." *Public Culture* 12 (2): 291–343.

Comaroff, John L. 1975. "Talking Politics: Oratory and Authority in a Tswana Chiefdom." In *Political Language and Oratory in Traditional Society,* ed. Maurice Bloch, 141–161. London: Academic Press.

Comaroff, John L., and Jean Comaroff. 2006. "Law and Disorder in the Postcolony: An Introduction." In *Law and Disorder in the Postcolony,* ed. Jean Comaroff and John L. Comaroff, 1–56. Chicago: University of Chicago Press.

Cooke, Bill, and Uma Kothari, eds. 2001. *Participation: The New Tyranny?* London: Zed Books.

Corrigan, Don H. 1999. *The Public Journalism Movement in America: Evangelists in the Newsroom.* Westport, Conn.: Praeger.

Cruikshank, Barbara. 1999. *The Will to Empower: Democratic Citizens and Other Subjects.* Ithaca, N.Y.: Cornell University Press.

Csordas, Thomas J., ed. 1994. *Embodiment and Experience: The Existential Ground of Culture and Self.* Cambridge: Cambridge University Press.

de Bruijn, Mirjam, Francis B. Nyamnjoh, and Inge Brinkman, eds. 2009. *Mobile Phones: The New Talking Drums of Africa.* Bamenda: Langaa Research and Publishing Common Initiative Group.

Devereux, Stephen, and Zoltan Tiba. 2006. "Malawi's First Famine, 2001–2002." In *The New Famines,* ed. Stephen Devereux, 143–177. New York: Routledge.

de Vries, Hent. 2001. "In Media Res: Global Religion, Public Spheres, and the Task of Contemporary Comparative Religious Studies." In *Religion and Media,* ed. Hent de Vries and Samuel Weber, 3–42. Stanford, Calif.: Stanford University Press.

Dewey, John. 1927. *The Public and Its Problems.* New York: Swallow Press.

Dewey, Susan. 2009. "'Dear Dr Kothari . . .': Sexuality, Violence against Women, and the Parallel Public Sphere in India." *American Ethnologist* 36 (1): 124–139.

De Witte, Marleen. 2003. "Altar Media's *Living Word:* Televised Charismatic Christianity in Ghana." *Journal of Religion in Africa* 33 (2): 172–202.

Diawara, Mamadou. 1997. "Mande Oral Popular Culture Revisited by the Electronic Media." In *Readings in African Popular Culture,* ed. Karin Barber, 40–48. Oxford: James Currey.

Dickey, Sara. 1993. *Cinema and the Urban Poor in South India.* Cambridge: Cambridge University Press.

Dinges, John. 2000. "Public Journalism and National Public Radio." In *Public Journalism and Political Knowledge,* ed. Anthony J. Eksterowicz and Robert N. Roberts, 91–118. Lanham, Md.: Rowman and Littlefield.

Dirks, Nicholas B., ed. 1992. *Colonialism and Culture.* Ann Arbor: University of Michigan Press.

Donnelly, Jack. 1989. *Universal Human Rights in Theory and Practice.* Ithaca, N.Y.: Cornell University Press.

Dorwald, Andrew, and Jonathan Kydd. 2004. "The Malawi 2002 Food Crisis: The Rural Development Challenge." *Journal of Modern African Studies* 42 (3): 343–361.

Dumont, Louis. 1980. *Homo Hierarchicus: The Caste System and Its Implications*. Chicago: University of Chicago Press.

———. 1986. *Essays on Individualism: Modern Ideology in Anthropological Perspective*. Chicago: University of Chicago Press.

Durán, Lucy. 1995. "*Jelimusow*: The Superwomen of Malian Music." In *Power, Marginality and African Oral Literature*, ed. Graham Furniss and Liz Gunner, 197–207. Cambridge: Cambridge University Press.

Durham, Deborah. 2002. "Uncertain Citizens: Herero and the New Intercalary Subject in Postcolonial Botswana." In *Postcolonial Subjectivities in Africa*, ed. Richard Werbner, 139–170. London: Zed Books.

Dyzenhaus, David, ed. 1998. *Law as Politics: Carl Schmitt's Critique of Liberalism*. Durham, N.C.: Duke University Press.

Dzimbiri, Lewis B. 2002. *Industrial Relations, the State and Strike Activity in Malawi*. Ph.D. thesis, Keele University, United Kingdom.

Ekeh, Peter P. 1975. "Colonialism and the Two Publics in Africa: A Theoretical Statement." *Comparative Studies in Society and History* 17 (1): 91–112.

Ellis, Stephen. 1999. *The Mask of Anarchy: The Destruction of Liberia and the Religious Dimension of an African Civil War*. London: Hurst.

Englund, Harri. 1996a. "Between God and Kamuzu: The Transition to Multiparty Politics in Central Malawi." In *Postcolonial Identities in Africa*, ed. Richard Werbner and Terence Ranger, 107–135. London: Zed Books.

———. 1996b. "Witchcraft, Modernity and the Person: The Morality of Accumulation in Central Malawi." *Critique of Anthropology* 16 (3): 257–281.

———. 1999. "The Self in Self-Interest: Land, Labour and Temporalities in Malawi's Agrarian Change." *Africa* 69 (1): 139–159.

———. 2002a. "The Village in the City, the City in the Village: Migrants in Lilongwe." *Journal of Southern African Studies* 28 (1): 137–154.

———. 2002b. "Introduction: The Culture of Chameleon Politics." In *A Democracy of Chameleons: Politics and Culture in the New Malawi*, ed. Harri Englund, 11–24. Uppsala: Nordic Africa Institute.

———. 2002c. *From War to Peace on the Mozambique-Malawi Borderland*. Edinburgh: Edinburgh University Press for the International African Institute.

———. 2003. "Christian Independency and Global Membership: Pentecostal Extraversions in Malawi." *Journal of Religion in Africa* 33 (1): 83–111.

———. 2004a. "Introduction: Recognizing Identities, Imagining Alternatives." In *Rights and the Politics of Recognition in Africa*, ed. Harri Englund and Francis B. Nyamnjoh, 1–29. London: Zed Books.

———. 2004b. "Gender-Relations in African-Language Literature: Interpretative Politics and Possibilities." *African Sociological Review* 8 (1): 154–175.

———. 2006. *Prisoners of Freedom: Human Rights and the African Poor*. Berkeley: University of California Press.

———. 2007a. "Witchcraft and the Limits of Mass Mediation in Malawi." *Journal of the Royal Anthropological Institute* 13 (2): 295–311.

———. 2007b. "Pentecostalism beyond Belief: Trust and Democracy in a Malawian Township." *Africa* 77 (4): 477–499.

———. 2008. "Extreme Poverty and Existential Obligations: Beyond Morality in the Anthropology of Africa?" *Social Analysis* 52 (3): 33–50.

Evans-Pritchard, E. E. 1931. "Sorcery and Native Opinion." *Africa* 4 (1): 22–55.

———. 1937. *Witchcraft, Oracles and Magic among the Azande.* Oxford: Clarendon Press.

Fardon, Richard. 1990. "Malinowski's Precedent: The Imagination of Equality." *Man (N.S.)* 25 (4): 569–587.

Fardon, Richard, and Graham Furniss. 2000. "African Broadcast Cultures." In *African Broadcast Cultures: Radio in Transition,* ed. Richard Fardon and Graham Furniss, 1–20. Oxford: James Currey.

Fassin, Didier. 2007. *When Bodies Remember: Experiences and Politics of AIDS in South Africa.* Translated by Amy Jacobs and Gabrielle Varro. Berkeley: University of California Press.

Fearon, James D. 1998. "Deliberation as Discussion." In *Deliberative Democracy,* ed. Jon Elster, 44–68. Cambridge: Cambridge University Press.

Ferguson, James. 1999. *Expectations of Modernity: Myths and Meanings of Urban Life on the Zambian Copperbelt.* Berkeley: University of California Press.

———. 2006. *Global Shadows: Africa in the Neoliberal World Order.* Durham, N.C.: Duke University Press.

———. 2009. "The Uses of Neoliberalism." *Antipode* 41 (1): 166–184.

Fernythough, Timothy. 1993. "Human Rights and Precolonial Africa." In *Human Rights and Governance in Africa,* ed. Ronald Cohen, Göran Hydén, and Winston P. Nagan, 39–73. Gainesville: University Press of Florida.

Finnegan, Ruth. 2007. *The Oral and Beyond: Doing Things with Words in Africa.* Oxford: James Currey.

Fleurbaey, Marc. 2007. "Poverty as a Form of Oppression." In *Freedom from Poverty as a Human Right: Who Owes What to the Very Poor?* ed. Thomas Pogge, 133–154. Oxford: Oxford University Press.

Fong, Vanessa L. 2007. "SARS, a Shipwreck, a NATO Attack, and September 11, 2001: Global Information Flows and Chinese Responses to Tragic News Events." *American Ethnologist* 34 (3): 521–539.

Fordred-Green, Lesley. 2000. "*Tokoloshe* Tales: Reflections on the Cultural Politics of Journalism in South Africa." *Current Anthropology* 41 (5): 701–712.

Fortes, Meyer. 1949. *The Web of Kinship among the Tallensi.* London: Oxford University Press.

Fortner, Robert S. 2005. *Radio, Morality, and Culture: Britain, Canada, and the United States, 1919–1945.* Carbondale: Southern Illinois University Press.

Fraenkel, Peter. 1959. *Wayaleshi.* London: Weidenfeld and Nicolson.

Fraser, Nancy. 1992. "Rethinking the Public Sphere: A Contribution to the Critique of Actually Existing Democracy." In *Habermas and the Public Sphere,* ed. Craig Calhoun, 109–142. Cambridge, Mass.: MIT Press.

Friedland, William H., and Carl G. Rosberg. 1964. "The Anatomy of African Socialism." In *African Socialism,* ed. William H. Rosberg and Carl G. Rosberg, 1–11. Stanford, Calif.: Stanford University Press.

Friedman, Marilyn. 2003. *Autonomy, Gender, Politics.* Oxford: Oxford University Press.

Furniss, Graham. 1996. *Poetry, Prose and Popular Culture in Hausa.* Edinburgh: Edinburgh University Press for the International African Institute.

———. 2005. "Video and the Hausa Novella in Nigeria." *Social Identities* 11 (2): 89–112.

Gardiner, Michael E. 2004. "Wild Publics and Grotesque Symposiums: Habermas and Bakhtin on Dialogue, Everyday Life, and the Public Sphere." In *After Habermas: New Perspectives on the Public Sphere,* ed. Nick Crossley and John Michael Roberts, 28–48. Oxford: Blackwell.

Geschiere, Peter. 1997. *The Modernity of Witchcraft: Politics and the Occult in Postcolonial Africa.* Charlottesville: University Press of Virginia.

———. 2006. "Witchcraft and the Limits of the Law: Cameroon and South Africa." In *Law and Disorder in the Postcolony,* ed. Jean Comaroff and John L. Comaroff, 219–246. Chicago: University of Chicago Press.

Geschiere, Peter, and Francis B. Nyamnjoh. 1998. "Witchcraft as an Issue in the 'Politics of Belonging': Democratization and Urban Migrants' Involvement with the Home Village." *African Studies Review* 41 (1): 69–91.

Gifford, Paul. 1998. *African Christianity: Its Public Role.* London: Hurst.

———. 2004. *Ghana's New Christianity: Pentecostalism in a Globalizing African Economy.* London: Hurst.

Ginsburg, Faye D. 1993. "Aboriginal Media and the Australian Imaginary." *Public Culture* 5 (3): 557–578.

———. 2002. "Screen Memories: Resignifying the Traditional in Indigenous Media." In *Media Worlds: Anthropology on New Terrain,* ed. Faye D. Ginsburg, Lila Abu-Lughod, and Brian Larkin, 39–57. Berkeley: University of California Press.

Glasser, Theodore L. 1999. Introduction. In *The Idea of Public Journalism,* ed. Theodore L. Glasser, 3–18. New York: Guilford Press.

Gluckman, Max. 1955. *The Judicial Process among the Barotse of Northern Rhodesia.* Manchester: Manchester University Press.

———. 1963. "Gossip and Scandal." *Current Anthropology* 4 (3): 307–315.

———. 1965. *The Ideas in Barotse Jurisprudence.* New Haven, Conn.: Yale University Press.

———. 1975. "Anthropology and Apartheid: The Work of South African Anthropologists." In *Studies in African Social Anthropology,* ed. Meyer Fortes and Sheila Patterson, 21–39. London: Academic Press.

———. 2006 [1961]. "Ethnographic Data in British Social Anthropology." In *The Manchester School: Practice and Ethnographic Praxis in Anthropology,* ed. T. M. S. Evens and Don Handelman, 13–22. New York: Berghahn.

Gluckman, Max, J. Clyde Mitchell, and J. A. Barnes. 1949. "The Village Headman in British Central Africa." *Africa* 19 (2): 89–106.

Goodale, Mark. 2009. *Surrendering to Utopia: An Anthropology of Human Rights.* Stanford, Calif.: Stanford University Press.

Goodin, Robert E. 2003. *Reflective Democracy.* Oxford: Oxford University Press.

Goody, Ester. 1982. *Parenthood and Social Reproduction: Fostering and Occupational Roles in West Africa.* Cambridge: Cambridge University Press.

Government of Malaŵi. 2008. *2008 Malaŵi Millennium Development Goals Report.* Lilongwe: Ministry of Economic Planning and Development.

Graeber, David. 2004. *Fragments of an Anarchist Anthropology.* Chicago: Prickly Paradigm Press.

Grätz, Tilo. 2000. "New Local Radio Stations in African Languages and the Process of Political Transformation: The Case of Radio Rurale Locale Tanguiéta in Northern Benin." In *African Broadcast Cultures: Radio in Transition,* ed. Richard Fardon and Graham Furniss, 110–127. Oxford: James Currey.

Gray, John. 2000. *Two Faces of Liberalism.* Cambridge: Polity.

Green, Maia. 2005. "A Discourse on Inequality: Poverty, Public Bads and Entrenching Witchcraft in Post-Adjustment Tanzania." *Anthropological Theory* 5 (3): 247–266.

Gulbrandsen, Ørnulf. 1991. "On the Problem of Egalitarianism: The Kalahari San in Transition." In *The Ecology of Choice and Symbol: Essays in Honour of Fredrik Barth,* ed. Reidar Gronhaug, Gunnar Haaland, and Georg Henriksen, 81–110. Bergen: Alma Mater Forlag.

Gunner, Liz. 2000. "Wrestling with the Present, Beckoning to the Past: Contemporary Zulu Radio Drama." *Journal of Southern African Studies* 26 (2): 223–237.

Guyer, Jane I. 1993. "Wealth in People and Self-Realization in Equatorial Africa." *Man (N.S.)* 28 (2): 243–265.

———. 2007. "Prophecy and the Near Future: Thoughts on Macroeconomic, Evangelical, and Punctuated Time." *American Ethnologist* 34 (3): 409–421.

Gwengwe, John W. 1964. *Cinyanja Cina*. Lusaka: Kenneth Kaunda Foundation.

———. 1965. *Sikusinja ndi Gwenembe*. Blantyre: Macmillan Malawi.

Haas, Tanni. 2007. *The Pursuit of Public Journalism: Theory, Practice, and Criticism*. New York: Routledge.

Habermas, Jürgen. 1989. *The Structural Transformation of the Public Sphere: An Inquiry into a Category of Bourgeois Society*. Translated by Thomas Burger, with Frederick Lawrence. Cambridge, Mass.: MIT Press.

———. 1996. *Between Facts and Norms: Contributions to a Discourse Theory of Law and Democracy*. Translated by William Rehg. Cambridge, Mass.: MIT Press.

Hackett, Rosalind I. J. 1998. "Charismatic/Pentecostal Appropriations of Media Technology in Nigeria and Ghana." *Journal of Religion in Africa* 28 (3): 258–277.

———. 2006. "Mediated Religion in South Africa: Balancing Airtime and Rights Claims." In *Religion, Media, and the Public Sphere*, ed. Birgit Meyer and Annelies Moors, 166–187. Bloomington: Indiana University Press.

Hallward, Peter. 2009. "Staging Inequality: Rancière's Theatrocracy and the Limits of Anarchic Equality." In *Jacques Rancière: History, Politics, Aesthetics*, ed. Gabriel Rockhill and Philip Watts, 140–157. Durham, N.C.: Duke University Press.

Hamilton, Carolyn, ed. 2002. *Refiguring the Archive*. Cape Town: David Philip.

Hannerz, Ulf. 2004. *Foreign News: Exploring the World of Foreign Correspondents*. Chicago: University of Chicago Press.

Hansen, Karen Tranberg. 2000. *Salaula: The World of Second-Hand Clothing and Zambia*. Chicago: University of Chicago Press.

Haraway, Donna. 2003. *The Companion Species Manifesto: Dogs, People, and Significant Otherness*. Chicago: Prickly Paradigm Press.

Harrigan, Jane. 2003. "U-Turns and Full Circles: Two Decades of Agricultural Reform in Malawi, 1981–2000." *World Development* 31 (5): 847–863.

Harrison, Lawrence E., and Samuel P. Huntington, eds. 2000. *Culture Matters: How Values Shape Human Progress*. New York: Basic Books.

Hastrup, Kirsten. 2001. "To Follow a Rule: Rights and Responsibilities Revisited." In *Human Rights on Common Grounds: The Quest for Universality*, ed. Kirsten Hastrup, 57–74. The Hague: Kluwer Law International.

Hasty, Jennifer. 2005. *The Press and Political Culture in Ghana*. Bloomington: Indiana University Press.

———. 2006. "Performing Power, Composing Culture: The State Press in Ghana." *Ethnography* 7 (1): 69–98.

———. 2010. "Journalism as Fieldwork: Propaganda, Complicity, and the Ethics of Anthropology." In *The Anthropology of News and Journalism: Global Perspectives*, ed. S. Elizabeth Bird, 132–148. Bloomington: Indiana University Press.

Henry, Neil. 2007. *American Carnival: Journalism under Siege in an Age of New Media*. Berkeley: University of California Press.

Herman, Edward S., and Noam Chomsky. 2002. *Manufacturing Consent: The Political Economy of the Mass Media*. New York: Pantheon Books.

Hertel, Shareen, and Lanse Minkler. 2007. "Economic Rights: The Terrain." In *Economic Rights: Conceptual, Measurement and Policy Issues*, ed. Shareen Hertel and Lanse Minkler, 1–35. Cambridge: Cambridge University Press.

Hickey, Samuel, and Giles Mohan, eds. 2004. *Participation, from Tyranny to Transformation? Exploring New Approaches to Participation in Development.* London: Zed Books.

Hilhorst, Dorothea. 2003. *The Real World of NGOs: Discourses, Diversity and Development.* London: Zed Books.

Hirschkind, Charles. 2006. *The Ethical Soundscape: Cassette Sermons and Islamic Counterpublics.* New York: Columbia University Press.

Hirschmann, Nancy J. 1992. *Rethinking Obligation: A Feminist Method for Political Theory.* Ithaca, N.Y.: Cornell University Press.

———. 2003. *The Subject of Liberty: Toward a Feminist Theory of Freedom.* Princeton, N.J.: Princeton University Press.

Hountondji, Paulin J. 1983. *African Philosophy: Myth and Reality.* Translated by Henri Evans. Bloomington: Indiana University Press.

Howard, Rhoda. 1990. "Group versus Individual Identity in the African Debate on Human Rights." In *Human Rights in Africa: Cross-Cultural Perspectives,* ed. Abdullahi A. An-Na'im and Francis M. Deng, 159–183. Washington, D.C.: Brookings Institution.

Howell, Signe. 1997. Introduction. In *The Ethnography of Moralities,* ed. Signe Howell, 1–22. New York: Routledge.

———. 2006. *The Kinning of Foreigners: Transnational Adoption in a Global Perspective.* Oxford: Berghahn.

———. 2009. "Adoption of the Unrelated Child: Some Challenges to the Anthropological Study of Kinship." *Annual Review of Anthropology* 38: 149–166.

Hultin, Niklas. 2007. "'Pure Fabrication': Information Policy, Media Rights, and the Postcolonial Public." *PoLAR: Political and Legal Anthropology Review* 30 (1): 1–21.

Humphrey, Caroline. 1997. "Exemplars and Rules: Aspects of the Discourse of Moralities in Mongolia." In *The Ethnography of Moralities,* ed. Signe Howell, 25–47. New York: Routledge.

Hund, John. 2004. "African Witchcraft and Western Law: Psychological and Cultural Issues." *Journal of Contemporary Religion* 19 (1): 67–84.

Hutchins Commission. 1947. *A Free and Responsible Press.* Chicago: University of Chicago Press.

Iggers, Jeremy. 1998. *Good News, Bad News: Journalism Ethics and the Public Interest.* Boulder, Colo.: Westview Press.

Ilboudo, Jean-Pierre. 2000. "Prospects for Rural Radio in Africa: Strategies to Relate Audience Research to the Participatory Production of Radio Programmes." In *African Broadcast Cultures: Radio in Transition,* ed. Richard Fardon and Graham Furniss, 42–71. Oxford: James Currey.

Iliffe, John. 1987. *The African Poor: A History.* Cambridge: Cambridge University Press.

———. 2005. *Honour in African History.* Cambridge: Cambridge University Press.

Irvine, Judith. 1993. "Insult and Responsibility: Verbal Abuse in a Wolof Village." In *Responsibility and Evidence in Oral Discourse,* ed. Jane Hill and Judith Irvine, 104–134. Cambridge: Cambridge University Press.

Ishay, Micheline R. 2004. *The History of Human Rights: From Ancient Times to the Globalization Era.* Berkeley: University of California Press.

James, Allison. 2007. "Giving Voice to Children's Voices: Practices and Problems, Pitfalls and Potentials." *American Anthropologist* 109 (2): 261–272.

James, Wendy. 1998. "'One of Us': Marcel Mauss and 'English' Anthropology." In *Marcel Mauss: A Centenary Tribute,* ed. Wendy James and N. J. Allen, 3–26. Oxford: Berghahn.

Jenkins, Henry. 2006. *Convergence Culture: Where Old and New Media Collide.* New York: New York University Press.

Jimu, Ignasio Malizani. 2008. *Urban Appropriation and Transformation: Bicycle Taxi and Hand-cart Operators in Malawi.* Bamenda: Langaa Research and Publishing Common Initiative Group.

Jones, Ben. 2009. *Beyond the State in Rural Uganda.* Edinburgh: Edinburgh University Press for the International African Institute.

Jul-Larsen, Eyolf, and Peter Mvula. 2009. "Security for Many or Surplus for the Few? Customary Tenure and Social Differentiation in Southern Malawi." *Journal of Southern African Studies* 35 (1): 175–190.

Kaag, Mayke. 2007. "Aid, *Umma,* and Politics: Transnational Islamic NGOs in Chad." In *Islam and Muslim Politics in Africa,* ed. Benjamin F. Soares and René Otayek, 85–102. New York: Palgrave-Macmillan.

Kalyvas, Andreas. 2008. *Democracy and the Politics of the Extraordinary: Max Weber, Carl Schmitt, and Hannah Arendt.* Cambridge: Cambridge University Press.

Kamchedzera, Garton S. 1998. "The Rights of the Child in the Christian Context." In *Faith at the Frontiers of Knowledge,* ed. Kenneth R. Ross, 75–93. Blantyre: Christian Literature Association in Malawi (CLAIM) for Kachere Series.

Kamm, F. M. 2004. "The New Problem of Distance in Morality." In *The Ethics of Assistance: Morality and the Distant Needy,* ed. Deen K. Chatterjee, 59–74. Cambridge: Cambridge University Press.

Kanyongolo, Fidelis Edge. 1995. "The Law and Practice of Censorship in Malawi: A Critical Review." In *Church, Law and Political Transition in Malawi 1992–94,* ed. Matembo S. Nzunda and Kenneth R. Ross, 75–88. Gweru: Mambo Press for Kachere Series.

———. 2005. "Land Occupations in Malawi: Challenging the Neoliberal Legal Order." In *Reclaiming the Land: The Resurgence of Rural Movements in Africa, Asia, and Latin America,* ed. Sam Moyo and Paris Yeros, 118–141. London: Zed Books.

———. 2008. "Law, Land and Sustainable Development in Malawi." In *Land and Sustainable Development in Africa,* ed. Kojo Sebastian Amanor and Sam Moyo, 83–99. London: Zed Books.

Kapferer, Bruce. 2002. "Outside All Reason: Magic, Sorcery and Epistemology in Anthropology." *Social Analysis* 46 (3): 1–30.

Kaplan, Robert. 1994. "The Coming Anarchy: How Scarcity, Crime, Overpopulation, and Disease Are Rapidly Destroying the Social Fabric of Our Planet." *Atlantic Monthly* (February): 44–76.

Kasoma, Francis P. 2002. *Community Radio: Its Management and Organisation in Zambia.* Lusaka: Zambia Independent Media Association.

Kayambazinthu, Edrinnie, and Fulata Moyo. 2002. "Hate Speech in the New Malawi." In *A Democracy of Chameleons: Politics and Culture in the New Malawi,* ed. Harri Englund, 87–102. Uppsala: Nordic Africa Institute.

Kelly, Paul. 2005. *Liberalism.* Cambridge: Polity.

Kerr, David. 1995. *African Popular Theatre: From Pre-colonial Times to the Present Day.* London: James Currey.

Kimenyi, Mwangi S. 2007. "Economic Rights, Human Development Effort, and Institutions." In *Economic Rights: Conceptual, Measurement and Policy Issues,* ed. Shareen Hertel and Lanse Minkler, 182–213. Cambridge: Cambridge University Press.

Kipnis, Andrew. 2007. "Neoliberalism Reified: *Suzhi* Discourse and Tropes of Neoliberalism in the People's Republic of China." *Journal of the Royal Anthropological Institute* 13 (2): 383–400.

Kishindo, Pascal J. 1998. "Politics of Language in Contemporary Malawi." In *Democratization in Malawi: A Stocktaking,* ed. Kings M. Phiri and Kenneth R. Ross, 252–280. Blantyre: Christian Literature Association in Malawi (CLAIM) for Kachere Series.

Kishindo, Paul. 2004. "Customary Land Tenure and the New Land Policy in Malawi." *Journal of Contemporary African Studies* 22 (2): 213–225.

Klaits, Frederick. 2010. *Death in a Church of Life: Moral Passion during Botswana's Time of AIDS.* Berkeley: University of California Press.

Kopytoff, Igor. 1964. "Socialism and Traditional African Societies." In *African Socialism,* ed. William H. Rosberg and Carl G. Rosberg, 53–62. Stanford, Calif.: Stanford University Press.

———. 1987. "The Internal African Frontier: The Making of African Political Culture." In *The African Frontier: The Reproduction of Traditional African Societies,* ed. Igor Kopytoff, 3–84. Bloomington: Indiana University Press.

Kopytoff, Igor, and Suzanne Miers. 1977. "African 'Slavery' as an Institution of Marginality." In *Slavery in Africa: Historical and Anthropological Perspectives,* ed. Suzanne Miers and Igor Kopytoff, 3–81. Madison: University of Wisconsin Press.

Kreide, Regina. 2007. "Neglected Injustice: Poverty as a Violation of Social Autonomy." In *Freedom from Poverty as a Human Right: Who Owes What to the Very Poor?* ed. Thomas Pogge, 155–181. Oxford: Oxford University Press.

Kuper, Adam. 1999. *Culture: The Anthropologists' Account.* Cambridge, Mass.: Harvard University Press.

Kydd, Jonathan, and Robert E. Christiansen. 1982. "Structural Change in Malawi since Independence: Consequences of a Development Strategy Based on Large-Scale Agriculture." *World Development* 10 (5): 355–375.

Kymlicka, Will. 1995. *Multicultural Citizenship: A Liberal Theory of Minority Rights.* Oxford: Oxford University Press.

LaMay, Craig L. 2007. *Exporting Press Freedom: Economic and Editorial Dilemmas in International Media Assistance.* New Brunswick, N.J.: Transaction Publishers.

Larkin, Brian. 2008. *Signal and Noise: Media, Infrastructure, and Urban Culture in Nigeria.* Durham, N.C.: Duke University Press.

Latour, Bruno. 2005. *Reassembling the Social: An Introduction to Actor-Network Theory.* Oxford: Oxford University Press.

Lekgoathi, Sekibakiba Peter. 2009. "'You Are Listening to Radio Lebowa of the South African Broadcasting Corporation': Vernacular Radio, Bantustan Identity and Listenership, 1960–1994." *Journal of Southern African Studies* 35 (3): 575–594.

LeMahieu, D. L. 1988. *A Culture for Democracy: Mass Communication and the Cultivated Mind between the Wars.* Oxford: Clarendon Press.

Lindholt, Lotte. 2001. "The African Charter: Contextual Universality." In *Human Rights on Common Grounds: The Quest for Universality,* ed. Kirsten Hastrup, 117–138. The Hague: Kluwer Law International.

Lippmann, Walter. 1922. *Public Opinion.* New York: Free Press.

———. 1925. *The Phantom Public.* New York: Harcourt Brace.

Lonsdale, John. 2004. "Moral and Political Argument in Kenya." In *Ethnicity and Democracy in Africa,* ed. Bruce Berman, Dickson Eyoh, and Will Kymlicka, 73–95. Oxford: James Currey.

Lumumba-Kasongo, Tukumbi. 2005. "The Problematics of Liberal Democracy and Democratic Process: Lessons for Deconstructing and Building African Democracies." In *Liberal Democracy and Its Critics in Africa: Political Dysfunction and the Struggle for Social Progress,* ed. Tukumbi Lumumba-Kasongo, 1–25. London: Zed Books.

Lwanda, John. 2008. "Poets, Culture and Orature: A Reappraisal of the Malawi Political Public Sphere, 1953–2006." *Journal of Contemporary African Studies* 26 (1): 71–101.

Mackenzie, Catriona, and Natalie Stoljar, eds. 2000. *Relational Autonomy*. Oxford: Oxford University Press.

Macola, Giacomo. 2010. *Liberal Nationalism in Central Africa: A Biography of Harry Mwaanga Nkumbula*. New York: Palgrave Macmillan.

Mafeje, Archie. 1998. "Anthropology in Post-Independence Africa: End of an Era and the Problem of Self-Redefinition." *African Sociological Review* 2 (1): 1–43.

Magalasi, Mufunanji. 2008. "Malawian Popular Commercial Stage Drama: Origins, Challenges and Growth." *Journal of Southern African Studies* 34 (1): 161–177.

Magubane, Bernard Makhosezwe. 1999. "The African Renaissance in Historical Perspective." In *African Renaissance: The New Struggle*, ed. Malegapuru William Makgoba, 10–36. Cape Town: Tafelberg.

Mahmood, Saba. 2001. "Feminist Theory, Embodiment, and the Docile Agent: Some Reflections on the Egyptian Islamic Revival." *Cultural Anthropology* 16 (2): 202–235.

———. 2005. *Politics of Piety: The Islamic Revival and the Feminist Subject*. Princeton, N.J.: Princeton University Press.

Malawi Broadcasting Corporation. 1998. *Report and Accounts for the Year Ended 30th June 1998*. Blantyre: Malawi Broadcasting Corporation.

Malkki, Liisa. 1997. "News and Culture: Transitory Phenomena and the Fieldwork Tradition." In *Anthropological Locations: Boundaries and Grounds of a Field Science*, ed. Akhil Gupta and James Ferguson, 86–101. Berkeley: University of California Press.

Malkki, Liisa, and Emily Martin. 2003. "Children and the Gendered Politics of Globalization: In Remembrance of Sharon Stephens." *American Ethnologist* 30 (2): 216–224.

Malunga, Chiku. 2010. *Oblivion or Utopia: The Prospects for Africa*. Lanham, Md.: University Press of America.

Mama, Amina. 1997. "Shedding the Masks and Tearing the Veils: Cultural Studies for Post-Colonial Africa." In *Engendering African Social Sciences*, ed. Ayesha Imam, Amina Mama, and Fatou Sow, 61–80. Dakar: Council for the Development of Social Science Research in Africa (CODESRIA).

Mamdani, Mahmood. 1996. *Citizen and Subject: Contemporary Africa and the Legacy of Late Colonialism*. Princeton, N.J.: Princeton University Press.

———. 1998. *When Does Reconciliation Turn into a Denial of Justice?* Pretoria: HSRC Publishers.

Mandala, Elias C. 2005. *The End of Chidyerano: A History of Food and Everyday Life in Malawi, 1860–2004*. Portsmouth, N.H.: Heinemann.

Mankekar, Purnima. 1999. *Screening Culture, Viewing Politics: An Ethnography of Television, Womanhood, and Nation in Postcolonial India*. Durham, N.C.: Duke University Press.

Manyeka, Matthias. 1990. *Mlereni Mwana*. Limbe: Popular Publications.

Manyozo, Linje. 2005. "The Practice of Participation in Broadcasting for Development in Post-Independent Malawi." *Journal of Social Development in Africa* 20 (1): 77–105.

Mapanje, Jack. 2002. "The Orality of Dictatorship: In Defence of My Country." In *A Democracy of Chameleons: Politics and Culture in the New Malawi*, ed. Harri Englund, 178–187. Uppsala: Nordic Africa Institute.

Marwick, M. G. 1965. *Sorcery in Its Social Setting: A Study of the Northern Rhodesian Ceŵa*. Manchester: Manchester University Press.

Matza, Tomas. 2009. "Moscow's Echo: Technologies of the Self, Publics, and Politics on the Russian Talk Show." *Cultural Anthropology* 24 (3): 489–522.

Mazrui, Alamin. 2009. "Language and the Media in Africa: Between Old Empire and the New." In *Media and Identity in Africa*, ed. Kimani Njogu and John Middleton, 36–48. Edinburgh: Edinburgh University Press for the International African Institute.

Mazzarella, William. 2004. "Culture, Globalization, Mediation." *Annual Review of Anthropology* 33: 345–367.

Mbazira, Christopher. 2007. "Bolstering the Protection of Economic, Social and Cultural Rights in Malawi under the Malawian Constitution." *Malawi Law Journal* 1 (2): 220–231.

Mbembe, Achille. 2001. *On the Postcolony*. Berkeley: University of California Press.

Mbiti, John S. 1970. *African Religions and Philosophy*. Portsmouth, N.H.: Heinemann.

Mchakulu, Japhet Ezra July. 2007. "Youth Participation in Radio Listening Clubs in Malawi." *Journal of Southern African Studies* 33 (2): 251–265.

McLagan, Meg. 2002. "Spectacles of Difference: Cultural Activism and the Mass Mediation of Tibet." In *Media Worlds: Anthropology on New Terrain,* ed. Faye D. Ginsburg, Lila Abu-Lughod, and Brian Larkin, 90–111. Berkeley: University of California Press.

Merry, Sally Engle. 2006. *Human Rights and Gender Violence: Translating International Law into Local Justice*. Chicago: University of Chicago Press.

Meyer, Birgit. 1998. "'Make a Complete Break with the Past': Memory and Post-colonial Modernity in Ghanaian Pentecostalist Discourse." *Journal of Religion in Africa* 27 (3): 316–349.

———. 2004. "'Praise the Lord': Popular Cinema and Pentecostalite Style in Ghana's New Public Sphere." *American Ethnologist* 31 (1): 92–110.

Meyer, Birgit, and Annelies Moors, eds. 2006. *Religion, Media, and the Public Sphere*. Bloomington: Indiana University Press.

Mhone, Guy C. Z. 1992. "The Political Economy of Malawi: An Overview." In *Malawi at the Crossroads: The Post-Colonial Political Economy,* ed. Guy C. Z. Mhone, 1–33. Harare: Southern African Political Economy Series (SAPES).

Mitchell, J. Clyde. 1956. *The Yao Village: A Study in the Social Structure of a Nyasaland Tribe*. Manchester: Manchester University Press.

Miyazaki, Hirokazu. 2004. *The Method of Hope: Anthropology, Philosophy, and Fijian Knowledge*. Stanford, Calif.: Stanford University Press.

Mkamanga, Emily. 2000. *Suffering in Silence: Malawi Women's 30 Year Dance with Dr. Banda*. Glasgow: Dudu Nsomba.

Mkandawire, Richard. 1992. "The Land Question and Agrarian Change in Malawi." In *Malawi at the Crossroads: The Post-Colonial Political Economy,* ed. Guy C. Z. Mhone, 171–187. Harare: Southern African Political Economy Series (SAPES).

Mkandawire, Thandika. 2005. "African Intellectuals and Nationalism." In *African Intellectuals: Rethinking Politics, Language, Gender and Development,* ed. Thandika Mkandawire, 10–55. London: Zed Books.

Moore, Sally Falk. 1986. *Social Facts and Fabrications: "Customary" Law on Kilimanjaro, 1880–1980*. Cambridge: Cambridge University Press.

Moorman, Marissa J. 2008. *Intonations: A Social History of Music and Nation in Luanda, Angola, from 1945 to Recent Times*. Athens: Ohio University Press.

Moran, Mary H. 2006. *Liberia: The Violence of Democracy*. Philadelphia: University of Pennsylvania Press.

Morris, Brian. 1996. *Chewa Medical Botany*. Hamburg: Lit-Verlag.

Moto, Francis. 2001. *Trends in Malawian Literature*. Zomba: Chancellor College Publications.

Mtenje, Alfred. 2002. "English Imperialism and Shifting Attitudes towards African Languages: The Case of Malawi." In *Talking Freedom: Language and Democratisation in the SADC Region,* ed. Karsten Legère and Sandra Fitchat, 53–65. Windhoek: Gamsberg Macmillan.

Mudimbe, V. Y. 1988. *The Invention of Africa: Gnosis, Philosophy, and the Order of Knowledge*. Bloomington: Indiana University Press.

———. 1994. *The Idea of Africa*. Bloomington: Indiana University Press.

Mutua, Makau. 2002. "The Banjul Charter: The Case for an African Cultural Fingerprint." In *Cultural Transformation and Human Rights in Africa*, ed. Abdullahi A. An-Na'im, 68–107. London: Zed Books.

Myers, Mary. 2000. "Community Radio and Development: Issues and Examples from Francophone West Africa." In *African Broadcast Cultures: Radio in Transition*, ed. Richard Fardon and Graham Furniss, 90–101. Oxford: James Currey.

Mytton, Graham. 1983. *Mass Communication in Africa*. London: Edward Arnold.

———. 2000. "From Saucepan to Dish: Radio and TV in Africa." In *African Broadcast Cultures: Radio in Transition*, ed. Richard Fardon and Graham Furniss, 21–41. Oxford: James Currey.

National Statistical Office. 1971. *Radio Listenership Survey, August 1970–January 1971*. Zomba: National Statistical Office.

———. 1972. *Radio Listenership Survey, February 1971–July 1971*. Zomba: National Statistical Office.

———. 2002. *1998 Malawi Population and Housing Census: Analytical Report*. Zomba: National Statistical Office.

———. 2003. *Malawi DHS EdData Survey 2002: Education Data for Decision-Making*. Zomba: National Statistical Office.

———. 2010. *2008 Population and Housing Census: The Main Report*. Zomba: National Statistical Office.

Neale, Tim. 2004. "Malawi's Media: 2004 and Beyond." In *The Power of the Vote: Malawi's 2004 Parliamentary and Presidential Elections*, ed. Martin Ott, Bodo Immink, and Christian Peters-Berries, 181–194. Blantyre: Christian Literature Association in Malawi (CLAIM) for Kachere Series.

Negt, Oskar, and Alexander Kluge. 1993. *Public Sphere and Experience*. Translated by Peter Labanyi, Jamie Owen Daniel, and Assenka Oksiloff. Minneapolis: University of Minnesota Press.

Newell, Stephanie. 2002. Introduction. In *Readings in African Popular Fiction*, ed. Stephanie Newell, 1–10. Oxford: James Currey.

Ngoma, Sylvester, and Wisdom Nkhoma. 2002. *Nsinjiro Za Chiyankhulo*. Blantyre: Macmillan Malawi.

Niehaus, Isak. 2007. "Death before Dying: Understanding AIDS Stigma in the South African Lowveld." *Journal of Southern African Studies* 33 (4): 845–860.

Nieuwenhuys, Olga. 1996. "The Paradox of Child Labor and Anthropology." *Annual Review of Anthropology* 25: 237–251.

Nordmann, Charlotte. 2006. *Bourdieu/Rancière: La Politique entre sociologie et philosophie*. Paris: Éditions Amsterdam.

Ntarangwi, Mwenda. 2009. *East African Hip Hop: Youth Culture and Globalization*. Urbana: University of Illinois Press.

Ntarangwi, Mwenda, David Mills, and Mustafa Babiker, eds. 2006. *African Anthropologies: History, Critique and Practice*. London: Zed Books.

Nthala, S. J. 1964. *Mawu Okuluẃika M'Chinyanja*. Lusaka: Zambia Educational Publishing House.

Nussbaum, Martha C. 1995. "Human Capabilities, Female Human Beings." In *Women, Culture, and Development: A Study of Human Capabilities*, ed. Martha C. Nussbaum and Jonathan Glover, 61–104. Oxford: Clarendon.

———. 2000. *Women and Human Development: The Capabilities Approach*. Cambridge: Cambridge University Press.

———. 2004. "Women and Theories of Global Justice: Our Need for New Paradigms." In *The Ethics of Assistance: Morality and the Distant Needy,* ed. Deen K. Chatterjee, 147–176. Cambridge: Cambridge University Press.

Nyamnjoh, Francis B. 2003. "Chieftaincy and the Negotiation of Might and Right in Botswana Democracy." *Journal of Contemporary African Studies* 21 (2): 233–250.

———. 2004. "Reconciling 'the Rhetoric of Rights' with Competing Notions of Personhood and Agency in Botswana." In *Rights and the Politics of Recognition in Africa,* ed. Harri Englund and Francis B. Nyamnjoh, 33–63. London: Zed Books.

———. 2005a. *Africa's Media, Democracy, and the Politics of Belonging.* London: Zed Books.

———. 2005b. "Fishing in Troubled Waters: *Disquettes* and *Thiofs* in Dakar." *Africa* 75 (3): 295–324.

Ochs, Elinor, and Lisa Capps. 2001. *Living Narrative: Creating Lives in Everyday Storytelling.* Cambridge, Mass.: Harvard University Press.

ODI (Overseas Development Institute). 2010. *Millennium Development Goals Report Card: Measuring Progress across Countries.* London: ODI Publications.

Ogbondah, Chris W. 2002. "Media Laws in Political Transition." In *Media and Democracy in Africa,* ed. Göran Hydén, Michael Leslie, and Folu F. Ogundimu, 55–80. Uppsala: Nordic Africa Institute.

Oldham, Paul, and Miriam Anne Frank. 2008. "'We the Peoples . . .': The United Nations Declaration on the Rights of Indigenous Peoples." *Anthropology Today* 24 (2): 5–9.

Onwudiwe, Ebere. 2001. "A Critique of Recent Writings on Ethnicity and Nationalism." *Research in African Literatures* 32 (3): 213–228.

Oomen, Barbara. 2005. *Chiefs in South Africa: Law, Power and Culture in the Post-Apartheid Era.* Oxford: James Currey.

Opoku-Mensah, Aida. 2000. "The Future of Community Radio in Africa: The Case of Southern Africa." In *African Broadcast Cultures: Radio in Transition,* ed. Richard Fardon and Graham Furniss, 165–173. Oxford: James Currey.

Paley, Julia. 2004. "Accountable Democracy: Citizens' Impact on Public Decision Making in Postdictatorship Chile." *American Ethnologist* 31 (4): 497–513.

Parkin, David. 1980. "The Creativity of Abuse." *Man (N.S.)* 15 (1): 45–64.

Parry, Jonathan. 1974. "Egalitarian Values in a Hierarchical Society." *South Asian Review* 7 (2): 95–121.

Patel, Nandini. 2000. "Media in the Democratic and Electoral Process." In *Malawi's Second Democratic Elections: Process, Problems, and Prospects,* ed. Martin Ott, Kings M. Phiri, and Nandini Patel, 158–185. Blantyre: Christian Literature Association in Malawi (CLAIM) for Kachere Series.

Pedelty, Mark. 1995. *War Stories: The Culture of Foreign Correspondents.* New York: Routledge.

Pelican, Michaela. 2009. "Complexities of Indigeneity and Autochthony: An African Example." *American Ethnologist* 36 (1): 52–65.

Peters, Pauline E. 1997. "Revisiting the Puzzle of Matriliny in South-Central Africa." *Critique of Anthropology* 17 (2): 125–146.

———. 2002. "Bewitching Land: The Role of Land Disputes in Converting Kin to Strangers and in Class Formation in Malawi." *Journal of Southern African Studies* 28 (1): 155–178.

———. 2009. "Challenges in Land Tenure and Land Reform in Africa: Anthropological Contributions." *World Development* 37 (8): 1317–1325.

Peters, Pauline E., and Daimon Kambewa. 2007. "Whose Security? Deepening Social Conflict over 'Customary' Land in the Shadow of Land Tenure Reform in Malawi." *Journal of Modern African Studies* 45 (3): 447–472.

Peterson, Mark Allen. 2010. "Getting the News in New Delhi: Newspaper Literacies in an Indian Mediascape." In *The Anthropology of News and Journalism: Global Perspectives,* ed. S. Elizabeth Bird, 168–181. Bloomington: Indiana University Press.

Pfaffe, Joachim Friedrich, ed. 2000. *Local Languages in Education, Science and Technology.* Zomba: Centre for Language Studies.

Pierre, Jemima. 2006. "Anthropology and the Race of/for Africa." In *The Study of Africa, Volume One: Disciplinary and Interdisciplinary Encounters,* ed. Paul Tiyambe Zeleza, 39–61. Dakar: Council for the Development of Social Science Research in Africa (CODESRIA).

Pincione, Guido, and Fernando R. Tesón. 2006. *Rational Choice and Democratic Deliberation: A Theory of Discourse Failure.* Cambridge: Cambridge University Press.

Pitcher, M. Anne, and Kelly M. Askew. 2006. "African Socialisms and Postsocialisms." *Africa* 76 (1): 1–14.

Pogge, Thomas W. 2002. *World Poverty and Human Rights: Cosmopolitan Responsibilities and Reforms.* Cambridge: Polity.

———. 2007. "Severe Poverty as a Human Rights Violation." In *Freedom from Poverty as a Human Right: Who Owes What to the Very Poor?* ed. Thomas Pogge, 11–53. Oxford: Oxford University Press.

Power, Joey. 2010. *Political Culture and Nationalism in Malawi: Building Kwacha.* Rochester, N.Y.: University of Rochester Press.

Pratten, David. 2007. *The Man-Leopard Murders: History and Society in Colonial Nigeria.* Bloomington: Indiana University Press.

Prins, Harald E. L. 2002. "Visual Media and the Primitivist Perplex: Colonial Fantasies, Indigenous Imagination, and Advocacy in North America." In *Media Worlds: Anthropology on New Terrain,* ed. Faye D. Ginsburg, Lila Abu-Lughod, and Brian Larkin, 58–74. Berkeley: University of California Press.

Rabinow, Paul. 2003. *Anthropos Today: Reflections on Modern Equipment.* Princeton, N.J.: Princeton University Press.

Rancière, Jacques. 1989. *The Nights of Labor: The Workers' Dream in Nineteenth-Century France.* Translated by John Drury. Philadelphia: Temple University Press.

———. 1991. *The Ignorant Schoolmaster: Five Lessons in Intellectual Emancipation.* Translated by Kristin Ross. Stanford, Calif.: Stanford University Press.

———. 2004. *The Philosopher and His Poor.* Translated by John Drury, Corinne Oster, and Andrew Parker. Durham, N.C.: Duke University Press.

Rao, Ursula. 2010. "Empowerment through Local News Making: Studying the Media/Public Interface in India." In *The Anthropology of News and Journalism: Global Perspectives,* ed. S. Elizabeth Bird, 100–115. Bloomington: Indiana University Press.

Reith, John C. W. 1924. *Broadcast over Britain.* London: Hodder and Stoughton.

Richards, Audrey I. 1956. *Chisungu: A Girl's Initiation Ceremony among the Bemba of Zambia.* London: Faber and Faber.

Richards, Paul. 1996. *Fighting for the Rainforest: War, Youth and Resources in Sierra Leone.* Oxford: James Currey.

Riches, David. 2000. "The Holistic Person, or, The Ideology of Egalitarianism." *Journal of the Royal Anthropological Institute* 6 (4): 669–685.

Ricoeur, Paul. 1991. "Narrative Identity." In *On Paul Ricoeur: Narrative and Interpretation,* ed. and translated by David Wood, 188–199. New York: Routledge.

———. 1992. *Oneself as Another.* Translated by Kathleen Blamey. Chicago: University of Chicago Press.

Riles, Annelise. 2006. "Anthropology, Human Rights, and Legal Knowledge: Culture in the Iron Cage." *American Anthropologist* 108 (1): 52–65.

Rio, Knut M., and Olaf H. Smedal. 2009. "Hierarchy and Its Alternatives: An Introduction to

Movements of Totalization and Detotalization." In *Hierarchy: Persistence and Transformation in Social Formations,* ed. Knut M. Rio and Olaf H. Smedal, 1–63. Oxford: Berghahn.

Robbins, Joel. 2007. "Continuity Thinking and the Problem of Christian Culture: Belief, Time, and the Anthropology of Christianity." *Current Anthropology* 48 (1): 5–38.

Rose, Nikolas. 1999. *Powers of Freedom: Reframing Political Thought.* Cambridge: Cambridge University Press.

Ross, Fiona. 2003. *Bearing Witness: Women and the Truth and Reconciliation Commission in South Africa.* London: Pluto Press.

———. 2007. "Linguistic Bearings and Testimonial Practices." In *Discourse and Human Rights Violations,* ed. Christine Anthonissen and Jan Blommaert, 101–113. Amsterdam: John Benjamins.

Ross, Hester F. 1998. "'All Men Do Is Love, Love . . .': Context, Power and Women in Some Recent Malawian Writing." In *Democratization in Malawi: A Stocktaking,* ed. Kings M. Phiri and Kenneth R. Ross, 168–194. Blantyre: Christian Literature Association in Malawi (CLAIM) for Kachere Series.

Rotberg, Robert I., and Dennis Thompson, eds. 2000. *Truth versus Justice: The Morality of Truth Commissions.* Princeton, N.J.: Princeton University Press.

Sadouni, Samadia. 2007. "New Religious Actors in South Africa: The Example of Islamic Humanitarianism." In *Islam and Muslim Politics in Africa,* ed. Benjamin F. Soares and René Otayek, 103–118. New York: Palgrave-Macmillan.

Sahlins, Marshall. 1972. *Stone Age Economics.* Chicago: Aldine-Atherton.

———. 1993. *Waiting for Foucault.* Cambridge: Prickly Pear Press.

Sandel, Michael. 1982. *Liberalism and the Limits of Justice.* Cambridge: Cambridge University Press.

Sanders, Todd. 2008. "Buses in Bongoland: Seductive Analytics and the Occult." *Anthropological Theory* 8 (2): 107–132.

Scannell, Paddy, and David Cardiff. 1991. *A Social History of British Broadcasting, Volume One, 1922–1939: Serving the Nation.* Oxford: Blackwell.

Schapera, Isaac, ed. 1937. *The Bantu-Speaking Tribes of South Africa.* London: Routledge & Sons.

———. 1938. *A Handbook of Tswana Law and Custom.* London: Oxford University Press.

———. 1965. *Praise-Poems of Tswana Chiefs.* Oxford: Clarendon Press.

Schatzberg, Michael. 2002. *Political Legitimacy in Middle Africa.* Bloomington: Indiana University Press.

Schmitt, Carl. 1985. *Political Theology: Four Chapters on the Concept of Sovereignty.* Translated by George Schwab. Cambridge, Mass.: MIT Press.

Schneider, Leander. 2007. "High on Modernity? Explaining the Failings of Tanzanian Villagisation." *African Studies* 66 (1): 9–38.

Schoffeleers, Matthew. 1999. *In Search of Truth and Justice: Confrontations between Church and State in Malawi 1960–1994.* Blantyre: Christian Literature Association in Malawi (CLAIM) for Kachere Series.

Schudson, Michael. 1999. "What Public Journalism Knows about Journalism but Doesn't Know about Public." In *The Idea of Public Journalism,* ed. Theodore L. Glasser, 118–133. New York: Guilford Press.

Schulz, Dorothea E. 2006. "Morality, Community, Publicness: Shifting Terms of Public Debate in Mali." In *Religion, Media, and the Public Sphere,* ed. Birgit Meyer and Annelies Moors, 132–151. Bloomington: Indiana University Press.

Scott, James C. 1985. *Weapons of the Weak: Everyday Forms of Peasant Resistance.* New Haven, Conn.: Yale University Press.

Sen, Amartya. 1992. *Inequality Reexamined.* Oxford: Oxford University Press.

Sengupta, Arjun. 2007. "Poverty Eradication and Human Rights." In *Freedom from Poverty as a Human Right: Who Owes What to the Very Poor?* ed. Thomas Pogge, 323–344. Oxford: Oxford University Press.

Shipton, Parker. 2007. *The Nature of Entrustment: Intimacy, Exchange, and the Sacred in Africa.* New Haven, Conn.: Yale University Press.

Simpson, Anthony. 2003. *"Half-London" in Zambia: Contested Identities in a Catholic Mission School.* Edinburgh: Edinburgh University Press for the International African Institute.

———. 2009. *Boys to Men in the Shadow of AIDS: Masculinities and HIV Risk in Zambia.* New York: Palgrave Macmillan.

Sindima, Harvey J. 1995. *Africa's Agenda: The Legacy of Liberalism and Colonialism in the Crisis of African Values.* Westport, Conn.: Greenwood Press.

———. 2002. *Malawi's First Republic: An Economic and Political Analysis.* Lanham, Md.: University Press of America.

Singer, Peter. 2009. *The Life You Can Save: Acting Now to End World Poverty.* New York: Picador.

Sirianni, Carmen, and Lewis Friedland. 2001. *Civic Innovation in America: Community Empowerment, Public Policy, and the Movement for Civic Renewal.* Berkeley: University of California Press.

Skinner, Quentin. 1998. *Liberty before Liberalism.* Cambridge: Cambridge University Press.

Smith, Daniel Jordan. 2007. *A Culture of Corruption: Everyday Deception and Popular Discontent in Nigeria.* Princeton, N.J.: Princeton University Press.

Smith, James Howard. 2008. *Bewitching Development: Witchcraft and the Reinvention of Development in Neoliberal Kenya.* Chicago: University of Chicago Press.

Solway, Jacqueline, ed. 2006. *The Politics of Egalitarianism: Theory and Practice.* Oxford: Berghahn.

Spitulnik, Debra. 2000. "Documenting Radio Culture as Lived Experience: Reception Studies and the Mobile Machine in Zambia." In *African Broadcast Cultures: Radio in Transition,* ed. Richard Fardon and Graham Furniss, 144–163. Oxford: James Currey.

———. 2002. "Mobile Machines and Fluid Audiences: Rethinking Reception through Zambian Radio Culture." In *Media Worlds: Anthropology on New Terrain,* ed. Faye D. Ginsburg, Lila Abu-Lughod, and Brian Larkin, 337–354. Berkeley: University of California Press.

Ståhlberg, Per. 2002. *Lucknow Daily: How a Hindi Newspaper Constructs Reality.* Stockholm: University of Stockholm.

———. 2006. "On the Journalist Bent in India: Encounters with the Near Familiar." *Ethnography* 7 (1): 47–67.

Stambach, Amy. 2000. *Lessons from Mount Kilimanjaro: Schooling, Community, and Gender in East Africa.* New York: Routledge.

Stephens, Sharon. 1995. "Children and the Politics of Culture in 'Late Capitalism.'" In *Children and the Politics of Culture,* ed. Sharon Stephens, 3–48. Princeton, N.J.: Princeton University Press.

Stokes, Susan S. 1998. "Pathologies of Deliberation." In *Deliberative Democracy,* ed. Jon Elster, 123–139. Cambridge: Cambridge University Press.

Stolcke, Verena. 1995. "Talking Culture: New Boundaries, New Rhetorics of Exclusion in Europe." *Current Anthropology* 36 (1): 1–24.

Strathern, Marilyn. 1985. "Discovering 'Social Control.'" *Journal of Law and Society* 12 (2): 111–134.

———. 1988. *The Gender of the Gift: Problems with Women and Problems with Society in Melanesia.* Berkeley: University of California Press.

————. 1991. *Partial Connections.* Lanham, Md.: Rowman and Littlefield.

————. 2004. "Losing (Out on) Intellectual Resources." In *Law, Anthropology, and the Constitution of the Social: Making Persons and Things,* ed. Alain Pottage and Martha Mundy, 201–233. Cambridge: Cambridge University Press.

Swidler, Ann, and Susan Cotts Watkins. 2009. "'Teach a Man to Fish': The Sustainability Doctrine and Its Social Consequences." *World Development* 37 (7): 1182–1196.

Sykes, Karen. 2005. *Arguing with Anthropology: An Introduction to Critical Theories of the Gift.* New York: Routledge.

Talbott, William J. 2005. *Which Rights Should Be Universal?* Oxford: Oxford University Press.

Tarnopolsky, Christina. 2007. "Platonic Reflections on the Aesthetic Dimensions of Deliberative Democracy." *Political Theory* 35 (3): 288–312.

Tate, Winifred. 2007. *Counting the Dead: The Culture and Politics of Human Rights Activism in Colombia.* Berkeley: University of California Press.

Taylor, Michael. 1982. *Community, Anarchy, and Liberty.* Cambridge: Cambridge University Press.

Temkin, Larry S. 1993. *Inequality.* Oxford: Oxford University Press.

ter Haar, Gerrie. 2007. "Introduction: The Evil Called Witchcraft." In *Imagining Evil: Witchcraft Beliefs and Accusations in Contemporary Africa,* ed. Gerrie ter Haar, 1–30. Trenton, N.J.: Africa World Press.

ter Haar, Gerrie, and Stephen Ellis. 2009. "The Occult Does Not Exist: A Response to Terence Ranger." *Africa* 79 (3): 399–412.

Thiong'o, Ngugi Wa. 2005. "Europhone or African Memory: The Challenge of the Pan-Africanist Intellectual in the Era of Globalization." In *African Intellectuals: Rethinking Politics, Language, Gender, and Development,* ed. Thandika Mkandawire, 155–164. London: Zed Books.

Thomas, Lynn M., and Jennifer Cole. 2009. "Thinking through Love in Africa." In *Love in Africa,* ed. Jennifer Cole and Lynn M. Thomas, 1–30. Chicago: University of Chicago Press.

Tsing, Anna Lowenhaupt. 2005. *Friction: An Ethnography of Global Connection.* Princeton, N.J.: Princeton University Press.

Tuchman, Gaye. 1978. *Making News: A Study in the Construction of Reality.* New York: Free Press.

Turner, Terence. 2002. "Representation, Politics, and Cultural Imagination in Indigenous Video: General Points and Kayapo Examples." In *Media Worlds: Anthropology on New Terrain,* ed. Faye D. Ginsburg, Lila Abu-Lughod, and Brian Larkin, 75–89. Berkeley: University of California Press.

Turner, Victor W. 1968. *The Drums of Affliction: A Study of Religious Processes among the Ndembu of Zambia.* Oxford: Clarendon Press.

UNDP (United Nations Development Programme). 2001. *Malawi Human Development Report 2001.* Lilongwe: UNDP.

Unger, Peter. 1996. *Living High and Letting Die: Our Illusion of Innocence.* Oxford: Oxford University Press.

Vail, Leroy. 1983. "The State and the Creation of Colonial Malawi's Agricultural Economy." In *Imperialism, Colonialism, and Hunger: East and Central Africa,* ed. Robert I. Rotberg, 39–87. Boston, Mass.: Lexington Books.

Vail, Leroy, and Landeg White. 1989. "Tribalism in the Political History of Malawi." In *The Creation of Tribalism in Southern Africa,* ed. Leroy Vail, 151–192. Berkeley: University of California Press.

————. 1991. *Power and the Praise Poem: Southern African Voices in History.* Charlottesville: University Press of Virginia.

Valadez, Jorge M. 2001. *Deliberative Democracy, Political Legitimacy, and Self-Determination in Multicultural Societies.* Boulder, Colo.: Westview.

van de Port, Mattijs. 2006. "Visualizing the Sacred: Video Technology, 'Televisual' Style, and the Religious Imagination in Bahian Candomblé." *American Ethnologist* 33 (3): 444–461.

van der Veur, Paul R. 2002. "Broadcasting and Political Reform." In *Media and Democracy in Africa,* ed. Göran Hydén, Michael Leslie, and Folu F. Ogundimu, 81–105. Uppsala: Nordic Africa Institute.

van Dijk, Rijk A. 1995. "Fundamentalism and Its Moral Geography in Malawi: The Representation of the Diasporic and the Diabolical." *Critique of Anthropology* 15 (2): 171–191.

Vaughan, Megan. 1987. *The Story of an African Famine: Gender and Famine in Twentieth-Century Malawi.* Cambridge: Cambridge University Press.

Vesperi, Maria D. 2010. "When Common Sense No Longer Holds: The Shifting Focus of News Production in the United States." In *The Anthropology of News and Journalism: Global Perspectives,* ed. S. Elizabeth Bird, 257–269. Bloomington: Indiana University Press.

Vokes, Richard. 2007. "Charisma, Creativity, and Cosmopolitanism: A Perspective on the Power of the New Radio Broadcasting in Uganda and Rwanda." *Journal of the Royal Anthropological Institute* 13 (4): 805–824.

Wagner, Roy. 1981. *The Invention of Culture.* Chicago: University of Chicago Press.

Wahl-Jorgensen, Karin. 2010. "News Production, Ethnography, and Power: On the Challenges of Newsroom-Centricity." In *The Anthropology of News and Journalism: Global Perspectives,* ed. S. Elizabeth Bird, 21–34. Bloomington: Indiana University Press.

Warner, Michael. 2002. *Publics and Counterpublics.* New York: Zone Books.

Wedell, George. 1986. "Three Priorities for Action." In *Making Broadcasting Useful: The African Experience,* ed. George Wedell, 285–296. Manchester: Manchester University Press.

Weiss, Brad. 2009. *Street Dreams and Hip Hop Barbershops: Global Fantasy in Urban Tanzania.* Bloomington: Indiana University Press.

Wenar, Leif. 2007. "Responsibility and Severe Poverty." In *Freedom from Poverty as a Human Right: Who Owes What to the Very Poor?* ed. Thomas Pogge, 255–274. Oxford: Oxford University Press.

Wendland, Ernst. 2005. *Sewero!: Christian Drama and the Drama of Christianity in Africa.* Blantyre: Christian Literature Association in Malawi (CLAIM) for Kachere Series.

Werbner, Richard. 2004. *Reasonable Radicals and Citizenship in Botswana: The Public Anthropology of Kalanga Elites.* Bloomington: Indiana University Press.

West, Harry G. 2005. *Kupilikula: Governance and the Invisible Realm in Mozambique.* Chicago: University of Chicago Press.

———. 2007. *Ethnographic Sorcery.* Chicago: University of Chicago Press.

White, Landeg. 1987. *Magomero: Portrait of an African Village.* Cambridge: Cambridge University Press.

———. 2007. "The Language and Practice of Human Rights in Malawi." *Journal of Southern African Studies* 33 (4): 885–886.

Widlok, Thomas, and Wolde Gossa Tadesse, eds. 2005. *Property and Equality, Vol. 1: Ritualisation, Sharing, Egalitarianism.* Oxford: Berghahn.

Williams, David. 2008. *The World Bank and Social Transformation in International Politics: Liberalism, Governance, and Sovereignty.* New York: Routledge.

Williams, Melissa. 2000. "The Uneasy Alliance of Group Representation and Deliberative Democracy." In *Citizenship in Diverse Societies,* ed. Will Kymlicka and Wayne Norman, 124–152. Oxford: Oxford University Press.

Williams, Raymond. 1983. *Keywords: A Vocabulary of Culture and Society.* London: Flamingo.

Wilson, Richard A. 1997. "Representing Human Rights Violations: Social Contexts and Subjectivities." In *Human Rights, Culture and Context: Anthropological Perspectives,* ed. Richard A. Wilson, 134–160. Ann Arbor, Mich.: Pluto Press.

———. 2001. *The Politics of Truth and Reconciliation in South Africa: Legitimizing the Post-Apartheid State.* Cambridge: Cambridge University Press.

———. 2007. "Tyrannosaurus Lex: The Anthropology of Human Rights and Transnational Law." In *The Practice of Human Rights: Tracking Law Between the Global and the Local,* ed. Mark Goodale and Sally Engle Merry, 342–369. Cambridge: Cambridge University Press.

Winnick, Dinah. 2008. "On *Coming of Age in Second Life:* An Interview with Tom Boellstorff." *Anthropology News* 49 (7): 21.

Wiredu, Kwasi. 1990. "An Akan Perspective on Human Rights." In *Human Rights in Africa: Cross-Cultural Perspectives,* ed. Abdullahi A. An-Na'im and Francis M. Deng, 243–260. Washington, D.C.: Brookings Institution.

———. 2009. "An Oral Philosophy of Personhood: Comments on Philosophy and Orality." *Research in African Literatures* 40 (1): 8–18.

Yang, Mayfair Mei-hui. 2002. "Mass Media and Transnational Subjectivity in Shanghai: Notes on (Re)Cosmopolitanism in a Chinese Metropolis." In *Media Worlds: Anthropology on New Terrain,* ed. Faye D. Ginsburg, Lila Abu-Lughod, and Brian Larkin, 189–210. Berkeley: University of California Press.

Yarrow, Tom. 2008. "Life/History: Personal Narratives of Development amongst NGO Workers and Activists in Ghana." *Africa* 78 (3): 334–358.

Zeleza, Paul Tiyambe. 2003. *Rethinking Africa's Globalization, Volume 1: The Intellectual Challenges.* Trenton, N.J.: Africa World Press.

———. 2004. "Introduction: The Struggle for Human Rights in Africa." In *Human Rights, the Rule of Law, and Development in Africa,* ed. Paul Tiyambe Zeleza and Philip J. McConnaughay, 1–18. Philadelphia: University of Pennsylvania Press.

———. 2009. "The Media in Social Development in Contemporary Africa." In *Media and Identity in Africa,* ed. Kimani Njogu and John Middleton, 19–35. Edinburgh: Edinburgh University Press for the International African Institute.

Zingani, Willie T. 1984. *Njala Bwana.* Limbe: Popular Publications.

———. 2004. *Kwangwala Wopusa.* Blantyre: Christian Literature Association in Malawi (CLAIM).

Index

HARRI ENGLUND is Reader in Social Anthropology at the University of Cambridge. His book *Prisoners of Freedom: Human Rights and the African Poor* (2006) is winner of the Amaury Talbot Prize of the Royal Anthropological Institute.